Learning
Business Statistics
with
Microsoft® Excel

Learning
Business Statistics
with
Microsoft® Excel

John L. Neufeld
University of North Carolina at Greensboro

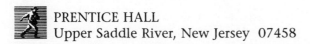
PRENTICE HALL
Upper Saddle River, New Jersey 07458

Library of Congress Cataloging in Publication Data

Neufeld, John L.
    Learning Business Statistics with Microsoft Excel / John L. Neufeld.
    p. cm.
    Includes Bibliographical reference and index.
    ISBN 0-13-234097-6
    1. Commercial Statistics. 2. Microsoft Excel for Windows
(Computer File) 3.Commericial Statistics--Computer Programs.
I. Title.
HF1017.N47 1997   96-4136
519.5'0285'5369--dc20   CIP

Director of Production and Manufacturing: Joanne Jay
Managing Editor: Katherine Evancie
Project Manager: Susan Rifkin
Manufacturing Manager: Vincent Scelta
Manufacturing Buyer: Alana Zdinak
Design Director: Patricia Wosczyk
Interior Design: Mediamark
Editor-in-Chief: Richard Wohl
Aquisitions Editor: Tom Tucker
Executive Marketing Manager: Nancy Evans
Cover Design: Bruce Kenselaar
Production Coordinator: David Cotugno

©1997 by Prentice Hall, Inc.
A Simon & Schuster Company
Upper Saddle River, N.J. 07548

Printed in the United States of America
10 9 8 7 6 5 4 3 2

ISBN 0-13-234097-6

Prentice-Hall International (UK) Limited, *London*
Prentice-Hall of Australia Pty. Limited, *Sydney*
Prentice-Hall of Canada, Inc., *Toronto*
Prentice-Hall Hispanoamericana, S.A., *Mexico*
Prentice-Hall of India Private Limited, *New Delhi*
Prentice-Hall of Japan, Inc., *Tokyo*
Simon & Schuster Asia Pte. Ltd., *Singapore*
Editora Prentice Hall do Brasil, Ltda., *Rio de Janeiro*

To Karol, Paul, Adam, and Margot. Thanks.

Brief Contents

Detailed Contents

Preface

▼ To the Student

This book is intended for the student learning business statistics who likes the idea of using Excel to help that learning. If you already know Excel, using that knowledge to help you learn statistics probably seems like a good idea. If you don't know Excel, or don't feel fully comfortable with it, using this book will enable you to learn it and become better at using it. No knowledge of Excel is assumed and the use of Excel is explained with clear and easy to follow steps.

There is a *synergy* between knowing computers and knowing statistics. Knowing how to use computers not only will help you solve practical statistical problems, *it can also help you understand statistical concepts*. The computer can empower you. Like any good tool, a computer enables you to do things you could not do without it. When you learn statistics, a computer will enable you to literally see statistical concepts which otherwise could only be imagined. An example of this is a sampling distribution, a concept involving the selection of all possible samples from a population. This fundamental concept of statistics would be much easier to understand if you didn't have to depend entirely on your imagination. In a lesson in this book you will be guided in using Excel to select 1,000 samples from a population and in a single graph observe how a sampling distribution actually looks. You will then easily explore how changes in the population affect this sampling distribution. Concepts which might otherwise seem abstract can be brought to life through the use of computers and thereby made easier to understand. Too many people approach statistics as a topic to memorize rather than to understand, and these people are never comfortable with the use of statistics. A good working knowledge of statistics doesn't require a rigorous mathematical approach, but it does require an *intuitive* understanding. Using computers to explore statistical concepts can make that intuition easier to acquire.

There are other good reasons why a knowledge of computers in general, and Excel in particular, would be useful. Too often, people try to learn a program like Excel by itself without a place to apply it. This is a very inefficient way to learn how to use a computer. For most people, computers are not so inherently interesting as to be an appropriate subject in themselves. You don't learn how to hammer by studying hammers. You learn how to hammer by needing to hit a nail. You learn computers by having a need the computer can help you fulfill. Do you need to learn business statistics? That's the nail. That's what you should focus on. Using this book will enable you to learn Excel not for its own sake, but because it's going to help you learn business statistics.

If you already have a good working knowledge of Excel, you may feel that some of the steps in the beginning are too detailed. This feeling will not persist. My assumption is that by the end of the book, everyone will have learned Excel. As the book progresses, the Excel instructions become less detailed and less effort is made to explain the features of Excel. Excel is rich with features, and there are many alternative ways of accomplishing the same end. Even if you feel you know Excel well, you may well learn some new tricks from this book which will help you use Excel more efficiently.

- This is not a book you just sit down and read at your desk (unless your desk has a computer). *This is a book you need to use with a computer.* Many of the paragraphs of this book have bullets (like this one). These paragraphs contain step-by-step instructions for you to carry out on your computer.

Using this book will help you learn business statistics, but it won't make the process automatic. Although the approach is often step-by-step, you must not follow the steps mindlessly. The objective of the steps is not to get the computer to display a particular number, it's to help you understand either a statistical concept or the process of solving a statistical problem. After you have completed a series of steps, reflect on what you have done. Read carefully the paragraphs which do not have bullets; they are designed to help you integrate your computer experiences with your growing understanding of statistical concepts and methods. Do the exercises at the end of each chapter *before* you look up the answers. Applying the methods you have learned in the text to a new problem can sometimes seem like a struggle, but it is in this struggle that learning occurs. You can test your understanding by doing the problems at the end of each chapter after the first. Getting through a chapter and yet being unable to do the problems indicates that you need to devote more thought to what the chapters are leading you through. Answers to most of the questions are in an appendix and are provided to enable you to check your work and thus your level of understanding.

This book is primarily intended for use in an undergraduate or MBA introductory college business or economics statistics course. You may find this book's approach helpful for such a course even if it is not required by the instructor. It also can be used by those who wish to learn the fundamentals of business statistics (and Excel) and who are not taking a formal course.

▼ To the Professor

I have had almost twenty years of experience as both a teacher and a user of statistics. During that time there has been tremendous advance in computing technology. This has brought about enormous change in the practice of statistics in business and by researchers. Sadly, it has had almost no effect on the pedagogy of statistics. As every college instructor knows, this is not owing to a lack of commercially available texts. You, like I, are probably inundated with textbooks and advertisements for textbooks, most of which are almost identical in their pedagogical approach. The problem is not that computers are ignored. Hardly a text today is published without an optional or accompanying data diskette. Most texts illustrate computer printouts in their pages. Many have supplements dealing with a particular software package—Minitab, SAS, and, increasingly, Excel. All of this, however, is very much of an add-on. The pedagogy of most texts has hardly changed over the past 20 years, and doesn't really depend on computers at all.

Most statistical programs have really been developed with the researcher or statistical user in mind, not the student. This is enormously valuable to those using statistics because it makes it easy to do complex statistical analysis on larger and larger sets of data. The intended users of these packages are expected to already understand the statistical concepts implemented in their code. It is, of course, important for students to gain some familiarity with these tools since that is how statistics is actually done. Unfortunately, these programs may hinder learning for the very reason that they are so easy to use. Why struggle with an understanding of regression when it can be done with a few mouse clicks? The response to this has tended to be a separation between *learning* statistics, which is done by hand or with a calculator, and *using* statistics, which is done with a computer. Even the widespread use of statistical tools has had remarkably little effect on pedagogy. How many textbooks continue to use the critical value approach as the primary method of teaching hypothesis testing even though the standard for computer programs is p values? Although both approaches are obviously equivalent, p values are more intuitive, but they are not as convenient to use with statistical tables. Statistical tables have more and more become used only by students. For most uses of statistics (certainly not all), they are an anachronism foisted upon students.

How is the approach used in this book different? Excel differs from most special purpose statistical packages in its versatility in handling all types of numeric manipulations, and it is easier for most computer novices to use than a statistical program. Consider the generation of a new variable. To do this in most statistical programs, you merely write an equation showing the new variable as a calculation of existing variables. Those of us who are used to using statistics have no difficulty visualizing this as operating on each of many observations generating a new value for each. Compare this to the approach with Excel. Each observation is seen as a row in a spreadsheet. A formula is entered into a new cell to calculate a new value using the values in existing cells. This value appears as soon as the formula is finished. That formula is then copied down the column, and the new value is immediately visible. This is inherently more visual and more intuitive than the approach taken by most statistical packages. Although it may not be more convenient for the researcher, it is preferable for the student.

Excel contains procedures much like those in the standard packages which automatically do such analyses as regression. These are fully covered in this book. What sets the approach of this book apart, however, are the other ways in which Excel is used to help students understand statistical concepts. Consider Chapter 8. Students explore the concepts of Type I and Type II error by performing 1,000 hypothesis tests in which the Null Hypothesis is either known to be correct or known to be wrong. A table showing the outcome of these tests is constructed, and the student actually sees the impact of significance level on incidence of Type I error and the impact of the difference between hypothesized and actual population parameter on the incidence of Type II error. Or consider Chapter 14 . If you, like many of us, think it is a good idea for students to have some experience estimating a simple regression by hand, you may like the approach taken there. Rather than immediately introducing the student to the use of the Regression Tool, the computer is first used to explore regression's concepts. Students experiment with trying to fit a line to data by guessing the regression coefficient. The regression coefficients are introduced by having the student construct the type of table which would be used in an estimation by hand. The relationship between the values in that table and scatter plots are also shown. Is this better than simply calculating the coefficients by hand? Yes. First the arithmetical drudgery is eliminated, and it becomes a simple matter to change the data estimated. Students can see the difference in the calculations between data which are well-fit by a regression line and for which there is no clear relationship.

This book should be used by instructors who are interested in pedagogical innovation. It probably is best used as a supplemental text to a more conventional textbook. Its use requires a commitment to computers, and students will have to spend many hours working through the instructions. This is probably best done in a lab setting where all students are working together, but it can be done out of class. You will have to provide reinforcement in your lectures to the concepts students are working through. The careful step-by-step approach used in this book makes it possible for students to proceed on their own, but some will have a tendency to focus too much on the steps and may not fully grasp the concepts unless you reinforce them by referring to the process they go through on the computer.

The traditional approach to teaching statistics has been exhaustively worked out and is backed by enormous quantities of instructional material. Such a course is difficult for students to learn, but it is not a particularly difficult course to teach. This is probably a factor in the subject's pedagogical inertia. The approach used in this book is new. It will undoubtedly be improved. I believe that by using it you will provide greater value to your students. Your course may become more exciting and more effective, but it will not be easier for you. It is my fervent hope that the approach taken here will be taken up by others and that we will have a choice among high quality material which makes effective use of computers in the pedagogy of statistics.

▼ Which Version of Excel?

This book was primarily written using Excel 5.0 for Windows 3.1. This is almost identical to Excel 5.0 for the Macintosh. The two versions share the same software manual. The differences arise primarily from the different mouse and keyboard used by the two systems. I have tried in the text to accommodate Macintosh users, but I have not tested this book on a Macintosh. I anticipate no problems in using it on a Macintosh, and I would appreciate any observations or comments from Macintosh users on improvements I could make for them.

Microsoft also has released Excel 7.0 for Windows 95. (There was no Excel 6.0.) Although the new version has a few minor enhancements, including cosmetics, version 7.0 is primarily the same as version 5.0. The biggest changes are in the help system and in the dialog boxes used for reading or writing files. Although most of the screen captures in this book come from version 5.0, users of version 7.0 will have no difficulty. When the differences were substantial, I have separate instructions for the two versions. Since students are more likely to know which version of Windows they are using than which version of Excel, I have referred to 7.0 as the Windows 95 version and to 5.0 as the Windows 3.1 version.

It is possible to use version 5.0 in Windows 95, however, and the windows in that case will be something of a hybrid. Since the discussions of the two separate versions are brief and together, I do not expect this to cause any problem.

▼ The Data Diskette

A data diskette is required for several of the lessons in this book. By *not* including the diskette with the book, Prentice Hall is able to charge a lower price than would otherwise be necessary. Copies of the diskette can be provided by Prentice Hall representatives. The data can also be downloaded from the internet in the form of a program in a file named *neufeld.exe*. Download the file, have a blank formatted diskette ready, and run the program from a DOS prompt or by choosing "Run" from the "File" menu of the Windows 3.1 Program Manager. The program will give you instructions and then write all of the data files to a diskette. If this program is placed on a network, students can run it individually to create their own data diskettes. The file can be downloaded either from Prentice Hall's anonymous ftp site, ftp.prenhall.com, in the directory pub/be/decision_science.d-012/neufeld/bus.stat, or from my WWW site given at the end of this preface.

▼ A Note on Student Computer Files

All of the lessons have students develop material in Excel workbooks. The instructions tell them to save their work frequently so that a computer problem will not cause them to lose what they have already done. It is best if these files are not saved to diskette while doing a lesson. It takes significantly longer to save a file to a diskette than a hard disk or network disk. When the student is finished working, the file can be copied to a diskette in situations where students cannot permanently store files on a local hard disk or network drive.

In some cases (including chapters 6 and 8) the files required to store the workbooks will become too large to fit on a diskette. Either hard disks or network drives will have to be used in these cases. Compression/decompression utilities (like PKZip, WinZip, and others) can be used to shrink the file so that it will fit on a diskette. A set of utilities to do this is included on the data diskette, and instructions for their use can be found in Appendix D. Your computing center may have alternative programs which are easier to use.

▼ Acknowledgments

Many people have helped me in developing this book by reading and working through chapters and making comments to me and by talking with me about computers, statistics, and pedagogy. At my own institution I owe a particular debt to Elizabeth Anthony, Andy Brod, Mike Evans, Terry Seaks, and Judy Tuttle. I am also grateful for the reviews and comments I have received from those at other institutions, including Kent S. Borowick at Baylor, Teresa Dalton at University of Denver, Paul J. Fields at the Naval Postgraduate School, Phillip C. Fry at Boise State University, Mehran Hojati at University of Saskatchewan, and Joseph Zaremba at SUNY Geneseo. Thanks also to Tom Tucker, the Decision Sciences Editor at Prentice Hall, who has been patient and encouraging, and to Diane Peirano, Audrey Regan, and Patricia Wosczyk at Prentice Hall.

My greatest thanks go to the hundreds of students who have shared classrooms with me and from whom I have learned more than I have ever taught.

I wish I could promise that this book is without error. I know from experience the frustration to student and professor alike of encountering errors in textbooks, especially statistics texts. It's only with this project that I have learned how truly difficult it is to eliminate all errors in a book of this sort. It is my intention to have a list of errata available at my World Wide Web site, whose address is given below. Please check it if you think you have found an error, and let me know if you have discovered a new error.

If you have any comments, suggestions, or criticisms you would like to share with me, I will welcome them.

John L. Neufeld
Department of Economics
University of North Carolina at Greensboro
Greensboro, NC 27412

email: **john_neufeld@uncg.edu**

WWW: **http://www.uncg.edu/bus_stat/**

Chapter 1

Introduction to Excel

Microsoft Excel is one of the most widely used computer programs. It belongs to the category of programs known as *spreadsheets*. Other well-known spreadsheet programs include Quattro Pro and Lotus 1-2-3. It's the versatility of spreadsheet programs that makes them so popular. When there is a need to analyze numerical data and prepare reports on that analysis, a spreadsheet program can often make the job easy. Spreadsheets are used by accountants, salespeople, managers, and nearly everyone working in business today. The ability to use a spreadsheet is a skill you will find useful in many different careers.

Spreadsheets have not traditionally been used for statistical analysis. Computers have long been used for statistical analysis, and computer programs to do that analysis existed long before the first spreadsheet program. As the use of computers became more widespread, statistics programs continued to develop even as the popularity of spreadsheets became firmly established for other types of quantitative analysis. Many excellent statistics packages, such as Minitab, SPSS, and SAS, are in wide use today. Spreadsheet programs also continued to develop, including the capability of doing statistical analysis. The current spreadsheet programs have considerable statistical capabilities, all you will need for the typical introductory college business statistics course.

Why use a spreadsheet program for statistics? There are two excellent reasons. First, spreadsheets are easier to learn and use than are traditional statistics programs. Although most statistics programs are constantly improved, they continue to show their mainframe heritage in the way they require users to use cryptic commands much like a programming language. By contrast, spreadsheets use a newer interface which, for most people, is more intuitive than the command language approach. In addition, the market for spreadsheet programs is huge, and the companies developing for that market can afford to devote enormous resources to develop any competitive advantage. Ease of use is one of the most important competitive advantages, and producers of spreadsheet programs are constantly working to improve their programs' ease of use. The much smaller market for statistical programs makes it difficult for ease of use to receive as much attention. The other big advantage of using a spreadsheet for statistics is that, unless you become a professional statistician, you are far more likely to be using a spreadsheet in your career than a statistical package. For most businesspeople, the need to do statistical analysis will be occasional. If you use a spreadsheet program for other purposes, statistical analysis will be easier (and will more likely be done) if you can use that same software.

Specialized statistical programs do have important advantages over spreadsheets. Most statistical programs provide a far greater variety of statistical procedures than does Excel. Even for those procedures which Excel does provide, statistical programs often provide additional or optional information not available with Excel. If your study of statistics goes much beyond the first course, you will need to learn to use a statistical program. If your career requires frequent statistical analysis or analysis near the "cutting edge" of statistical sophistication, you will need to learn and use a specialized statistical package. There is, however, every expectation that the statistical capabilities of spreadsheet programs like Excel will improve as new versions are released, and the role of spreadsheet programs in statistical analysis is likely to grow.

This chapter is designed to introduce you to Excel's basic features and operations. If you are familiar with any Windows or Macintosh program, some of the material here will be familiar to you, and you may be able to skim it. Some of the material is unique to Excel, and, unless you are already familiar with Excel, you should go over it more carefully.

▼ Using a Mouse

Although it is possible to use Excel without a mouse, it is not recommended. It takes most people a little practice to get used to using a mouse, so don't worry if you initially have difficulty controlling the mouse pointer. If you are using an IBM compatible PC, your mouse will have two buttons. Some PCs have a mouse with three buttons, but the middle button is not used with Excel. If you are using a Macintosh, your mouse will have only a single button. Many actions require that you position the mouse pointer at a particular location on the screen and click the mouse button. On a PC, most actions involve clicking the left button, but a few require clicking the right button. In this book, "clicking" a particular location on the screen will mean placing the mouse pointer on that location and then quickly pressing and releasing the *left* mouse button. If the right button is to be used, it will be clearly stated. Sometimes an action will require "double clicking." This means you position the

mouse pointer and push the button quickly twice in a row. On a PC, double clicking is always done with the *left* mouse button. New users often
find double clicking tricky at first, but it too will come with time.

▼ Starting Excel

- If you are using Windows 95, click the "Start" button on the lower left
  of your screen. A menu will open. Click "Programs." On the new
  menu, look for the Excel icon (shown on the left) and click it. If you
  don't find the Excel icon, look for an icon titled Microsoft Office in
  the shape of a folder and click it. The Excel icon will be in the window
  which opens.

Microsoft Excel

- If you are using Windows 3.1, look in the Program Manager for a Program Group icon titled "Excel" or "Microsoft Office." Double click
  that icon. When it opens, look for the Excel Icon (shown on the left)
  and double click it.

- If you are using a Macintosh, look for the lower icon in Finder and
  double click it.

When Excel starts, it will be in a *window*. That window may fill your machine's screen, or it may only fill a portion of the screen.

- If the window fills only a portion of your screen, make it fill the entire
  screen by clicking a special place on the upper right-hand corner of the
  window. In Windows, this is called the maximize button and looks like
  ◢ in Windows 3.1 and ❐ in Windows 95. On a Macintosh, it is
  called a zoom box.

Once the Excel window fills the screen, it should look approximately like
the picture on the next page. Don't worry if your window isn't exactly
like that shown. Excel allows a user to change some aspects of its appearance. This may have been done with your Excel.

Pay attention to the names shown for various parts of the screen. You
will likely want to refer back to this picture as those names are used later
in this book.

- Practice moving the mouse pointer by moving your mouse. It's important that you be able to accurately place the mouse pointer on part of
  the screen. Notice that the shape of the mouse pointer changes as you
  move to various parts of the screen. The shape of the mouse pointer
  changes to indicate the kind of operation you can do with the mouse
  in that portion of the screen.

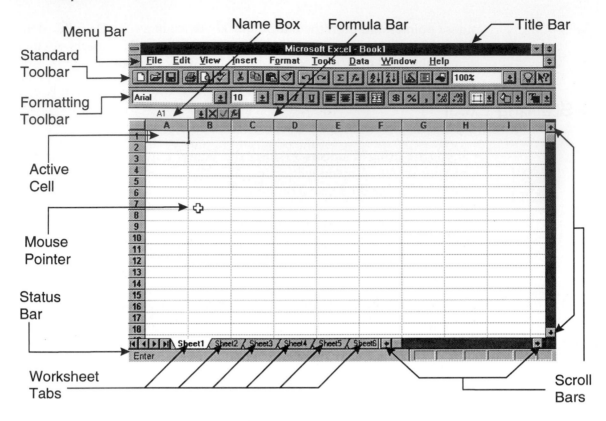

As long as you have the mouse pointer in the central part of the screen (the *cells*), it has the shape of a white plus sign ✛. This shape indicates that you can use the mouse pointer to *select cells* (which will be discussed below). Move the mouse pointer into the formula bar and it changes to this "I-beam" shape: I . When the mouse pointer has this shape, Excel will allow you to *enter numbers or letters* from the keyboard. Move the mouse pointer to the button bars, the Menu Bar, or the title bar, and the mouse pointer will have the shape of an arrow pointing to the upper left: ↖ .

As you use Excel, you will discover that there are other shapes the mouse pointer can take. These shapes indicate the operation Excel expects you to make. Sometimes, when you are having difficulty getting Excel to do what you want, the shape of the mouse pointer will clue you to what Excel thinks you should be doing.

Let's take a quick tour of the main Excel screen from top to bottom. The features mentioned here will be discussed in more detail later.

▼ The Title Bar

The *Title Bar* on top tells us what is in this window. As you use Excel, you will find that some operations open windows *within* the main Excel window. These "sub windows" will generally also have a Title Bar indicating the operation that window performs. For the main Excel window, this includes the name of the application (Microsoft Excel) and the name of the *workbook* (Book1). When you use Excel, you create a workbook which can be saved in a file. Another common name for what Excel calls a workbook is a *spreadsheet*.

If you are using Windows 3.1, at the extreme left of the Title Bar you will see the Control-Menu Box : ▬. Most windows have this box. Double clicking this box will generally close the window. In the case of the main Excel window, this will end the Excel session.

If you are using Windows 95, you will find the Close Box ✖ on the right side of the Title Bar. Most windows will have this box. Clicking it will generally close the window, and clicking the Close Box in the main Excel window will end the Excel session.

- Click the Close box or double click the Control-Menu Box. A window may open with a question of whether or not you wish to "save the changes in 'Book1'?" If you see this window (and you may not), place the mouse pointer directly on the word "No" and click the (left) mouse button. Your Excel session will end.

Many windows will have buttons or menu items which will close them, but using the Close Box or Control-Menu Box will work with virtually any window.

- Start Excel again by clicking or double clicking the Excel icon.

▼ The Menu Bar

Below the Title Bar is the Menu Bar.

- Place the mouse pointer over the word **View**. If you are using a PC, click the left mouse button. If you are using a Macintosh, push and hold the mouse button.

The View menu will open as shown on the top left of the next page. Notice the check marks beside "Formula Bar" and "Status Bar." These two features can be either *on* or *off*. The check marks indicate that both are currently *on*.

- Place the mouse pointer over the words "Formula Bar" and click the (left) mouse button (on a PC), or release the mouse button (on a Mac). The Formula Bar will disappear from your screen.

- Again open the View menu. Notice that the check mark beside "Formula Bar" is now gone (the feature is *off*). Choose "Formula Bar" as you did above (click on a PC, release button on a Mac).

The Formula Bar will reappear. If you lose the Formula Bar (or the Status Bar), this is the way you get them back. Be sure that they are showing whenever you use this book.

Some of the menu choices are followed by an ellipsis (...). This indicates that if you make that choice, there will be further choices to make. Sometimes Excel will open a submenu when a menu choice with an ellipsis is made. At other times a *dialog window* will open. A dialog window will give you the opportunity to make further choices.

- Open the View menu and select "Toolbars...."

A window (like that shown below) will open, showing the names of all of Excel's toolbars. When Excel is first started, the toolbars which are visible are the Standard and Formatting toolbars. These are the ones shown on the screen picture on page 4. (The Standard toolbar is on top in that picture, but may not be on your screen.) In the dialog window shown, there are X marks in the boxes beside "Standard" and "Formatting."

- Place the mouse pointer on the word "Standard" and click the (left) mouse button. Do the same on the word "Formatting." The Xs in the boxes will disappear.

- Click the rectangle in the upper right corner with "OK" in it.

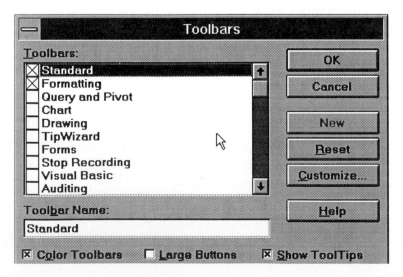

The window will close, and both toolbars will be gone from your screen.

- Open the View menu again, and click "Toolbars..." again. When the window opens, click again on the words "Standard" and "Formatting," so the Xs return and the dialog window again looks like that shown above.

- Click "OK."

Your Excel screen should now look like that shown on page 4. Whenever you are using this book, you should be sure that you start Excel with the Standard and Formatting toolbars showing (and no others). Use the procedures you have just practiced if needed to be sure these toolbars are showing when you start an Excel session.

▼ Using the Toolbars

There are two toolbars shown in the Excel screen on page 4. The top bar is called the *standard* toolbar and the lower bar is called the *formatting* toolbar. On your screen the bars might be interchanged.

Each toolbar consists of a group of icons or "buttons" (also called "speed buttons"). The buttons are the little squares, each with a symbol in it. You "press" a button by placing the mouse pointer over the button and clicking the (left) mouse button. When you do this, the button will appear to be pressed; it will seem recessed and its color will lighten slightly. Most of the buttons perform operations which also could be performed by using the menus. The buttons are a convenience because they are faster to use than the menus, and they are always visible. The menus are designed to be organized logically by operation, while the buttons are meant to provide an easy way of accessing the most frequently used operations. Excel provides extensive facilities for the user to control what buttons are shown and even to define new buttons. If you are interested, consult the Excel manual.

- Place the mouse pointer over one of the buttons, but don't click a mouse button.

Look at the status bar. A brief description of a speed button's function appears *before* you activate it by clicking.

- If you are using a PC place the mouse pointer on a speed button and leave it there a few seconds without clicking a mouse button.

Notice that the name of the button will appear directly below the button. Macintosh users can activate a similar feature by selecting "Show Balloons" from the Help icon menu near the right end of the Menu Bar.

▼ Getting Help—The Help Speed Button

One of Excel's most useful features is its extensive on-line help. Even experienced Excel users will sometimes forget how to do a certain operation or will be unsure how a particular function works in Excel. Rather than having to search through a thick manual, Excel can give you instructions directly from the program itself. It can be useful, but it's not perfect. Sometimes the instructions don't tell you exactly what you want to know. Other times finding the information you want can be a problem. Excel tries to help with this latter problem by giving you several different ways of getting to the help system. One way is through the Help menu on the Menu Bar. At times, a special help speed button will be available. The Help speed button is on the right side of the standard toolbar on the main Excel screen.

- Find the Help speed button: ▨ and click it.

Notice that this changes the mouse pointer to a new shape similar to the icon shown on the button: ▨ . This is the Help mouse pointer.

If you use the Help mouse pointer to click on a speed button, Excel will open a Help window explaining the function of that speed button. The Help window will provide much more information than you saw on the status bar. The status bar description (and balloon help) are designed to help you find the button which performs an operation you already are familiar with. The Help window is designed to explain how to use an operation you are not familiar with.

The Help pointer can also be used to get help on a menu operation.

- With the Help mouse pointer, click on the View menu and then click on the words "Formula Bar" just as you did above to open the dialog window enabling you to make the Formula Bar disappear and reappear.

This time, instead of the Formula Bar disappearing, a Help window appears on your screen as shown on the next page. This window explains what clicking "Formula Bar" on the View menu does.

▼ The Help System—Windows 95

(Skip this section if you are using Windows 3.1.)

In addition to the Help button, Windows 95 has the Answer Wizard which can provide answers to an enormous number of questions. Let's suppose that you want information on how to enter dates in an Excel worksheet.

- Click on **Help** on the right side of the Menu Bar. The "Help" menu will open as shown below. Select "Answer Wizard." The Answer Wizard dialog window will open.

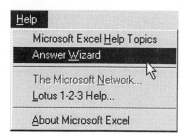

- In the top field of the Answer Wizard dialog window enter "entering dates" as shown in the picture below. Click the "Search" button to the right of the field. Excel is not picky about exactly what you put in this field. Instead of "entering dates," you could have put "enter dates," or "How do I enter dates?", or just "dates." All will work.

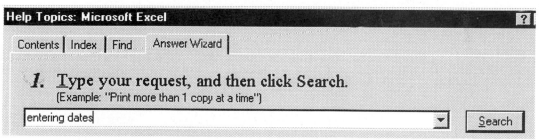

You will notice a number of topics in the large bottom field of the Answer Wizard dialog window (shown below) under the general headings "How Do I," "Tell Me About," and "Programming and Language Reference." Each line of text under each of these headings is a topic about which Excel's Answer Wizard can provide additional information.

- Under "How Do I" select "Type a date or a time." The background around that topic will become dark and the letters will become light (see picture below). Click the ⸢Display⸣ button at the bottom of the dialog window. A Help window will open explaining how to enter date and time information.

- Read the information in the help window. Use the "Page Down" key to see the information at the bottom. Notice the "For more information, click ⸢»⸣ " in the text. This is a *hyperlink* button and allows you to get additional information.

- Place your mouse pointer directly over the button. Notice the pointer changes to the shape of a hand pointing a finger ⸢🖱⸣. When the mouse pointer is in this shape, click the left mouse button. A new help window will appear providing you with additional information.

Some of the Help windows also contain *hypertext*, words which function like the reference button in the sense that, when clicked, a new Help window appears. Hypertext may appear as underlined or as a different color in the Help window. You can easily determine if certain words are hypertext, or if a symbol is a reference button by placing the mouse pointer over it. If the pointer changes to the pointing-hand shape, clicking the left mouse button will bring you a new help window.

▼ The Help System—Windows 3.1

(Skip this section if you are using Windows 95.)

- On the right side of the Menu Bar, locate the **Help** menu item. Open the menu using the method appropriate for your machine (PC or Mac—see page 5). The menu which opens is shown on the left.

- Select the submenu "Search for Help on ..." which is shown highlighted on the left.

If you observe carefully, you will notice that two windows open. A Help window much like that seen before opens, and a Search window opens directly over the Help window. The Search window has two parts. The top part consists of a list of search words in alphabetic order. The bottom part has a list of topics for each search word.

- In the top field of the Search dialog window, enter the phrase "entering dates" one letter at a time. Observe the behavior of the list of words and phrases in the field immediately below the one where you are entering text. Each word or phrase is a subject on which Excel can provide additional information. When you type the letter "t," the entry "entering, dates" will be visible in that window.

- Click "entering, dates" so that it becomes highlighted (white letters on a dark background). Click the "Show Topics" button on the upper right portion of the dialog window.

Sometimes several topics will appear in the bottom field. In that case, you would select the one you wanted to see by highlighting it. In this case, only one topic, "Entering a date or time" appears, and it is already highlighted. Your window should look like the picture below. If you had started the search process by entering "dates" instead of "entering dates" in the first search field, you would have been led to this same topic.

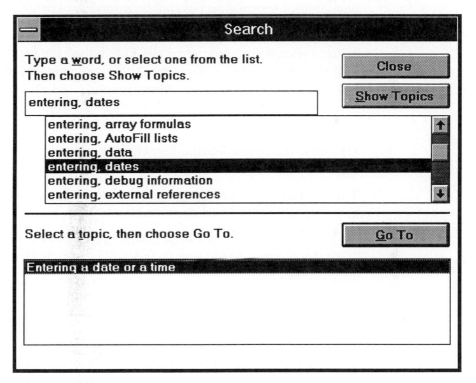

- Click the "Go To" button on the right side of the dialog window. A How To window will appear explaining how to enter dates. Read the information in the window. You can use the "Page Down" key on the keyboard to see the information at the bottom.

At the end of the information in the Help window, Excel provides other help topics related to the one in the window. Notice that these topics are underlined and may be in a different color. This distinctive appearance identifies them as *hyperlinks*. Clicking on these words will cause Excel's help to provide you with additional information.

- Place your mouse pointer on the "Assigning a number, date, or time format" hyperlink in the Help window. Notice that the mouse pointer changes to a small pointing hand: 🖑 .

- Click the (left) mouse button. A new How To window appears. Notice that it also has hypertext.

▼ Moving a Window

At this point you should have either one or two windows on top of your spreadsheet covering the information below. Suppose you want to see the portion of a spreadsheet covered by a window. Fortunately, nearly every window with a Title Bar can be moved.

- Place your mouse pointer on the Title Bar of the Help window (or one of the help windows). Press the (left) mouse button, and, while the button is depressed, move the mouse pointer. An outline of the window will move with the pointer. Move it away from where the Help window is now located.

- Release the mouse button. The Help window will move to where you positioned the outline.

This operation is called *dragging* the window. As you will see below, dragging can be used in Excel to move other objects.

- Close the Help window or windows. This can be done by double clicking the Control-Menu Box (Windows 3.1) or clicking the Close Box (Windows 95)..

▼ The Active Cell

The heart of an Excel workbook is the *cells* in the central part of the window. Each of the cells has an address determined by the row and column in which the cell is located. At the top of each column is a *column heading* with a letter, and to the left of each row is a *row heading* with a number. A cell's address is the letter of its column followed by the number of its row. In the section of the worksheet shown on the next page, the active cell is in column A and row 1. Its address is therefore A1. Notice that this address is shown in the Name Box. The Name Box shows the address of the active cell.

The active cell is the cell in which you can enter data. You can tell which cell is the active cell because it is surrounded by a special border, the ac-

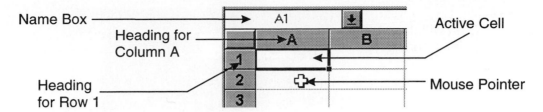

tive cell border: [▭]. A cell is made active by placing the mouse pointer in the cell and clicking the (left) mouse button.

- Make cell C2 active.

If you have done this correctly, the Name Box will contain the address "C2."

▼ Selecting Cells

The active cell is always a single cell. Some operations in Excel involve more than a single cell and require that you *select* a *range* of cells. A selection of cells is usually a rectangular block of cells. Since it is rectangular, it can be referred to by the cell addresses of its corners. Excel requires these addresses be separated by a colon. For example, suppose we wanted to select the rectangular array of cells consisting of cells A1, B1, A2, B2, A3, and B3. The four corners of this array are A1, B1, B3, and A3. This book will use the convention of referring to the array by the addresses of the upper left cell (A1 in this case), and the lower right cell (B3). This range would be referred to as A1:B3. Select this range of cells by doing the following.

- Place the mouse pointer on cell A1 and press and hold the (left) mouse button.

You will see cell A1 immediately become the active cell.

- While continuing to press the mouse button, drag the mouse pointer to cell B3 and release the mouse button (as illustrated on the next page).

The selected region of cells will include the active cell (A1 in this case). The other cells in the selected region will be black.

- Press the Tab key repeatedly and notice how the active cell changes within the selected region. Press the Enter key repeatedly and notice the same behavior.

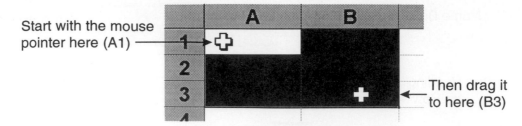

Start with the mouse pointer here (A1)

Then drag it to here (B3)

▼ Entering Data

Data are entered into the active cell from the keyboard. There are three types of data which can be entered:

1. Numbers. When you use Excel for statistical or other quantitative analysis, numbers are the starting point of the analysis.

2. Text. Text should be used liberally in an Excel workbook to document the numbers and calculations to make it easy to remember what the numbers mean. Excel is capable of producing beautiful tables which can be used in reports. Every table should have text defining the rows and columns.

3. Formulas. Much of the work done by Excel will be in formulas you enter where you tell Excel the calculations you want done.

▼ Numbers

To enter a number in the active cell, simply type the number on your keyboard. To complete the entry of a number, press the Enter key.

As you enter the number specified below, notice the following:

1. As you enter a number, the characters you type appear in the cell and in the Formula Bar.

2. As you enter a number, a vertical line called the *insertion point* shows where the next character you type will appear. As long as the insertion point is visible, you can correct typing errors with the backspace key. Once you press the Enter key, the insertion point will disappear.

	A	B
1		100.5
2		

Insertion Point

- Click cell B1 (make it the active cell). This should also remove the black selected region.

- Enter the number "100.5" (don't enter the quotation marks). Observe the formula bar as you enter the number. Press the Enter key when you are finished.

▼ Editing a Cell

It is easy to edit a cell which already has an entry by placing the mouse pointer in the cell and double clicking. This will cause both that cell to become the active cell and the insertion point to appear within the cell. When you first were entering the number, the insertion point was always to the right of the last character you typed. When you edit a cell, you can move the insertion point by using the left or right cursor (arrow) keys or by positioning the mouse pointer exactly where you want the insertion point and clicking. This lets you add a character in the middle without re-typing the rest of the number. You can erase the character to the right of the insertion point by pressing the Delete key. The Back Space key deletes the character to the left of the insertion point.

- Double click cell B1. You should see the insertion point in the cell.

- Place the mouse pointer between the decimal point and the "5," and click the mouse button.

Notice that when a cell has been double clicked and is ready for editing, the mouse pointer changes shape. The new shape (the "I-beam") makes it easier to point precisely where you want the insertion point to be. Clicking between the decimal point and the "5" will cause the insertion point to appear at that location.

- Type the character "4" (without the quotation marks), and press the Enter key.

The contents of cell B1 should now be 100.45.

It is also possible to edit the contents of a cell in the Formula Bar.

- Make cell B1 the active cell, but don't double click the cell.

- Move the mouse pointer to the Formula Bar. Place the mouse pointer to the right of the "5" and click.

An insertion point will appear at the end of the number.

- Type a "6" (without the quotation marks). Press the Enter key.

The value of cell B1 should now be 100.456.

▼ Entering Text

Entering text is as simple as entering numbers.

- Double click cell A1.

- Type the following text (without the quotation marks): "The First Number."

Notice that before you press the Enter key, the text which you enter goes beyond the right border of cell A1 and causes the contents of cell B1 to disappear.

	A	B
1	The First Number	
2		

After the Enter key is pressed, the contents of B1 reappear, but part of the text is covered as shown below.

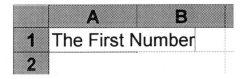

	A	B
1	The First N	100.456
2		

- Click cell A1 to again make it the active cell, but don't double click.

Notice the Formula Bar. The full text appears there. Even though cell A1 on the worksheet is not wide enough to show the entire text, *it is there*. Excel stores the entire text correctly. It displays what it can given the available space.

Excel behaves similarly with numbers. It keeps track of all decimal places even if the cell is too narrow to display them all and even though the value displayed in the cell may be rounded. The full number is stored and can be seen in the Formula Bar when the cell containing the number is made active.

- Click cell A2.

- Enter the following text (without the quotation marks): "The Second Number."

- Press the Enter key. The cells should look like the following picture.

	A	B
1	The First N	100.456
2	The Second Number	

Notice this time that the full text appears even after the Enter key is pressed. This is because cell B2 is empty. If something is later entered into that cell, part of the text in A2 would disappear just as you saw in the first row.

▼ Changing the Width of a Column

If you increase the width of column A, the full text of cell A1 can be viewed in the cell.

Carefully place the mouse pointer on the border between the heading for column A and the heading for column B. (Row and column headings are shown on page 13.) When you have it correct, the pointer will change to new shape: ✛. This is the *column width* mouse pointer.

The column headings and mouse pointer should look like the following picture.

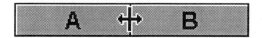

- Once you see the column width mouse pointer, press and hold the (left) mouse button, and *drag* the headings boundary to the right. Position the mouse pointer so that it is approximately over the "B" in the next column's heading (no need to be precise). Release the mouse button.

The width of column A will increase and move the columns to the right further to the right.

- Again position the mouse pointer on the boundary between the heading for column A and that for column B. This time, *drag* the boundary to the left about halfway across the current width of column A (more or less on the A). Release the mouse button. This enables you to reduce the width of a column.

Although this method gives you complete control over column width, it is hard to know exactly how wide to make the column to display its contents without wasting space. Fortunately, there is a shortcut when you want simply to make a column wide enough to display the cell contents.

- Again position the mouse pointer on the boundary between the headings of columns A and B. Instead of dragging, double click without moving the mouse.

The width of column A will immediately adjust to display the text in the cells in that column. The cells should look like the picture below.

	A	B
1	The First Number	100.456
2	The Second Number	

▼ An Editing Shortcut—Text Highlighting

Suppose that we wanted to change the word "First" in cell A1 to "1st," and the word "Second" to "2nd." One way of doing this would be to first erase the word "First" and then enter "1st." There will be many times when you will want to replace one thing with another, and there is a useful shortcut for this operation.

- Double click cell A1 so that you can edit it.

- Place the insertion point immediately to the left of the "F" in "First."

- Move the mouse pointer so that it is on the insertion point.

- Press and hold the (left) mouse button.

- Move the mouse pointer to the right (across the word "First") while continuing to press the mouse button.

As the mouse pointer moves across the letters, notice that the colors switch from black letters on a white background to white letters on a black background. This is called *highlighting* the letters.

- Continue moving the mouse until you have highlighted the word "First" and only the word "First." Release the mouse button.

Your screen should look like the picture below.

- On your keyboard type "1st" (without the quotation marks).

	A	B
1	The First Number	100.456
2	The Second Number	

As soon as you begin typing, the highlighted text ("First") is deleted and new text appears in its place. Your screen should look like the picture below.

	A	B
1	The 1st Number	100.456
2	The Second Number	

- Press the Enter key to complete the cell editing.

This "text highlighting" can be used anywhere in Excel (including dialog windows) when you want to edit text. "Text" in this sense means anything you could enter from the keyboard, including numbers and formulas.

- Practice the technique by changing the word "Second" in cell A2 to "2nd." Be sure to press the Enter key.

- Use the method described above (page 17) to have Excel automatically adjust the width of column A to fit the data in the column. Although this was used above to expand the column's width, the same method can also reduce a column's width.

Your screen should look like the following picture.

	A	B
1	The 1st Number	100.456
2	The 2nd Number	

▼ Entering Formulas

- Make cell C1 the active cell.

- Enter (without the quotation marks): "=3+2" and press the Enter key.

- Again make cell C1 the active cell.

You indicate to Excel that you are entering a formula when you first enter an equals sign. Notice that cell C1 appears to have a "5" but that the Formula Bar shows the formula you entered. (See the picture on the next page.)

This formula, of course, directs Excel to add 3 and 2.

C1	±	=3+2

	A	B	C
1	The 1st Number	100.456	5
2	The 2nd Number		

- Edit cell C1 and change the plus sign to a minus sign (-). Press Enter. Cell C1 should have a 1.

- Change the minus sign to a forward slash (/). This is the symbol for division, and the formula now directs Excel to divide 3 by 2. Press Enter and cell C1 should have 1.5.

- Change the forward slash to an asterisk (*). There is no real multiplication sign on a computer keyboard, and Excel uses the asterisk for that purpose. Press Enter, and cell C1 will have a 6, the product of 3 and 2.

- Change the asterisk to a carat ($^\wedge$). This is Excel's symbol for exponentiation, raising a number to a power. Press Enter and cell C1 will have the value of 3^2 or 9.

▼ Order of Arithmetic Operations

When a long formula with several operations is entered, Excel uses the standard "order of precedence" to determine which operations to do first. This means that first exponentiation will be done. Multiplication and division will be done next. Addition and subtraction will be done last. You can control the order in which operations are done by using parentheses.

- Enter "=(3+2)*6" (without quotation marks) in cell C1 and press Enter.

The value will be 30. Excel first does the operation inside the parentheses by adding 3 and 2. The result of that operation, 5, is then multiplied by 6.

- Enter "=3+(2*6)" in cell C1 and press the Enter key.

This time the value is 15. Excel first multiplies 2 times 6 and then adds the result (12) to 3.

- Enter "=3+2*6" in C1 with no parentheses. Press the Enter key.

Again, the answer is 15 because the order of precedence causes Excel to do the multiplication before the addition. It's a good idea to freely use parentheses in any formula with more than one operation so that you will be sure that the calculations will be done in the order you want. Remember that you always have to explicitly use the asterisk to indicate multiplication, even if you use parentheses. In mathematics, notation like (2)(3) is often understood to mean that the two values should be multiplied. With Excel, however, the multiplication must always be explicitly shown by an asterisk.

In addition to the basic arithmetic operations, Excel has a large number of mathematical functions. These functions can be entered directly in a formula. For example, suppose we wanted to calculate the square root of 9.

- In cell C1 enter "=sqrt(9)" and press the Enter key.

Cell C1 should now show a "3." The square root function has the name "sqrt" in Excel. Notice that the "9" is in parentheses and immediately follows the "sqrt." The "9" is called an argument of the function; it's the value we want the function to work on. Some functions have more than one argument. A few functions have no arguments. Regardless of the number of arguments, they all appear within a single set of parentheses. If there is more than one argument, they are separated by commas. If there are no arguments, the function name is followed by empty parentheses "()."

- Make C1 the active cell. Notice the Formula Bar.

Excel converts the function name to uppercase. You can enter a function name either in uppercase or lowercase, but it will always appear in the Formula Bar as uppercase.

As you will learn later, Excel has a very clever feature which makes its built-in functions much easier to use. This feature is called the Function Wizard, and much use will be made of it in this book.

▼ Using Cell Addresses in Formulas

A particularly useful and powerful facility in Excel is the ability to create formulas which refer to a cell whose contents are used in the calculation.

- Enter the following formula in cell C2 (without the quotes): "=b1+10." Press the Enter key.

The value displayed in cell C2 should be 110.456, which is the number in cell B1 plus the number 10.

Use the up-arrow cursor key to make C2 the active cell again. Notice that in the formula bar, the contents of the cell are displayed as

=B1+10. Just as in the case of the SQRT function, Excel changes a cell address to uppercase letters even if you enter it in lowercase.

- Click cell B1 to make it the active cell (but don't double click). Enter the number "50" (without the quotation marks). Press the Enter key.

Notice that entering something new in an active cell which already has something in it simply erases the old contents and replaces it with the new. What does cell C2 now show? It should have the value 60, the contents of cell B1 (now 50) plus 10.

- Change the value of cell B1 to -20. Press the Enter key.

No matter what value you enter in cell B1, the displayed value of cell C2 will be 10 more. In this case, 10 more than -20 is -10.

It is also possible to enter a cell address by pointing to it with the mouse pointer.

- Make cell C3 the active cell. Begin a formula by entering an equals sign (=). Move the mouse pointer over cell B1 and click the (left) mouse button once.

A "B1" should be entered into the formula in cell C3 immediately after the equals sign.

- Enter a plus sign (+). Move the mouse pointer directly over cell C1 and click the (left) mouse button once.

The formula in cell C3 should now be "=B1+C1."

- Press the Enter key.

The value of cell C3 should display as -17, assuming that B1 has the value -20 and C1 has the value 3. Remember that C1 contains a formula ("=sqrt(9)"), not a number. As long as a cell *displays* a number, its address can be used within a formula even though that number is the result of a formula.

- Change cell C1's value to 50. What now is the value of cell C3?

Cell C3 should now display 30. Whenever the value of a cell changes, the displayed value of any cell containing a formula which references that cell will also change. This very important feature makes it possible to set up a workbook to analyze a particular *type* of problem and easily use it to handle different data by simply changing the numbers in cells referenced by equations in other cells which do the real analysis.

▼ Scientific Notation

Sometimes the result of a calculation will be an extremely large or an extremely small number. When this happens, Excel uses a format which is similar to what is called *scientific notation*.

- Make C1 active and enter the formula "=55 ^ 13." Press the Enter key.

This formula directs Excel to calculate 55^{13}, which is a very large number. Cell C1 will have the value 4.21E+22. (Your display might show other numbers between the "1" and the "E.") In scientific notation, this number would be:

$$4.21 \times 10^{22}$$

where 10^{22} is twenty-two 10s all multiplied together. This number is a 1 followed by 22 zeros. The "E" in this notation is short for "exponent." In the scientific notation shown above, the "22" is called the *exponent* of 10. To represent this number in the notation we are most familiar with, the decimal place would have to be shifted 22 (the amount of the exponent) places to the right of where it is in 4.21. So this number is a bit larger than 4 followed by 22 zeros.

If you are not used to scientific notation, you probably don't feel comfortable with it. Excel can convert the number to the more familiar notation for you.

- Make cell C1 the active cell. Find the Comma Style speed button on the formatting toolbar: ▪. Click it.

The reason the cell contents become "########" is that the cell is not wide enough to display the number in the format you have chosen.

Have Excel automatically adjust the cell width by double clicking the border between the heading for the C column and the D column. Is this better? The number may be easier for you to make sense of now, but it takes up a lot of space.

Very small numbers in this notation have negative exponents.

- Make cell D1 active and enter "=1/(55 ^ 13)." Press the Enter key.

This directs Excel to calculate 1 divided by the same huge number it just calculated. This, of course, will be very small. Excel will show it as 2.37E-23. Notice that the exponent is *negative* (-23). To see this number in standard notation, we would have to shift the decimal place 23 positions to the *left* of where it is in 2.37.

To get Excel to show you the number in more familiar notation, do the following.

- Manually increase the width of column D by dragging the border between the heading of columns D and E to the right. Make column D about as wide as column C.

- Make D1 the active cell.

- Click the Comma Style speed button.

You may be surprised that cell D1 appears to contain zero. This is because the Comma Style button sets the cell to display only two decimal places. Another speed button will increase the number of displayed decimal places.

- Click the Increase Decimal speed button: [icon]. You will have to click it many times before you see enough decimal places to display this number.

Here again, although this format is probably easier for you to read than Excel's scientific format, it takes up much more space. Numbers like this will occasionally be produced by some statistical procedures, and it is best (but not essential) to get used to Excel's standard representation of them.

▼ Error Codes

Some calculations cannot be done and result in an error. In these cases, Excel displays an *error value* in the cell. Let's see what they look like. The examples discussed below are going to involve making pretty obvious errors, ones you might be very unlikely to make. As your use of Excel becomes more sophisticated, however, errors become much more subtle and less obvious than these examples.

- In cell D1 enter the formula "=10/0" (without quotes). Press the Enter key.

This formula instructs Excel to divide the number 10 by zero, although division by zero is not defined. Instead of a value, cell D1 contains the error value "#DIV/0!" All Excel error values begin with "#." It's not hard to see that this error value warns of division by zero.

- Make D1 the active cell. Look at the Formula Bar.

As in the case of a valid calculation, the formula bar shows us that Excel continues to store the formula in the cell and simply displays the answer as an error value.

- Edit the formula, changing the "0" to a "5." Press the Enter key.

A nonerror value ("2") now appears in cell D1.

You are likely to encounter other error values as you work with Excel. The meaning of some of them may not be so obvious. Whenever Excel does something unexpected, a good first place to turn is the on-line help.

Suppose you wanted to use Excel to take the absolute value of a number, and were unsure of the name Excel uses for the absolute value function. One reasonable approach to this problem is to guess.

- Enter in cell D1 the formula "=absval(-10)" without the quotation marks. Press the Enter key.

At this point you can probably guess what the error value, "#NAME?," means. Suppose, however, that you needed an explanation of the error message. This is an excellent opportunity to experiment with Excel's extensive on-line help system.

- Use the on-line help system to view Excel's help window for the "#NAME?" error code. Start by entering the code in the Answer Wizard (Windows 95) or in the Search window of Help (Windows 3.1).

You will notice in the Help window that there are several possible causes for the error listed, including "Misspelling the name of a function." This is likely confirmation that we have misspelled the name of Excel's function to take the absolute value. How can we determine what the correct spelling is?

- Use Excel's help system to search for the name of the Excel formula which determines the absolute value. Do this by asking for help for "absolute value." If you are using Windows 95, one of the topics the Answer Wizard offers is on the ABS worksheet function. If you are using Windows 3.1, ABS is the only topic offered. Choose that topic. It is apparent from the information given in the help window that "ABS" is the absolute value function.

- Close the Help window.

- Edit the formula in cell D1 to change "absval" to "abs." Press the Enter key. The error value should be replaced by 10—the absolute value of −10

▼ The Scroll Bars

Excel displays only a portion of a worksheet on your computer screen. It frequently will be necessary to view the other cells. Think of your screen as a small window on a very large worksheet. To view portions of the worksheet which are not currently visible you need to move your screen's window on the worksheet until it is over the cells you want to see. One way of doing this is to use the scroll bars.

There are two scroll bars. The horizontal scroll bar moves the screen window horizontally, while the vertical bar moves the window vertically. The parts of the scroll bar are shown in the picture below. Note that the scroll bars on your screen will be longer than those shown below, and your screen will probably include worksheet tabs.

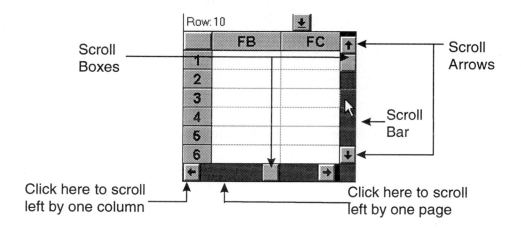

Each scroll bar has a scroll box and two scroll arrows. The position of the scroll box within the scroll bar shows the relative position of the screen window on the worksheet. For example, in the picture above, the scroll box is at the top of the vertical scroll bar, indicating that the screen window is at the top of the worksheet. The first row of the worksheet is visible.

The scroll box in the horizontal scroll bar, on the other hand, is more or less in the middle of the scroll bar. The visible portion of the worksheet is to the right of the first column (column A). To move the screen window over the worksheet, you move the scroll box within its scroll bar.

- On your worksheet, place the mouse pointer on the bottom scroll arrow of the vertical scroll bar on the right of your screen. Click the (left) mouse button once.

The screen window will move down one row. The top row visible on your screen should be row 2 and the bottom row should be one row below that which was originally visible.

- Place the mouse pointer on the vertical scroll bar so that it is below the scroll box and above the scroll arrow. Click the (left) mouse button once.

The screen window will scroll down by a "page" (the total number of rows displayed). All of the rows now visible are below what was the bottom row. Anytime you click the mouse pointer on any part of the scroll bar below the scroll box but above the scroll arrow, the screen window will move down a page. If you click the scroll bar above the scroll box, the screen window will move up a page.

- Place the mouse pointer directly on the scroll box. Press and hold the (left) mouse button. While holding the mouse button, slowly move the scroll box up. Notice the name box. Position the scroll box so that the name box contains "Row: 10." Release the mouse button.

Row 10 should now be the top row on your screen.

- Experiment with the horizontal scroll bar by clicking the scroll arrows, scroll bars, and moving the scroll box.

▼ Worksheets and Worksheet Tabs

An Excel worksheet, as you have seen, contains far more cells than can be seen on your screen at one time. In addition, an Excel *workbook* contains many *worksheets*. Tabs for some of these worksheets can be found at the bottom of the Excel window to the left of the horizontal scroll bar. The current worksheet is "Sheet1," and you will notice that the tab for that worksheet appears on top and is lighter than the other worksheet tabs.

- Click the "Sheet2" tab.

Notice that a blank worksheet appears with all the columns set to their original width. Notice also that the "Sheet2" tab now appears to be on top and is the lightest tab.

- Click the "Sheet1" tab.

The previous worksheet reappears.

Worksheets give you a way to help you organize the information in a workbook. In addition, some operations in Excel create new worksheets. As you will see, some worksheets will contain a graph rather than cells.

Not all of the tabs for the available worksheets may be visible. The visible tabs can be scrolled using the special scroll arrows immediately to the left of the worksheet tabs. The functions of those arrows are described in the picture below.

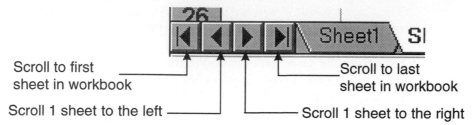

Scroll to first sheet in workbook

Scroll to last sheet in workbook

Scroll 1 sheet to the left

Scroll 1 sheet to the right

- Click each of the worksheet tab scroll arrows and observe its operation.

In addition to entering data in cells, you can also put values in cells by filling, copying, and moving cells. "Filling" refers to the ability within Excel to automatically extend a sequence of values.

▼Copying and Moving Cells

- Click the "Sheet2" worksheet tab so that you can work with a clean worksheet.

Excel provides a number of different methods to copy or move cells. It is common to want to copy the contents of a single cell to several adjacent cells, either in the same row or the same column. As will be discussed below, this is a particularly useful operation when the cell to be copied contains a formula, but the procedure will work when the cell contains text or numbers.

- Enter the number "1" (without quotes) in cell A1. Press the Enter key.

- Click cell A1 to again make it the active cell, but don't double click since you don't want to edit the cell.

Look carefully at the border around the active cell. In the lower right corner there is a small square called the *fill handle*. Carefully position the mouse pointer over the fill handle. When you have it correctly positioned, the pointer will change from a thick white cross to a thin black cross as shown in the picture on the next page.

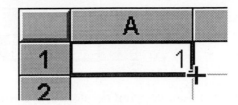

- Click and hold the (left) mouse button while it is in the shape of a black cross. Drag the mouse pointer down column A until the selection frame includes cell A10. Release the mouse button. Cell A1 will be white, and cells A2 through A10 will be black.

- Release the mouse button.

The "1" originally in cell A1 has been copied to all the cells in the range.

- Press the "Delete" or "Del" key on your keyboard. This will erase the contents of the selected range. (The "Del" key on the numeric keypad will only work if NumLock is *off*).

- Click cell A1 and enter the word "Total" (without quotes). Press the Enter key. Reselect cell A1.

- Position the mouse pointer over the lower right corner so that it changes into a black cross.

- Hold the mouse button and drag to the *right* until the selection boundary includes the cell at the top of row E. Release the mouse button.

The word "Total" will have been copied to all of the cells within the selected region A1 through E1.

- Erase the contents cells A1 through E1 using the Delete key.

▼ Filling Cells

- Enter the number "1" in cell A1 and the number "2" in cell B1.

- Select the cell range A1:B1.

- Place the mouse pointer over the square in the lower right corner of the selection boundary until it becomes a black cross, as shown in the picture at the top of the next page.

- With the mouse pointer in the shape of a black cross, click and hold the (left) mouse button and drag the selection outline to the right along the first row until it includes cell G1. Release the mouse button.

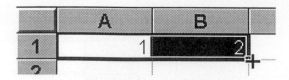

Rather than copying the contents of cells A1 and B1 to the other cells, Excel continues the series begun in those cells, with cells A1 through G1 containing the number 1 through 7.

- Erase the contents of the cells in the first row.

- Put the number "5" (no quotes) in cell A1 and the number "10" in cell A2.

- Create a selected region containing cells A1 and A2 by placing the mouse pointer in the center of cell A1, pressing and holding the (left) mouse button, dragging the mouse pointer to the center of cell A2, and releasing the mouse pointer in cell A2.

- Place the mouse pointer over the small square in the lower right-hand corner, press the (left) mouse button, and drag the selection outline down to cell A10. Release the mouse button.

Since cells A1 and A2 had values which differed by 5, Excel extended the series by adding 5 to each number. Try repeating the process after putting "2" in A1 and "4" in A2. Try again with "1920" in A1 and "1930" in A2. Excel's ability to fill a range of cells is an excellent demonstration of intelligence in a computer program.

Excel's ability to fill with certain text values is even more remarkable.

- Follow the steps above (p. 29) that you used to copy the word "Total" from cell A1 to E1, except use the word "Monday" instead of "Total" (without quotation marks).

Instead of copying, Excel fills the cells with the other names of the days of the week!

- Excel can also fill (and copy) several series at once. To see this, enter the values shown below in the first row of the worksheet. Excel recognizes the value in cell A1 as a date, but it, and all the others, should be entered in the same way as you enter text.

- Select the region from A1 to G1. Do this by placing the mouse pointer on A1, holding down the (left) mouse button, and dragging the selec-

	A	B	C	D	E	F	G
1	2/25/96	Mon	Jan	january	Week 1	1st	1st Quarter

tion boundary to the right until it includes G1. Your screen should look like the picture below:

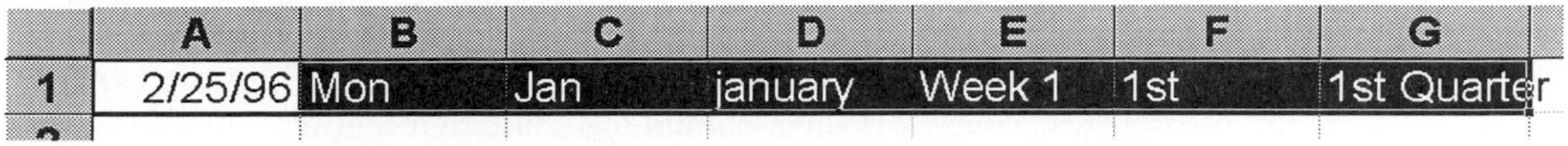
A
B
C
D
E
F
G
1
2/25/96
Mon
Jan
january
Week 1
1st
1st Quarter

- Notice that the selected region has a small square in the lower right corner the same as that which you used earlier to copy and fill. Place the mouse pointer over that square until it becomes a black cross.

- When the mouse pointer is a black cross, press the (left) mouse button and drag the mouse pointer downward until the selection boundary includes row 15. Release the mouse button.

Notice that Excel has filled each column in the selected region. If you look carefully at each series, you will notice some remarkable examples of Excel's built-in intelligence:

Look at the dates in the first column. Notice that the date after 2/29/96 is 3/1/96. Not only does Excel know how many days are in each month, it also knows that 1996 is a leap year.

If a name begins with a lowercase letter (like "january" in cell D1), Excel will fill the series with names all beginning with lowercase letters.

Compare the series in columns F and G. Excel knows that there are only four "Quarters," and begins renumbering after the fourth.

▼ Moving and Copying Regions of Cells

Excel provides a method for moving and copying cells using the mouse. Let's use this method to move the information in columns E, F, and G one column to the right so that column E is cleared.

- Select the region of cells from E1 to G15. Do this by dragging the mouse pointer (with the mouse button pressed) from cell E1 to cell G15.

- Position the mouse pointer on a boundary (any of the four boundaries will work) of the Selected Region. When it is correctly positioned, its shape will change from a white cross to a white arrow: .

- While the mouse pointer is in the shape of an arrow, press and hold the (left) mouse button.

- With the mouse button pressed, move the mouse pointer to the right. After you have moved at least one column, an outline of the selected region will appear which moves with the mouse pointer.

- Position the outline so that it is in columns F, G, and H, in the first fifteen rows. Your worksheet should look like that below.

	A	B	C	D	E	F	G	H
1	2/25/96	Mon	Jan	january	Week 1	1st	1st Quarter	
2	2/26/96	Tue	Feb	february	Week 2	2nd	2nd Quarter	
3	2/27/96	Wed	Mar	march	Week 3	3rd	3rd Quarter	
4	2/28/96	Thu	Apr	april	Week 4	4th	4th Quarter	
5	2/29/96	Fri	May	may	Week 5	5th	1st Quarter	
6	3/1/96	Sat	Jun	june	Week 6	6th	2nd Quarter	
7	3/2/96	Sun	Jul	july	Week 7	7th	3rd Quarter	
8	3/3/96	Mon	Aug	august	Week 8	8th	4th Quarter	
9	3/4/96	Tue	Sep	september	Week 9	9th	1st Quarter	
10	3/5/96	Wed	Oct	october	Week 10	10th	2nd Quarter	
11	3/6/96	Thu	Nov	november	Week 11	11th	3rd Quarter	
12	3/7/96	Fri	Dec	december	Week 12	12th	4th Quarter	
13	3/8/96	Sat	Jan	january	Week 13	13th	1st Quarter	
14	3/9/96	Sun	Feb	february	Week 14	14th	2nd Quarter	
15	3/10/96	Mon	Mar	march	Week 15	15th	3rd Quarter	

- When the outline is correctly positioned, release the mouse button.

The selected region will move to the new area and column E will be empty. This method of moving a region of cells is called the *drag and drop* method. You drag a region of cells (holding the mouse button down) and drop it where you want it.

There is also a drag and drop method of copying a region of cells. Let's use it to copy the days of the week in column B to the now empty column E.

- Select the region of cells from B1 to B15.

- Place the mouse pointer over the border of the selected region so that its shape changes to a white arrow.

- With the mouse pointer in the shape of an arrow press and hold the Ctrl key (PC) or OPTION key (Mac) on your keyboard. A small plus sign will appear beside the arrow.

- Continue to press the Ctrl or OPTION key and also press and hold the (left) mouse button. Drag the selected region outline until it is over column E.

- Release the mouse button first and then release the keyboard key.

The days of the week will be copied to column E and will also still be in column B.

▼ Copying and Moving Formulas—Relative Cell Addresses

Special attention has to be paid when formulas containing cell addresses are moved or copied. Let's examine the way Excel handles these situations.

- Click the "Sheet3" sheet tab so that this exercise may be done on a blank worksheet.

- Enter the letters and numbers in cells A1 through B3 and C1 as shown below.

	A	B	C
1	1st Value	2nd Value	Sum
2	1	10	
3	2	20	
4			

Use Excel's fill capability to extend the series in columns A and B through row 10.

- Select the region A2:B3, then drag the small rectangle in the lower right corner down until the selection boundary includes row 10.

Column A should show the series of numbers from 1 through 9, while column B should shown 10, 20, 30, up to 90.

- Enter this formula in cell C2 (without quotation marks): "=a2+b2."

The value displayed in cell C2 should, of course, be "11."

- Move cell C2 to C3. A single cell can be moved exactly like a larger selected region. Click C2 to make it the active cell, place the mouse pointer on a boundary of the cell until the pointer turns into a white arrow, then hold the (left) mouse button and drag the cell boundary until it is in cell C3. Release the mouse button.

Moving the formula from C2 to C3 shouldn't change it. It still should display "11." The formula bar should show "=A2+B2" when C3 is active. *Moving* a cell with a formula doesn't change it. This may not surprise you since moving a number or text also doesn't change the value entered in a cell. *Copying* a formula, however, *may* change it in a way which can be quite useful.

- Move the formula from C3 back to C2.

- Now *copy* the formula from C2 to C3. Use the drag and drop method.

Instead of "11," cell C3 should display "22."

- Click on cell C3 to make it the active cell.

- Drag the rectangle in the lower right-hand corner down until the selection boundary includes cell C10.

- The displayed value of each cell will differ. Cell C4 shows "33," while cell C5 shows "44," and so on.

- Click on cell C6 to make it the active cell and observe the cell's contents in the formula bar.

Instead of "=A2+B2," the contents of C6 are "=A6+B6." When the formula was copied, the cell addresses were changed.

- Click on each of the cells in column C from C2 to C9, and observe the formula in each cell in the formula bar.

Each cell contains a formula adding the values in the two cells immediately to the left. Thus cell C2 adds the numbers in columns A and B which are in the same row (2) as cell C2. The formula in cell C4 does the same, only since C4 is in row 4, the two cells whose values are added are also in row 4.

When you put the formula "=A2+B2" in cell C2, Excel interpreted the addresses "A2" and "B2" as *relative* cell addresses. Excel determined where those cells were *relative* to the cell containing the formula. Thus cell A2 is two cells to the left of cell C2, and B2 is one cell to the left of cell C2. When the formula in C2 is copied to another cell, those addresses are changed to the addresses of the cells which are in the same position *relative* to the copied formula's position. For example, the formula in cell C4 adds the value of the cell two cells to the left of C4 (which is A4) and the value of the cell which is one cell to the left of C4 (which is B4).

This ability of Excel to change cell addresses in this way is very useful. Many spreadsheet problems will require performing the same calculations on several rows or several columns of numbers. With relative cell addressing, you need only specify the calculation in a formula for one of the rows or columns, and then copy that formula to the other rows or columns.

Let's take a look at the use of relative cell addresses on operations involving columns. Suppose that we want the cells in row 11 to display the sum of the numbers in the column above. Thus cell A11 would show the sum of A2 through A10, B11 would show the sum of B2 through B11, and C11 would show the sum of C2 through C11.

Let's start by entering the formula in A11 to add the numbers in A2 through A10.

- Click cell A11 to make it the active cell.

Summing a row or column is such a common operation on a spreadsheet that Excel provides a speed button specifically for that operation.

- Find the AutoSum button on the Standard Toolbar **Σ** and click it.

Excel will insert the formula in cell A11 which it *thinks* you want. You should see the following in that cell: =SUM(A2:A10). The most likely error Excel might make is to guess the wrong cell addresses you want added. To help you correct the cell addresses, Excel has already highlighted them in the formula. In this case, however, Excel has guessed correctly.

- Press the Enter key and the sum of the column, 45, will display in cell A11.

- Copy cell A11 to B11 and C11. B11 should display 450 and C11 should display 495.

▼ Absolute versus Relative Cell Addresses

Suppose that we would like column D to contain the percentage each value in column C is of the total for column C. The sum of the values in column C is 495, so we would like cell D2 to indicate what percentage of 495 is 11 (the value in C2). Cell D3 should indicate what percentage of 495 is 22, and so on.

- In cell D1 enter the text label "Percent" without quotation marks.

- In cell D2, enter the following formula (without quotation marks): "=c2/c11." Press the Enter key.

The value 0.022222 should be displayed in D2. Note that this is a proportion rather than a percentage. To convert a proportion to a percentage, we must multiply by 100. Excel, however, has a special formatting which allows a proportion to *display* as a percentage.

- Make D2 the active cell. Click the Percent Style speed button **%** on the Formatting Toolbar.

The value 2% will be displayed.

- Click the Increase Decimal speed button ▨ on the Formatting Toolbar twice.

The value 2.22% should now be displayed. The Percent Style button formats the cell but doesn't change its value. If C2 were used in a mathematical formula, the value which would be used would be 0.022222, not 2.22.

- Copy the formula in D2 to D3.

Although our objective is for D3 to calculate C3 as a percentage of the total, this clearly did not happen. Instead, D3 shows an error (#DIV/0!). This error indicates an attempt to divide a number by 0.

- Make D3 the active cell and observe the formula in the formula bar.

The formula in D3 is =C3/C12. But this is not correct. C12 is blank. What we want is for the value in C3 to be divided by the value in C11, not C12. The problem is that when the formula in D2 (=C2/C11) was copied, the C2 was changed to C3 and the C11 was changed to C12. What we wanted, however, was for just the C2 to be changed. The way to do this is to make the C12 in the formula in D2 an *absolute* address which won't change when it is copied.

Double click cell D2 so that you can edit it.

Highlight the C11 in the formula so that you can edit that portion of the formula.

With the C11 appearing as white against a black background, press the F4 function key. The "C11" should change to "$C$11". The dollar signs make the address absolute. Without the dollar signs, the address is relative. An absolute address will not change if it is copied to another cell, while a relative address will change.

You can also make an address absolute by manually entering the "$" rather than using the function key.

- Press the Enter key to indicate that you have finished editing the cell.

- Copy cell D2 to cells D3 through D10.

Each of the cells should now display a correct value. Examine the formulas in several of the cells. Notice that in each of them the numerator is the cell address of the cell immediately to the left, while the divisor is always "$C$11."

Notice also that Excel has copied the formatting to the cells. Thus each cell appears as a percentage with two decimal points.

- Copy the formula in cell C11 (which sums column C) to cell D11 so that D11 will have the sum of the number in column D.

Are you surprised that the value is 1 instead of 100? Although the percentages add up to 100%, remember that the numbers in the cells in column D are *proportions*, not percentages. The Percent Style button causes them to be displayed as percentages, but the numbers which are added are all between 0 and 1. Of course, we could use the Percent Style on D11 to make it also display as a percentage.

Congratulations! You have now learned enough Excel to begin to use it to explore data and perform statistical analysis. You will be introduced to new features but this will always be done in the context of using Excel to explore statistics. Don't be surprised if you need to refer back to this chapter. As time goes on, you'll remember more and more about Excel, and you will find the discussions in this book will deal increasingly with statistics and decreasingly with Excel.

Chapter 2

Descriptive Statistics

Chances are that what you think of today as *statistics* is more precisely called *descriptive statistics*. There are many times when a businessperson will need to understand information provided by a collection of numbers—such as sales figures, labor turnover, expenditure records, and many more. We mortals do not have the ability to look at more than a handful of numbers and immediately have a sense of the information those numbers contain. To get a sense of the information contained in a huge collection numbers, we have to summarize, or we have to convert the numbers into a chart or graph.

Vision is our keenest sense. You take advantage of that sense when you use graphics to represent the information in numbers. Before computers, graphical representations of data were difficult and time consuming to do well. Computers, and programs like Excel, make it easy to prepare graphics, although it still takes some skill to know how to use graphics effectively.

Data summaries, or descriptive statistics, are also important. Most of your study of statistics will not be of descriptive statistics. It will be of *inferential statistics*. Inferential statistics provides us with a way to investigate the characteristics of a *population* when we only have data from a *sample*. A common example is a poll which provides information on the attitudes of an entire electorate by questioning only a tiny proportion of all the people in that electorate. The techniques of inferential statistics require calculating numerical summaries of the sample data and using them to develop information about the population.

▼ Using Graphics in Excel

Let's explore Excel's graphics capability through the use of an example using data on the size of the civilian work force in the United States, classified by gender.

Start Excel (if you have not already done so).

The data for this example are available in the Excel worksheet named labor.xls. To read that worksheet into Excel, do the following:

- If you are using the data diskette for this book, insert the diskette in the A drive on your computer. If the files on that diskette have been copied to a hard drive or a network drive, skip this step and substitute the appropriate drive letter for "a:" in the instructions below.

- Click the Open ![open icon] speed button on the standard toolbar.

If you are using Windows 3.1, the following dialog window will open.

1. Select "a:" in the "Drives" field.

2. Double click "chap_2" in the "Directories:" field.

3. Select "labor.xls" in the "File Name:" field.

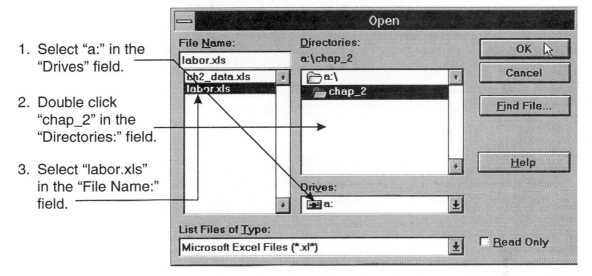

- Click the arrow beside the "Drives:" field (![arrow icon]) and a selection menu will open. Select the small picture of a diskette drive with "a:" beside it as shown in the picture.

The "Directories" field (above the "Drives" field) will show a list of the directories (or folders) on the diskette. Each directory's name corresponds to a chapter for which there is data.

- Find the folder named "chap_2." This is the subdirectory in which the labor.xls file is located. Place the mouse pointer on the folder icon or on the words "chap_2" and double click the (left) mouse button. The icon will change to an open folder and file names will appear in the "File Name" field on the left side of the dialog window.

- Find "labor.xls" in the "File Name" field. Select it. Your dialog window should now look like the picture above with "labor.xls" in the top field below "File Name." Click "OK." The dialog window will close and your screen should show the worksheet shown on page 40.

- If you are using Windows 95, click the downward-pointing arrow beside the smaller upper "Look in:" field at the top of the dialog window. A list of all local and network drives will appear. Select "3½ Floppy (A:)" (below "My Computer"). You can make this selection by double clicking or by clicking once to highlight and then clicking the "Open" button on the right side of the window

The field should look like the picture below.

- The larger field below the one pictured above shows the contents of your selection. A list of directories (folders) on the diskette will appear. Locate 📁 Chap_2 and place the mouse pointer directly on it. Either double click the left mouse button or click once to highlight followed by a click on the "Open" button.

- The contents field should now show the Excel files located within the Chap_2 directory. Open 📄 Labor. The dialog window will close and Excel will load the workbook as shown below.

	A	B	C
1	Civilian Labor Force (1,000)		
2	Year	Males	Females
3	1960	46,388	23,240
4	1970	51,228	31,543
5	1975	56,299	37,475
6	1980	61,453	45,487
7	1983	63,047	48,503
8	1984	63,835	49,709
9	1985	64,411	51,050
10	1986	65,422	52,413
11	1987	66,207	53,658
12	1988	66,927	54,742
13	1989	67,840	56,030
14	1990	68,234	56,554
15	1991	68,411	56,893
16	1992	69,184	57,798
17	1993	69,633	58,407

These data show the size of the civilian labor force by gender for several recent years. The numbers provide information on how the total labor force size has changed and how the proportion of the labor force consisting of women has changed. This information would be much easier to understand, however, if it were shown in a chart. Let's use Excel to create such a chart.

You have the option in Excel to place a chart on the same worksheet as the data or to place it on a worksheet by itself. For this exercise, you will do the latter.

- Open the Insert menu by clicking the mouse pointer on "Insert" on the Menu Bar at the top of the Excel window.

- Click "Chart" on the menu and then click "As New Sheet."

Excel will start the Chart Wizard, which provides a sequence of dialog windows for you to specify details about the type of chart you want. In the first step you tell Excel which data you wish displayed as a chart.

- Place the mouse pointer on cell A2 and press the (left) mouse button. While continuing to press the button, drag the mouse pointer to cell C17.

This is exactly the same operation you would perform if you were selecting the cell range A2:C17. Instead of turning the selected cells black, however, the range becomes surrounded by a moving dashed line, which is called a "marquee." In addition, the range address is automatically inserted into the address field of the Chart Wizard dialog window. The dialog window should look like that shown below.

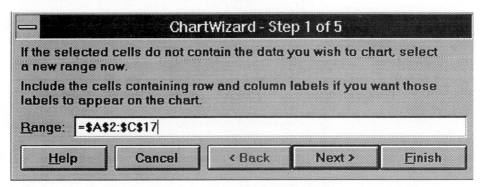

Check the address in the field on your computer with that shown. When you are sure they are the same, click the "Next" button.

A new dialog window will open for you to choose what type of chart you want Excel to create. For this example, let's suppose that you want a vertical bar chart. Excel uses the term "Bar" only for horizontal bar charts. Vertical bar charts are called "Column" charts. Excel's terminology is not standard, but the pictures make clear the type of chart.

- Select the Column chart as shown in the following diagram by double clicking it or by clicking once and then clicking the "Next" button.

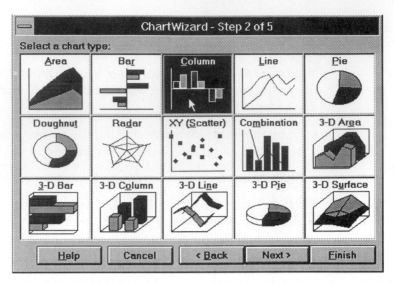

The next dialog window enables you to choose the type of vertical bar chart. Excel doesn't try to name these choices and provides only a number and picture for each choice.

- Choose the stacked bar chart which Excel gives the number 3 as shown below. Notice that numbers 5, 9, and 10 are different versions of stacked bar charts which could be used. The choice of which chart to make depends on what aspect of the data you want to emphasize.

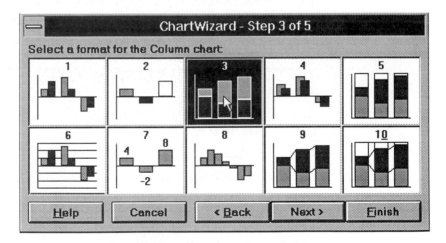

The choices you have now made enable the remaining dialog windows to show a preview of the chart Excel will prepare. As you change the dialog window settings, the preview chart will change to reflect those choices.

The fourth dialog window concerns details about how Excel interprets the data. At the top of the window, Excel wants to know whether the data are rows or columns. In this case the data are in columns and the radio button beside "Columns" should be chosen. Excel should have already guessed this. They are named "radio buttons" because only one of the set can be chosen, like the station buttons in a car radio.

The next field tells Excel whether the "First" (that is, leftmost) column is to be used to label the bars or should be interpreted as data. If you look at the preview chart, you will see that the bars are consecutively numbered. They should be labeled with the year. Since years are numbers, Excel has incorrectly assumed that they are data rather than labels. Change the "0" to a "1" by clicking the small arrow pointing up.

In the last field Excel should have already determined that the first row (which contains the words "Year," "Males," and "Females") should be used for legend text. The completed dialog window should look like the one below titled "Step 4 of 5."

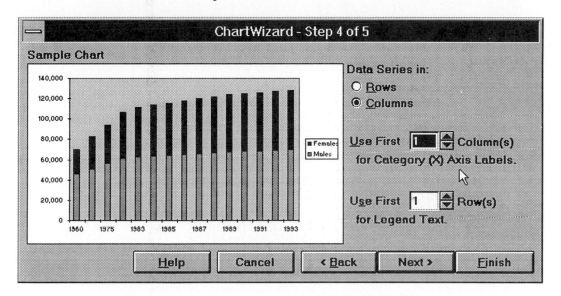

- Make any changes in the dialog window on your machine so that it matches the one shown here. Then click the "Next" button.

The final dialog window allows you to decide whether or not you want a "Legend" (showing which part of the bar corresponds to males and which part to females). A legend is a good idea when a chart displays more than one data series. This chart displays two data series (males and females), and the legend will show which part of the chart goes with each series. You also can specify a title for the chart and labels for both the horizontal (X) and vertical (Y) axis. As you will see below, all of the decisions you make now can be changed later.

- Add the chart and axis titles shown in the dialog window on the next page and click the "Finish" button.

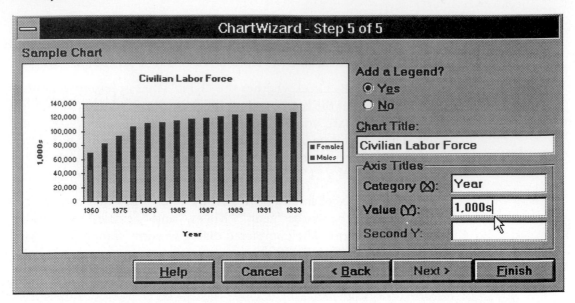

The completed chart will appear on your screen on a worksheet named "Chart1."

- Save the work you have done up to this point by clicking the Save speed button 🖫 on the standard toolbar. Get in the habit of frequently clicking the button to ensure that a computer problem will not result in losing your work.

Let's examine some ways in which this chart might be changed. Suppose we wanted to make the following changes:

1. Convert the chart to a 3-D type bar chart.

2. Change the title to "Civilian Labor Force by Gender."

3. Change the bars from colors to gray-scale patterns which will show on a non color printer.

4. Print the chart.

Many other changes are possible, but these will demonstrate how you can change an existing chart.

▼ Changing the Chart Type

- Click "Format" on the Menu Bar at the top of the Excel window so that the Format menu will drop down.

- Select "Chart Type" from the Format menu. The "Chart Type" dialog window will open.

- At the top of the dialog window (shown below) is a field labeled "Chart Dimension" with two radio buttons. Click the "3-D" button. You will notice that the pictures illustrating chart types will change.

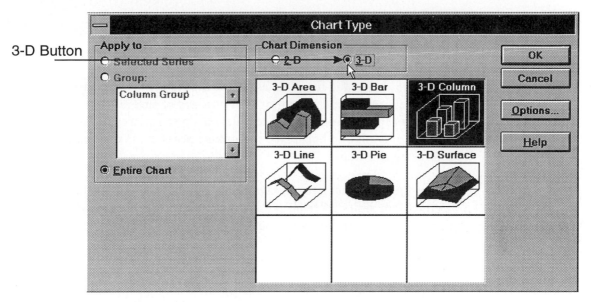

- Select "3-D Column" by double clicking on that picture or by clicking once to select it and then clicking the "OK" button.

The display will return to the worksheet with the chart. As you see, the bars now appear three dimensional, and the data for males and females are represented by bars in different rows. Unfortunately, the taller bars representing males are in front of the bars representing females. It is difficult to see the bars representing females. The chart would be much better if the bars for females were in front of those for males. This is a change Excel can easily make.

- Open the "Format" menu on the Menu Bar.

- Choose "3-D Column Group" from the Format menu which opens. This will open the "Format 3-D Column Group" dialog window.

- Click the "Series Order" folder tab. Above the preview in the dialog window a list titled "Series Order" contains the names of the two rows of bars: "Males" and "Females."

- Select "Males" (unless it is already selected). Click the "Move Down" button.

- The preview will change to show the bars representing females in front of those representing males. Click the "OK" button to have the change made to the chart on the worksheet.

The next step is to change the colors used in the bars to gray-scale patterns which print better on black and white printers.

▼ Changing the Chart Colors

- Place the mouse pointer directly over one of the bars in front representing a data value for females. Click the (left) mouse button once. Small squares should appear at four corners of several (but not all) of the bars representing data on females. If these squares do not appear or appear only on one bar, place the mouse pointer off the chart, click, and retry this step.

- Open the "Format" drop-down menu from the Menu Bar. Choose "Selected Data Series..." from the Format menu. The "Format Data Series" dialog window will open.

- Select the "Patterns" file folder tab.

- In the central part of the dialog window is a panel showing various colors. Place the mouse pointer over a shade of gray and click the mouse button. Observe the rectangle in the dialog window labeled "Sample." Its color should change to the selected shade of gray.

- Find the "Pattern" controls below the colors and place the mouse pointer on the downward-pointing arrow like this: Pattern: [ ] ▾. Click the mouse button.

- A window containing patterns and colors will open. Find this pattern ▨, place the mouse pointer on it, and click the mouse button. The "Sample" field should show this pattern.

- Click the "OK" button. The changes will be shown in the chart on the worksheet.

- Place the mouse button over one of the (still colored) bars representing a data value for males. Click the mouse button. Squares should now appear around most of the bars representing male data points.

- Use the same procedure used for the female data bars to change the male data bars to a gray pattern. Use a different pattern and a different shade of gray (or use black). Return the display to the chart on the worksheet with the changes showing.

▼ Changing the Chart Title

It is easy to make changes to the chart title or to either of the axis titles. These changes include moving the titles, changing the fonts, adding colors, and more. In this example you will change the title from "Civilian Labor Force" to "Civilian Labor Force by Gender."

- Place the mouse button on the chart title ("Civilian Labor Force"), and click the mouse button. A border will appear around the title indicating that the title is "active."

- Place the mouse pointer within the border around the title. The pointer will change to the I-beam shape used for editing.

- Place the I-beam pointer just to the right of the word "Force" and click the mouse button. An insert cursor will appear at that position.

- Use the keyboard to enter " by Gender."

- Place the mouse pointer off the chart and click the mouse button. This will remove the border from around the title so that it will no longer be active.

- Click the "Save" speed button.

When text on the chart is active, the format menu can be used to change fonts, font size, and color. By placing the mouse pointer on the border, the entire title can be dragged to a different location.

The connection between a chart in an Excel workbook and the data on which that chart is made is dynamic. That is, if the data change, those changes will be immediately reflected in the chart. To see this, do the following:

- Click the worksheet tab titled "Civilian Labor Force."

- Change the word in cell B2 from "Males" to "Men," and change the word in cell C2 from "Females" to "Women"

- Return to the chart by clicking the "Chart1" worksheet tab. Notice how the labeling on the chart has changed.

In this example, a change of labels in the data changed the labels in the chart. If, however, the numbers in any of the cells containing data were changed, the height of the bars in the chart would also change.

▼ Previewing a Printout

Although there is a Print speed button, you can often save time and paper by previewing a printout before it is actually printed.

- With the chart displayed on your screen, open the "File" menu from the Menu Bar. Select "Print Preview."

The Print Preview screen opens. The lower part of the screen shows you a very good representation of how the actual printout will appear. Notice that there is a header at the top of the page, above the chart ("Chart1"), and a footer below the chart ("Page 1"). If you look closely at the chart, you may notice a few minor differences between the appearance of the chart as it will print and its appearance on a worksheet.

- Place the mouse pointer on the part of the screen showing the chart. Notice the pointer is shaped like a small magnifying glass ✑.

- Place the mouse pointer over the chart legend. (The chart legend tells which bars are which.) Click the (left) mouse button. An enlarged view of the area around the mouse pointer will enable you to examine details more closely.

- Notice the mouse pointer has returned to being an arrow. Click the mouse button again, and the view will return to its original magnification.

- The upper part of the screen has a row of buttons. Click the Setup... button. This will open the Page Setup dialog window, which will have several file folder tabs at the top. Each allows you to control different aspects of how the printout will appear.

▼ Changing Headers and Footers on a Printout

- Click the Header/Footer tab. The dialog window should look like that shown on the next page.

There are two ways of changing the headers and the footers which will appear on the printed page. Excel has a number of preset headers and footers which show such things as today's date and the name of the owner of the Excel software (which was entered when the program was installed). In addition, you can enter a "custom" header or footer, which will allow you to use anything for a header or footer. If, for example, you were submitting a printout from Excel in response to a homework as-

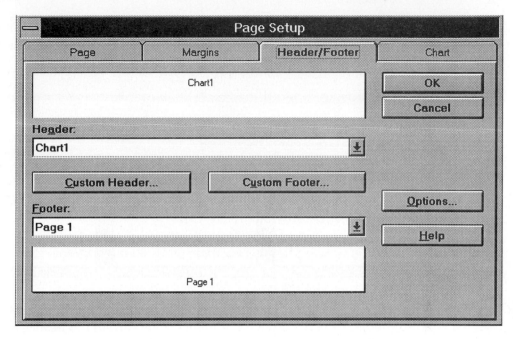

signment, you might want to have the course name and your name appear in the header.

The instructions below will show you how to eliminate all footers and how to put your name at the top right of the page. The current header ("Chart1") and the current footer ("Page 1") appear twice in the dialog window. Each appears in a one-line window with a downward pointing arrow, and each appears below that window in a small preview window.

- Click the downward arrow ![arrow] for the footer (now "Page 1"). A list will open with a scroll bar to the right.

- The list contains the built-in footers which you could choose to use. At the top of the list (use the scroll bar) you will find "(none)." Click this choice.

The one-line window should now contain "(none)," and the preview window below it should be completely blank.

- Click the ![Custom Header...] button on the dialog window. The header dialog window will open. The window has three fields for you to enter headers for the left, center, and right-hand portions of the header. The center section should currently have "&[Tab]," which is an Excel code meaning that the name of the worksheet will be entered.

- Click the mouse pointer in the window for the center section and erase what is now there.

- Click the mouse pointer in the window for the right section and enter your name. The window should look like the picture below (except with your name, of course).

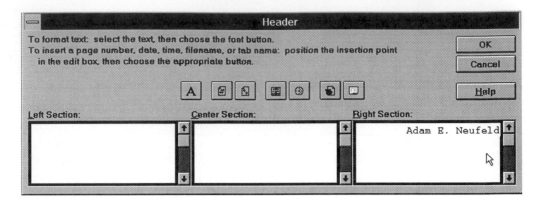

- Click the "OK" button to return to the Page Setup dialog window. Check the two preview windows to be certain the header and footer are correct. If they are, click the "OK" button. This will return you to the Print Preview screen, with the new header and footer displayed.

- Click the Print... button. One or more dialog windows will open concerning the print. If Windows has been properly set up, just click "OK" in each of these dialog windows, and your chart will be printed.

- Be sure to save the worksheet in its final form by clicking the Save button.

▼ Numerical Summaries

Before returning to graphical displays, let's consider the issues of numerical summaries. There are a couple of approaches to descriptive statistics, the mean-variance approach and the quantile approach. Both approaches are frequently used, but the former is much more important in inferential statistics. One method starts with the *mean,* the other with the *median.*

When a set of numbers is reduced to a single descriptive statistic, that statistic should give the maximum information about the set of numbers. The mean (or arithmetic mean) is commonly known as the average, by far the most widely used descriptive statistic. The other commonly used measure of central location is the *median,* which, in a sense, lies in the middle of a set of numbers. Let's use Excel to examine the differences between these two measures. We can use Excel's built-in *functions* which save us from having to specify exactly how the statistic is calculated.

- Drop down the "File" menu from the Menu Bar and click "New." If you are using Windows 95, a dialog window entitled "New" will open. Simply click the "OK" button. A new workbook will open.

- Double click the worksheet tab "Sheet1." A dialog window will open enabling you to rename the worksheet. Rename it to "Num Smry."

- Drop the "File" menu again and click "Save As…." A window will open similar in appearance to the "Open File" dialog window discussed earlier (page 5). Enter the name "chap2.xls" in the "File Name:" field which is at the top left of the Windows 3.1 dialog window and second from the bottom in the Windows 95 dialog window. The file will be saved to the same drive and directory as the last file read or saved. Unless you have interrupted your session, this would be the "labor" worksheet. Windows 3.1 will open a "Summary Info" dialog window which you can close by simply clicking "OK."

- In the first column (cells A1:A5), enter the numbers 10, 20, 30, 40, 50.

- In cell A7, enter the label "Mean" (without quotes).

- In cell A8, enter the label "Median" (without quotes).

- Click on cell B7 to make it active.

▼ Using the Function Wizard

- With cell B7 active, click the Function Wizard Button ⬛. A dialog window which gives you access to all of Excel's built-in functions will appear. The window contains two lists. The one on the left is labeled "Function Category" and the one on the right is labeled "Function Name." Both lists have scroll bars which can be used to see choices not immediately visible.

- In the "Function Category" list choose "Statistical" by placing the mouse pointer on that word and clicking the mouse button once. The word will then appear in white letters with a black background, and the choices in the "Function Name" list will change.

- In the "Function Name" list choose "AVERAGE." The dialog window should look like the picture at the top of the next page. Notice the brief description of the function whose name has been chosen.

- Click the "Next>" button. A second dialog window will appear for the AVERAGE function. Although different functions will have differ-

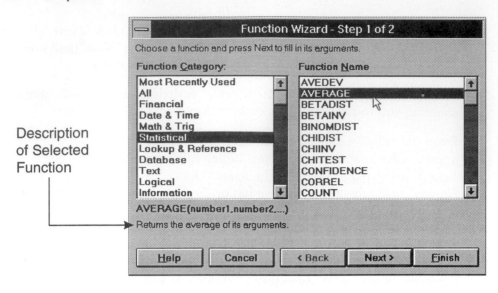

Description
of Selected
Function

ent second dialog windows, all have certain features in common, as shown in the picture below.

Function
Description

Arguments
Description

Cell Address
of Arguments

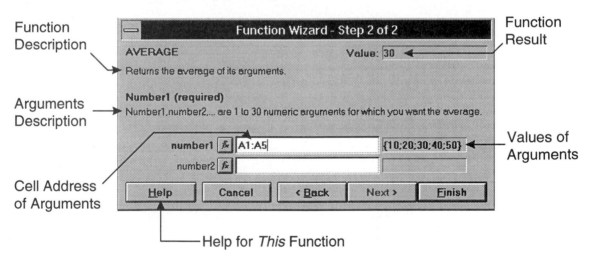

Function
Result

Values of
Arguments

Help for *This* Function

A function will have an *argument* or *arguments* from which it will derive a *result*. (Arguments are also often called *parameters*.) In the case of the AVERAGE function, the numbers to be averaged are the arguments and the value of the average is the result.

Notice the dialog window provides a brief description of the function and a description of the arguments. Two fields are provided for you to tell Excel the cell addresses (or values) of the arguments. The first one is labeled **number1** (in bold). The bold indicates that Excel requires you to provide information in this field. The second field, number2, is not bold. You may use this field, but you don't have to. Usually it won't be used.

- Does the dialog window cover the cells with the data you want averaged (A1:A5)? If it does, move the window out of the way. (See page 12 if you have forgotten how to move a window.)

- Place the mouse pointer in the "number1" field and click. An insertion point will become visible.

- The data for which you want the average are in cells A1:A5. Although this address could be entered with the keyboard, instead use your mouse to perform the operation to "select" cells A1 through A5. When you finish, these cells will have a moving "marquee" surrounding them.

- Immediately to the right of the field where you have entered the addresses is a field in which Excel shows the *values* in those cells (10, 20, 30, 40, and 50). Checking this field helps you be sure you have given Excel the correct cell addresses.

- At the top right of the dialog window is a field labeled "Value:" in which Excel will show the function result. You should see "30" in this field, which is the average of 10, 20, 30, 40, and 50. If there is no number in the value field, you have not responded to the dialog window correctly. Check your dialog window with the example above.

- Click the "Finish" button at the bottom of the dialog window.

The dialog window will close and cell B7 should show "30." Look at the Formula Bar. It should contain "=AVERAGE(A1:A5)." This is what the Function Wizard has entered into the cell. You could achieve the same result by entering this yourself, but it is usually wise to use the Function Wizard unless you are very familiar with a particular Excel function.

- Use the Function Wizard to have Excel calculate the median of the numbers in cells A1:A5 and place the result in cell B8. The median function is in the same category as the mean function ("Statistical") and has the name MEDIAN. Be sure to check the formula bar that an Excel function has been entered. When you finish, your worksheet should look like the picture at the top of the next page.

▼ Exploring the Difference Between the Mean and the Median

For the data originally entered, the mean and median are the same, 30. To understand differences and the advantages and disadvantages of each of these measures, let's experiment with the types of changes which can cause these two statistics to differ.

	A	B
1	10	
2	20	
3	30	
4	40	
5	50	
6		
7	Mean	30
8	Median	30

- Change the value of the number in cell A5 from 50 to 523. The value of the mean changes to 124.6, but the value of the median does not change.

In a list of five numbers sorted in order, the median will always be the third number. The median divides the list into two equal-sized groups: those that are smaller than the third number (the first two numbers) and those that are greater (the fourth and fifth).

- Change the value of the number in cell A1 from 10 to -100. The mean will fall to 102.6, but the median remains unchanged. The list of numbers is still in order, and 30 is still the third number. There are still two numbers in the list greater than 30 and two numbers smaller than 30.

- Change the value of the number in cell A1 from -100 to 55. In addition to the mean changing, the median also changes—to 40. 30 is still the third number in the list, why has the median changed to 40? With 55 as the first number, the list is no longer in order. Let's resort the list.

▼ Using the Sort Buttons

- Select the cell region A1:A5.

- Click the Sort Ascending button ![Sort Ascending icon]. The list is put in order, and 40 is now the third number.

If the number of numbers in the list is odd (like 5), and the list is put in order, the median will always be the middle number. What if the number of numbers in the list is even?

- Double click cell B7. Change the "A5" in the formula "=AVERAGE(A1:A5)" to "A6."

- Change the "A5" in the formula in cell B8 to "A6."

- Enter the number 610 in cell A6.

The mean showing in cell B7 should now be 213, and the median showing in cell B8 should now be 47.5. The number of numbers in the list is now 6. There is no single middle number. Instead, the numbers in positions 3 and 4 are in the middle. In a sense, we can think of the middle as lying halfway between position 3 and position 4. There is, of course, no number, between the 40 in position 3 and the 55 in position 4. Instead, the median is defined as the number *halfway between* the two values 40 and 55. This is the same as the average of 40 and 55:

$$\frac{40+55}{2} = \frac{95}{2} = 47.5.$$

- Change the number in cell A6 from 610 to 40. What is the median now?

Remember that the median will be halfway between the number in position 3 and the number in position 4 only if the list is sorted. Putting the value 40 at the end of the list makes the list out of order.

- Resort cells A1:A6 using the method described on page 54 (be sure to include A6 in the selected region). Is the median now halfway between the number in position 3 and the number in position 4? If you have done this correctly, both A3 and A4 should have the value 40.

- Change the number in position 4 (cell A4) from 40 to 42. The median is now 41, the number halfway between 40 and 42.

- Change the number in cell A6 from 523 to 521. The median should still be 41, and the mean should change to 118.

These examples only looked at sets of five and six numbers, but the definition of the median can be applied to any size set. If the set of numbers is ordered from highest to lowest the median will either be the value of the middle number (if the set has an odd number of numbers) or halfway between the values of the two middle numbers (if the set has an even number of numbers).

▼ Measures of Dispersion

If the first and most important descriptive statistic is a measure of location, what is the second most important? For the mean-variance approach, it is the *variance* or *standard deviation* of the data. These are both closely related measures of dispersion—they indicate how far the individual data items are likely to be from the mean. Although Excel has built-in functions to calculate the variance and standard deviation, we will first use Excel to calculate these "by hand" to better see exactly what they measure.

The formulas for the sample variance and standard deviation are:

$$\text{variance} = s^2 = \frac{\sum (x - \bar{x})^2}{n-1}$$

$$\text{standard deviation} = s = \sqrt{s^2}$$

The instructions below will direct you in the construction of a worksheet to calculate these formulas.

- Place the mouse pointer on the heading for Row 1 and click the mouse button to select the entire first row. (See page 13 for the location of the Row Heading).

- Open the "Insert" menu on the Menu Bar and choose "Rows." This will insert a new row above the numbers on the worksheet, moving down the rows already there.

- In cell A1 enter the label "x" (without the quotes).

- Skip cell B1 and enter in cell C1 the label "x bar."

- Enter in cell D1 the label "x-x bar."

- Enter in cell E1 the label "(x-x bar)2."

- Select C2 to make it the active cell and begin entering a formula by typing an equals sign ("=").

- Place the mouse pointer on cell B8 (where the mean is now displayed), and press the mouse button. Look at the formula bar. You should see "=B8."

- Before pressing the Enter key, press the F4 (on a PC) or the COMMAND and T key (on a Mac) to make the address absolute. The formula bar should show "=$B$8."

- Press the Enter key and the mean, 118, should be displayed in cell C2. (Note: It is important to follow the instructions in entering a *formula* and not just the *number* result.)

- Copy the formula in cell C2 to cells C3 through C7. The absolute address in cell C2 should copy unchanged, and all the cells in column C should display the same value (118).

Column D will be used to calculate the difference between each of the x values in column A and the mean of all of the x's in column C. Enter the formula in cell D2 to calculate the difference between the value of x in row 2 (the number in cell A2 which is 20) and the mean of the x's in cell C2.

- Make D2 the active cell, and enter "=" to start a formula. Place the mouse pointer on cell A2 and click the mouse button. Enter a minus sign "-." Place the mouse pointer on cell C2 and click the mouse button. The formula in the cell and on the formula bar should be "=A2-C2." Notice that relative addresses are used in this formula.

- Press the Enter key, and cell D2 should show -98.

- Copy the formula in cell D2 to cells D3 through D7.

Since relative addressing was used in D2, the address will change as it is copied to each cell. In each case, the number will be the difference between the value of x (column A) for that row and the mean of all of the x's (118) which appears in column C of each row. Cell D7, for example, should display 403.

Column E will be used to square the difference between each x value and the mean of the x's.

- Make cell E2 active and enter the formula "=D2^2." Press the Enter key and the value 9604 should be displayed.

- Copy the formula in cell E2 to cells E3 through E7.

- Have you remembered to save this worksheet as you work on it? If not, do it now, and do it periodically as you continue to change it.

Because relative addressing was used in E2, the displayed values in E3 through E7 should differ, each being the square of the value displayed in the corresponding cell of column D. Cell E7 should display 162409.

The next step is to sum the values in column E. Although not required by the calculations, the values in column D will also be summed.

- In cell C8 enter the label "Sum."

- In cell D9 enter the label "Variance," and in Cell D10 enter the label "Std Dev."

- Make D8 the active cell. Use the AutoSum button, Σ, to put the sum of cells D2 through D7 in D8. You must press the Enter key for the result to be displayed. The displayed value in D8 should be 0.

- Make E8 the active cell and use the AutoSum button to put there the sum of cells E2 through E7. The displayed value should be 195586.

Cell E8 evaluates $\sum (x - \bar{x})^2$, the numerator of the formula for the variance (page 56). The next step is to divide this by the denominator, $n - 1$. The number of data values (n) in this table is 6, and $n - 1$ therefore is 5.

- Enter the formula in cell E9 which will divide the value in cell E8 by 5. The value displayed in E9 should be 39117.2.

- Enter the formula in cell E10 which will calculate the square root of the value in cell E9. This requires using the built-in square root function. One way of doing this is to use the function wizard button. The Function Category is "Math & Trig," and the Function Name is SQRT. The value displayed in cell E10 should be 197.7807.

Check the appearance of your worksheet with the illustration below. If you spot a difference, do not simply change cells in your worksheet so they contain the numbers displayed by the corresponding cells in the illustration. The x values in the A column are going to be changed. Many of the cells contain formulas, and if you do not enter the correct formulas, the effects of changing the x values will not be correctly calculated.

	A	B	C	D	E
1	x		x bar	x-x bar	(x-x bar)2
2	20		118	-98	9604
3	30		118	-88	7744
4	40		118	-78	6084
5	42		118	-76	5776
6	55		118	-63	3969
7	521		118	403	162409
8	Mean	118	Sum	0	195586
9	Median	41		Variance	39117.2
10				Std Dev	197.781

Notice that the sum of the x-x bar (D) column is 0. Some of the numbers in the column are negative and one is positive. Could this be a coincidence of the particular x values used in this example?

The numbers in column E2:E7 are the squares of those in D2:D7. Squaring a number always produces a positive result, and the numbers in E2:E7 are all positive. As long as any of the number in D2:D7 are nonzero, the sum in cell E8 must be a positive number.

If most of the numbers in a set of numbers are close to the mean, the differences between each number and the mean will be relatively small, the square of those differences will also be relatively small, and the variance and standard deviation will also be relatively small. Two different sets of numbers could have the same mean and yet differ in how far the individual numbers tended to be from that mean. Let's consider some examples.

- Enter the following numbers in cells A2:A7:
    80, 85, 90, 100, 110, 135.
  As you enter each number, notice that the worksheet immediately changes the calculated values, including the mean shown in column C. Once all six numbers have been entered, the displayed mean should be 100 and the displayed standard deviation should be 20.24846. Observe the values in column D, which show the difference between each x value and the overall mean.

- Copy the contents of cells A2:E10 to A12:E20. If you have forgotten how to copy a set of cells, review the method given on page 32. You now have two tables to calculate variances and standard deviations. (The formulas in C12:C17 still equal B8 instead of B18 since the copied references were absolute. As long as B8 equals B18 this will not cause a problem.)

- Now enter the following set of numbers in A2:A7:
    20, 40, 60, 80, 195, 205.
  These numbers have the same mean, 100, but a higher standard deviation, 80.06248. Again observe the values in column D.

- Compare the two sets of numbers in column A in the two tables on your worksheet. Both sets of numbers have the same mean, but the top set has greater *dispersion*. Compare the differences in column D between the numbers in each set and the mean. All of the numbers in the top set are greater in absolute value than the corresponding numbers in the bottom set. The individual values in the top set tend to be further from the mean than those in the bottom set, and this difference between the two sets is dispersion. The measures of dispersion, variance and standard deviation, are thus larger for the top set than the bottom set.

- Save the worksheet.

▼ Copying a Range of Cells to a New Worksheet

In the previous chapter you learned a method for using the mouse to copy or move a range of cells. Although convenient, this method is difficult to use if the range is very large or if there is a need for the move or copy to occur between worksheets. Another procedure is preferable for these situations. This procedure involves use of the *Windows clipboard,* a kind of holding area. You *copy* a selected range of cells to the clipboard and then *paste* the range from the clipboard to a new location. Let's do this in preparation for the use below of the Descriptive Statistics Analysis Tool.

- Select cells A1:A7.

- Click the Copy speed button ▣. This will copy the contents of the selected cell to the clipboard. Notice that a moving marquee appears around the selected range.

- Click the worksheet tab "Sheet2."

- Select cell A1 to make it the active cell.

- Click the Paste button ▣. Cells A1:A7 on this worksheet will now be a copy of those on worksheet "Num Smry."

The procedure to move a range of cells is much the same. Instead of clicking the Copy button after the range of cells is selected, the Cut button ▣ would be clicked. Like the Copy button, the Cut button copies the selected range to the clipboard. The Cut button also erases the selected range of cells after the Paste button is clicked.

- Rename "Sheet2" to "Desc Stats Tool."

▼ Using the Descriptive Statistics Tool

In addition to the built-in functions, Excel contains a set of analysis tools which is very useful for a number of statistical analyses. The analysis tools generally perform more complex calculations than does any single function. The results provided by an analysis are written to more than a single cell. For some of the procedures, the results will fill many cells. An important difference between the analysis tools and the built-in functions is that there is not a link between the cells containing the input and the output of an analysis tool as there is between the cells containing the arguments of a function and the displayed value of the cell with the equation containing the function. The output of an analysis tool is numbers; these numbers will not change unless the analysis tool is rerun and the new results overwrite the old.

The Analysis Tools are provided by Excel's Analysis ToolPak. Although the Analysis ToolPak is a standard part of Excel, it must be specifically installed. Excel is often set up without the Analysis ToolPak; fortunately, it is easy to add it after installation (see Appendix A).

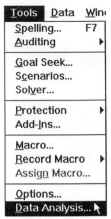

- Open the "Tools" menu on the Menu Bar. It should appear similar to the picture at the left. If "Data Analysis…" is not on your Tools menu, then the Analysis ToolPak has not been installed on your system. See Appendix A for instructions on adding the Analysis ToolPak.

- Click "Data Analysis…." The Data Analysis dialog window will open.

- Choose "Descriptive Statistics" by double clicking it or by clicking it once and then clicking the "OK" button. The Descriptive Statistics dialog window will open.

- The first field in the dialog window is labeled "Input Range," and the window opens with an insertion point in it. Use the same mouse operation you would use to select the cell range A1:A7. A moving marquee will appear around that range of cells, and the address "$A$1:$A$7" will appear in the field. As an alternative to using the mouse, the cell address A1:A7 could be entered directly into the field.

- Click the mouse pointer in the box beside "Labels in First Row." An "x" or check should appear in the box.

This box needs to be clicked because the cell in the first row (A1) contains a label rather than data. If the first field were given the cell range A2:A7, then the box beside "Labels in First Row" should *not* be checked because the first row (cell A2 in this case) contains data, *not* a label. When an Analysis Tool is told the first row contains a label, that label will be used in the tool's output.

At the bottom of the dialog window is a section called "Output Options." Three radio buttons enable you to specify where you want the output placed. "Output Range" results in the output being placed on this worksheet. "New Worksheet Ply" causes Excel to create a new worksheet with the results, and "New Workbook" creates a new workbook with the results.

- Click the "Output Range" radio button.

- Immediately to the right of the words "Output Range" is an input field. Click the mouse pointer in this field so an insertion point will appear.

- Click cell B1. The address "$B$1" will appear in the "Output Range" field. This establishes the upper left hand corner of the section of the worksheet where the Tool will place the results.

- Click the box beside "Summary Statistics" at the bottom of the dialog window. If you don't, Excel will skip most of the output.

When you have finished with the dialog window, it should look like the illustration below.

```
┌────────────────────────────────────────────────────────────┐
│ ▬               Descriptive Statistics                       │
├──────────────────────────────────────────────────┬─────────┤
│ ┌─Input─────────────────────────────────────────┐ │ ┌─────┐ │
│ │ Input Range:          [$A$1:$A$7        ]      │ │ │ OK  │ │
│ │                                                │ │ └─────┘ │
│ │ Grouped By:           ◉ Columns                │ │ ┌──────┐│
│ │                       ○ Rows                   │ │ │Cancel││
│ │                                                │ │ └──────┘│
│ │ ☒ Labels in First Row                          │ │ ┌─────┐ │
│ │                                                │ │ │Help │ │
│ │ ☐ Confidence Level for Mean:  [95   ] %        │ │ └─────┘ │
│ │                                                │ │         │
│ │ ☐ Kth Largest:        [1          ]            │ │         │
│ │                                                │ │         │
│ │ ☐ Kth Smallest:       [1          ]            │ │         │
│ └────────────────────────────────────────────────┘ │         │
│ ┌─Output options───────────────────────────────┐  │         │
│ │ ◉ Output Range:       [$B$1             ]      │  │         │
│ │ ○ New Worksheet Ply:  [                 ]      │  │         │
│ │ ○ New Workbook                                 │  │         │
│ │ ☒ Summary statistics    ▷                      │  │         │
│ └────────────────────────────────────────────────┘ │         │
└────────────────────────────────────────────────────┴─────────┘
```

- Click the "OK" button.

The results of the Descriptive Statistics tool will be in columns B and C and in rows 1 through 16. If your results occupy only three rows, you forgot to click the square beside "Summary Statistics," and you will need to recall the Descriptive Statistics Tool, correct the error, and then re-click "OK."

When an Excel Analysis Tool finishes, the region where the results are placed will be selected. The Analysis Tool does not adjust the width of the columns so that you can see all of the labels.

- Make sure the region containing the output is still selected.

- Open the "Format" menu on the Menu Bar.

- On the drop-down menu, click "Column." A cascading menu will appear.

- Click "AutoFit Selection" as shown on the top of the next page. The width of columns B and C will automatically adjust.

- Click any visible cell on the worksheet to deselect the region with the results.

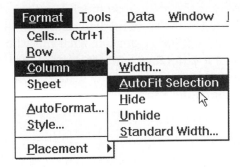

As you can see, the Descriptive Analysis Tool automatically provides a number of descriptive statistics.

- Compare the mean, variance (called "Sample Variance"), and standard deviation with those on the "Num Smry" worksheet. Do they agree? (They should.)

- Click the "Desc Stats Tool" worksheet tab to make that the active worksheet.

- Change the "205" in cell A7 to "305." Do any of the descriptive statistics provided by the Analysis Tool change?

As discussed earlier, no link is maintained between the input of an Analysis Tool and its output. Thus when one of the data items changes, the Analysis Tool output is not automatically updated. To update the output of the Analysis Tool, it would have to be rerun.

Let's try the Descriptive Statistics Tool on another set of data.

- Open the workbook "ch2_data.xls" (Windows 3.1) or "Ch2_data" (Windows 95).

This workbook contains several worksheets. The first provides data by state on the median value of owner occupied houses. (Data are from U.S. Bureau of the Census, *Statistical Abstract of the United States: 1994* (114th edition.), p. 736.

- Select the Housing worksheet.

- Use the Descriptive Statistics Tool to summarize the data on the median value of owner occupied homes. Have Excel put the results in the region beginning with cell C1. Don't forget to use Format...Column...AutoFit Selection to adjust the column widths.

- If you have done this correctly, the mean should be 84209.80392, while the median is 68900.

Why is the median so much less than the mean in this case? The average value for the state medians is over $84,000, but only half the values exceed $68,900. Consider what must be true about the set of numbers for such a difference to exist. Insight into this question involves understanding more about the distribution of data than location and dispersion. A graphical approach may provide this insight.

▼ Histograms

One of the best ways to graphically describe a set of data is with a histogram chart. Many statistics texts describe a number of graphical techniques for describing data, but many of them, including stem-and-leaf charts and frequency polygons are simply variations of histograms.

A histogram groups data into a relatively small number of intervals. A vertical bar chart shows the number of observations in each interval. Let's use Excel to produce a histogram chart of the data on median house value by state. We first must determine the intervals. Although Excel can automatically determine the intervals into which the data are grouped, doing that step manually may produce a better histogram.

From the descriptive statistics, we can tell that the minimum value in the data is 45200 and the maximum is 245300. The range is 245,300 − 45,200 = 200,100. The intervals should be equally sized, but Excel's histogram tool always makes the first and last intervals open ended (no minimum for the first, no maximum for the last). If eight intervals were used, each would be slightly over 25,000 ($^{200,100}/_{8}$). The intervals would be those shown in the table of the top of the next page.

Since the largest value in this set of data is 245,300, it lies just above the upper bound of the largest interval. Since the difference is slight, including this value in the largest interval will bend the rules only slightly. Since Excel makes the last interval open we will simply make that interval contain all data values greater than or equal to 220,000.

For the Histogram Tool to use the intervals (Excel calls them *bins*) which we have selected, the upper bounds of each interval, except the first and last, must be entered into a section of cells somewhere on the worksheet. Let's use the vertical section beginning with cell C18.

• Enter the value 45000 in cell C18 and the value 70000 in cell C19.

These are the lower and upper bounds of the first interval. Excel will actually determine the number of observations in the data *less than* 70000

Interval	More than...	But not more than ...
1	45,000	70,000
2	70,000	95,000
3	95,000	120,000
4	120,000	145,000
5	145,000	170,000
6	170,000	195,000
7	195,000	220,000
8	220,000	245,000

rather than *between* 45000 and 70000. Even though the 45000 is ignored by Excel, it should be included to provide for the first interval

- Use Excel's "fill" capabilities (see page 29) to complete the rest of the series (95000, 120000, 145000, 170000, 195000, 220000) in cells C20:C25. These values correspond to the values in the right-most column of the table above except that the last one is omitted.

Now you are ready to use the Histogram tool.

- Open the "Tools" menu on the Menu Bar and select "Data Analysis...."

- When the Data Analysis dialog window opens, select "Histogram." The Histogram dialog window will open.

- The first field of the dialog window is "Input Range," and an insertion point should already be in that field. You need to enter here the cell addresses which contain the state median housing values. Because of the length of the list (greater than can be shown on the screen without scrolling) you may find it awkward to use the normal mouse actions. Let's look at an alternative method for selecting a large number of cells.

▼ Selecting a Range of Cells with the Keyboard

It is possible to use the normal technique of selecting a range of cells by placing the mouse cursor on the first one, pressing and holding the mouse button, and dragging down the column. If you move the pointer below the last visible cell in the column, the worksheet will begin to scroll up. If you move the pointer back up into the cell area, the scrolling will stop. This scrolling can be hard to control, however.

When selecting large regions, it is often easier to use the keyboard than the mouse. Once a cell is selected (by any means) the selected region can be expanded by pressing a "Shift" key while using the cursor (arrow) keys. Here are step-by-step instructions for this case:

- Select *any* cell in column B. That cell's address will appear (as an absolute address) in the dialog window's Input Range field.
- Press the End key on your keyboard. Release the End key and press the up arrow cursor key. The worksheet will scroll up, cell B1 will have a marquee, and $B$1 will appear in the Input Range field.
- Press and hold a "Shift" key on your keyboard. Press and release the "End" key on your keyboard. While holding a "Shift" key also press the down arrow key. The selected region will immediately move down to include all cells until an empty cell is reached. The cell addresses $B$1:$B$52 should appear in the dialog window's Input Range field.

The region is now selected and we can turn our attention to the rest of the dialog window.

- The next field in the dialog window is "Bin Range." Click the mouse pointer in this field so that it will have an insertion point. The cell addresses which should go in the field are those containing the interval boundaries: C18:C25.
- Click "Labels" so an x appears in the small box.
- Click the mouse pointer in the "Output Range" radio button and then click the mouse pointer in the Output Range field. Click the mouse pointer in cell C27, or enter that address directly in the field.
- Select "Chart Output" at the bottom of the dialog window by clicking the square just to the left of those words so that an x appears.

The histogram dialog window should look like that which appears on the top of the next page. If you have entered any cell addresses directly, it is OK if they appear as relative rather than absolute addresses.

- Click the "OK" button.

Two types of output will appear: a table and a chart. Both provide the same information; the chart is simply a graphic representation of the table. Let's make the chart taller.

- Place the mouse pointer inside the chart and click the (left) mouse button *once*. Small squares (called "handles") should appear at each of the four corners and in the middle of each of four sides. The one at the top of the chart should look like this —▪—.

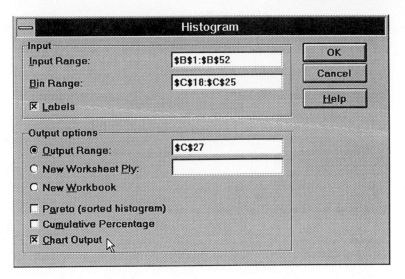

- Place the mouse pointer directly over the handle on the middle of the top border of the chart. When it is in the correct position, the mouse pointer will change shape to an arrow with two heads pointing up and down ⇕ .

- With the mouse pointer in the double-arrow shape, press the (left) mouse button and drag the mouse pointer up by two or three cell heights. You should see the boundary around the chart move with the mouse pointer.

- Release the mouse pointer. You have resized the chart to make it taller. It should look like the picture at the top of the next page.

This histogram shows data which are *right-* or *positively skewed.* Most of the data are close to the lower bound, but there are a number of extremely high values. From the output of the Descriptive Statistics tool, we know that the median for the data is $68,900. Since this value lies within the interval represented by the first bar, that interval must contain more than half of all state median housing values.

▼ Printing the Worksheet

The process of printing a worksheet is very similar to that of printing a chart. If the amount of information on a worksheet is not too great, it is often useful to have Excel print the entire worksheet on a single sheet of paper. Excel will then reduce the size of charts and print so it will fit on a page. To avoid having Excel reduce things until they are too small, it is useful to have the information on the worksheet in as compact a rectangular area as possible.

Histogram

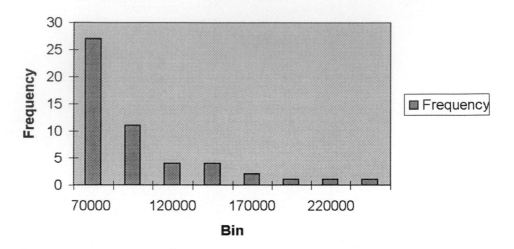

To better examine the layout of the worksheet, you can have Excel reduce the size at which things on the worksheet are displayed on your monitor.

- On the standard toolbar, click the down arrow to the right of the zoom control `100%` ⬍ . A list of zoom factors will open.

- Click on 75%. If you cannot see the entire list of states, change the zoom factor to 50% or 25%. Do not worry if the words or numbers become unreadable.

In order to make the information on the worksheet more compact, you should move the histogram chart down and to the left.

- Place the mouse pointer approximately in the center of the histogram chart and click the mouse button once so that the "handles" appear in the chart's border.

- With the mouse pointer in the approximate center of the chart, press and hold the (left) mouse button. You can now drag an outline of the chart to a new location. When you release the mouse button, the chart will move to the new position.

- Move the chart down and to the left as shown in the illustration on the next page.

- Open the File menu on the Menu Bar. Select "Page Setup."

- When the Print Preview dialog window opens, click the "Page" folder tab.

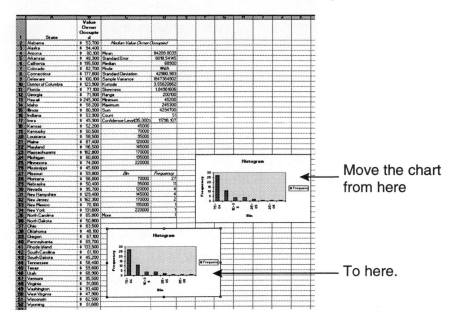

Move the chart from here

To here.

- You have a choice between two orientations: *Portrait* and *Landscape*. You should choose Portrait whenever the material you want printed will better fit the page in a vertical orientation than a horizontal orientation. That's the case here, so click the Portrait radio button.

- In the "Scaling" section, click the radio button to the left of "Fit to," and be sure the numbers in the following fields are both 1 (for pages wide and tall). This tells Excel to reduce the print so that everything will fit on one sheet. The dialog window should look like the picture at the top of the next page.

- Click the "Header/Footer" folder tab, put your name in the header and eliminate the footer. Click the "OK" button.

- Click the "Print" button at the top of the Print Preview screen.

- When your screen returns to the worksheet, change the zoom factor back to 100%.

Look at the table produced by the histogram tool in your printout (cells C27:D35 of your worksheet). This table shows the number of observations in each interval. The first interval contains 27 observations, confirming that over half are in this interval. The extreme large values increase the value of the mean but not the median. Finding that the mean is larger than the median (as in these data) is an indication of positive skew. Notice that the output of the Descriptive Statistics tool includes a measure for skewness (1.84961606). For positively skewed data like these, the skewness measure will be positive.

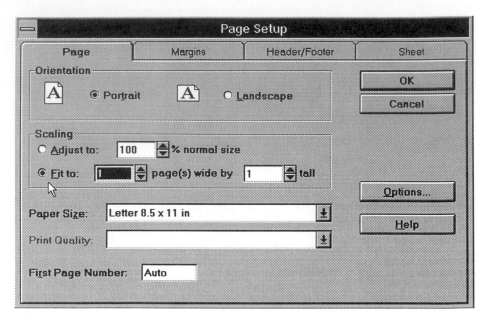

▼ Sorting the Data

The construction of the histogram will be clearer if you examine the state median housing data sorted by value. This is easy for Excel. Recall that we used the Sort button earlier. Now we look at another method of sorting which gives us a little more control than the Sort button.

- Select the range of cells including both the state names and the median housing values. Because of the amount of data, this is best done by using the keyboard. First select cell A1 by clicking the mouse pointer on that cell. Next, hold down a "Shift" key and press the right arrow key once. This will extend the selected region one cell to the right to include cell B1. Continue pressing a "Shift" key and press in sequence the End key and the down-arrow key. The selected region will include all the cells in columns A and B down to the bottom of the list, row 52.

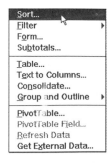

- With the region A1:B52 selected, open the Data menu on the menu toolbar and choose "Sort" (see illustration to the left). The Sort dialog window will open.

The Sort dialog window enables you to specify multiple sort keys. In this case only one is needed. Excel will sort the entire selected region. The purpose of the dialog window is to tell Excel which column to sort the region by. The first column contains the state names and the second contains the median housing value. Sorting the region by the first column would alphabetize by state name (which is how it is currently ordered). Instead, we want it sorted by the second column.

At the bottom of the dialog window you will find two radio buttons allowing you to choose either "Header Row" or "No Header Row." This determines whether the dialog window refers to the column by the column's letter (A or B) or the column label in the first row ("State" or "Value Owner Occupied").

- Select the "Header Row" radio button.

- Click the small down arrow to the right of the top "Sort By" field. In the list which opens, choose the column containing the median state housing value. Your dialog window should look like the picture below.

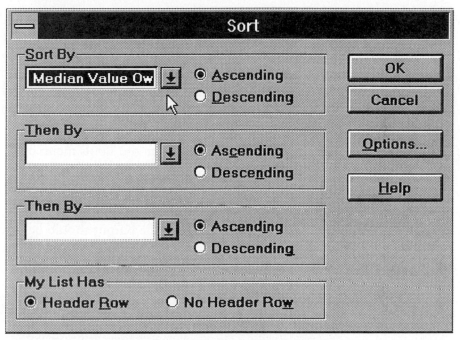

- Click the "OK" button. Excel will sort the data. Scroll your worksheet so that you can examine the top of the list (cells A2 and B2 at the top of your screen).

Scroll down until you find a state whose median housing value exceeds $70,000. You have to go pretty far down in the list until you reach New Mexico, which has a median of $70,100. Continue scrolling down until you reach a state with a median value over $95,000. You need only look down a few states before reaching Vermont whose median value is $95,500. Notice how few states you need to go down before reaching the next interval boundary, $120,000. Each $25,000 increase in median housing value requires moving down fewer states in the list. This confirms what the histogram tells us: although the range of median housing values is quite large, most of them are concentrated near the bottom, below $70,000.

▼ Let Excel Choose the Intervals

It's much quicker and easier to let Excel choose the interval widths than to determine them yourself, but Excel's choices are often not ideal. Let's look at this with a different set of data.

- Click the "Deterg" worksheet tab to bring it to the front and make it active. This worksheet contains information on the cost per load of a number of different liquid and powder laundry detergents available for sale at a single supermarket.

- Sort the data on the worksheet (A1:C36) so that the detergent with the lowest cost per load is at the top and the one with the highest cost per load is at the bottom. You can select the region by first clicking the mouse pointer on cell A1, then, while holding down a "Shift" key, press the right arrow key twice. While continuing to hold down a "Shift" key, press the End key and the down-arrow key. To sort, choose from the Menu Bar "Data...Sort...."

- Choose the Data Analysis from the Tools menu on the Menu Bar and select Histogram.

- When the Histogram dialog window opens, enter the locations of the Cost/Load data in the input range, click the "Labels" and "Chart Output" boxes, and specify that the output should be placed beginning in cell D2. Clear the "Bin Range" field so that it is blank. The dialog window should look like the picture below.

- Click the "OK" button. The results should look like those shown below.

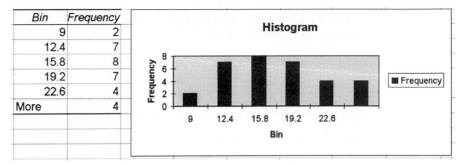

Bin	Frequency
9	2
12.4	7
15.8	8
19.2	7
22.6	4
More	4

- Compare this histogram with that for the housing data.

In this chart, most of the observations are in the middle rather than close to lowest or highest values. This is reflected in the chart by the fact that the tallest bars are in the center rather than on one side. This distribution is less skewed or more *symmetric* than that of the housing data. If a distribution were perfectly symmetric, and you were to draw a vertical line in the center of the histogram chart, the portion of the chart to the left of the line would be a mirror image of that to the right. In such a case, the mean and the median would be the same value.

- Use the Descriptive Statistics tool to calculate descriptive statistics for the detergent cost/load data. Have the output placed in the region beginning with D20.

How do the mean and median compare? The median for these data is 15 while the mean is a bit more than 16.2. These are much closer together, although the fact that the mean is still greater than the median indicates some positive skew. This is confirmed by the positive coefficient of skewness which is slightly over .50. Although positive, this is less than that of the housing data which was just under 1.85. Perfectly symmetric data would have a skewness coefficient of zero and negatively skewed data would have a negative coefficient of skewness.

When the Histogram Tool chooses its own intervals, it forms six intervals, which is a reasonable number, but may not be the most logical grouping for the problem at hand. Unfortunately, the first interval usually consists only of those observations with the minimum value in the data set. For continuous data only one observation may have the minimum value. Excel's self-chosen first interval will thus often have only one observation, although there were two observations for these data.

▼ Embellishing the Histogram Charts

You have already learned how to increase the height of the chart. There are many other changes you can make to the appearance of the chart.

Place the mouse pointer approximately in the middle of the detergent histogram chart and double click the (left) mouse button. This will "activate" the chart, allowing you to edit it. You can determine that it has been activated by noticing the active mode boundary which surrounds it: ▨▨▨. If you single click on the title of the chart ("Histogram") an active mode boundary will also surround it. When you move the mouse pointer into that boundary, it will change to an insertion point, allowing you to change the title.

- Change the title of the histogram chart to "Distribution of Detergent Costs per Load" (without the quotation marks).

Clicking on other parts of the chart will enable you to make changes to those parts. Double clicking will typically cause a menu to appear, permitting you to change such characteristics as color.

If you print from Excel while a chart is is activated, only the chart will print, and it will fill the output page just as it did when the chart was placed on its own worksheet.

When a chart has been activated, the Menu Bar items change. They become the same as they did when a chart was on a separate worksheet.

- With the histogram chart activated, open the "Format" menu on the menu toolbar. Choose "Chart Type...." In the dialog window which opens, click the sample "Line" chart. After it darkens, click the "OK" button.

Your histogram chart has become a frequency polygon chart.

▼ Run Charts

The last descriptive statistic we will consider in this chapter is the run chart which has important application to quality control. Although a run chart is a simple plot of a set of data, it incorporates additional information: order or time. Let's look at an example.

- Click the "Wait" worksheet tab to bring it into view.

This worksheet shows the waiting time spent by each of 36 patients in a physician's office on a single day. The data are ordered so that the first number represents the waiting time of the first patient. The second number is that of the second patient, and so on.

Suppose that we want to determine whether or not there appears to be a problem with the process which this physician uses to schedule his patients. Let's first use the tools already discussed to examine this issue.

- Use the Descriptive Statistics tool to produce descriptive statistics on patient waiting time.

The mean waiting time for patients in this office is a little over 24.5 minutes, which may indicate a problem. The slightly lower median (23 minutes) suggests a slight positive skew which is confirmed by the skewness coefficient. A histogram would show that waiting time was approximately symmetric, as might be expected. None of this establishes clearly whether or not there is a problem. Let's see what can be learned from a run chart.

- From the Menu Bar, open the Insert menu. Choose "Chart," then "As New Sheet."

- In the dialog menu for the first step of the Chart Wizard, indicate that the range of cells to use is that containing the patient waiting time (including the label). This should be B1 through B37. Click the "Next" button.

- In the dialog menu for the second step, choose "XY (Scatter)." Click the "Next" button.

- The third-step dialog window allows you to choose the type of scatter plot. Notice that the sample scatter plots used to illustrate the choices show plots with two data series. For the run charts discussed here, only one data series (patient waiting time) will be shown. The different types are identified only with a number.

- The best plot type for a run chart is one which shows each data point and connects them with a line. This choice is number 2 as shown in the picture at the top of the next page. Choose it and click the "Next" button. The remaining dialog windows will provide a small view of what your graph will look like.

- Check the Step 4 dialog window to be sure that it indicates that the data are in columns (not rows), that 0 columns are being used for X data, and that 1 row is used for legend text. If necessary change the settings to agree with these. Click the "Next" button.

A legend only is useful if a chart has more than one data series and more than one line. In such a case, a legend would tell which line went with

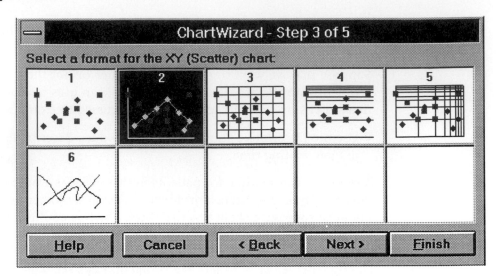

which data series. Since only one data series is used in this case, the legend should be eliminated.

- Click the "No" radio button under "Add a Legend?". Click the "Finish" button. Your chart should look like the one below.

Patient Waiting Time

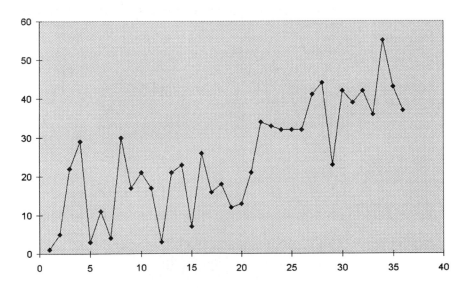

The large up and down movements of the graph suggest the physician often spends an amount of time with a patient which differs substantially from the amount of time scheduled for that patient. In addition, there is an overall pattern to the graph—as the graph moves to the right it had a tendency to move up. This indicates that the average wait for patients seen later in the day is greater than the average wait for patients seen earlier in the day. This suggests that the physician tends to spend a longer time with a patient than the scheduled time. Perhaps too many patients are being scheduled each day.

Univariate (one-variable) descriptive statistics do not reveal the problems with patient waiting time which are clear from the run chart. This is because a run chart shows a relationship between time or sequence (first, second, etc.) and the value of the variable to be analyzed while ordinary descriptive statistics cannot show this relationship. Run charts are used as an aid to understanding a repeated *process*. The manufacturing of a product is such a process, and run charts can be an important tool in quality control for identifying and diagnosing problems. A problem should be suspected whenever the run chart shows a clear pattern, such as a tendency to trend upwards (or downwards). Excessive variation can also be evidence of a problem.

▼ Exercises

1. Use Excel to produce a frequency polygon chart of patient waiting time. Does the picture of the distribution appear symmetrical? Print the polygon chart with your name on the page header.

2. The worksheet named "GDP per cap" provides an international comparison of per capita GDP valued by purchasing power parity for OECD countries in 1991. This measures the value of economic production per person in each country adjusted for differences in prices by country and is an indicator of average economic well-being by country.

   • Sort the data by per capita GDP from lowest to highest so you can easily tell which countries are at the top and which are at the bottom.

   • Produce a histogram chart showing the number of countries with per capita GDP between $0 and $4,000, between $4,001 and $8000, between $8,001 and $12,000, and so on. Do the data appear skewed? If so, in which direction is the skew?

   • Calculate descriptive statistics for these data. Which statistics, if any, confirm the judgment you made about direction of skew above?

   • Print the worksheet on a single sheet of paper showing the list of countries and GDP per capita sorted by GDP per capita, the descriptive statistics, and the histogram chart. Put your name in the header at the top of the page.

3. Amalgamated Hardware is a producer of specialty bolts for the automotive and aircraft industries. One of their products is a 20-centimeter high-strength bolt. The process used to manufacture that bolt is designed to produce bolts whose average length is 20 centimeters. The length of the bolts is carefully controlled, but some process variation is impossible to remove. When the process is operating normally, this variation is completely random. Amalgamated calculates the average length of a sample of the bolts produced each day. The worksheet "Bolt Length" contains the data for 100 consecutive samples. The average of these 100 numbers is 20.0063, which seems high to management.

- Investigate the source of any possible problem by producing a run chart of the sample lengths. Do you see any pattern in the run chart which might indicate an equipment problem or other problem? If so, what is it?

Chapter 3

Discrete Random Variables and Probability Distributions

Random variables and their probability distributions are the basis of inferential statistics. In this chapter you will explore the relationship between the distribution of a random variable and the distribution of data. You will start with one kind of random variable—discrete—and one way of representing a probability distribution—a table. In later chapters you will learn how to work with discrete probability distributions represented as mathematical formulas or Excel formulas and how to work with continuous random variables. Understanding random variables and probability distributions will help you make sense of sampling distributions.

▼ Probability Distributions

The value of a random variable can never be known in advance of its selection. If you toss a die, for example, you can't be certain before the toss what number will come up (assuming the die is not loaded!). You do, however, know the *set of possible values*. The toss of a die must result in an integer value between 1 and 6. The probability distribution of a random variable gives you this information and also provides you with the probability associated with each possible value.

Sometimes random variables have outcomes which are not quantitative. The outcome of a coin toss, for example, is heads or tails, not a number. The gender of newborn child is also not a number. These nonquantitative outcomes must be represented as numbers to be usable in Excel. Usually, any integers will suffice, such as 0 for tails and 1 for heads.

Suppose your statistics professor assigns grades purely by chance. You have no idea what your grade will be, but you do know the probability distribution which is shown in the table on the next page:

Grade	Probability
4	.10
3	.20
2	.35
1	.25
0	.10

Remember that Excel's operations require the values of random variables to be numeric. Thus rather than represent the grades as A, B, C, D, and F, they are represented by integers with 4 for A, 3 for B, and so on.

- Start Excel with a new blank workbook.

- Enter this table into an Excel worksheet using Columns C and D and rows 1 through 6. Put the labels "Grade" and "Probability" in cells C1 and D1 respectively. Your worksheet should like the picture below.

	A	B	C	D
1			Grade	Probability
2			4	0.1
3			3	0.2
4			2	0.35
5			1	0.25
6			0	0.1
7				

- Open the File menu on the Menu Bar and choose "Save As...." Save the workbook in a file named "CHAP3.XLS."

- An important property of a probability distribution is that the probabilities must all sum to 1.0. Check that this is true in your worksheet by selecting cell D7 and clicking the AutoSum button Σ. Excel should respond by showing a formula to sum cells D2 through D6.

- Press the Enter key and the number 1 should appear in cell D7 confirming that the sum of the probabilities is 1.

▼ Mean and Variance of a Probability Distribution

Let's have Excel calculate the mean and variance of this distribution. We will then explore the *meaning* of the mean and variance of a probability distribution. The formula for the expected value or mean of a probability distribution is:

$$E(x) = \mu = \sum (x \cdot P(x)).$$

Where $P(x)$ is the probability of the random variable having the value x.

When calculating a formula like this, it is often best to have Excel perform the calculations on the expression within the summation $(x \cdot P(x))$ for each x value and then sum the result of these calculations across all x values. This is the procedure used to calculate the variance and standard deviation of a sample in Chapter 2. This will be done by having cell E2 contain the product of the value of x in cell C2 and the value of $P(x)$ in cell D2. Cells E3 through E6 will have the corresponding products for the values in those rows. The sum of these products will be the expected value.

- To document what you will be doing, enter the label "Mean" in cell E1 and the word "Variance" in cell F1.

The mean or expected value will be calculated in column E and the variance in column F.

- Select cell E2.

- Type an equals sign (=) to let Excel know that you are entering a formula.

- Move the mouse cursor to cell C2 and click the left mouse button. That cell address (C2) should appear after the equals sign in the formula in cell E2. Notice that this is a *relative* address, not an *absolute* address, since there are no $ signs in the address.

- Enter the Excel multiplication symbol (*), and then point to cell D2 and click the left mouse button. The formula appearing in cell E2 should be =C2*D2.

- Press the Enter key or click the check mark in the formula bar, and the formula should be replaced by its value, 0.4.

The next step is to copy this formula to the other cells in column E.

- Use the mouse cursor to select cell E2.

- Position the mouse cursor on the fill handle and drag the fill handle downward (while pressing the left mouse button) until the selection border surrounds cells E2 through E6.

- Release the mouse button.

Each cell in the selected region of column E should contain the product of the numbers in columns C and D for that row. Check this by selecting cell E5 and checking the formula bar. The formula which should appear should be =C5*D5.

The last step is to calculate the sum of the values in cells E2 through E6.

- Select cell E7 and use the AutoSum ∑ button to have Excel automatically enter the formula summing cells E2 through E6. Press the Enter key, and the expected value of the probability distribution (1.95) should appear in cell E7.

We will explore the meaning of a probability distribution's expected value below. First, let's use Excel to calculate the variance of this probability distribution.

The formula for the variance of a probability distribution is given by the following formula:

$$\text{VAR}(x) = \sigma^2 = \sum (x - \mu)^2 P(x).$$

The structure of this formula is similar to that of the expected value—a summation of separate terms for each value of x. We will use the same strategy to calculate the formula as we used in that case. In cells F2 through F6 Excel will calculate the value of the expression within the summation (Σ) for the value of x for that row. In F2 we will put the formula to calculate this expression for $x=4$. That formula will then be copied to cells F3 through F6 and cell F7 will sum these values.

- Select cell F2 and type an equals sign followed by a left parenthesis.

- Click the mouse pointer on cell C2 (the value of x for that row), and "C2" should appear after the left parenthesis in the formula in cell F2.

- Type a minus sign and click cell E7. Cell E7 contains the expected value, the "μ" in the formula. Since we will want to copy the formula in this cell to the cells below E2, this address must be made an absolute rather than a relative address. Do this by pressing the F4 function key once. This should change the E7 in the formula to $E$7.

- Type a right parenthesis.

The expression within the parenthesis, "=(C2-$E$7)," corresponds to the "$(x - \mu)$" in the formula for the variance.

- To square the quantity in parentheses, enter " ^ 2" after the right parenthesis.

The formula now corresponds to the expression $(x - \mu)^2$ in the formula for the variance. All that remains is to multiply this by the probability of x, $P(x)$.

- Enter the multiplication symbol, *, and click cell D2. The formula in cell F2 should be "=(C2-$E$7)^2*D2." Press Enter or click the check mark in the formula bar and the value 0.42025 will appear in the cell.

- Copy the formula in cell F2 to cells F3 through F6.

- Check to be sure that the copying is correct by examining the value of cell F5. It should be 0.225625. If this is not the value, check the formula bar or double click cell F2 to see the formula in the cell. It should be =(C5-$E$7)^2*D5.

If this is not the formula in cell F5, you probably entered the wrong formula in cell F2. Go back to cell F2 and be sure the formula there is =(C2-$E$7)^2*D2, then recopy it to cells F3 through F6.

- Use the AutoSum button to place the sum of the values of cells F2 through F6 in cell F7. This is the variance of the distribution.

If you have done everything correctly, your spreadsheet should look like the picture below.

	A	B	C	D	E	F
1			Grade	Probability	Mean	Variance
2			4	0.1	0.4	0.42025
3			3	0.2	0.6	0.2205
4			2	0.35	0.7	0.00088
5			1	0.25	0.25	0.22563
6			0	0.1	0	0.38025
7				1	1.95	1.2475
8						

Thus the mean of the probability distribution is 1.95 and the variance is 1.2475. But what is the connection between the mean and variance of a probability distribution and the mean and variance of a set of data? Let's examine that relationship.

▼ Probability Distributions and Data

If we choose one student at random from the class whose grades are described by the probability distribution, there is no way we can know for certain what grade that student will receive. If, however, many students are chosen, the distribution of those grades should be similar to that given by the probability distribution. We can see this by taking advantage of Excel's ability to choose random variables from a probability distribution, a capability provided by Excel's Analysis ToolPack.

- Select the Tools menu from the Menu Bar. Choose "Data Analysis…" from the menu which opens.

- Choose "Random Number Generation" from the list in the Data Analysis dialog window. You may need to scroll the list down before you see this choice. The random number generation dialog window will open.

Let's start by having Excel draw one random number from the probability distribution on our worksheet.

The first two fields in the dialog window for which we must provide information are labeled "Number of Variables" and "Number of Random Numbers." You must enter a number in each field. The labeling of many of these fields is confusing. Despite the way the fields are labeled, the total number of random numbers Excel will draw is the *product* of the numbers you enter in these two fields. Excel will put the random numbers in a rectangular array on your worksheet. The value you put in the "Number of Variables" field determines how many columns Excel will use for the random numbers. The value you put in the "Number of Random Numbers" field determines the number of rows Excel will use. The names Excel uses are consistent with standard statistical practice where data are usually arranged in rectangular arrays with each observation in a separate row and each variable in a separate column.

- Since our first use of the random number generator will be to generate only one random number, enter the number 1 in both the "Number of Variables" field and the "Number of Random Numbers" field.

The third field in the dialog window is labeled "Distribution." It is here that you tell Excel what kind of random number you wish generated.

- Click on the small downward-pointing arrow ▣ beside the Distribution field.

This will open a list of distributions.

- Choose the "Discrete" distribution.

The distribution you choose determines which fields appear in the dialog window. When Discrete is chosen, the fourth field in the dialog window is labeled "Value and Probability Input Range." In this field you must put the cell addresses of the probability distribution table showing each possible value for the random variable and the probability of that value.

- Click the mouse pointer in the field labeled "Value and Probability Input Range." An insertion point should appear in the field.

- Use the mouse or the keyboard to enter the cell addresses for columns C and D, rows 2 through 6. Note that you do not include the column labels in the first row. If you use the mouse, the cell addresses will appear as an absolute address, but you may enter a relative address with the keyboard.

- Click the radio button beside "Output Range:," and then click the mouse pointer in the adjacent field so that an insertion point will appear. Click the mouse button in cell A1. The absolute address $A$1 will appear in the field. An alternative to pointing at the cell is to type A1 directly into the field. When you have finished, the dialog window should look like the picture below.

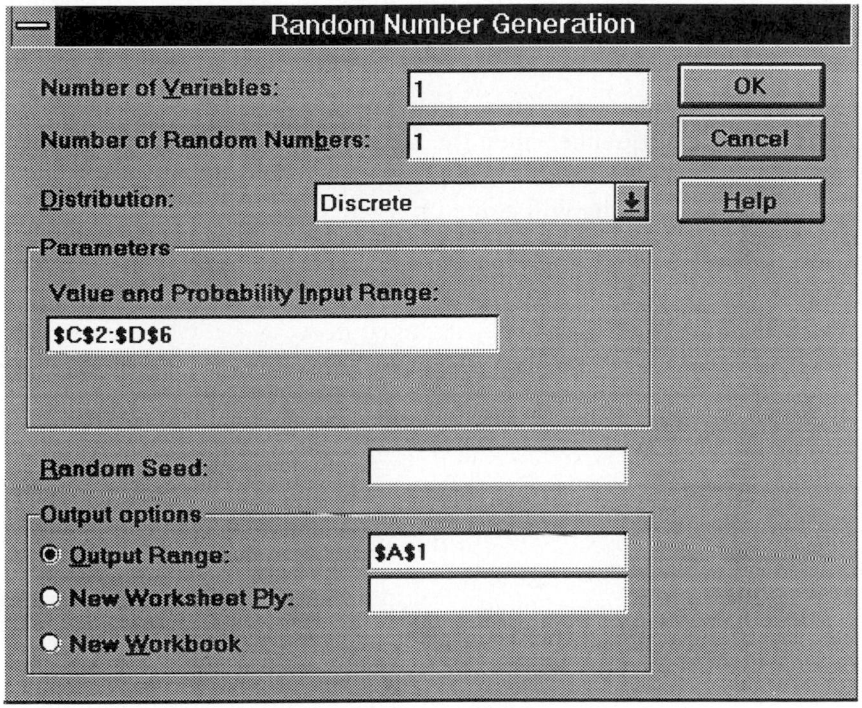

- Click the "OK" button. The dialog window will disappear and cell A1 will contain one of the integers 0 through 4. Since this is a random number, it is impossible to predict in advance what that number will be. Make a mental note of what the number is so that when you repeat this process you can observe how the value changes.

- Open the Tools menu again and again choose Data Analysis.

- When the Data Analysis dialog window opens, notice that Random Number Generation is already chosen. Click the "OK" button. The Random Number Generation dialog window will open.

- Notice that the fields you previously filled out in the Random Number Generation dialog window retain those values. Again, simply click the "OK" button. A warning window will open.

The warning window appears because you have asked the Random Number Generation tool to put a random number in cell A1, but cell A1 already has a value. Putting a new value there will destroy or *overwrite* the value already there. Excel is concerned that this may be a mistake. In this case it is not.

- Simply click the "OK" button on the warning window. A new value will be written to cell A1.

Is the new value the same as the old?

- Select a dozen different new random numbers by repeating this sequence: open the Tools menu, select Data Analysis, click the "OK" button in the next three windows which open. Try to predict which value will come up next. Tally the number of times each comes up in the table below by placing a mark in the "Tally" column each time that value appears.

Value	Tally	Count
4	_____	_____
3	_____	_____
2	_____	_____
1	_____	_____
0	_____	_____

Sum

- After you have chosen and tallied all 12 random numbers, enter the total number of times each value occurred. Check your answer by summing these numbers. They should sum to 12.

Let's use Excel to automate the process of drawing many random numbers and tallying how many times each different value occurs.

- Recall the Random Number Generation dialog window (Tools, Data Analysis, "OK").

- Change the value in the Number of Random Numbers field from 1 to 1000. Click "OK" in this window and in the warning window.

Excel will generate 1,000 different random values and place them in column A (A1:A1000). This will, of course, take a bit longer than generating a single random number. While Excel is generating the numbers, you will be able to move the mouse pointer around, but you won't be able to do anything else. You can tell Excel is still busy if the mouse pointer is in the shape of an hourglass.

The next step will be to look at the distribution of these random numbers. We will tally the number of 4's, 3's, 2's, 1's, and 0's and also determine the proportion of the total made up of each of these values. In addition, we will calculate the mean and standard deviations of this group of numbers and compare all this to the probability distribution. We will also look at how these proportions change as the number of random numbers increases.

The thousand values in A1:A1000 are, of course, a sample of 1,000 random numbers. Rather than generating more samples, we will take the ten numbers in A1:A10 as a sample of ten random numbers and the 100 numbers in A1:A100 as a sample of 100 random numbers.

Use columns G, H, and I in the same rows as the probability distribution which will be used to count the number of times each value of the random variable occurs in each of the three samples we will look at.

- Label cell G1, H1, and I1 as shown below.

	G	H	I
1	10 values	100 values	1000 values

In cell G2 we will have Excel put a count of the number of times the value "4" occurs in cells A1:A10. In cell H2 we will put a count of the number of times the value "4" appears in cells A1:A100, and in cell I2 we will put a count of the number of times the value "4" appears in A1:A1000. In cells G3, H3 and I3, we will put a count of the number of times the value "3" appears in each of the same ranges. Rows 4, 5, and 6 will contain similar counts for values "2," "1," and "0." Excel has a useful function named COUNTIF for just this purpose.

- Select cell G2. Click the Function Wizard button 🔧.

- In the Function Wizard dialog window choose "Math & Trig" for function category and "COUNTIF" for function name. Click the "Next" button.

The COUNTIF function has two arguments: *range* and *criteria*. The *range* argument is the cell addresses where you want Excel to determine the count for a specific value and *criteria* is the value you want counted.

- Enter "$A$1:$A$10" (without quotes) in the range field.

The range field is given as an absolute address so that it can be copied without its value changing.

- Click the mouse pointer in the criteria field and then click cell C2. The cell address, C2, will go in the field.

- Press the F4 function key three times. The "C2" in cell G2 should become "$C2." If you have difficulty, use the keyboard to put "$C2" in the criteria field.

- Click the "Finish" button. Check to be sure the value in cell G2 really is the number of 4's in cells A1:A10.

The value for which we want a count in cell G2 is the value "4." Rather than put a "4" directly in the field, we have put a cell address containing that value from the Grade column. The *column* part of the address "$C2" is absolute. If we copy that cell's formula to a cell in a different column, the formula in the copied cell will always refer to column C. The *row* part of the cell address is relative. If the formula is copied to a different row, the formula in the copied cell will change to refer to the same row as the copied cell.

- Copy the contents of cell G2 to cells G3:G6. Check by clicking on cell G6 and verifying that the formula there is "=COUNTIF($A$1:$A$10,$C6)."

- Further check your results by using the AutoSum button in cell G7 to calculate the sum of the values in cells G2:G6. The sum should be 10.

The formulas in cells H2:H6 should be just like those in G2:G6 except the range should be A1:A100 instead of A1:A10.

- Copy the formula in cell G2 to H2.

- Select cell H2. Change the "$A$1:$A$10" in the formula to "$A$1:$A$100." The change can be made either in the formula bar or directly in the cell by first double clicking H2.

- Copy cell H2 to H3:H6.

- Use the AutoSum button in H7 to determine the sum of the values in H2:H6. If done correctly, the sum should be 100.

- Follow a similar procedure to put formulas in cells I2:I6. The formulas in column I should refer to A1:A1000 for their range.

- Check your work in column I by using I7 to sum the values of I2:I6. The sum should be 1000.

You now have a table counting the number of times each value appears in the sample. To compare these numbers to the probability distribution, we need to convert the count of values to a proportion of the total. That proportion can then be directly compared to the probability in the distribution.

Let's make a comparison table in the region C9:G17.

- Copy the contents of cells C1:C6 to C9:C14. This will provide the first column of the new table giving the possible grade values. The easiest way of copying a small number of cells is to first select the cells to be copied, place the mouse pointer on the cell boundary, and, while pressing the Ctrl key (PC) or OPTION key (MAC), drag the selection outline to the location where you want the copy.

- Copy the contents of cells G1:I1 to D9:F9. This will give a row of labels across the top of the table.

- Enter the label "Distribution" (without quotes) in cell G9.

- Copy the contents of cells D2:D6 to G10:G14.

- Enter the labels "Mean" in cell C15 and "Variance" in cell C16.

Cells G15 and G16 should contain the mean and variance of the distribution which are calculated in cells E7 and F7.

- Select cell G15 and enter the formula "=E7." Select cell G16 and enter the formula "=F7."

This section of your worksheet should look like the picture at the top of the next page. This provides the distribution probabilities for comparison with the sample proportions which need still to be calculated.

Next we will put formulas in cells D10:F14 which will calculate the proportion of each sized sample which is equal to the value given in the appropriate row of column C. To calculate the proportion, we want to take the number of times each value occurs in each sample (which is in G2:I6) and divide by the sample size (which is in G7:I7). So each of the cells in D10:F14 will divide the value of a cell in G2:I6 by the value of a cell in G7:I7. For example, cell D10 will contain the proportion of 4's in the sample of 10. This is calculated by dividing the value of cell G2 by the value of cell G7. If we copy this formula to another cell in D10:F14,

	C	D	E	F	G
9	Grade	10 values	100 values	1000 values	Distribution
10	4				0.1
11	3				0.2
12	2				0.35
13	1				0.25
14	0				0.1
15	Mean				1.95
16	Variance				1.2475

we would like both the row and column of the numerator cell to change. We would also like the denominator column to change from G to H to I for the different cell sizes. We do not, however, want the denominator's *row* to change. The row must be 7. This can be done by making the column reference relative and the row reference absolute.

- Select cell D10. Enter an equals sign to start the formula.

- Click cell G2. "G2" will be written in the formula. Enter the division symbol ("/" without the quotes). Click cell G7 (which displays "10," and then press the F4 function key twice. The "G7" in the formula should change to "G$7," which makes the row reference absolute. The formula in D10 should be "=G2/G$7."

- Press the Enter key. The value displayed in D10 will be a number between 0 and 1.

- Copy the formula in D10 to the rest of the cells in the region D10:F14. One way to do this is to copy cell D10 down to D11:D14. With D10:14 as the selected range, you can copy the column to the right by dragging the fill handle of the selected region two columns to the right.

Each of the cells in D10:F14 should display a number between 0 and 1. The five proportions in each column will sum to 1.0.

Next put formulas in rows 15 and 16 to calculate the mean and variance of each set of numbers.

- Use Excel's built-in function (by using the Function Wizard) in cell D15 to calculate the average of cells A1:A10. Similarly, in cell E15 calculate the average of cells A1:A100 and in cell F15 calculate the average of A1:A1000.

- In cells D16, E16, and F16, use Excel's built-in function to calculate the sample variance of A1:A10, A1:A100, and A1:A1000, respectively.

The table can be made more readable by formatting. Let's format the numbers so that all the proportions, probabilities, and summary statistics are displayed with three positions to the right of the decimal point.

- With the mouse select the region D10:G16. This is the region whose values are to be formatted.

- Click the Decrease Decimal button on the formatting toolbar ![Decrease Decimal]. All of the displayed numbers in the selected region should now show only one digit in each cell.

- Click the Increase Decimal button on the formatting toolbar ![Increase Decimal] three times. Each time you click the button, an additional digit to the right of the decimal point appears. With three clicks, the digits to the right of the decimal point will be displayed. The displayed values are rounded. No change is made to the values which Excel would use for calculation.

For the proportion receiving each of the grade values and for the mean and variance, notice the pattern that exists as you move to the right. As the number of random numbers increases, the proportion which each value has is usually closer to the probability given by the probability distribution. Sometimes this doesn't happen. The exceptions generally occur when the smaller data set happened to have a proportion which was already very close to the distribution probability. Increasing the size of the data set might result in a proportion that was further from the distribution probability, but this is not what usually happens.

Similarly, as the size of a data set of random numbers increases, the mean and variance of those data generally approach the mean and variance of the probability distribution. In all cases, the values associated with 1,000 numbers should be quite close to those of the probability distribution. Increasing the number of values would bring them even closer, but it should be clear that there is not a lot of room for further improvement. Although a single value of a random variable cannot be predicted, the characteristics of a moderately large number of random variables can be predicted with a fairly high degree of accuracy.

▼ Turning Off Automatic Calculation

With this worksheet, it is easy to look at a different set of random numbers. Excel will, however, recalculate the values of all of the formulas in the worksheet each time a single random number is generated. The process of picking new random numbers will be speeded up if we turn off Excel's automatic calculation.

- Open the Tools menu on the Menu Bar and choose "Options...." The Options dialog window will open.

- The Options dialog window has many tab folders. Click on the "Calculation" tab folder.

- In the top left of the dialog window is a region titled "Calculation" with several radio buttons. Click the "Manual" radio button. The dialog window should look like the picture below.

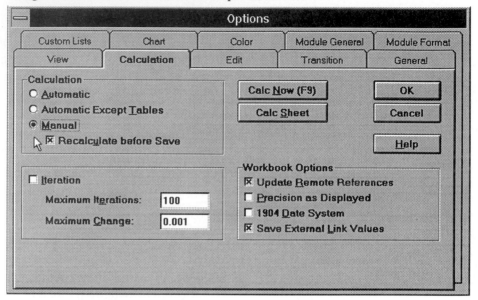

▼ New Random Numbers

Let's generate a new set of random numbers.

- Open the Tools menu, choose Data Analysis and Random Number Generation.

If you have done this chapter in a single session with Excel, the Random Number Generation dialog window will already have the fields filled out. If not, refer to the picture on page 85, except change the value in the Number of Random Numbers field from 1 to 1000.

- Click the "OK" button.

- Give Excel the OK to overwrite existing data.

Wait until the mouse pointer is no longer in the shape of an hourglass. Notice that because you set calculation to manual, neither of the tables summarizing the random numbers will have changed until you tell Excel to do a recalculation.

- Tell Excel to recalculate by pressing the F9 function key. You should see the values in the table change.

Look at the new table. You should, of course, see some differences, but the general pattern should be the same. The larger the sample of random numbers, the closer its distribution, mean, and variance will tend to be to those of the probability distribution. You can think of the probability distribution as a description of an infinitely large set of random numbers drawn from that distribution.

▼ Exercises

1. Use the formatting buttons to enhance the appearance of the table in C9 through G16. Use formatting to set the row and column headings apart from the data in table. Use font changes or style changes to further enhance the visual distinction between the headings and the data.

   When you are finished, print out the enhanced table with your name in the header. Here is how to print just the table (not the entire worksheet).

   - Select the region C9:G16 (the new table).

   - Open the File menu on the Menu Bar and choose "Print...." The Print dialog window will open.

   - At the top of the dialog window under "Print What," click the "Selection" radio button.

   - Click the "Print Preview" radio button on the right side of the window.

   - Click the "Setup..." button at the top of the Print Preview screen.

   - Use the "Page" folder in the Setup dialog window to increase the scaling to a number greater than 100%. This will enlarge the selection to be printed so that it will fill more of the page.

   - Use the "Margin" folder in the Setup dialog window to center the table horizontally and vertically.

   - Use the Header/Footer folder to put your name and a title on the page header.

   - Click the "OK" button in the dialog window.

   - Click the "Print..." button at the top of the Print Preview page.

2. An investor is considering purchasing shares of newly issued stock. Suppose many companies are issuing stock this year The percentage one year return to each stock can be treated as an independent random number following the same distribution shown below:

Percentage Profit	Probability
-100	.10
-60	.20
-10	.15
+10	.15
+60	.25
+100	.15

Use Excel to calculate the mean and variance of this distribution.

Use Excel's random number generator to simulate the one-year return to different sized portfolios consisting of stocks with the probability distribution shown above:

• a portfolio of equal amounts of five company's stocks.

• a portfolio of equal amounts of 50 company's stocks.

• a portfolio of equal amounts of 500 company's stocks.

For each portfolio determine the proportion of stocks providing each level of profit and the mean and standard deviation of each portfolio. Create a chart comparing these proportions and summary statistics with the probability distribution like the chart prepared in this chapter. Enhance the appearance of your chart, put your name and a title on the header, and print it out.

Chapter 4

The Binomial Distribution

A number of probability distributions occur so often in practical situations that mathematical formulas for their distributions have been developed. These formulas make it easier to solve problems using these distributions, especially since Excel has built many of the most popular formulas into Excel functions. When a distribution is important enough to get this kind of special attention, it also gets a name. The distribution we will look at in this chapter is the *binomial* distribution. There is one mildly confusing feature of the way distributions are named. The name of a distribution is always singular. For example, the distribution we will look at in this chapter is always called *the* binomial distribution. In reality, however, the binomial distribution is not a single distribution in the same way as the distribution of grades discussed in a previous chapter was a single distribution. The binomial distribution is really a family of distributions. There are an infinite number of different binomial distributions. They all have certain characteristics in common, and they share a common formula.

A random number from the (or a) binomial distribution can be thought of as being generated by a random process which has two possible outcomes, one of the outcomes is of particular significance and is usually termed *success*. The other is termed *failure*. The random process occurs a fixed number of times. The probability of success each time is constant and independent of whether or not a success has occurred any of the other times. The binomially distributed random number is the count of the number of successes which have occurred.

Two things make one binomial distribution different from another. These are the probability that the random process will produce a success and the number of times that the process is repeated. These are the variables of the binomial distribution. Most authors symbolize the probability of the random process resulting in success with p, although some use π. The number of trials is usually symbolized with n.

An example may make this easier to understand.

An automobile salesperson has discovered from experience that two out of every ten persons she takes for a test drive in a new automobile eventually buy a car from her. Suppose one evening she takes five people for a test drive. What is the probability that none of them purchase a car from her?

The random variable here is the number of persons who purchase a car from the salesperson out of the five taken for a test drive. The random process here is the one determining whether or not a person taken for a test drive ends up buying a car. That process has two outcomes: the person buys a car or the person does not buy a car. The outcome we want to count is the first, so we will call the outcome "buying a car" a success. The question tells us that the probability of success is two in ten or .20. In other words, $p=.20$. Furthermore, we know that five people are taken on a test drive, so $n=5$.

Recall that a probability distribution tells us all the possible values which the random variable can equal and the probability associated with each of those values. What are the possible values for this random variable? In other words, what values are possible for the number of people who buy a car out of five who take a test drive? Clearly the lowest value is zero; it is possible that none of those who take a test drive will buy a car. The highest value is five; all of the people who take a test drive might buy a car. All of the integer values in between are also possible. The number of people who buy a car is thus 0, 1, 2, 3, 4, or 5. These are the possible values for the random variable (which we will symbolize as x). For this problem we are to determine the probability that $x = 0$.

Let's further explore this problem by using Excel to simulate the situation.

▼ Simulating a Binomial Problem

- Start Excel and open a new workbook.

- Save the workbook as chap4.xls.

The Random Number Generation Tool will be used to simulate the random process of a test driver deciding either to buy or not to buy a car. The first step is to enter a probability distribution for this random process. To buy or not to buy; that is the first question.

Since Excel requires that the outcomes of a random process be represented as numbers, we will use "0" to represent the outcome of *not* buying a car and "1" to represent the outcome of buying a car. The probability of "1" is .20; the probability of "0" is thus .80 (1.00 − 0.20 = 0.80).

- Enter the label "Outcome" in cell H1 and "Probability" in cell I1.

- In cell H2 enter the number "1" (without quotes), which stands for buying a car, and in I2 enter the number ".20" (without quotes), which is the probability that the person taking the test drive will buy a car. This is the value of p discussed above.

- In cells H3 enter the number "0" (without quotes), which stands for not buying a car. The probability of not buying a car is $1 \sim p$. In this case that probability is 0.80, but instead of entering that number, enter the formula "=1-I2" in cell I3 so that later changes in p will cause this probability to be changed automatically. The displayed value should be 0.8.

Now let's use the Random Number Generation Tool to simulate the outcome associated with *one* person taking a test drive.

- Open the Tools menu, select "Data Analysis...," and choose "Random Number Generation." The Random Number Generation dialog window will open.

- Enter "1" for both Number of Variables" and "Number of Random Numbers."

- Choose "Discrete" for the Distribution. In the "Value and Probability Input Range" put the address for the cell range containing the probability distribution you just entered for whether or not a test driver becomes a buyer, H2:I3.

- Choose "Output Range," and have the Random Number Generation Tool put the output in cell A1.

The completed dialog window should look like the picture at the top of the next page.

- Click the "OK" button in the dialog window.

Look in cell A1. Did the test driver buy the car (cell A1 has a "1") or not (cell A1 has a "0")?

- Try another customer by opening the Tools menu again, choosing "Data Analysis," and clicking "OK" in the next three dialog windows which open. See how many times you have to do this before you find a test driver (or another test driver) who decides to buy (that is, before you get a 1 (or another 1) in cell A1.

Let's now simulate an entire evening of five test drivers.

- Open the Tools menu and choose "Data Analysis" again. Click "OK" to recall the Random Number Generation dialog window.

Random Number Generation		
Number of <u>V</u>ariables: `1`		OK
Number of Random Num<u>b</u>ers: `1`		Cancel
<u>D</u>istribution: `Discrete` ↧		<u>H</u>elp

Parameters

Value and Probability <u>I</u>nput Range:

`$H$2:$I$3`

<u>R</u>andom Seed: _____

Output options
- ⦿ <u>O</u>utput Range: `$A$1`
- ○ New Worksheet <u>P</u>ly: _____
- ○ New <u>W</u>orkbook

- Change the number "1" in the "Number of Variables" field to "5." Click "OK," and then click "OK" again in the overwrite warning window.

Five numbers will fill the range A1:E1. How many of them are 1's? Although it is not difficult to spot and count the 1's among the 0's, let's have Excel do this for us automatically. One way would be to use the COUNTIF function. A perhaps simpler method would be to simply have Excel add all five numbers together. Since the numbers must each be either 0 or 1, the sum of the five numbers will always equal the number of 1's.

- Select cell F1.

- Click the AutoSum button ▣. The formula to add A1:E1 will automatically be entered in cell F1. Press the Enter key.

Cell F1 now contains a count of the number of 1's in cells A1:E1. This number is a simulation of the number of people out of five test drivers who will buy a car. It is this number in cell F1 which is the binomially distributed random variable.

Try the simulation five to ten times by opening the Tools menu, choosing "Data Analysis" and clicking the "OK" button in the next three dialog boxes. What is the largest number of buyers you get in these simulations? What do you think is the most likely number of buyers the salesperson will get after taking five people on test drives? Your experience should convince you that often none of the five test drivers will purchase a car. Car sales is a tough business.

Rather than repeatedly simulate the purchase decisions of five test drivers, let's have Excel do this for us.

- Recall the Random Number Generation dialog window and change "Number of Random Numbers" from 1 to 1000. Click the "OK" button.

After a delay, Excel will fill the range of cells A1:E1000 with 0's and 1's. We can interpret each row in this range as a separate simulation of the purchase decision of five test drivers.

The next step is to copy the formula in cell F1, which tells the number of 1's in row 1, down column F until a similar sum is available for each row. This could be done by selecting cell F1 and dragging its fill handle down to cell F1000. This is tricky to do, however, because the region is so large. Here is an alternative.

- Click the mouse pointer in the Name Box. (See page 4 if you have forgotten where the Name Box is.) The current value will become highlighted, and you will be able to enter a new value.

- Enter "f1:f1000" (without quotation marks) in the Name Box. Press the Enter key.

The entire region F1:F1000 becomes selected.

- Open the Edit menu on the Menu Bar. Select "Fill." A cascade menu will open to the right, as shown on the next page.

- Select "Down" from the cascade menu. The menu will disappear, and the formula in F1 will be copied to all the cells in the selected region. Column F will provide the number of 1's in each of 1,000 rows. These values in column F are values for specific instances of the binomially distributed random variable, the number of people who buy cars out of five who take test drives.

The next step is to count the number of times each possible different value occurs in column F, determine the proportion of times each value occurs, the average and standard deviation of the values and compare these with the values given by the binomial distribution functions.

The procedure we will use here is very similar to that used in the previous chapter. Two tables will be created on this worksheet. The first one will tally the number of the times each possible value for the number of car buyers occurs in the first 10 rows, the first 100 rows, and the entire

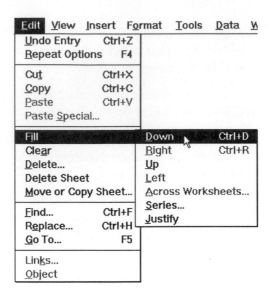

1,000 rows. A second table will convert these counts to proportions and compare them to the probabilities generated by the binomial function. This table will also compare the means and standard deviations of the three groups of rows to those of the binomial distribution.

▼ Counting the Number of Car Buyers

- Prepare labels for the first table in the positions shown in the picture below.

The word "nights" is used in the labels to refer to the fact that the car salesperson takes five people on a test drive in an evening.

- Use the Function Wizard to create an Excel formula in cell I6 using the COUNTIF function to count the number of times the value "5" appears in the range F1:F10. Make the cell addresses in the "range" field *absolute* so they will not change when you copy the formula to other

	H	I	J	K
5	Sales	10 nights	100 nights	1000 nights
6		5		
7		4		
8		3		
9		2		
10		1		
11		0		
12	sum			

cells. In the "criteria" field put the cell address for the "5" in H6. Make the column reference *absolute* and the row reference *relative* so that if you copy the formula to cells in other rows, the criteria will always refer to cells in column H.

The number displayed in cell I6 will be an integer between 0 and 10. The most likely value is 0.

- Copy the contents of cell I6 to cells I7:I11. If the addresses have been specified properly, each cell should display the number of times the value in that row of column H occurs F1:F10. Check this!

- Check the result by selecting cell I12 and clicking the AutoSum button. Press Enter. The displayed value should be 10.

- Copy the formula in cell I6 to cell J6. Double click cell J6 to edit the formula.

- Change the $F$1:$F:$10 in cell J6 to $F$1:$F:$100.

- Copy cell J6 to J7:J11. These cells should display a count of the number of times each value occurs in F1:F100.

- Select cell J12, click the AutoSum button, and press the Enter key. The sum of J6:J11 should be 100.

- Copy cell J6 to K6. Double click cell K6 so that you can edit the formula.

- Change the $F$1:$F$100 in cell K6 to $F$1:$F$1000. K6 should now display the number of times the value "5" appears in all 1,000 rows of column F.

- Copy the formula in K6 to K7:K11. Each cell should show the number of times the corresponding value in row H occurs in the 1,000 rows of column F.

- Select cell K12 and use the AutoSum button to add the numbers in K6:K11. Verify that the sum is 1,000.

This table gives the results of simulating the car buying behavior of 10, 100, and 1,000 groups of five test drivers. Don't be surprised if there are no cases in which all five drivers bought cars. As we will see, the probability of this is quite low.

The next step is to create a table where these numbers are summarized and converted to proportions and compared to the probabilities from the binomial distribution.

- Put the second table in the cells H14:L22 on your worksheet. Set up labels for this table as shown in the illustration below. Many of these labels can be easily copied from the previous table without retyping.

	H	I	J	K	L
14	Sales	10 nights	100 nights	1000 nights	binomial
15	5				
16	4				
17	3				
18	2				
19	1				
20	0				
21	mean				
22	std dev				

- Select cell I15. Enter in this cell the formula to divide the value of cell I6 (the number of times all five drivers purchased cars in the group of ten) by the value of cell I12 (the total size of the group of ten—10). Make the row of the address for this latter number absolute but the column relative (I$12). Press the Enter key.

- Copy the formula in cell I15 to cells I16:I20. The values of I15:I20 should sum to 1.

- With the region I15:I20 selected, drag the fill handle to the right copying the cells in column I to columns J and K.

- Check the formula in cell K20 by selecting that cell. The formula bar should show its formula to be "=K11/K$12."

- Enter the formula in cell I21 to calculate the mean of F1:F10, in cell J21 to calculate the mean of F1:F100, and in cell K21 to calculate the mean of F1:F1000. Using the Excel function to do this is explained on page 50.

- Enter the formulas in cells I22, J22, and K22 to calculate the sample standard deviations for F1:F10, F1:F100, and F1:F1000, respectively. The name for the function in Excel which calculates sample standard deviations is STDEV. It can be found with the Function Wizard in the "Statistical" category. Only one argument need be supplied—the range address of the cells for which the standard deviation is to be calculated. This argument should be identical to that used in the AVERAGE function to calculate averages in row 21.

▼ Using the BINOMDIST Function

Cell L15 is to contain the probability that if five people are taken on a test drive, all five will eventually buy a car if the probability that one will buy a car is .20. Another way of saying this is that we want the probability of five successes in five trials given that the probability of success is .20.

- Select cell L15.

- Click the Function Wizard button. Choose "Statistical" category. Under function name choose BINOMDIST. Click the "Next>" button.

The BINOMDIST function has four arguments:

1. **number_s**—short for number of successes. This is the value of the random variable for which we want a probability. Most textbooks symbolize this as x. For cell L15, this argument should be 5 because we want the probability that all five test drivers will buy a car.

2. **trials**—This argument is the number of trials. Most textbooks symbolize this as n. This is one of the two variables distinguishing one binomial distribution from another. For cell L15 this value should be 5 because five people test drive a car in each evening.

3. **probability_s**—short for probability of success. Most textbooks abbreviate this either as p or as π. This is the other binomial distribution variable. For cell L15 this value should be .20 because there is a .20 probability that any one test driver will purchase a car. Rather than enter this number directly, enter the address of cell I2 where the value 0.20 was entered for use by the Random Number Generation Tool.

4. **cumulative**—This argument determines whether Excel provides the probability that the random variable is *equal* to x (the value given in the first argument), or the probability that the random variable is *less than or equal* to x. The latter is commonly called the cumulative probability. As we will see, this is quite useful for dealing with many binomial problems. For cell L15, however, we want the probability that the number of buyers is equal to 5, not less than or equal to 5 (which must be true). We tell Excel we don't want a cumulative probability by putting the word "false" (without quotes) or the number 0 into the argument field. If we did want a cumulative probability, we would put "true" or the number 1.

- Enter the values of the arguments in the BINOMDIST dialog window. The value in the "value" field in the upper right-hand corner of the window will show 0.00032 when the correct argument values are entered.

- Use the Function Wizard to enter equations using the BINOMDIST in cells L16 through L20. The arguments for BINOMDIST in each of these cases will be the same as in L15 except for the first, the number of successes. With the correct arguments, the displayed values of L16, L17, L18, L19, and L20 will be 0.0064, 0.0512, 0.2048, 0.4096, and 0.32768. If you choose to copy L16 to L16:L20, be sure you have converted the proper cell addresses in the formula in L15 to absolute.

The last step is to put the mean and the standard deviation of the binomial distribution in cells L21 and L22. If we symbolize the two variables of the binomial distribution, the number of trials, and the probability of success on a single trial, as n and p, respectively, the formulas for the mean and standard deviation are:

$$\text{mean} = \mu = np$$
$$\text{standard deviation} = \sigma = \sqrt{np(1-p)}$$

We will later examine the effect of changes in the value of p on this worksheet, but the value of n will not be changed from 5. The value of p is given in cell I2.

- Enter the Excel formula in cell L21 to calculate the mean of the binomial distribution by multiplying the number 5 (n) by the value of cell I2 (p). The answer should be 1.

- Enter the following formula (without the quotes) in cell L22 to calculate the standard deviation of the binomial distribution: "=SQRT(5*I2*(1-I2))." The correct value is 0.894427.

- Select the range I15:L22. Use the Increase (and/or Decrease) Decimal button to have all the cells in the selected range display four digits after the decimal point.

- Save the workbook—now and often.

Examine the table. You should see the same general pattern in this table as you saw in the last chapter. As the number of nights increases, the proportion of times the numbers of buyers equaled any of the six numbers should get closer to the binomial probability shown in column L. If the value happened to be very close to the true probability for a smaller number of nights, it might diverge as the number of nights went up, but the divergence should be small. It is even more likely that the mean and standard deviation of the number of sales will get closer to the mean and standard deviation of the distribution as the number of sales goes up.

Notice that you shouldn't be surprised if in your simulation the salesperson never got all five test drivers to buy a car. As we can see from the probabilities in column L, the chance of this happening is .0003, which is less than 1 in 3,000.

The answer to the question given at the beginning of this chapter is that the probability that *none* of the five people test driving the car will purchase one from the salesperson is .3277 (in cell L20). This is the binomial probability of zero successes in five trials given a probability of success in each trial of .20.

▼ Exploring Other Binomial Distributions

Let's use this worksheet to explore a different binomial distribution, one with a different value of p.

- Because of the large amount of calculations on this worksheet, use the Options dialog window from the Tools menu to switch calculation from automatic to manual. More detail on how to do this can be found on page 91.

The great baseball player Babe Ruth came to bat 8,399 times in his illustrious career. 714 of those times he hit a home run. What is the probability that if the Babe came to bat five times in a game he would hit at least one home run?

To use the binomial distribution, we have to assume that the probability of the Babe hitting a home run was constant and independent and equal to $^{714}/_{8399}$. Counting a home run as a *success,* the probability is equivalent to the probability of one or more successes in five trials given a probability of success of $^{714}/_{8399}$.

There are two differences between this problem and the previous car salesperson problem: the value of p has changed, and the values of x for which a probability is needed have also changed. In the car salesperson problem we wanted to determine the probability that $x = 0$ (no test driver would purchase a car). In this problem we wish to determine the probability that $x \geq 1$ (at least one home run will be hit).

We will use this worksheet not only to calculate the probability, but also to simulate the Babe's batting performance in a game.

- The value of p is in cell I2. There are two ways of entering the value in the cell. Excel will allow you to enter a fraction by entering a zero, followed by a space, followed by the fraction. To do this, select cell I2 and enter "0 714/8399" without the quotes and with a space after the

"0." An alternative would be to have Excel do the implied division by entering the formula "=714/8399" (no quotes, of course).

If you enter the value as a fraction, when you press the Enter key, the fraction in its reduced form (4/47) will be displayed immediately (if the cell is selected, the decimal equivalent will appear in the formula bar). None of the other cells have changed their value, however, because the workbook is set for manual calculation. Cell I3, which is supposed to equal $1 - p$ still displays 0.8.

- Recalculate the workbook by pressing the F9 function key.

This changes not only the value of cell I3 (to 0.91499) but also the binomial distribution calculations in cells L15:L22. In fact, these values are sufficient to answer the question. Let's redo the simulation, however.

- Recall the Random Number Generation dialog window from the Data Analysis list chosen from the Tools menu.

If you are still in the same Excel session you were when you generated the simulations for the car buyers, all the fields in the dialog window will already have the correct values. If they do not, look back at the illustration on page 98. Change the value in the Number of Variables field at the top to 5 and the value of the Number of Random Numbers field to 1000.

- Click the "OK" button in the Random Number Generation dialog window. When the overwrite warning window appears, click the "OK" button in it.

- After the random numbers have been generated, recalculate the workbook by pressing the F9 function key. This will update the tables which determine the number and proportion of successes and the mean and standard deviation for the first 10 simulations, the first 100 simulations, and the entire 1,000 simulations.

Look at the table again. Confirm the same general pattern you saw before. As the number of simulations increases, the statistics become closer to those of the binomial distribution given in column L.

You might notice that the displayed value for the probability that the Babe would get five home runs is .0000. Does that mean the probability is zero that he would hit a home run each time at bat? The answer is no. The probability is not zero, but it is so low that when rounded to four decimal places it displays as zero.

- Increase the width of column L to about twice its normal width.

- Click the Increase Decimal button nine times. The displayed probability in L15 is now clearly not exactly zero, but it is a small number.

What is the probability that the Babe would hit at least one home run? This probability is not directly available in the table, but it can be easily calculated. What needs to be determined is the probability that x is greater than or equal to 1 or $P(x \geq 1)$. This can also be stated as $P(x = 1$ or $x = 2$ or $x = 3$ or $x = 4$ or $x = 5)$. Since these outcomes are mutually exclusive, this probability can be calculated by adding $P(x = 1)$ plus $P(x = 2)$ and so on.

- Select cell M19. Click the AutoSum button, but do not press Enter.

When the AutoSum button is clicked, Excel makes a guess about which cells you wish to add. In this case, Excel assumes you want to add the row adjacent to cell M19 (H19:L19), which is wrong. Fortunately, Excel makes it easy for you to change the cells to be summed by "highlighting" them so that you need only enter the cell address range you want and it will replace the one Excel guessed. In this case we want to add L15 (which is $P(x = 5)$) to L16, L17, L18, and L19.

- Select the range L15:L19 with the mouse pointer. You should see the formula in cell M19 change to "=SUM(L15:L19)."

- Now press the Enter key. The correct value, 0.3587, will be displayed in M19. (If your display shows "####," use the Decrease Decimal button to reduce the number of displayed decimal points to four or increase the width of column M.)

An alternative way of coming up with the same answer would have been to calculate $1 - P(x = 0) = 1 - 0.6413 = 0.3587$.

- Double click the "Sheet1" worksheet tab and change its name to "Simulate" (without quotes).

- Change Excel's calculation back to automatic. Open the Tools menu, choose "Options…," click the "Calculation" folder tab in the dialog window, click the "Automatic" radio button in the upper left-hand corner. Click the "OK" button in the dialog window.

- Save the worksheet.

▼ Using Excel to Solve Binomial Word Problems

Most statistics texts provide binomial tables for use in solving word problems involving the binomial distribution. Instead of a table, Excel's BINOMDIST function can be used. Compared to a table, BINOMDIST is easier to use, more accurate, and can be used to solve a wider variety of problems than any binomial table. To solve a binomial word problem, however, you still must figure out what the problem is asking for, the same as you would if you were to use a table. First you have to be sure the problem really is one requiring the binomial distribution. Next you must come up with answers to the following three questions:

1. What is the value of p (the probability of success on a single trial) for the binomial distribution for this question?

2. What is the value of n (the number of trials) for the binomial distribution for this question?

3. For what value or values of x (the binomially distributed random variable) is a probability being asked for?

The third question is the one most likely to be answered erroneously. A systematic approach can help. Once you have determined the value of n (the answer to the second question), you know the set of possible values for x—the integers between 0 and n, including 0 and n. A useful visual aid is to write down the set of possible integers (assuming the set is not too large). Once that is done, determine which integers within the set satisfy the condition in the question for which you want to determine a probability.

There is more than one correct way of using BINOMDIST to solve any binomial word problem. The discussion below will recommend two procedures. One procedure will be used if the probability for only a single value of x is needed. The other procedure is for use when the probability of x being within a range of values is required.

▼ Using BINOMDIST with a Single *x* Value

We saw the BINOMDIST function used to calculate the actual probabilities that each possible number of test drivers would become car purchasers. Although BINOMDIST was used to determine the probabilities of six different x values (0, 1, 2, 3, 4, and 5), a probability was assigned to only a single x value. The method described below is essentially similar to that used previously.

- Double click the "Sheet2" worksheet tab. Change the worksheet's name to "1 value."

- In cell A1, enter the label "n" (without quotes). In cell A2, enter the label "p" (also without quotes). The adjacent cells (B1 and B2) will be where you put the variables of the binomial distribution.

- In cell A4, enter the label "x." You will put the value of x for which you want a probability in cell B4.

- In cell A6, enter the label "Prob." The formula to calculate the probability will go in cell B6.

- Select cell B6, click the Function Wizard button, and choose BINOMDIST in the "Statistical" category.

- The "number_s," or number of successes, is the value of x for which we want a probability. This value will go in cell B4. Click the mouse pointer in the "number_s" field and then click cell B4 so that its address will go in that field.

- The "trials" field is where the binomial variable n goes. Click the mouse pointer in this field and then click cell B1 to put its address in the field.

- The "probability_s" field is where the binomial variable p goes. Click the mouse pointer in this field and the click cell B2 to put its address in the field.

- In this case we do not want the cumulative distribution. Click the mouse pointer in the "cumulative" field and enter the word "false" (without quotes).

- Click the "Finish" button.

Since nothing is currently entered in cells B1, B2, and B4, the BINOMDIST function will interpret those cells as containing zeroes and will provide a result of 1, which is meaningless in this case. Let's try applying this worksheet to some specific problems.

What is the probability that the toss of two dice will result in two ones?

A "success" in this problem is getting a one. The number of trials is two, since two dice are thrown. Therefore, $n = 2$. The probability of success on a single trial is the probability that a single die will have a one when tossed. Since there are six sides to a die, and only one side has a one, the probability of rolling a one with one die is $\frac{1}{6}$. Therefore, $p = \frac{1}{6}$. The number of success for which we want a probability is two. Therefore, $x = 2$.

- Enter (without quotes) "2" in cell B1, "0 1/6" (space after "0") in cell B2, and "2" in cell B4.

The answer, 0.027778, will appear immediately in cell B6.

Consider another problem:

A television manufacturer is considering purchasing a chassis component from an independent supplier. In order to test the supplier's quality, the TV manufacturer takes a random sample of 100 components and tests them to see how many are defective. Suppose the component manufacturer's process results in 99% of the chassis components being defect-free. What is the probability that none of the components in the sample chosen by the TV manufacturer will have a defect?

The wording of this problem is trickier than the previous problem. The first step is to decide what outcome is to be considered a "success." The second sentence of the problem suggests that finding a part to be defective is what is to be counted, that is, a defective part is a "success." The next sentence, however, tells the probability of a part being defect-free. A part is either defective or defect-free. The question can be answered by taking either of these outcomes as a "success," although that decision affects the determination of the values of n, p, and x.

Let's take the finding that a part is defective as a "success." The number of trials, n is the number of parts the TV manufacturer tests, 100. The problem tells us that 99% of the parts are defect-free. Thus 1% are defective and the probability of a part being defective, p, (a "success") is .01. We are asked the probability that none of the parts have a defect, so the value of x for which we want a probability is 0.

- Enter 100, .01, and 0 in the appropriate cells. The probability that none of the parts will be defective, .366032, will appear in cell B6.

- Observe cell B2. You entered ".01" but what is displayed is a "0" in the middle of the cell. Why is that?

When you previously entered 0 1/6 in the cell, you not only set a value for the cell, you also set a *format*. To have the cell display the number as you expected, you must change the format.

- Select cell B2.

- Open the Format menu on the Menu Bar. Select "Style…." The Style dialog window will open.

- Set the dialog window so that the Style Name displayed in "Normal." If the window does not come up with that name, click the downward pointing arrow beside the Style Name field and choose "Normal." Click the "OK" button in the window.

- Save your workbook.

Cell B2 should now display 0.01 as you expect.

▼ Using BINOMDIST with a Range of *x* Values

If the range of values includes only a few numbers, one way of determining the probability that the random variable will fall within the range would be to determine the probability associated with each value in the range and add these probabilities together. A different procedure will be used here, one which will work whether the number of values in the range is large or small. This method will use *cumulative* probabilities.

Consider the following problem:

If a fair coin is tossed ten times, what is the probability that the number of heads will be between four and six?

Remember that the outcomes of a binomial random variable are mutually exclusive. If we want the probability that an outcome will have one of several values, we want the sum of the probabilities the outcome will equal each value. In this problem, we want the probability that the number of heads is four or five or six. Although we could determine this by adding the probability that the number of heads is four to the probability that the number is five and the probability that the number is six, cumulative probabilities offer an easier method.

The cumulative probability that the number of heads is six is the probability that the number of heads is zero or one or two or three or four or five or six. This is more than we want. Since we want the probability only of four, five or six, we need to subtract the probability that the number of heads is zero, one, two or three. But this is simply the cumulative probability that the number of heads is three. The difference between the cumulative probability that the number of heads is three and the cumulative probability that the number of heads is six is the probability that the number of heads is four, five, or six.

Notice that if we want the probability of the number of heads being between four and six, we have to subtract from the cumulative probability that *x* is six the cumulative probability that *x* is *three,* one less than the lower bound of four.

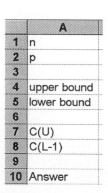

	A
1	n
2	p
3	
4	upper bound
5	lower bound
6	
7	C(U)
8	C(L-1)
9	
10	Answer

- Double click the "Sheet3" worksheet tab and change its name to "Range of Values."

- Enter labels in column A as shown in the picture on the left.

As in the previous worksheet, the values of *n* and *p* will go in cells B1 and B2. The upper and lower bounds of the interval will go in cells B4 and B5. Cell B7 will contain the cumulative probability of the upper bound, and cell B8 will contain the cumulative probability of the lower bound *minus one*. Cell B10 will contain the difference.

- Select cell B7. Call up the Function Wizard's BINOMDIST dialog window.

- For the number of successes argument, enter the cell address for the upper bound. For the trials and probability of success arguments, enter the relevant cell address.

- Click the mouse pointer in the "cumulative" field and enter the word (without quotes) "true." Click the "Finish" button. The value "1" will appear in the cell.

- Select cell B8. Again call up the BINOMDIST dialog window.

- For the number of successes, you want the lower bound *minus one*. Click the mouse pointer in the "number_s" field to put the insertion point in the field, click the cell which will contain the lower bound and then enter "-1." The field should contain "B5-1," which instructs to Excel to take the value in cell B5 and subtract 1.

- Enter the same values in the other fields as you did for cell B4. Remember to enter "true" in the "cumulative" argument field.

- Click the "Finish" button. Do not be alarmed that the cell displays the "#NUM!" Error.

- Select cell B10. Enter a formula which will take the value of cell B7 and subtract the value of cell B8. Once you press the Enter key, this cell will also display the "#NUM!" Error.

Let's put the data for this problem in the appropriate cells. In this problem we will count Heads, so getting a heads from a coin toss is a "success." The coin is tossed ten times. The probability of success on each toss is .50.

- Enter the correct values for *n* and *p* in cells B1 and B2.

The range of values for which we want a probability is 4 to 6. Thus 6 is the upper bound of the range and 4 is the lower bound.

- Enter these values in the appropriate places in cells B4 and B5.

Your worksheet should look like the illustration at the top of the next page.

The results of the calculations done on the worksheet tell us that the probability of getting six or fewer heads in ten tosses of a fair coin is .82813. The second probability shown, .17188, is the probability of get-

	A	B
1	n	10
2	p	0.5
3		
4	upper bound	6
5	lower bound	4
6		
7	C(U)	0.82813
8	C(L-1)	0.17188
9		
10	Answer	0.65625

ting *three* or fewer heads—remember that this is cumulative probability of the lower bound *minus one*. The probability of getting between four and six heads is thus .65625.

Consider this similar problem:

If a fair coin is tossed 100 times, what is the probability that the number of heads will be between 40 and 60?

Notice the similarity between this question and the previous question. The number of coin tosses and the range boundaries have both been multiplied by ten. The proportion of possible values within the requested range is the same for both problems. Does it seem to you that the answer to this problem will be the same as that of the previous problem?

- Change the values of n, the lower bound, and the upper bound to the values for this problem. The answer is 0.9648, substantially higher than that of the previous problem.

Why the difference? In the beginning of this chapter and in the previous chapter you saw that the larger a sample of random numbers, the more likely it is to resemble the probability distribution which generated the numbers. In both of these problems, the center of the range for which a probability was sought was the mean or expected value ($n\,p$, when $n =$ 10, $n\,p =5$ and when $n = 100$, $n\,p = 50$). A larger sample is more likely to have an actual probability closer to the mean (or expected value) than a smaller sample.

▼ Open-Ended Ranges

Sometimes the range of values for which you want a probability is open-ended. That is, only a lower bound or an upper bound is given. Consider these two questions about 100 coin tosses. "What is the probability that the number of heads will be greater than or equal to 60?" is an example of a range with no upper bound, while "What is the probability that the number of heads will be less than or equal to 45?" refers to an interval with no lower bound. For the binomial distributions, the ranges are not really unbounded, because x can never be less than zero or more than n.

The first question is equivalent to asking, "What is the probability that the number of heads is between 60 and 100?"

- Use the worksheet to answer this question by using these values for the upper and lower boundaries. The answer you should get is .028444.

Notice the two probabilities in cells B7 and B8. Cell B7 shows that the cumulative probability of the number of heads being 100 is 1. If you toss a coin 100 times, the number of heads *must* be less than or equal to 100. Cell B8 shows the probability of getting 59 or fewer heads. One minus that probability is the probability of 60 or more heads.

The second question is equivalent to asking, "What is the probability that the number of heads will be between zero and 45?"

- Put these upper and lower bounds in the appropriate place in your worksheet.

The "#NUM!" error appears as it did when you were first setting up the formulas. The reason for this error is that cell B8 calculates the cumulative probability of 1 less than the lower bound in cell B5. When cell B5 contains zero (or is blank), B8 tries to calculate the cumulative probability of −1. Since x cannot possibly equal −1, an error is generated.

What we want, of course, is the cumulative probability of 45, and this value is provided in cell B7 (.184101). We can use the worksheet to handle this type of problem, but we have to look for the answer in a different place.

▼ The Wording of Binomial Word Problems

As was mentioned at the beginning of the chapter, decoding the language of a binomial word problem is often the hardest part to solving the problem, especially when the problem is asking for the probability of a range of values for the random variable. This, of course, is not a computer problem or a statistics problem, it's an English problem. Most people taking a statistics course think English is the least of their worries, but when you are faced with solving a binomial word problem (especially on a test), it's the English that will often fail you.

The table below is meant to be an aid to help you decode word problems. When you try to solve a word problem, you must first determine the values of n, p, and the upper and lower bounds for x. The table is designed to help you with the last determination.

What is the probability that in n trials with probability of success in each trial of p, the number of success will be...

	Lower Bound	Upper Bound
...at least y.	y	n
...at most y.	0	y
...more than y.	$y + 1$	n
...fewer than y.	0	$y - 1$
...not fewer than y.	y	n
...not more than y.	0	y

▼ Exercises

1. Suppose the postal service has a delivery goal of delivering 90% of all first-class mail within the same city on the day after mailing. If this goal is achieved, and 100 items of mail are chosen at random to test delivery time, what is the probability that...

   a) at least 90 will be delivered by the next day?

   b) more than 95 will be delivered by the next day?

   c) all 100 pieces will have been delivered by the next day?

   d) fewer than 90 will have been delivered by the next day?

2. Suppose the proportion of automobiles of a certain make which require warranty service is .15. If a particular dealer sells 500 cars...

   a) What is the expected number of cars sold by that dealer which will require warranty service?

   b) What is the standard deviation of the number of cars which will require warranty service?

c) What is the probability that the number of cars requiring repair will exactly equal the expected value?

d) What is the probability that the number of cars requiring repair will be within two standard deviations of the mean (more than the mean minus two times the standard deviation and less than the mean plus two times the standard deviation)?

3. Format and print out the table in the "Simulate" worksheet showing the simulated and predicted probabilities of Babe Ruth hitting different numbers of home runs for a game in which he batted five times (cells H14:L21). Put a title in the center of the header of your printout which says "Computerized Babe Ruth" (don't put quotes in your title). Put your name on the right side of the header.

4. The "Range of values" worksheet generated an error message if a lower bound of zero was used, as discussed at the end of the chapter. Figure out a way to use the IF function (in the "Logical" category) to alter your worksheet so that the correct answer appears in cell B10 when any valid value between zero and n (including zero) is put in cell B8 as the lower bound of a range.

Chapter 5

The Normal Distribution

The normal distribution is important for two reasons. First, many real-world random variables are either normally distributed or have distributions which can be closely approximated with the normal distribution. Second, properties of the normal distribution place it at the foundation of traditional inferential statistics. Indeed, its importance is suggested by its name. (Another name for the normal distribution is the *Gaussian* distribution.)

Like the binomial distribution (and all other named distributions), there is not a single normal distribution. There are an infinite number of normal distributions. Any binomial distribution could be identified by the value of its variables—the number of trials (n) and the probability of success on a single trial (p or π). Similarly any normal distribution can be completely identified by the values of two variables—μ and σ. These are the same symbols used for the mean and standard deviation of a population (or probability distribution). They are used for the variables of the normal distribution because the mean of the normal distribution *is* the value of the first variable, and the standard deviation of the normal distribution *is* the value of the second variable. Using the same symbols makes that a snap to remember.

An important difference between the normal distribution and the binomial distribution is that the normal distribution is *continuous* while the binomial distribution is *discrete*. A binomially distributed random variable must have an integer value; a normally distributed random variable can have noninteger values. Between any two integer values there are an infinite number of different values which a normally distributed random variable can equal. Like all continuous random variables, the probability that a normally distributed random variable will equal any *specific* value is zero. Nonzero probabilities can only be assigned to a *range* of values. It is thus not meaningful to ask the probability that a normally distributed random variable exactly equals 2, for instance, because 2 is a specific value and the probability is zero. We could ask the probability that a normally distributed random variable has a value between 1 and 2 or between 1.99 and 2.01. The probability associated with these ranges of values would be nonzero.

Continuous probability distributions are represented by a probability *density* function which differs from the probability *distribution* function used to represent discrete random distributions like the binomial. Probability density functions are often shown graphically. Like a discrete distribution function, the horizontal axis shows the set of values which the random variable could equal. Unlike a discrete distribution function, the vertical axis does not show probability; instead it shows density. A range of values of a continually distributed random variable would define a line segment on the horizontal axis. The *area* between the density function and that segment equals the probability that the random variable will equal a value within that range. Calculating these areas might seem difficult, but Excel provides built-in functions which will do those calculations easily. Density functions are often represented graphically, and we will see an example shortly.

In addition to being continuous, the normal distribution (*all* normal distributions) are *unbounded*. This means that a normally distributed random variable could take on any value from $-\infty$ to $+\infty$. As we will see, the probabilities associated with intervals far from the mean are very small. So small, in fact, that for practical purposes the distribution can be treated as bounded.

Before looking at how those calculations can be done in Excel, let's look at the shape of the normal density function and how that shape is affected by the values of the distributions variables, μ and σ.

▼ Graphing the Normal Density Function

The directions below will direct you in preparing a chart of two normal density functions. One will be the "standard" normal function which has a mean of 0 and a standard deviation of 1. The other will be a general normal density function with values for the mean and standard deviation which are taken from worksheet cells and which you will be able to change. Before the chart can be drawn, a table must be created giving a set of x values and the density values associated with each of these x values.

• Start Excel with a new blank worksheet and save it as chap5.xls.

• In cell A1 enter the label "x." Column A will be used for the values of the random variables.

- In cell B1 enter the label "general." Column B will be used for the general normal density values.

- In cell C1 enter the label "standard." Column C will be used for the standard normal density values.

- Enter the label "mu" in cell D1 and "sigma" in cell D2.

- Enter the value "0" in cell E1 and "1" in cell E2. These cells will hold the variables for the general normal distribution. Initially they will be the same as the values for the standard normal distribution.

In column A, starting with cell A2, we will put the series of numbers starting with −5 and going to +5. Each time we move down a cell, the value will increment by 0.1. Thus cell A2 will be −4.9, cell A3 will be −4.8, and so on. How many cells will be needed? The general formula is to take the difference between the ending and starting value, divide by the increment, and add 1. Thus if we were going from a to b by increment i, the formula would be: $\dfrac{b-a}{i} + 1$. For this case: $\dfrac{5-(-5)}{.01} = 101$. Therefore if the series starts in cell A2, it will end in cell A103.

There are a number of ways of having Excel create the series, but since over 100 cells are involved, using the mouse could be tricky. Try the following method instead.

- Enter "-5" in cell A2.

- Click the mouse pointer in the Name Box, and then enter "a2:a103." Press the Enter key and that region will be selected. The location of the Name Box is shown on page 4.

- Open the Edit menu on the Menu Bar. Click "Fill." A cascade menu will open. Choose "Series...." These menus are shown at the top of the next page.

- The Series dialog window will open. This window allows you to specify how you want Excel to create a series. In this case you want a *linear* series, which means the increment value will be constant, and you want the increment to be 0.1. The increment is referred to in the dialog window as "Step Value."

- Click the mouse pointer in the "Step Value" field and enter the value 0.1. The window looks like the second picture on the next page.

- Click the "OK" button and you should see the series in the selected region.

Next we will put the values for the density functions in columns B and C.

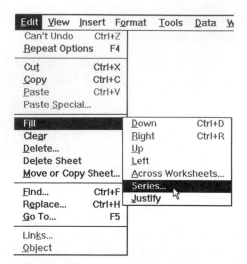

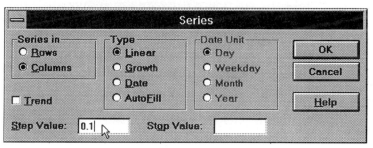

- Select cell B2. Click the Function Wizard button. In the "Statistical" category, choose the NORMDIST function, and click the "Next>" button.

The NORMDIST function has three arguments:

1. **x**—the value of the random variable for which the density is to be determined. Enter a *relative* address for cell A2, which contains −5. The relative address will change to refer to the cell in the same row of column A when the formula is copied down the column.

2. **mean**—the mean of the normal distribution. Enter an *absolute* address for cell E1 which contains a 0. When the formula is copied down the column, this reference will remain to cell E1.

3. **standard_dev**—the standard deviation of the normal distribution. Enter an *absolute* address for cell E2 which contains a 1.

4. **cumulative**—Enter the word "false" (without) quotes. This will cause the function to provide the density value. If the word "true" were entered, the cumulative probability would be provided.

The dialog window should look like the illustration on the next page.

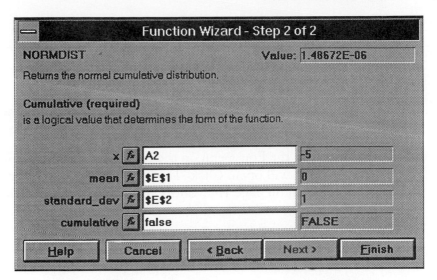

Click the "Finish" button. The value which appears in cell B2 is 1.49E-06 which could also be written as .00000149. Remember that this very small number is *not* a probability.

The density values for the standard normal distribution will go in column C. The standard normal distribution is the normal distribution with $\mu = 0$ and $\sigma = 1$.

- Select cell C2. Click the Function Wizard Button and choose NORMDIST again. Use the same values in the argument fields you used above *except* enter the number 0 in the "mean" field and the number 1 in the "standard_dev" field (as shown below). Click the "Finish" button. The same value should appear in cell C2 as appears in cell B2.

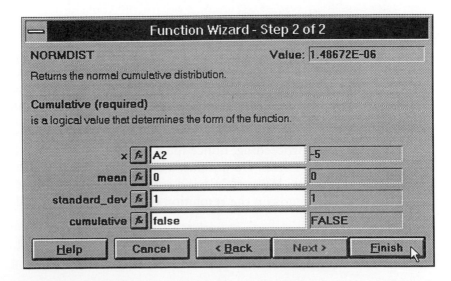

Next the formulas in cells B2 and C2 must be copied down the columns. Recall that the last value in column A is in A103. The formulas in B2 and C2 need to be copied down to row 103. The instructions below use a method similar to that used to generate the series in column A.

- Click the mouse pointer in the Name Box. Enter the range address B2:C103. Press the Enter key and the range will be selected.

- Open the Edit menu on the Menu Bar. Choose "Fill," and a cascade menu will open. Click "Down" on the cascade menu. These menus are shown on page 100. Check row 52. Column A should display a 0. Columns B and C should both display the value 0.398942.

- Save your worksheet now and often!

The last part is to have Excel graph the density values in columns B and C against the x values in column A. The instructions below will direct you to create a graph which will share your screen with the values of μ and σ in cells E1 and E2. This will enable you to change those values and immediately see the change in the density function without scrolling your screen or changing worksheets. In an earlier chapter you saw the Histogram Tool place a chart on an existing worksheet. You can create your own chart on a worksheet by using the Chart Wizard button.

- Use your worksheet's horizontal and vertical scroll bars so that cell D1 is in the upper left corner of your screen and columns A, B, and C should not be visible.

- Click the Chart Wizard button ▨. As you move the mouse pointer back to the worksheet cells, notice that it has a new shape: ⁺▥ .

The Chart Wizard mouse pointer allows you to determine exactly where on your worksheet the graph will go. The graph will be a rectangle, and you determine where it goes by using the mouse to establish two opposite corners (usually the upper left and lower right). Be careful not to move the mouse pointer beyond the boundaries of the cells which are visible because this will cause your worksheet to scroll and the graph will be larger than the visible portion of your worksheet.

Before proceeding, notice the address of a cell in the lower right corner of your screen. Do not pick a cell which is partially off the screen; pick a cell whose lower right-hand corner is clearly visible. (The address of this cell depends on the resolution of your screen and will differ among computers).

- Place the Chart Wizard mouse pointer roughly in the center of cell D3. This will be the upper left corner of your graph.

- With the Chart Wizard mouse pointer in cell D3, press and hold the (left) mouse button.

- With the mouse button pressed, drag the Chart Wizard mouse pointer to the approximate center of the cell in the lower right corner of your screen you found above. Be careful not to drag it too far because you do not want Excel to scroll the worksheet.

- When the mouse pointer is in the correct position, release the mouse pointer.

A series of Chart Wizard dialog windows will appear. These are the same dialog windows you saw when you had Excel create a graph on a separate worksheet.

- The first Chart Wizard dialog window provides a field for you to place the address of the cells which you want graphed. Using the keyboard, enter the following in that field: "=a1:c103" (without the quotes). Click the "Next >" button.

- The second Chart Wizard dialog window enables you to choose the type of chart or graph you want. Choose "Line" (on the top row of choices), and click "Next>."

- The third Chart Wizard dialog window enables you to choose the type of line chart you want. For the purpose of this chart, it is best if the simplest line chart is used which does not place markers on the points and does not draw a gridline. Choose number 2. Click the "Next >" button.

- In the next dialog window (Step 4) you must tell Excel that the first column contains the X axis values. Change the "0" to a "1" so that the box says, "Use First 1 Column(s) for Category (X) Axis Labels." You should see an immediate change in the small preview graph in the window.

- Click the "Finish" button.

- If necessary, use the worksheet scroll bars so that cell D1 is again in the upper left-hand corner of the visible portion of your worksheet. You should be able to see both the values of μ and σ in cells E1 and E2. The picture following the next few steps shows what should appear on the screen.

Excel has decided how to label the x axis. Let's explicitly control that.

- Place the mouse pointer inside the graph and double click to "activate" the graph. You can tell it has been activated by the active mode border which will surround the graph (see the picture below).

- Place the mouse pointer directly on the horizontal (*x*) axis where it is not close to the charted line (near the center of the axis). Click the (left) mouse button once. Two small squares (or *handles*) will appear at each end of the horizontal axis indicating that the axis has been *selected*.

The working area of your worksheet should look like the picture below.

Axis Selection Handles

Active Mode Border

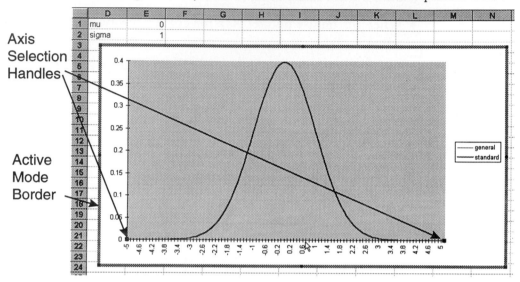

- Open the Format menu on the Menu Bar. The first choice should be "Selected Axis...." Click the mouse pointer on that choice. The Format Axis dialog window will open.

- Click the "Scale" folder tab.

- Change the value of the "Number of Categories Between Tick-Mark Labels" field to five. The dialog window should appear like the picture at the top of the next page.

- Click the "OK" button.

- Take the chart out of active mode by clicking the mouse pointer off the chart on a worksheet cell (such as cell D1). The active mode border will disappear.

Each tick mark corresponds to a value in column A of the worksheet. The tick marks are therefore at intervals of 0.1 since the values in column A differ by 0.1. By telling Excel that you want labels every five tick marks, you get labels spaced every $5 \times 0.1 = 0.5$.

There appears to be only one graph on your screen, but actually there are two which are identical. Both are the standard normal distribution in which $\mu = 0$ and $\sigma = 1$. You may recognize the shape of the graph; it is

Format Axis

Patterns	Scale	Font	Number	Alignment

Category (X) Axis Scale

Value (Y) Axis Crosses
at Category Number: `1`

Number of Categories
between Tick-Mark Labels: `5`

Number of Categories
between Tick Marks: `1`

☐ Value (Y) Axis Crosses between Categories
☐ Categories in Reverse Order
☐ Value (Y) Axis Crosses at Maximum Category

[OK]
[Cancel]
[Help]

often referred to as "bell-shaped." The peak of the graph occurs right above the value 0 on the horizontal axis.

Consider the density graph of the standard normal distribution shown below. Both shaded regions have the same width on the *x* axis. This means

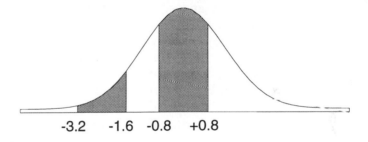

$$-3.2 \quad -1.6 \ -0.8 \ +0.8$$

that both represent equal-sized intervals of the random variable. The left region represents the interval from −3.2 to −1.6, while the central region represents the interval from −0.8 to +0.8. Both represent intervals of 1.6. The central region, however, is taller and has a much greater area than the left region. Since the area of the region equals the probability of the interval, this means that a random variable with the standard normal distribution is much more likely to have a value within the range of −0.8 to +0.8 than it is to have a value within the range −3.2 to −1.6. The places where the density function is furthest above the horizontal axis correspond to the values on the horizontal axis which are most likely to occur.

Notice on your worksheet how close the density function is to the horizontal axis to the left of −3.5 and to the right of +3.5. There doesn't seem to be any space at all between the horizontal axis and the density function line. The area of the region for the interval between 3.5 and

5.0, for example, looks like it would be zero. In fact the density function line *is* above the horizontal axis and so the region would not be exactly zero. It *would* be so small that it could practically be taken as zero. Although the standard normal distribution is unbounded, the probabilities associated with any region to the left of −3.5 or to the right of +3.5 are so very small that they can practically be treated as zero. For practical purposes, then, the standard normal distribution can be regarded as bounded between −3.5 and +3.5. Other normal distributions will also have practical (but not theoretical) boundaries.

Let's examine the effect which changes in the value of μ and σ have on the shape of the density function.

- Select cell E2 (the value of σ, the standard deviation) and change the value from 1 to 1.1. The two density functions are now both clearly visible. Look at the legend to determine which is the "general" normal density function. That is the one which has changed.

- Change cell E2 from 1.1 to 2 in steps of 0.1. Observe the change in the density function with each change in σ.

Increasing the standard deviation makes the curve more "spread out." It also causes the "peak" to be less high. This second change is necessary to keep the entire area below the entire curve at a constant 1.0.

- Change cell E2 back to 1. Now change it to 0.9. Continue decreasing the value of E2 to 0.5 in steps of 0.1. Pay attention to which curve is the "general" normal density function and which is the "standard" normal density function. Pay attention also to the vertical axis scale.

The "standard" normal density function curve looks like it is going down, but in terms of the axis values, it is really not changing. Instead, the "general" normal density function is getting taller. This causes Excel to redraw the "standard" curve so that both will fit in the fixed space.

Decreasing the standard deviation makes the curve higher and more "pinched." What is the meaning of these changes? A normally distributed random variable drawn from a distribution with small standard deviation is more likely to have a value near the mean than is a normally distributed random variable drawn from a distribution with a large standard deviation. The area of an interval around the mean (like the central region in the preceding picture) will be greater the higher the curve, which happens when the standard deviation is small. The area of an interval away from the mean (like the left region in the preceding picture) will be smaller if the curve is more "pinched" as also happens with a small standard deviation.

Observe now the effect of a change in μ.

- Change the value of E2 back to 1.

- Select cell E1 which contains the mean. Change it to 0.5. Continue increasing the value of E1 by steps of 0.5 to 4.0. Observe the chart. Then change it back to 0 and decrease it by steps of −0.5 to −4.0.

As you see, changing the value of μ shifts the curve right or left. The peak is always above μ, no matter what its value. Since the peak marks the value which the random variable is most likely to be close to, you can see that mean is always the value which normally distributed random variables are likely to be close to.

- Double click the "Sheet1" worksheet tab and change its name to "Density."

- Save the workbook.

▼ Determining Probabilities from Intervals

Most problems involving the normal distribution fall into two categories: 1) determining the probability of a normally distributed random variable having a value within a given interval, and 2) determining an interval within which the value of a normally distributed random variable will fall with given probability. The first type of problem will be considered first.

- Double click the "Sheet2" worksheet tab and change its name to "Probability."

The normal distribution has a property which made it a particularly convenient distribution to use in the precomputer days. If we want to find the probability of a randomly distributed variable having a value within a given interval, it is an easy matter to find a corresponding interval for a different normal distribution with the same probability. The importance of this property is that once the relationship between intervals and probabilities is worked out for one particular normal distribution (that is, one particular set of values for μ and σ), a problem involving another normal distribution could be easily transformed to the one for which the probabilities had been worked out. The distribution to which all intervals were converted is the standard normal distribution we have seen where μ = 0 and σ = 1.

Suppose we have a problem involving determining the probability of a normally distributed random variable having a value within a known interval. That interval will be defined by one or more boundary values. The process of transforming those boundary values to the equivalent values in the standard normal distribution is called the *z transformation*. If the normal distribution of concern in the problem has a mean equal to μ and a standard deviation equal to σ, the *z* transformation is given by the formula:

$$z = \frac{x - \mu}{\sigma}$$

Another name for the standard normal distribution is the *z* distribution, and the value of a standard normal interval boundary corresponding to the value of the interval boundary in a different normal distribution is called a *z* value.

With a computer program like Excel, it would be possible to avoid the *z* transformation. As you have seen, the NORMDIST function has arguments for the mean and standard deviation of the distribution which interests you. The *z* transformation is, however, easy, even trivial, in a spreadsheet. Furthermore, the use of *z* values and the *z* transformation is so deeply ingrained in modern statistical practice that the methods discussed in this book will involve calculating and using the *z* value. Its importance is sufficiently great that Excel provides separate functions for the standard normal distribution.

The discussion below will first consider determining the probabilities associated with intervals in the *z* distribution. This will then be expanded to an interval for any normal distribution.

▼ Determining Probabilities for *z* Intervals

All intervals for the normal distribution can be classified into one of three types or can be divided into subintervals which can each be classified into one of three types. The first type is bounded from above. It has only one boundary value and the relevant probability is the probability that a standard normal random variable will be less than that value. The second type is bounded from both sides and has two boundary values. The probability we want is the probability that a standard normal random variable falls between these two values. The third type is bounded from below. It has only one boundary value, and the probability of interest is the probability that a standard normal random variable will be greater than the boundary value. Examples of these intervals with the shaded regions whose areas equal the desired probabilities are shown in the picture below. The "L" and "U" subscripts denote whether the boundary is upper or lower.

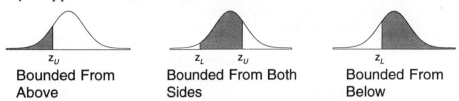

| Bounded From Above | Bounded From Both Sides | Bounded From Below |

- In cell B1 enter the label "Above," in cell C1 enter the label "Both," and in cell D1 enter the label "Below." These labels correspond to the three interval types pictured above, and the column of each label will be used to calculate the probability for that interval type.

- In cells A4 and A5 enter the labels "zu" and "zl." These will correspond to the boundaries pictured above.

- In cell A7 enter the label "Prob." Row 7 will be where probabilities will be displayed.

▼ Interval Bounded from Above

Suppose that we want to determine the probability that a standard normal random variable will have a value less than −1.0. This value would be an upper bound, and the interval is bounded from above.

- Enter the number "-1" in cell B4. This is the place for the upper bound value (z_U) for a region bounded from above.

- Select cell B7. Click the Function Wizard button and choose "NORMSDIST" from the "Statistical" category. Notice the "S" in the middle of this function's name. That "S" indicates that this is the function for the standard normal distribution.

The NORMSDIST function has only one argument, z, and the probability it provides is a cumulative probability, the probability that a standard normal variable will have a value less than or equal to the argument. This is exactly the type of probability desired in this problem.

- An insertion point should be in the "z" field. If not, click the mouse pointer in the field. Then click cell B4, and its address should appear in the field. Click the "Finish" button.

The probability of a standard normal random variable being less than −1.0 is 0.158655, the value which appears in cell B7.

▼ Interval Bounded from Both Sides

Suppose that we wanted to determine the probability that a standard normal random variable would have a value between −0.5 and 2.0. This is an example of an interval bounded from both sides. The probability of such an interval is determined by subtracting the probability of a standard normal variable being less than −0.5 from the probability of a standard normal variable being less than 2.0. This is illustrated in the picture below:

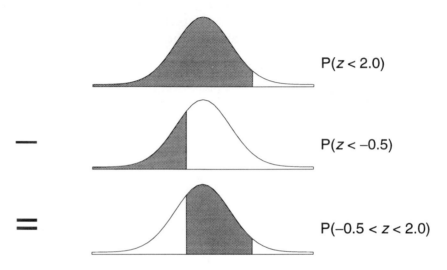

- Enter "2" and "-0.5" in the cells for the upper (z_U) and lower (z_L) bound of an interval with both bounds, C4 and C5 respectively.

Cell C7 should have a formula which subtracts the cumulative probability of the value in cell C5 from the cumulative probability in cell C4.

- Click the mouse pointer in cell C7.

- Enter an equal sign to begin the formula. When the Function Wizard is used after entering an equal sign, its function becomes a part of the formula rather than the whole formula.

- Click the Function Wizard button and select NORMSDIST. Make the z argument the cell address of the upper bound (z_U, cell C4). Click the "Finish" button. This part of the formula calculates the probability of a value below the upper bound.

Notice that cell C7 doesn't display a value but shows the beginning of a formula. You must now complete that formula.

- Enter a minus sign.

- Click the Function Wizard button again. Select NORMSDIST again. This time enter the cell address of the lower bound for the z argument (C5). This will calculate the probability of a value below the lower bound. Click the "Finish" button.

- Press the Enter key to end the formula and display its value.

The probability of a standard normal random variable having a value between −0.5 and 2.0 is 0.668712, the value which should be displayed in cell C7.

▼ Interval Bounded from Below

Suppose that we want to determine the probability that a standard normal random variable will have a value greater than 0.7. Recall that the area under the entire density function is 1.0. To determine the probability of a standard normal variable being greater than a given value, we simply subtract the probability of a standard normal variable being *less* than that value from 1.0. This is illustrated in the picture below.

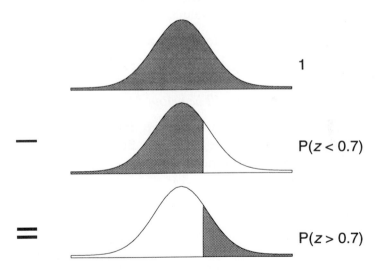

- Enter the value ".7" in cell D5.

- Click cell D7. Enter the formula which will calculate 1 minus the probability of a standard normal variable having a value less than that in D5. Press the Enter key.

The answer to this problem is 0.241964, and this value should appear in cell D7 in your worksheet.

- Save your workbook.

▼ Determining Probabilities for Intervals of Other Normal Distributions

Determining the probability of a normal variable with any value for the mean and standard deviation having a value within a given interval is a two-step process. The first step involves converting the boundary value or values to z values using the formula on page 128. First prepare labels for the new values which will have to be entered.

- In cells A9 and A10 enter the labels "mu" and "sigma" respectively. The adjacent cells in column B will be used to put the mean and standard deviation of the normal distribution.

- In cells A2 and A3 enter the labels "xu" and "xl" respectively. The adjacent cells in column B is where you will put the upper and lower bounds of the interval of values of the normal distribution for which a probability is wanted.

The entries in rows 4 and 5 will be changed so the upper and lower bound z values will be calculated from the corresponding upper and lower bound x values.

Consider the following problem:

Suppose Wednesday sales at a convenience store average $2,000 with a standard deviation of $500. What is the probability that sales for one Wednesday will be below $1,000?

The interval in this case is defined by its upper bound as shown in the diagram on the next page. Enter the relevant numbers from the problem in your worksheet.

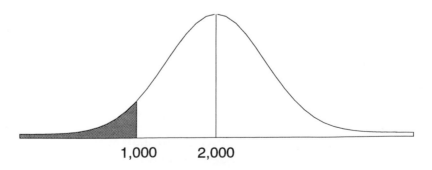

1,000   2,000

- Enter the upper bound, 1000, in cell B2.

- Enter the distribution's mean and standard deviation, 2000 and 500, in cells B9 and B10, respectively.

- Select cell B4. Enter the following formula which will standardize the value of the number in B2: "=(B2-B9)/B10." Verify that this is the z transformation shown on page 128. Press the Enter key.

The standardized value of 1,000 is -2, which appears in cell B4. The probability that sales on a single Wednesday will be less than $1,000 is the same as the probability of a standard normal random variable being less than -2. This probability is .02275, the value which appears in cell B7.

- Replace the number in C4 by a formula which will standardize the x value in cell C2. This formula should subtract the distribution's mean, which is cell B9, and divide the difference by the distribution's standard deviation, which is in cell B10. The formula should look similar to that in B4. Since there is no number in cell C2, Excel will treat the value of that cell as 0. The standardized value of 0 in this case is -4, and that is what should be displayed in C4 by the standardizing formula.

- Replace the number in C5 by a formula which will standardize the x value in cell C3. The absence of a number in C3 will also result in a standardized value of -4 appearing in C5.

- Replace the number in D5 by a formula which will similarly standardize the x value in D3. It, too, should initially display -4.

Use the worksheet to solve the following problem:

An automobile manufacturer has determined that the cars in a particular model line have fuel consumption which averages 27 miles per gallon with a standard deviation of 5 miles per gallon. What proportion of cars could be expected to have fuel consumption between 25 mpg and 30 mpg?

- Enter the distribution's mean and standard deviation (27 and 5) in the correct cells.

- This interval is bounded from both sides. The upper bound (x_U) is 30 and the lower bound (x_L) is 25. Enter these values in the appropriate location.

The correct answer, .381169 or about 38%, should appear in cell C7.

Try this problem:

A package delivery firm regularly sends trucks between two regional distribution centers. Through careful recordkeeping, it has discovered that the transit time is normally distributed with a mean of 10 hours and a standard deviation of 2.5 hours. What is the probability that a single truck would make the trip in less than 5 hours or more than 15 hours?

The interval described here is illustrated by the shaded areas in the diagram below. Note that this doesn't fit into any of the three categories in

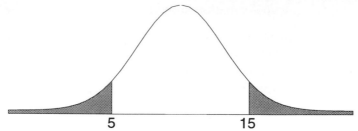

5   15

the worksheet. It can, however, be regarded as a combination of those three categories. Two approaches are possible:

1. The shaded region could be regarded as what's left over when the central region is taken out. Using this approach, you would determine the area of the region above the interval between 5 and 15 and subtract that from 1.0. Perform this subtraction in any handy available cell by using an Excel formula. Use the cell address of the central region for your formula.

2. The shaded region could be regarded as the combination of an interval defined by an upper bound and an interval defined by a lower bound. Using this approach, you would determine the area of the left-tail region bounded from above by 5 and add that to the area of the right-tail region bounded from below by 15. Do this addition in an available cell near that used above by using an Excel formula.

- Use both approaches to solve this problem. Verify that you get the same answer with each approach. The correct answer is .0455.

- Save your worksheet.

▼ Determining Intervals from Probabilities

A different type of problem which arises with the normal distribution (and other distributions) is one which you want to determine an interval within which a normally distributed random variable will fall with known probability. Most problems involve one of four types of intervals (illustrated below).

Left Tail   Right Tail   Two-Tailed   Central Region

The left-tail and right-tail regions are self-explanatory. An important characteristic of the two-tailed region is that *the areas of the two tails are equal.* The central region has the property that it is centered directly over the mean of the distribution. As a consequence, the two tails which lie outside the region are equal in area.

Let's set up an Excel worksheet which can handle these four cases.

- Double click the "Sheet3" worksheet tab and rename it to "Intervals."

- In the first row of cells, in B1 through E1, enter the labels "Left Tail," "Right Tail," "2-Tailed," and "Central Region."

- In the first column in cells, in A3 through A6 enter the labels "x1," "x2," "z1," and "z2." The rows with a "z" will be where the standard normal boundary values will appear. The rows with an "x" will have the *z* values converted to correspond with the specific normal distribution of a problem. For those areas which have a single boundary value (left and right tail), the cells adjacent to the x1 and z1 labels will be used. For the two-tail and central region areas, x1 and z1 will refer to the smaller boundary value and x2 and z2 to the larger.

- In cell A8 enter the label "Probability." We will put the probability corresponding to one of the four areas in cell B8.

- In cells A10 and A11 enter the labels "mu" and "sigma." The mean and standard deviation of a problem's normal distribution will be entered in cells B10 and B11.

Excel's NORMSDIST function is a standard normal cumulative distribution function. For problems of this type we need the inverse function, and Excel provides it in a function named NORMSINV. This function has one argument—probability. Excel interprets this as the area of a left tail and returns the corresponding *z* value. In the "Left Tail" diagram above, if the probability argument were equal to the area of the shaded region, the NORMSINV function would provide the *z* value which is the upper bound of the shaded region. This is the inverse of the NORMSDIST function which provides the value of the shaded area (representing a probability) when it is given *z* as an argument.

Suppose, for example, that we want to determine what value has the property that the probability of a standard normal random variable being less than that value is exactly .025? This situation is shown in the graph at the top of the next page, where the shaded left tail area is equal to .025 and we want to know what is the value of the boundary *z*.

- Enter the value .025 in cell B8.

- Select cell B5 (z1 for the left tail case), and click the Function Wizard button.

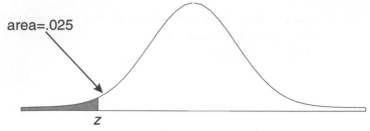

area=.025

z

- In the "Statistical" category, select NORMSINV.

- NORMSINV has a single argument, probability. Either click the mouse pointer on the cell containing the ".025" you entered above or directly enter that cell's address. Click the "Finish" button.

The answer, -1.95996, appears in cell B5. Let's check this by putting this value back in the "Probability" worksheet.

- Select cell B5. Click the "Copy" speed button 📋.

- Click the "Probability" worksheet tab to return to the previous worksheet.

What we want to do is to paste the value of cell B5 (*not* the formula) as the upper bound of an interval.

- Select cell B4. This is the cell where the value is to be pasted.

- Drop down the "Edit" menu by clicking the mouse pointer on "Edit" on the Menu Bar.

- Select "Paste Special..." A small dialog box will open.

- Select "Values" as shown in the picture below. Click "OK."

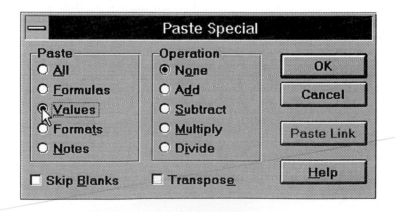

The value -1.95996 will display in cell B4. Look at the formula bar. Does it show the cell as containing a formula or a number? Look at cell B7. This shows the probability of a normally distributed random variable being less than -1.95996. This probability is .025, confirming that -1.95996 is the correct value.

- Click the tab to select the "Intervals" worksheet again.

▼ Going from a Standard Normal Boundary to a General Normal Boundary

What if the problem involves some normal distribution other than the standard normal? Once the answer to the standard normal version of a problem is determined, it is a simple matter to convert that boundary value to a corresponding value for any normal distribution.

Consider the following problem:

The time required for a package delivery firm to deliver a package is normally distributed with a mean of 10 hours and a standard deviation of 3 hours. What delivery time will be beat by only 2.5% of all deliveries?

This is the equivalent of the problem considered above in the context of a general normal distribution. If only 2.5% of deliveries take less time, the probability of a single delivery taking less time is .025. To convert a standard normal value, z, to the corresponding value, x, in a general normal distribution, the following formula can be used:

$$x = z\sigma + \mu$$

To implement this in Excel, first put the distribution's mean and standard deviation in the appropriate cells.

- Enter the value 10 in cell B10 and the value 3 in cell B11.

- Select cell B3. Enter the Excel formula which will take the z value in cell B5, multiply it by the standard deviation in cell B11, and then add the mean in cell B10.

The answer which appears in cell B3 should be 4.120117. The probability that a transit will require less than about 4.12 hours is .025.

▼ Determining the Boundaries of Other Interval Types— Right Tail

Determining the boundaries of other intervals with the NORMSINV function requires converting the probability associated with that interval into a left tail area. The properties of the standard normal distribution make this easy: the distribution is symmetric with mean 0, the area under the entire density function is 1.0, and, in the case of the two-tailed and central region intervals, the areas of the two tails are equal.

Suppose that we had a right-tail problem such as finding the value of z such that the probability of a standard normal variable being greater than z is exactly .25. This situation is depicted in the picture below. The shaded area is known to be .25, but what is the value of z?

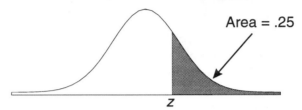

One way of solving this problem would be to subtract the area from 1. The difference would be the area to the left of z, which is what is needed for NORMSINV. Another approach would take advantage of the symmetry of the normal density function. Consider the diagram below.

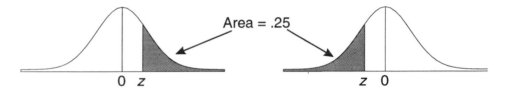

The picture on the left is the same as that above except for the addition of a vertical line at the zero mean. The picture on the right shows a normal density function with a shaded area on the left which has the same area, 0.25. How does the value of z in the picture on the left compare to that of z in the picture on the right? The symmetry of the normal density function ensures that each will be the same distance from the mean. Since the mean is zero, both z's will have the same absolute value but different signs. To find the z in the left diagram, we can use NORMSINV to find the z in the right diagram and put a minus sign in front of it to switch the sign.

Let's do this on the worksheet.

- Select cell C5. Start a formula by entering an equal sign.

- Enter a minus sign and then click the Function Wizard button. Select NORMSINV. The probability parameter should refer to cell B8.

- Click the "Finish" button. When the Function Wizard window closes, press the Enter key.

The value displayed in cell C5 should be 1.959961, the same as that displayed in B5, except for the sign. This is the boundary value for a probability of .025 remaining from the previous problem.

- Enter ".25" in cell B8.

The correct boundary value for this probability, 0.67449, now appears.

To solve a similar problem for a general normal distribution, this z value must be converted to an x value using the approach given on page 137.

- Enter the formula in cell C3 to convert the z value in cell C5 to the corresponding value for a normal distribution whose mean is in cell B10 and whose standard deviation is in cell B11.

The answer displayed in cell C5 should be 12.02347. Cells B10 and B11 still have the mean and standard deviation for the package delivery firm. This value can be interpreted as applying to that distribution. The probability of a delivery taking longer than 12.02347 hours is .25.

▼ Two-Tailed Intervals

The other two boundary types, the two-tailed and central region, are quite similar. Both have an upper and lower boundary which is the same distance from the mean—one above and the other below. The two types have areas (and probabilities) which are complementary—with the same pair of boundary values, they would sum to one. Finding the two boundaries, for example, which define a two-tailed area of .25 is the same as finding the two boundaries which define a central region area of .75.

Consider the two-tailed case. Since both tails have the same area, the area of the left tail is half the total. NORMSINV can easily do this:

- Select cell D5. The calculated value of the lower bound for the standard normal distribution will appear here.

- Click the Function Wizard button. Select NORMSINV.

- Enter "B8/2" in the field for the probability argument. Cell B8 holds the probability. This expression will pass half of that as the argument to NORMSINV. You should see "0.125" in the argument values field.

- Click the "Finish" button.

Cell B5 will show -1.15035, the value of z_1.

What about z_2, the boundary for the upper tail? It will have the same absolute value but the opposite sign of z_1.

- Select cell D6. Enter the formula to calculate the negative of the value in cell D5. Press the Enter key.

D6 will display 1.150349. Since there is no minus sign, an additional digit to the right of the decimal point is shown.

- Using the same approach as above (and as shown on page 137), enter the formula in cell D3 to convert the z value in cell D5 to the corresponding value in the normal distribution whose mean and standard deviation are given in cells B10 and B11.

- Enter the formula in cell D4 to similarly convert the z value in cell D6.

The value for x_1 in cell D3 should be 6.548952, and that for x_2 in cell D4 should be 13.45105. For the delivery firm, this means that there is a .25 probability that a delivery will require less than 6.548952 hours or more than 13.45105 hours. Another way of stating this is that there is a .75 $(= 1 - .25)$ probability that a delivery will take between 6.55 and 13.45 hours.

▼ Central Regions

Finding the boundaries of a central region of known area (or probability) is very similar to finding a confidence interval, an important form of statistical inference which you will study later. An example of a problem in which the central region is known is the following:

Within what range of delivery times, symmetrically distributed about the mean, will 25% of all package deliveries fall?

If the central region has an area of .25, the two tails have an area of $1 - .25 = .75$. The area of the two tails is one minus the area of the central region. The area of the left tail is half this, or .375. In this way, a central region problem can be converted to a two-tailed region problem. Recall that lower z boundary value for a two-tailed region was found by dividing the two-tailed region area by two.

- Select cell E5.

- Click the Function Wizard button and select NORMSINV.

- In the probability argument field enter "(1-B8)/2." The argument values field should display "0.375."

Cell B8 contains the probability or area of the central region. This expression will determine the area of the left tail and pass the result as an argument to NORMSINV.

- Click the finish button.

The value of z_1, -0.31864, will appear in cell E5. The upper bound, z_2, will have the same absolute value, but opposite sign, as z_1.

- Enter the formula in E6 to calculate the negative of the number in E5.

The last step is to convert the standard normal values z_1 and z_2 to general normal values x_1 and x_2 using the mean and standard deviation in cells B10 and B11.

- Enter the formulas in cells E3 and E4 to convert the values in E5 and E6 respectively.

The value displayed in E3 should be 9.044082, and that in E4 should be 10.95592. Since the probability in E8 is still .25, the probability of a delivery taking between approximately 9.0 and 10.9 hours is .25. We would expect 25% of delivery times to fall within that range.

- Save your workbook.

▼ The Normal Distribution as an Approximation to the Binomial

One of the reasons for the popularity of the normal distribution is that it can approximate many other distributions, including distributions which are inconvenient to work with without a computer. One of the distributions which has traditionally been approximated by the normal distribution is the binomial distribution. This approximation underlies the traditional approach to making statistical inferences about a population proportion. Although the use of computer programs like Excel makes this unnecessary, this approach still dominates in introductory statistics textbooks. In this section we will use Excel's graphics to compare various binomial probability distribution functions with their approximations using the normal distribution.

The variables of the binomial distribution are n and p (or π), the number of trials and the probability of success on a single trial, respectively. These must be converted to values for the normal distribution's μ and σ using the formulas for the mean and standard deviation of the binomial distribution:

$$\mu = np$$
$$\sigma = \sqrt{np(1-p)}$$

We will proceed by creating a binomial table for the case when $n =$ 1,000 and $p = .2$, add the corresponding normal approximation for each value of x and then graph the two distributions.

- Double-click the "Sheet4" worksheet tab and rename it to "Binom Approx"

- Place the following labels in the newly renamed worksheet.: "x" in A1, "P(x)" in B1, "Norm" in C1, "n" in D1, "p" in D2, "mu" in D3, and "sigma" in D4.

- Enter the initial value for n (1,000) in cell E1 and the initial value for p (.2) in cell E2.

- Enter the Excel formula in cell E3 to calculate μ as shown in the formula above.

- Enter the Excel formula in cell E4 to calculate σ as shown in the formula above. You will need to use the SQRT function which can be found in the Function Wizard in the "Math & Trig" category.

At this point your worksheet should look like the one below. Be sure E3

	A	B	C	D	E
1	x	P(x)	Norm	n	1000
2				p	0.2
3				mu	200
4				sigma	12.64911
5					

and E4 contain formulas (and not just numbers), because we will be changing the values of n and p and μ and σ need to automatically recalculate.

The values of x (which go from 0 to n) are to be placed in column A.

- Place the series of integers from 0 to 1000 in the range A2:A1002. The easiest way to do this is to first enter a "0" in A2, then select the region A2:A1002 using the Name Box, then drop the "Edit" menu on the Menu Bar, choose "Fill," then "Series...," and select a "Step Value" of 1. This same procedure was used earlier and described in more detail on page 119.

Each cell in column B will contain the binomial probability of getting the number of successes indicated by the value in that row in column A given the value of *n* in cell E1 and the value of *p* in cell E2. This is most easily done by entering a formula in B2 which uses a relative address to refer to *x* and absolute addresses to refer to *n* and *p*. The formula can then be copied to cells B3:B1001.

- Select cell B2.

- Click the Function Wizard button. Choose the BINOMDIST function in the "Statistical" category.

- The "number_s" argument is *x* and should have a *relative* address reference to cell A2.

- The "trials" argument is *n* and should have an *absolute* address reference to cell E1.

- The "probability_s" argument is *p* and should have an *absolute* address reference to cell E2.

- Enter the word "false" in the "cumulative" argument field so Excel will provide the probability for a single *x* value.

- Click the "Finish" button.

The value appearing in cell B2 should be 1.23E-97. This is a very small number, reflecting the fact that it is extremely unlikely that no success would occur in 1,000 trials if the probability of success in each trial were .2.

- Copy the formula in cell B2 down through cell B1002. The easiest way to do this is to use a method similar to that used to generate the series in column A. Select cells B2:B1002 using the Name Box. Open the "Edit" menu on the Menu Bar, and choose "Fill." Select "Down" (instead of "Series...").

Examine the probabilities. As you move down the list, the probabilities should first increase. The largest probability will correspond to a value for *x* of 200 (in cell B202). That probability is .031525. Check to be sure you have this value in your worksheet. If you do not, then you have made an error somewhere and need to recheck and redo the values in columns A and B.

Since the normal distribution is continuous, the probability of a normally distributed random variable equaling any specific value is always zero. In order to approximate a single binomial value, the corresponding range of values from the previous integer to the desired integer is used. For example, if we wanted to approximate the probability of getting exactly 15 successes, we would use the probability of a normally distributed random variable having a value greater than 14 and less than 15. This can be implemented using Excel's cumulative distribution functions by subtracting the probability the normal variable is less than 14 from the probability it is less than 15. The approximation could be improved (but seldom is) by using the "correction for continuity" discussed in an exercise below.

- Select cell C2. This cell will contain the probability of a normally distributed random variable (with the same values for μ and σ as the binomial distribution being approximated) having a value less than zero and more than $0 - 1 = -1$.

We want to be careful in the use of *relative* and *absolute* cell addresses so that the formula in cell C2 can be copied down to the other cells in column C. The references to the "x" values should be relative, since we want those to differ for each formula in column C. The references to μ and σ, however, should be absolute. The mean of the normal distribution is in cell E3 and the standard deviation is in cell E4, and those addresses must be fixed for all the formulas in column C.

Since the formula we want to enter must calculate the difference between two normal probabilities, the Function Wizard must be used *within* an equation rather than as the whole equation.

- Enter an equal sign. This signals the start of a formula.

- Click the Function Wizard button. Select the NORMDIST (*not* NORMSDIST) from the Statistical category.

- Set the "x" argument to be a *relative* reference to cell A2.

- Set the "mean" argument to be an *absolute* reference to cell E3, and the "standard_dev" argument to be an *absolute* reference to cell E4.

- Enter the word "true" in the field for the "cumulative" argument.

- Click the "Finish" button.

Instead of displaying a value, cell C2 displays a partial formula. The formula will be complete when we subtract the cumulative probability of an *x* value which is one less than the *x* value just calculated.

- Enter a minus sign. Click the Function Wizard button and again select NORMDIST.

- All of the arguments this time should be the same as those used above *except* the "x" argument. Instead of "A2," the argument should be "A2-1." This subtracts the number 1 from the value given in A2 (which should still be a relative address).

- Press the Enter key.

Cell C2 will now also display a 0. Although this number is, at least theoretically, greater than 0, it is so small (even smaller than the number in B2) that Excel sets it to 0. Check to be sure that your entry is correct by selecting C2 again and examining the formula which appears in the formula bar. It should be "=NORMDIST(A2,$E$3,$E$4,TRUE)-NORMDIST(A2-1, $E$3,$E$4,TRUE)."

- Copy cell C2 to cells C3 through C1002. Like other massive copies, this is best done by entering the range C2:C1002 in the Name Box and then using the "Edit...Fill...Down" menus sequence.

- Scroll down your worksheet until you see some nonzero values in column C. These values should generally be close to (but not equal to) those in the corresponding rows of column B.

Let's examine how good the approximation is graphically.

- Scroll your worksheet so that cell D1 is in the upper left-hand corner. Rows A, B, and C should not be visible.

We will use the large region of unfilled cells at the bottom of the screen to place the graph.

- Make a note of the address of the cell lying entirely in the lower right corner of your screen. That address will vary among computers depending on the screen resolution.

- Click the Chart Wizard button.

When you move the mouse pointer back into the region of cells, it will have the Chart Wizard shape. You can use this pointer to define the area on the worksheet where you want the graph to be placed.

- Place the mouse pointer approximately in the center of cell D5. Press and hold the (left) mouse button and drag the mouse pointer to the approximate center of the cell in the lower right corner of your screen (which you noted above). Release the mouse button.

- When the Step 1 window of the Chart Wizard appears wanting to know the range of cells whose data you want in the chart, enter "=a1:c1002." Click the "Next>" button.

- Click the sample graph headed "Combination" in the Step 2 window (second row). This will result in the true binomial distribution being displayed as a bar chart and the normal approximation being displayed as a line graph. Click the "Next>" button.

- In the Step 3 window choose the first format. It has the label "1" at the top. Click the "Next>" button.

- In the Step 4 window, you have to let Excel know that the first column contains the values for the horizontal ("Category (X)") axis. The value "0" in that middle field needs to be changed to "1." Make the change and click the "Next>" button.

- In the Step 5 window there is a question which asks "Add a Legend?" Click the button beside "No." This will give your chart a little more space.

- Click the "Finish" button.

- Readjust the scroll bars, if necessary, so that cell D1 is again in the upper left corner of your screen.

Your worksheet should look approximately like the picture below.

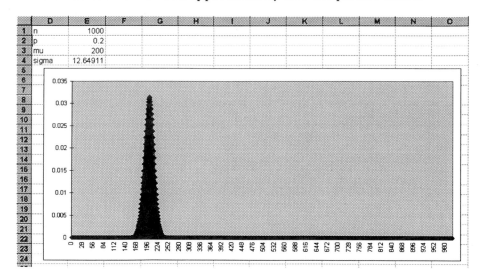

What this shows is a narrow bell-shaped curve centered over the value 200. It is difficult to see that there are two graphs. This can be made clearer by magnifying the image.

- Click the mouse pointer once inside the chart to select it.

- Click the mouse pointer in the field of the Zoom Control which is located on the standard toolbar 100% . Change the "100%" to "400%."

- Scroll the worksheet until the peak of the curve becomes visible.

Even at this magnification, the normal distribution line (which has diamond-shaped symbols connected by a line) may be difficult to distinguish from the differently colored bars. The bars are narrow and are obscured by the normal line, so it is not obvious that they are bars. If you look very carefully, you should notice a gap between the bars and the line on the right side of the peak but not on the left side.

- Using the Zoom Control, return the magnification to 100%. Rescroll your screen so that cell D1 is in the upper left-hand corner.

- Select cell E2 (which contains the value of p). Change the ".2" to ".5." Notice how this changes both the graph and the values of μ and σ (in cells E3 and E4).

- Experiment with other values of p, going from very small values (such as .0001) to very large values (.9999). Notice the extent to which the normal line closely follows the binomial bar chart.

With very large values of n (1,000 is a large value), the normal distribution is an excellent approximation of the binomial distribution. What if n is smaller?

- Change the value of p (cell E2) to .5 and the value of n (E1) to 100.

When n is 100, the maximum number of successes for the binomial distribution is also 100. If you were to examine column B below row 102, you would find all the cells displaying an error because the formulas they contain ask for the probability of a number of successes greater than 100. The normal approximation in column C does not have errors because the normal distribution is unbounded. All the probabilities are 0, however.

The chart needs to be modified so that the horizontal axis goes only from 0 to 100 rather than 1,000.

- Select the chart by placing the mouse pointer somewhere in it and clicking the (left) mouse button once. Do not double click.

- Click the Chart Wizard button. This will cause the Step 1 window of the Chart Wizard to reappear.

The row corresponding to 1,000 success is 1002 in your worksheet. The row corresponding to 100 successes is 102. The extra "2" are accounted for by the label in row 1 and the fact that the series starts with "0" in row 2 rather than "1."

- The field in the Step 1 window should be "=$A$1:$C$1002." Change the "1002" to "102" so that you have "=$A$1:$C$102." Click the "Finish" button. (If you click the "Next>" button or press the Enter key by mistake, simply click the "OK" button on the next window.)

The difference between the bar chart of the binomial distribution and the connected diamonds of the normal distribution should be much clearer in this chart. Notice how the normal approximation has a slight rightward shift compared to the binomial bars. The normal approximation is too small to the left of the peak (number of successes less than μ), and too large to the right.

- Change the value of p to from .5 to .05. The difference between the binomial and normal approximation should be even clearer. Experiment with other p values including both smaller values and large values just below 1.0.

The normal distribution generally does a better job of approximating the binomial distribution the closer p is to .50.

Try now an even smaller value for n.

- Change the value of p back to .50, and change the value of n to 20.

- Correct the horizontal dimension of the chart by selecting the chart (single click the mouse button with the mouse pointer inside the chart) and then click the Chart Wizard button.

- Change the "102" in the field in the Step 1 window to "22." The entire field should contain "=$A$1:$C$22." Click the "Finish" button.

For smaller sizes of n the normal distribution is a poorer approximation of the binomial.

- Experiment with different values for p when $n = 20$. Verify that the approximation seems best when p is close to .5.

▼ Exercises

1. The scores on an exam are approximately normally distributed with a mean of 75 and a standard deviation of 10. If the professor wants 10% of the class to receive the grade of A, then what is the minimum score a student can get and receive an A on the exam?

2. The weight of a loaf of bread produced by a bakery is normally distributed with a mean of 18 ounces and a standard deviation of .9 ounces. The bread is packaged with a wrapper which describes it as weighing 16 ounces. What proportion of the loaves of bread can be expected to weigh less than the amount shown on the package?

3. A company which produces fasteners for the automotive industry is evaluating a new bolt-making machine which makes a particular style

bolt with a weight which is normally distributed with a mean of 28 grams and a standard deviation of 1.16 grams. Within what interval, symmetrically distributed about the mean, will the weight of 95% of the bolts fall?

4. The speed of cars traveling a section of the interstate was found to be normally distributed with a mean of 62 mph and a standard deviation of 4.8 mph. What is the probability that a single car is exceeding the posted speed (55 mph)?

5. In examining the normal distribution as an approximation for the binomial, we did not use the correction for continuity. To approximate the binomial probability of receiving exactly x successes, the normal probability of getting a value between $x - 1$ and x was calculated. This was done by subtracting the cumulative probability of $x - 1$ from the cumulative probability of x. If the correction for continuity were used, the binomial probability of receiving exactly x successes would be approximated by the normal probability of getting a value between $x - 0.5$ and $x + 0.5$.

Print the graph you get showing the relationship between the binomial and normal approximations distributions *without* using the correction for continuity when $n = 10$ and $p = .2$. Put headings on the printout which identify this printout as *not* using the correction for continuity. Put your name in a footer of the chart. Then change the formulas in column C of your worksheet so they incorporate the correction for continuity. Reprint the graph, this time with a heading which identifies it as using the correction for continuity. What difference does the correction for continuity seem to make? (To print only the chart, activate it by double clicking the chart, then open the File menu from the Menu Bar and choose "Print Preview.")

Chapter 6

The Sampling Distribution of the Mean

Sampling distributions are the foundation of inferential statistics. The object of inferential statistics is to take data from a sample and gain knowledge about the population from which the sample was drawn. A good example are the TV rating services, such as Nielsen, which track the TV watching behavior of a sample of viewers and make inferences about the popularity of shows to all television viewers. A potential problem with this, which has occurred to anyone whose favorite show was canceled because of "low ratings," is that the sample might somehow not be "representative" of the population. How sure can we be that a couple of thousand viewers are going to be similar to the population of millions of television viewers? It's a logical question, and one that is addressed through the concept of a sampling distribution.

The information which we want to know about a population is usually a descriptive statistic, such as the mean or the proportion of the population which fits into a certain category. The population descriptive statistic is called a *parameter*. The parameter is a number, and we can easily imagine calculating this descriptive statistic if all population data were available. Because of difficulty or expense, collecting all the population data is not done. Instead, a sample is drawn from the population, and a descriptive statistic is calculated from the sample data. In the jargon of inferential statistics, the number calculated from the sample is a *statistic*. Once a sample is drawn and a statistic is calculated from the sample, that statistic becomes an *estimator* for the population parameter which we want to know. Since a sample may not be representative of the population, we also would like some indication of whether the sample statistic is likely to be a good estimator of the population parameter.

There are a number of techniques for selecting samples from a population. Unfortunately, many methods are not statistically valid in the sense that a statistic calculated from a sample should not be used to make an inference about the population parameter. Among those sampling techniques from which valid inferences can be made, the simplest is known as *simple random sampling*. In this technique, all items in the population have an equal probability of being chosen. Depending on the nature of the data to be analyzed, other valid techniques, such as stratified sampling, may make it possible to make equally valid inferences from smaller samples. They sometimes complicate the mathematics of the analysis, however, and for introductory statistics it is best to keep things as simple as possible.

With simple random sampling (or any other valid sampling technique), any value taken from a member of a sample is a random number since that member is chosen by a random process. Any sample statistic calculated from the sample values is also going to be a random number. A random number has a distribution. If we knew that distribution, we would have good information on the likelihood of a sample statistic being a good estimator of a parameter.

Sampling can be done *with replacement* and *without replacement*. When a sample is drawn with replacement, once an item is chosen for the sample from the population, that same item is replaced before a second item is selected for the sample. It is possible that the same population item might be chosen twice for the sample. When sampling is drawn without replacement, this cannot happen. If the population is very large compared to the sample, both techniques result in essentially equivalent samples, but this is not the case if the sample is close in the size to the population. Suppose a sample of ten people were chosen from the entire U.S. population. It wouldn't matter if the sampling were done with or without replacement, because it is unlikely that the same person could be chosen twice if sampling were done with replacement. On the other hand, if a sample of ten people were chosen from a class of thirty, it is very likely that someone would be chosen more than once if sampling were done with replacement. In practice, sampling is almost always done without replacement partly because with small populations this permits smaller samples to be used to make equally valid inferences. The simplest analysis, however, occurs if sampling is done *with replacement*. So that technique will be the one we will assume is used whenever it might make a difference.

▼ Simulating the Sampling Distribution of the Mean

Most people find the concept of a sampling distribution a little tricky when they first encounter it. It often seems a little nebulous or abstract. It is really a very concrete concept, however. We will investigate it here by using Excel to help us look at a specific sampling distribution of the mean.

Ideally, this would be done by calculating a mean from every possible sample which could be drawn from a population. Unfortunately, for even moderately large samples drawn from moderately large populations, the number of possible samples is astronomical. For example, suppose we were interested in estimating the average lifetime of a specific lot of 100 light bulbs by choosing and testing a sample of ten light bulbs. How many different samples are there in total?

How many different choices do we have for the first member of the sample? Any of the 100 bulbs in the population could be chosen. What about the second member? If the sampling is done with replacement, there are 100 choices for the second as well. The total number of distinct samples would be the product of 100 multiplied by itself 10 times, or 100^{10}. This is a huge number which could be written as a 1 followed by 20 zeroes! If we correct for the fact that some of these samples would be identical except for order, we still would have left so many samples that their number would have 14 digits to the left of the decimal point! If the sample size or population sizes were large, the number of samples would grow even faster.

Our approach will be to look at the means of a large enough number of samples that we can get a good notion of what the distribution of all sample means would look like.

▼ Drawing Samples with Excel

Excel has a sampling tool included with its analysis tools. Unfortunately, this tool will not take multiple samples. Taking a thousand samples one at a time is impractical. Fortunately, there is an alternative way to take samples within Excel which will permit multiple samples. Since this method is not completely obvious, the first step will be to explore exactly how it works.

- If you have not already done so, start Excel with a new blank workbook. If the workbook which displays is not empty, open the File menu on the Menu Bar, and click "New."

- Save the new workbook in a file named chap6.xls. (Note: this file should be saved on a hard disk or network drive; it will become too large for a diskette. For a method of storing it on diskette at the end of your session, see Appendix D.)

- In cell A1 enter the label "Population."

- In cells A2 through A6, enter five three-digit numbers. Use any numbers you like, but be sure all five are different.

- In cell C1 enter the label "Choose."

- In cell C3 enter the label "Value."

For the purposes of seeing how a sample can be chosen, the five numbers you have entered in cells A2 through A6 will be regarded as a population, and we will see how Excel's functions can be used to select values from this population.

- In cell D1, enter the number "1" (without the quotes).

This value will initially be used to determine which value in the population will be chosen.

- Click cell D3 to make it the active cell. Click the Function Wizard button.

- In the first Function Wizard window, select the Function Category "Lookup & Reference." In the Function Name list select INDEX and click the "Next>" button.

Some Excel functions, like the INDEX function, have more than one syntax. The next window which appears enables you to choose which version of the INDEX function you want. In this case, you'll take the second choice, which begins with "reference" rather than "array," although either one would work in this case.

- In the Step 1a window, click the second set of arguments (which begins with "reference") and then click the "OK" button. A familiar looking Function Wizard window will open.

- Only two of the arguments need to be provided. In the "reference" field provide the range address of the cells from which you want the Index function to make a selection. For this case, you want the population values whose range address is A2:A6.

- In the "row_num" argument field you should put an integer (or a cell address containing an integer) which tells which of the values in the reference field you want selected. We will enter this number in cell D1 so enter that address in the "row_num" field. Click the "Finish" button.

The number which shows in cell D3 should be the same as the number in cell A2. The INDEX function has used the "1" in cell D1 to select the first number in the range A2:A6.

- Enter the number "3" in cell D1. The third number in the range (the one in A4) should now be selected and appear in cell D3. Try entering other integers between "1" and "5" in D1 and verify the operation of INDEX.

- What happens if you enter "0," a negative number, or a number greater than 5 in cell D1?

Entering a value outside the range of 1 to 5 should produce an error message. In at least some versions of Excel, they do not. This is a bug in Excel which will not cause a problem as long as we are careful to use a valid number in the "row_num" argument.

To use the INDEX function as a device for sampling, a method for having it select a random value from the population is needed.

▼ Selecting a Random Value

Excel has a built-in function which provides a pseudo-random variable. A pseudo-random variable is the output of a sequence of mathematical operations which produces a series of numbers having most of the properties of random numbers. These numbers can be used as if they were genuine random numbers. For the problem of selecting a random value from a range of five values, we need a random integer between 1 and 5 inclusive. This is not the type of random variable directly provided by Excel, but it is not difficult to convert what Excel provides to what we need.

- In cell F1 enter the label "RAND." In cell F3 enter the label "Times 5." In cell F5 enter the label "CEILING."

- Select cell G1 to make it the active cell. Click the Function Wizard button.

- In the category "Math & Trig" select the function named RAND. Click the "Next>" button.

The next window which opens usually provides fields for you to enter values or cell addresses for the function arguments. The RAND function, however, has no arguments! The function description indicates a random number between 0 and 1 will be returned. This number is designed to be a *uniform* random number. All subintervals of fixed width within the 0-1 interval are equally likely to include the number generated by RAND. Notice that in the Value field, Excel has "Volatile" instead of a number. Although this may seem to indicate that your worksheet is likely to explode, Excel simply means that the value will change.

- Click the "Finish" button.

Look at the number in cell G1. If G1 is not the active cell, make it so. The number displayed will be a value between 0 and 1. That means it will be a positive decimal number with only zero to the left of the decimal point. Look at the formula bar to see the contents of G1. Like all functions, RAND is followed by a set of parentheses containing its arguments. Since RAND has no arguments, nothing is between the parentheses. If you enter the function directly into a cell, you must not forget the parentheses.

- Press the F9 function key on your keyboard. (If you have a Mac without an F9 key, hold down the Command key and press the = key.) Notice what happens to the value of cell G1. Press the F9 key repeatedly and observe G1.

When the F9 key is pressed, Excel recalculates the worksheet. Each time the worksheet is recalculated, a new value for the random variable will be displayed. Other things besides pressing the F9 key will cause Excel to automatically recalculate the workbook (and display a new value for the RAND function). If, for example, you change the contents of any cell, Excel will recalculate the workbook. This automatic recalculation can be turned off and should be turned off when a workbook has so much calculation which needs to be done that it annoyingly slows down entering or changing cells.

We need to convert the random number between 0 and 1 to a random integer between 1 and 5, inclusive. This will be done in two steps. The first step is to generate a random number between 0 and 5.

- Enter a formula in cell G3 which will multiply the number in cell G1 by 5 and display the result. Observe the displayed number. Press the F9 function key (or Command and =) several times and notice the range of values which appears. Pay particular attention to the value in the one's position.

When a random number between 0 and 1 is multiplied by any number n, the product is a random number between 0 and n. Multiplying the random number in cell G1 by 5 results in a random number between 0 and 5. The one's digit of that number will be 0 through 4.

The last step is to convert the random number between 0 and 5 to a random integer between 1 and 5.

- Make cell G5 active. Click the Function Wizard button.

- When the Step 1 Function Wizard window opens, select the "Math & Trig" function category. Select the function named CEILING and click the "Next>" button.

The description of the CEILING function given in the Step 2 window is unclear. What the ceiling function does is round *up* the value given as the "number" argument to the next value divisible by the value in the "significance" argument. In our case we want the value in cell G3 rounded up to the next value divisible by 1.

- Enter the cell address "G3" in the "number" argument field and the number "1" in the "significance" value field. Click the "Finish" button.

- Press the F9 (or Command and =) key several times. Notice that a random integer between 1 and 5 inclusive now appears in cell G5.

Next change the formula in cell D3 so that this random integer will be used to select the value from the population rather than the integer in cell D1.

- Click cell D3 to make it the active cell. Click the Function Wizard key. Since the INDEX function is already used in this cell, the Function Wizard will automatically assume you want to modify its arguments.

- Click the "OK" button in the window enabling you to choose which argument list you want. For our purposes, either argument list will work the same.

- When the next window appears, change the "row_num" argument so that instead of referring to the value entered in cell D1, it will refer to the random integer in cell G5. Click the "Finish" button.

- Press the F9 (or Command and =) key repeatedly and observe the value in cell D3. Each time you press F9, a value from the list in cells A2:A6 will appear in D3. Sometimes the same value will appear twice, but most times a new value will appear when F9 is pressed.

Excel is now drawing a random sample of size one from the population in cells A2:A6!

▼ Combining All Steps in One Formula— Functions Within Functions

One of the goals of the chapter is to use Excel to select 1,000 different samples. It will be much easier to do this if all the steps represented by calculations in different cells can be combined into a single formula which can be copied to produce a new sample value. Doing this will involve using the output of one function as an argument of another function. Excel has a facility for using the Function Wizard within another function argument to help with this.

- Select cell D4. Click the Function Wizard button. Under the category "Lookup & Reference," select INDEX. (Click the "Next>" button to move to the next window.)

- Click the "OK" button in the multiple argument lists window. The Step 2 INDEX window will appear.

- In the first argument field (which is called either "array" or "reference" depending on which argument list you chose), enter the cell addresses for the population in column A. Make these cell addresses absolute.

- Immediately to the left of the "row_num" argument field is a small Function Wizard button. (See picture below.) Click it.

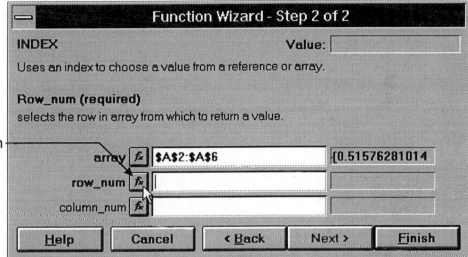

A new Step 1 Function Wizard window opens. Notice the title bar. The word "Nested" indicates that a function *inside* a function is being prepared.

- In the "Math & Trig" category select CEILING. The Step 2 Function Wizard will open.

The "number" argument field should contain an expression which calculates five times the random number returned by the RAND function.

- Begin the expression in the "number" argument field by entering "5*" (without the quotes). Then click the small Function Wizard Button alongside the "number" argument field.

A new Step 1 Function Wizard window will open. Notice that this one also has "Nested" in the title bar.

- From the "Math & Trig" category choose RAND.

- As before, since RAND has no arguments, there is nothing to put in the arguments window. Notice that the right most button is labeled "OK" instead of "Finish." Click it.

You've returned to CEILING's arguments window. This was the window from which you clicked the Function Wizard for RAND. Notice that the Function Wizard has completed the "number" argument so that it is now "5*RAND()."

- Enter the number "1" in the "significance" argument field. Remember that this will cause CEILING to scale the value in the "number" argument field up to the next integer value. Click the "OK" button.

- Excel moves you back to the INDEX function. Excel seems unable to remember which of the arguments list you chose previously and asks you again. Again, it doesn't really matter which you choose. Click the "OK" button.

Now you've moved back to INDEX's argument window. It was from this window that you called the Function Wizard for CEILING. This window does not have "Nested" in its title bar, and it has a "Finish" button instead of an "OK" button. Notice that the "row_num" argument field now has "CEILING(5*RAND(),1)." This is the expression which you built up by repeatedly calling the Function Wizard. You could have achieved the same effect by directly entering this expression into the "row_num" argument field.

- Click the "Finish" button.

Cell D4 should now, like cell D3, contain one of the five values in cells A2:A6. Press the F9 (or Command and =) key several times. Both of the values should change, although occasionally one of them will retain a previous value, and occasionally the two will have the same value.

- Copy cell D4 to cells D5 and D6. The easiest way to do this is probably to make D4 active and drag its fill handle down to D6.

Notice that cells D5 and D6 now also contain values from those in A2:A6.

- Press the F9 (or Command and =) key repeatedly and notice the values in D4:D6.

When you copied cell D4, the RAND function inside the formula in that cell was also copied. When Excel evaluates those copies, it makes a separate call to RAND for each cell. This means that the selections from A2:A6 in cells D4:D6 are all independent of each other (as well as the selection in cell D3). Cells D3:D6 now show a sample of size 4, selected with replacement, from a population of size 5. Every time you press F9, a new sample is chosen. Do not be surprised if two or more values of the sample are identical. When the sample size is nearly as large as the population size and sampling is done with replacement, this is normal.

We will now apply this technique to draw multiple larger samples from a much larger population.

▼ Setting Up a Population

- Double click the "Sheet2" worksheet tab and change its name to "Population."

Once we have the workbook set up, it will be easy to change the population from which the samples will be drawn. To begin with, a very simple population will be used—all of the numbers divisible by .5 between .5 and 100.

- Enter the number ".5" in cell A1.

- Enter the number "1.0" in cell A2.

- Select the region A1:A200. The easiest way to do this is probably to enter "a1:a200" in the Name Box and press the enter key.

- With A1:A200 selected, open the "Edit" menu on the Menu Bar. From the menu which drops down, select "Fill." A cascade menu will open. Select "Series…" from that menu. The Series dialog window will open.

- Just to the left of the center of the dialog window is a region titled "Type" which contains four selections with radio buttons. These selections are "Linear," "Growth," "Date," and "AutoFill." Select "AutoFill" by clicking the mouse pointer on the radio button just to the left of that choice. Click the "OK" button in the box.

The selected region A1:A200 should automatically fill with the series of numbers from .5 to 100 with each cell having a value which is .5 greater than the cell above it. The effect of using Series Fill with "AutoFill" is the same as if A1:A2 were selected and the mouse used to drag the fill handle to cell A200. When large regions (such as this) are involved, using the mouse is often not easy because of the difficulty of controlling Excel's scrolling.

▼ Setting Up a Dynamic Histogram

In order to better see the shape of the distribution of the population we have just created, it would be useful to have a histogram. In Chapter 2 you learned how to use the Histogram Tool. That is the simplest way of producing a histogram in Excel. Like all the output prepared by the analysis tools, the histogram tool is *static*—changes to the data are not immediately reflected in the histogram. To see the effect of changes in the data, the Histogram Tool would have to be rerun.

Instead of using the Histogram Tool, we can make a histogram using Excel's built-in functions. Although it is slightly more difficult, the histogram so constructed will be *dynamic*. Any changes we may make to the population data will be immediately shown in the histogram.

To make a dynamic histogram, we have to set up what Excel refers to as "bins," the intervals which each bar in the histogram will represent. Since the population values all fall between 0 and 100, let's use ten intervals whose upper bounds are 10, 20, 30, etc.

- In cells B1 through B10, enter the values 10, 20, 30, …, 100. Remember that one easy way of doing this is to enter "10" in cell B1 and "20" in cell B2. Then use the mouse to select cells B1:B2. After the two cells are selected, the fill handle can be dragged down to cell B10. When it is released, the series will be completed.

The next step is to have Excel count the number of population values within each interval. This can be done using the built-in function FREQUENCY. This function is an *array* function which produces a multinumber output. The rules for using such functions differ somewhat from those you have used earlier.

- Select cells C1:C10. The FREQUENCY function, like other array functions, has multiple outputs and we must start by showing the set of cells where the outputs must go.

- Click the Function Wizard button. In the "Statistical" category choose FREQUENCY.

- When the Step 2 window opens, you will see two argument fields. The "data_array" argument should be the cell addresses of the population data, A1:A200. The "bins_array" argument should be the cell addresses of the "bins," cells B1:B10. Enter these values in their respective fields.

- Click the "Finish" button. Be careful not to alter your worksheet before instructed below. The next step is where things are different.

When the Function Wizard window closes, you will see a number in cell C1, but not in any of the other cells in the selected region. Be careful not to lose the selection of cells C1:C10. If you do, reselect that region before the next step.

- With region C1:C10 selected, click the mouse pointer in the formula bar. The formula bar should contain the equation "=FREQUENCY(A1:A200,B1:B10)." It does not matter where in the formula bar the mouse pointer is clicked. The objective is for the formula bar to contain an insertion point, *or* for some part of the equation to be highlighted.

- On a PC, hold down the Ctrl and Shift keys. While holding them down, press the Enter key. On a Mac, hold down the Command key, and, while holding it down press the Return key.

Each of the cells in the selected region C1:C10 should display the number "20." Look at the formula bar. The entire formula should appear surrounded by braces (also called curly brackets) "{}." To provide an additional check against error, let's be sure that the numbers in C1:C10 sum to 200.

- Select cell C11. Click the AutoSum button. This will insert the equation to add cells C1:C10. Press the Enter key. If the value displayed in C11 is not 200, you have made an error somewhere.

The next step is to produce a histogram chart from these numbers. Notice the cell in the lower right corner of your worksheet. We will use the Chart Wizard, and you do not want to cause the worksheet to scroll when defining the chart outline.

- Click the Chart Wizard button. Place the Chart Wizard mouse pointer roughly in the center of cell D1. Press and hold the (left) mouse button, and drag the mouse pointer to the lower right corner of your worksheet. Do not get too close to the scroll bars, or your worksheet will begin scrolling! Release the mouse button.

- When the Step 1 window opens, you want to indicate the cells to be charted. They are B1:C10. One way of doing this is to place the mouse pointer in cell B1, click the (left) mouse button, and drag the pointer to C10 exactly as if you were selecting that region. Alternatively, you can enter "b1:c10" from the keyboard (without the quotes). Click the "Next>" button.

- Choose the "Column" chart in the top row of the Step 2 window. Click the "Next>" button.

- Select sample chart number 7 in the Step 3 window. This will result in the number represented by each bar being written above that bar. Click "Next>."

- In the Step 4 window change the middle field so that Excel will know to use the first column for the X axis labels. As soon as you make that change, all of the bars will be the same color. Click the "Next>" button.

- In the Step 5 window, select "No" for "Add a Legend." In the "Chart Title:" field enter "Population Histogram" without quotes. Click "Finish."

The histogram for this population should consist of ten bars of equal height, each with the number "20" above it.

The last thing to put on this worksheet is the population mean and standard deviation.

- Enter the label "Mean" in cell B13.

- Enter the formula in cell C13 to calculate the mean of the numbers in A1:A200. The Excel function has the name AVERAGE. The value displayed should be 50.25.

- Enter the label "Std Dev" in cell B14.

- Enter the formula in cell C14 to calculate the standard deviation of the numbers in A1:A200. Since these numbers constitute a population, you need to use the population standard deviation formula rather than the sample standard deviation formula. The Excel function to calculate a population standard deviation is STDEVP. The value displayed should be 28.86715.

- Save your workbook, now and often!

▼ Drawing the Samples

Double click the "Sheet3" worksheet tab and change its name to "Samples." On this worksheet we will have Excel draw 1,000 different samples of size 30 from the population of 200 on the "Population" worksheet. Because each sample value will require Excel to calculate the RAND function, which Excel normally does every time a cell's value is changed, it would be a good idea to turn automatic recalculation off.

- Open the "Tools" menu on the Menu Bar. Select "Options...."

- When the Options window opens, click the "Calculation" folder tab.

- In the upper left part of the window you will see a region titled "Calculation." Click the radio button beside "Manual." Click the small box below "Manual" to remove the "x" beside "Recalculate before Save." Click the "OK" button. These choices will prevent all automatic recalculation which will speed up data entry and saving the workbook. In order to get Excel to recalculate a worksheet, it will now be necessary to press the F9 (or Command and =) key.

The manual recalculation setting applies to this session, not this workbook. If you save the workbook and reopen it in a later session, automatic recalculation will be back on. If you plan to reopen this workbook, it would be a good idea to set recalculation to manual *before* you open it.

The next step is to enter a formula which uses the technique developed at the beginning of the chapter to draw a random value from the population.

- Select cell A1. Click the Function Wizard button.

- Choose the INDEX function. It is in the "Lookup & Reference" category. You may also find it in the "Most Recently Used" category.

- Click the "OK" button in the Step 1a (multiple arguments) window. The Step 2 window will open.

In the first argument field (named either "array" or "reference," depending on the choice you made in the multiple arguments list window) you need to place the cell addresses of the population. Since this is on a different worksheet (the Population worksheet) let's use the mouse.

- Make sure the insertion point is in the first argument field. Click the Population worksheet tab. The screen will switch to the Population worksheet with the Function Wizard on top. Notice that "Population!" has been entered in the argument field.

- Click the mouse pointer in cell A1 of the Population worksheet. Hold down the Shift key. While pressing the Shift key press first the End key and then the down arrow key. Then press the F4 (or Command and Y) keys to make this address absolute.

The argument field should contain "Population!$A$1:$A$200." This is the syntax which Excel uses to refer to a cell range on a different worksheet. This address could have been directly entered from the keyboard.

- Click the mouse pointer in the "row_num" argument field. Notice that this shifts the screen back to the Samples worksheet.

The "row_num" argument needs to be a random integer between 0 and 200 since there are 200 items in the population.

- Click the small Function Wizard button beside the "row_num" argument field. Select the CEILING function either from the "Math & Trig" or "Most Recently Used" category.

- When CEILING's Step 2 window opens, enter in the "number" argument field the expression "200*rand()" (without quotes). Enter the number "1" (without quotes) in the "significance" argument field. Click the "OK" button.

As you remember, RAND() will return a random number between 0 and 1. Multiplying this number by 200 results in a random number between 0 and 200. We could have used the Function Wizard, as was done on the Sheet1 worksheet, to have helped construct this expression. Once you know what it should look like, however, it is quicker to enter it directly. The number displayed in cell A1 should be one of the numbers in the population.

- It still doesn't matter what choice you make at the "multiple arguments" window. Click "OK."

- You should return to the INDEX Step 2 window. The "row_num" argument field should have "CEILING(200*RAND(),1)." If it does, click the "Finish" button.

Notice that the number displayed in A1 is one of the values from the population—a number between .5 and 200 which is divisible by .5.

- Copy the contents of cell A1 to cell A2.

The same number will be displayed in A1 and A2. This is not because of the sampling with replacement. It is because automatic recalculation was turned off.

- Press the F9 (or Command and =) keys.

Now cells A1 and A2 should display different population values. (It's possible that they *might* display the same value, but it's unlikely. If this happens, press the F9 key again. If it happens twice in a row, something is wrong.) You now have a sample ($n = 2$) drawn from a population ($N = 200$). Each recalculation results in a new sample of size 2. Let's increase this to a sample of size $n = 30$.

▼ The First Sample

To draw the first sample, we need to copy the formula in cell A1 to the next 29 cells to the right. This requires going beyond column Z since columns A through Z comprise only 26. After column A, Excel labels the columns AA, AB, AC, etc. After column AZ, Excel starts with BA, BB, BC, and so on. So we are not likely to run out of columns.

Since A through Z make up 26 columns, the 30th column is AD. So we want to copy the contents of A1 across the first row through cell AD1.

- Click the mouse pointer in the Name Box (whose location is shown on page 4). Enter "a1:ad1," and press the Enter key. The first 30 cells in row 1 will be selected.

- Open the "Edit" menu on the Menu Bar. Select "Fill." A cascade menu will open. Click "Right."

Cell A1 will be copied to the 29 cells to the right. All will display the same value because automatic recalculation is off. If the F9 key were pressed, the values would differ.

Next the formula will be put in cell AF1 to calculate the average of the 30 values displayed in A1:AD1.

- Select cell AF1. One way to do this is to enter "af1" in the Name Box and press the Enter key.

- Click the Function Wizard button. Select AVERAGE (from the "Statistical" category).

- Enter the range address "a1:ad1" in the "number1" argument field. Click the "Finish" button.

- Press the F9 (or Command and =) key. The value which appears in cell AF1 should be close to 50. Press the key again. The displayed value should change, but still be close to 50. If you press it repeatedly, most of the values displayed in AF1 should be between 40 and 60, but it is OK if occasionally a value appears outside that range.

▼ Drawing the Next 999 Samples

To draw an additional 999 samples and calculate the mean of each, all that is needed is to copy the cells in row 1 (columns A through AF) down through row 1000.

- Click the mouse pointer in the Name Box and enter "a1:af1000" (no quotes). Press the Enter key and this entire huge region will be selected.

- Open the Edit menu on the Menu Bar. Select "Fill." On the cascade menu choose "Down."

- A warning window may open saying "Selection is too large. Continue without Undo?" If it does, simply click the "OK" button.

This is a great deal of copying, and, depending on the speed of your computer, may take a while. A progress indicator on the status bar (whose location is shown on page 4) should reassure you that the copying is continuing.

▼ The Theoretical Distribution of Sample Means

Statistical theory tells us that the distribution of sample means should have a mean which is itself equal to the population mean:

$$\mu_{\bar{x}} = \mu$$

and a standard deviation which is related to the population standard deviation by the following formula:

$$\sigma_{\bar{x}} = \frac{\sigma}{\sqrt{n}}$$

Note that n is the size of each of the samples, not the total number of samples. For our case, $n = 30$ (*not* 1,000).

The 1,000 samples and sample means we have generated can be thought of as a sample drawn from the entire population of samples. The preceding two equations strictly hold for the entire set of sample means. Still, it would be interesting to see how close the mean and standard deviations of the sample means just generated are to the values which theoretically would hold for the entire set of sample means. Let's create a table for these values.

- In cell AG1 enter the label "Sampling Distribution." In cell AG3 enter the label "Theoretical." In cell AG4 enter the label "These Samples."

- Increase the width of column AG so that it is wide enough to hold the label in AG4.

- In cell AH2 enter the label "Mean," and in cell AI2 enter the label "Std Dev."

- In cell AH3, enter a formula which reads the population mean from the Population worksheet. Do this by making AH3 active. Then enter an equal sign to tell Excel you are beginning a formula. Then click the Population worksheet tab with the mouse pointer. Then click the cell containing the population mean (C13). Press the Enter key.

Pressing the Enter key will cause your display to shift back to the Samples worksheet with a value displayed in AH3.

- Again make AH3 active and observe the formula in the formula bar. Verify that it is "=Population!C13." Switch back to the Population worksheet and verify that the value displayed in AH3 in the Samples is indeed the population mean.

Notice again the syntax Excel uses when referring to a cell address on a different worksheet. The address begins with the name of the worksheet followed by an exclamation point. If you were to change the name of a worksheet, Excel would automatically change all formulas in the workbook which referred to cells on that worksheet.

The next step is to enter the formula which will calculate the theoretical standard deviation of sample means from the population standard deviation. Let's try entering this formula directly this time.

- Switch to the Population worksheet and note the cell address containing the population standard deviation.

- Switch back to the Samples worksheet and make cell AI3 active. Enter the following formula into the cell (without quotes): "=population!C14/sqrt(30)." Notice that it is OK to use a lowercase "p" in the formula even though the worksheet begins with an uppercase "P." Excel automatically corrects the case. The displayed value is 5.270397.

The next step is to add the formulas to calculate the mean and standard deviation of the sample means which are in the cell range AF1:AF1000.

- Select cell AH4. Enter the Excel formula which calculates the average of the numbers in the range AF1:AF1000.

- Select cell AI4. Enter the Excel formula which calculates the standard deviation of the numbers in the range AF1:AF1000. In this case you should use the *sample* standard deviation (STDEV) because the 1,000 sample means represent a sample of the huge set of all possible sample means.

If the sample values shown in the table do not seem as close to the theoretical values as they should, it might be because Excel has not recalculated the workbook. Until that is done, the samples have not really been picked!

- Press the F9 key (or Command and =). Recalculation could take a while. Look at the Status Bar for an indication of how it is progressing.

Once the recalculation is done, the theoretical mean and standard deviation should be very close to the mean and standard deviation of the 1,000 sample means. They will not be exactly the same because the 1,000 sample means are not the set of all possible sample means. Each time Excel recalculates the worksheet (you press F9), an entirely new set of 1,000 samples is chosen. Thus the mean and standard deviation of the 1,000 samples will change, but the theoretical mean and standard deviation, which are based on fixed population values, will not change.

▼ Examining the Distribution of Sample Means

The next step will be to create a dynamic histogram of the sample means which can be compared with that of the population. We will superimpose on the histogram a graph of the normal distribution with the mean and standard deviation of the sample means (in AH4 and AI4). The steps for setting up this histogram are very much like those used for the population histogram.

In order to provide more detail, 20 bars will be used for the histogram of sample means compared to the 10 bars used for the population histogram. This means 20 "bins" (or categories) must be created. Cells AG6:AG25 will be used for this. These bins will go from 5 to 100 by 5.

- Enter the number "5" in cell AG6 and the number "10" in cell AG7.

- Select the region AG6:AG7.

- Drag the fill handle down through AG25.

When you release the fill handle, the region AG6:AG25 should contain the series from 5, 10, 15, 20, ..., to 100 in AG25.

- Select the region AH6:AH25.

- Click the Function Wizard button. Choose FREQUENCY from the "Statistical" or "Most Frequently Used" category. The FREQUENCY dialog window will open.

- The "data_array" argument field should contain the addresses of the sample means, AF1:AF1000.

- The "bins_array" argument field should contain the addresses of the "bins," AG6:AG25.

- Click the "Finish" button.

The dialog window will close. The region AH6:AH25 will still be selected and AH6 will display a value (probably 0). Be careful to do nothing which would unselect AH6:AH25. If you accidentally unselect that region, then reselect it.

- With region AH6:AH25 still selected, click the mouse pointer in the formula bar so that either an insertion point appears there or part of the formula is highlighted.

- While holding down the Ctrl and Shift keys, press the Enter key. (On a Mac, hold down the Command key and press the Return key.)

Numbers should now display in all of the cells AH6:AH25. The cells at the beginning and end of the region are very likely to have 0's.

- Check the values in cells AH6:AH25 by using cell AH26 to determine the sum of the values in AH6:AH25. Use the AutoSum button. The displayed value should be 1,000.

Before charting these values, we will compare them to the amounts which would be predicted by the normal distribution.

▼ The Normal Distribution and the Central Limit Theorem

According to the central limit theorem, the distribution of sample means should be approximately normal if the samples are large enough. The size of the samples required for this depends on the population distribution. According to a widely used rule of thumb, sample sizes of at least 30 are sufficiently large to assume the distribution of sample means is normal. We will look at that by comparing the distribution of sample means with that which would occur if the sample means were normally distributed. Since the 1,000 sample means we are looking at are a tiny proportion of all the sample means, some mismatch between the actual distribution of the 1,000 sample means and the number predicted by the normal distribution is to be expected. The central limit theorem doesn't assure us that any 1,000 samples will be distributed *exactly* as predicted by the normal distribution, but the distribution should be close.

The range AI6:AI25 will be used for the values predicted by the normal distribution with μ given by the value in AH3 and σ given by the value in AI3. Cell AI6 will take the probability of a random variable with this normal distribution being less than the value given in cell AG6 and multiply it by 1,000. Cell AI7 will take the difference between the probability of a normal random variable being less than the value given in AG7 and the probability of it being less than the value in AG6 and multiply that difference by 1,000. The difference in the two probabilities equals the probability of the random variable being greater than the value in AG6 and less than the value in AG7. The formulas in the rest of the range will be similar to that of AG7. By the judicious use of absolute and relative addresses, we will be able to copy AG7 through the rest of the range.

The probabilities will be calculated using Excel's NORMDIST function which (unlike the NORMSDIST function) allows us to specify a value for the mean and standard deviation. An argument value controls whether this function provides the density or cumulative probability. We will use it to provide cumulative probability.

- Select cell AI6. Begin entering a formula by entering "=1000*" (without quotes).

- Click the Function Wizard button. Select the NORMDIST function in the "Statistical" category. The NORMDIST dialog box will open.

- The value for the "x" argument is the value in cell AG6. Enter the address AG6, not the number displayed in that cell.

- Cells AH3 and AI3 contain the theoretical mean and standard deviation of the distribution of sample means. Put these addresses in the argument fields for "mean" and "standard_dev," respectively.

- In the "cumulative" argument field enter the word "true" (without quotes). As soon as you finish, you should see the number "0" in the "Value" field at the top right of the window. Click the "Finish" button.

- Press the Enter key to end the formula.

The formula in cell AI7 will be similar except that it will use the difference between two cumulative normal probabilities.

- Select cell AI7. Enter "=1000*(" (without quotes). Notice the left parenthesis. The difference between the two cumulative normal probabilities will be inside the parenthesis so that the difference will be calculated before the multiplication by 1,000.

- Click the Function Wizard button and select NORMDIST.

- The "x" argument should contain a reference to the cell containing the "bin" value for this row (AG7). Make this a *relative* cell address so that it will automatically update when copied.

- As in the previous case, the "mean" and "standard_dev" arguments should refer to AH3 and AI3. Be sure to make these address references *absolute* since we do not want these addresses updated when the formula is copied.

- As before, enter "true" in the "cumulative" argument field. Click the "Finish" button.

The formula is not yet finished. We now have to subtract the probability of a normal variable being less than the value given by the previous row's "bin."

- The insertion point should be after the call to NORMDIST formed by the Function Wizard. Enter a minus sign. After the minus sign, click the Function Wizard button and select NORMDIST again.

- The only difference between this call to NORMDIST and the previous is that this time we want the "x" argument to refer to the address of the previous row's "bin" value (AG6). Make the reference to this address *relative*.

- Enter the same addresses in the "mean" and "standard_dev" argument fields as you did before (be sure to make them *absolute*). Enter "true" in the "cumulative" argument field as you did before. Click the "Finish" button.

- Finish the equation by first entering a right parenthesis to close the set of parentheses around the two calls to NORMDIST. Notice that since the last call to NORMDIST has parentheses around the arguments, there will be two right parentheses in a row at the end of your formula.

- Press the Enter key to end the formula, which should be:
  =1000*(NORMDIST(AG7,$AH$3,$AI$3,TRUE)-NORMDIST(AG6,$AH$3,$AI$3,TRUE))

It's a long formula, but it's not really complicated. Multiplying a probability by 1,000 give us the expected number of the 1,000 sample means which will fall within this range. The probability is the cumulative probability of a sample mean being less than the value in AG7 (10) minus the cumulative probability of a sample mean being less than the value in AG6 (5). The difference is the probability of a sample mean being between the numbers in AG6 and AG7. The entire function will tell us the expected number of sample means whose value will be between 5 and 10.

Unlike the value displayed in cell AI6, the value in AI7 is not zero, but it is a very small number such as 1.12E-11. We don't expect many sample means in this range, and it's not surprising if we don't have any.

- Copy the contents of cell AI7 to cells AI8 through AI25. Initially all the displayed values will be the same. Have the workbook recalculate. Check your work by verifying that the value in cell AI16 (the predicted number between 50 and 55) is 335.1918. The displayed value in cell AI25 should be 0.

▼ Charting the Sample Means

The next step is to have Excel chart the distribution of sample means and the normal prediction.

- Select the region of cells consisting of the "bins," the count of sample means in each interval and the predicted number from the normal distribution (AG6:AI25).

- Scroll the worksheet so that cell AJ1 is in the upper left corner of your screen. Your screen should show only blank cells.

- Click the Chart Wizard button. Place the mouse pointer in the approximate center of cell AJ1, press and hold the (left) mouse button, and drag the pointer to the approximate center of the cell at the bottom right of the screen. Be careful not to go beyond the cell boundaries because you don't want Excel to scroll the screen.

- Release the mouse pointer. The Step 1 dialog window of the Chart Wizard will appear. It should have the "Range" field already filled out with the address of the selected region (=$AG$6:$AI$25). Correct it if it does not and click the "Next>" button.

- Choose the "Combination" chart from the Step 2 dialog window. Click the "Next>" button.

- In the Step 3 dialog window, choose chart number 1. This will result in a combination bar chart and line plot with both charts using the same *y* axis scale. Click the "Next>" button.

- In the Step 4 dialog box, indicate that the first (1) column is to be used for the *x* axis labels. This will leave the chart with one set of bars. Click the "Next>" button.

- In the final (Step 5) dialog box, click the radio button so that Excel will *not* add a legend. Give the chart the title, "Central Limit Theorem." Click the "Finish" button.

- Scroll the worksheet so that you can see the entire chart. Press the F9 (or Command =) keys so that Excel will recalculate the workbook. Excel will select a new set of 1,000 samples and chart their sample means as a bar chart with the predicted values from the normal distribution shown as the line plot. Are they close?

- Click the "Population" worksheet tab. Compare the histogram of the population with that of the sample means on the "Samples" worksheet. Switch back and forth by alternately clicking each tab.

One obvious difference is that while population values go all the way from .5 to 100, the sample values tend to be clustered near the mean. Most of the bars in the sample means histogram have zero height. This is a consequence of the standard deviation of sample means (the *standard error*) being so much less than the standard deviation of the population. We can get a better impression of the distribution of sample means if we alter the range of values plotted so as to eliminate the values at each end for which the bar heights are near zero. Follow the procedure below to change the range of plotted sample values to those between 30 and 70.

- Select the "Samples" worksheet. Enter the number "32" in cell AG6 and the number "34" in cell AG7. Select the region AG6:AG7. Place the mouse pointer on the fill handle and (while holding the mouse button) drag the fill handle down to include cell AG25. Release the mouse button. Cells AG6:AG25 should display the series from 32 to 70 with an increment of 2.

- Scroll the worksheet so that you can see the entire chart of sample means. Press F9 (or Control =) to recalculate the worksheet. Try this several times. Each recalculation results in a new set of 1,000 samples and a new chart. The predicted normal distribution line plot does not change, although it may appear to because Excel may change the scaling of the vertical axis. Notice the "fit" between the line and the bars and how it changes with each set of samples.

Are you impressed with the closeness of the fit between line and bars, or are you disappointed that the fit is not perfect? For the fit to be perfect, we would have to plot all the sample means of which there are an astronomical number. (Writing out the number would require 28 digits to the left of the decimal point.) The 1,000 samples are thus a tiny proportion of the total, and randomness in the selection of the samples will prevent the fit from being perfect. The fit is *good*. How would changes in the distribution of the population affect this?

▼ Nonuniform Population

The uniform population which we have been using is quite different from the normal distribution, although it is symmetric. Suppose the population distribution differs even more from the normal distribution. Let's first try a bimodal distribution with no values near the mean.

- Click the "Population" worksheet tab.

We're going to use Excel's built-in Random Number Generation Tool as a handy method for quickly generating a large number of numbers which we will use as our population. This tool was used previously in Chapters 3 and 4.

- With the "Population" worksheet active, open the "Tools" menu on the Menu Bar. When the Menu Bar drops down, select "Data Analysis." The "Data Analysis" window will open enabling you to choose among the tools. If "Data Analysis" does not appear in your Tools menu, see Appendix A.

- Select the "Random Number Generation" tool. This will require scrolling down the list. One way of scrolling is to press the key for the first letter of the item you want ("r" in this case.)

Recall that in the first two fields of this tool, you indicate the number of columns and the number of rows in the range of cells in which you want the tool to enter numbers. Put the number of columns in the field which is labeled "Number of Variables" and the number of rows you want filled in the field labeled "Number of Random Numbers." For this exercise, we will select 200 numbers to be our population. All of them will go in column A, but we will use the Random Number Generation Tool to choose 100 numbers twice, rather than choosing all 200 at once.

- Enter the number "1" in the "Number of Variables" field and the number "100" in the "Number of Random Numbers" field.

- In the "Distribution" field select "Uniform." This selection will cause the next two fields to change.

When "Uniform" is chosen, the Random Number Generation Tool will generate values which are between the two values entered in the fields in the "Parameters" section labeled "Between" and "and." These values will be continuous, not integers.

- Enter values so that the Random Number Generation Tool will generate numbers between 0 and 20.

- Select the radio button beside "Output Range," and using either the mouse pointer or the keyboard, indicate that the numbers should start in cell A1. The window should look like that shown at the top of the next page.

```
┌─────────────────────────────────────────────────────────────┐
│ ▭            Random Number Generation                         │
├─────────────────────────────────────────────────────────────┤
│  Number of Variables:        [2              ]    [   OK   ]  │
│                                                               │
│  Number of Random Numbers:   [100            ]    [ Cancel ]  │
│                                                               │
│  Distribution:         [Uniform            ▼]     [  Help  ]  │
│  ┌─Parameters─────────────────────────────────┐               │
│  │                                            │               │
│  │  Between  [0      ]  and  [20     ]        │               │
│  │                                            │               │
│  │                                            │               │
│  └────────────────────────────────────────────┘              │
│  Random Seed:                [              ]                 │
│  ┌─Output options───────────────────────────┐                │
│  │  ◉ Output Range:       [$A$1          ]   │                │
│  │  ○ New Worksheet Ply:  [              ]   │                │
│  │  ○ New Workbook                          │                │
│  └──────────────────────────────────────────┘                │
└─────────────────────────────────────────────────────────────┘
```

- Click the "OK" button. Click the "OK" button on the window warning that you are about to overwrite some data. Column A (A1:A100) will fill with numbers.

You may wonder why the Random Number Generation Tool was used to generate these numbers rather than the RAND function. As you may have figured out, a uniform random variable between 0 and 100 could be generated by entering the equation "=100*RAND()." There is an important reason why the tool rather than the function was used.

- Select one of the numbers in column A (the one in A3, for example). Observe the value shown in the formula bar.

The formula bar shows that the number has more decimal places than are displayed in the cell. The important thing to note about the value displayed in the formula bar is that it is a *number*, not an *equation*. Had we used an equation with the RAND function, the value of the cells would have changed each time Excel did a recalculation. We have used the Random Number Generation Tool as a convenient way to get a large bunch of numbers for our population. The values in a population (*any* population) are not random. They are fixed.

The first half of our new population contains values between 0 and 20. Let's make the second half consist of values between 80 and 100.

- Recall the Random Number Generation Tool. You will find that the dialog box contains the values you previously entered. Three fields need to be changed. Make the two changes so that the tool will generate random numbers between 80 and 100. Change the "Output Range" field so that the numbers will start in cell A101 instead of A1. That will cause the numbers selected this time to be put in column A *after* the previous set of numbers between 0 and 20.

- Click all the "OK" buttons necessary to get Excel to generate the numbers chosen.

- Scroll your worksheet up so that the population histogram is visible. Press F9 (or Command =) to recalculate the workbook. Examine the population histogram.

The population histogram should show only four bars, two at the left and two at the right, reflecting the fact that the new population has no values between 20 and 80.

- Click the "Samples" worksheet tab and examine the histogram of sample means.

The mean of this new population will be very close to the mean of the previous population, and the chart should thus appear centered about as it did before. This population, however, has a larger standard deviation than did the previous population and so does the distribution of sample means. If you look at the "tails" of the distribution on each side of the histogram, you will see that they are above the horizontal axis. A slight increase in the range of values shown on the *x* axis would be desirable but is not absolutely necessary.

- Press F9 (or Command =) to select and chart a new set of 1,000 samples. Do this several times. How well do the sample means from this population fit the normal curve compared to the means of samples previously drawn from the uniform population?

You should see little or no difference. In other words, samples of size 30 drawn from this nonuniform population have means which seem normally distributed as do samples of the same size drawn from a uniform population. Despite the sharp difference in the shapes of the population distribution, the sample means have distributions which are the same shape!

Both of the populations we have considered are symmetric, as is the normal distribution. Will the same relationship hold if the population is sharply skewed?

▼ Skewed Population

We will use the Random Number Generation Tool to help create a skewed population. The procedure below is designed to create a skewed population whose mean is close to 50. This will minimize the need to make changes in the histograms.

- Click the "Population" worksheet tab.

- Run the Random Number Generation Tool four times. Several things will be the same each time the tool is used. The "Number of Variables" should always be 1. The "Distribution" should always be "Uniform." The radio button beside "Output Range" should be selected although the address will change. The fields which should be changed each run are the "Number of Random Numbers," the two fields giving the beginning and end values for the uniform random variables ("Between" and "and"), and the address for the "Output Range" field. The values are summarized in the table below.

Run	"Number of Random Numbers"	"Between"	"and"	"Output Range"
1	20	0	20	A1
2	40	20	40	A21
3	60	40	60	A61
4	80	60	80	A121

These four sets of random numbers will completely overwrite your previous population in column A with a new set of numbers.

- Press F9 (or Command =) to recalculate the workbook. Examine the population histogram.

The population histogram should clearly show that the data are left (or negatively) skewed. As you look from left to right, there should be a clear tendency for the histogram bars to get taller, although sometimes a bar may be slightly lower than the one to its left. An example of one of these population histograms is shown on the next page. Yours will differ somewhat since it will be based on different random numbers.

- Click the "Samples" worksheet tab and look at the histogram of the sample means.

Population Histogram

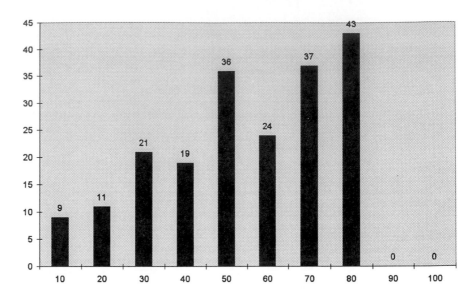

This population has a smaller standard deviation (and smaller standard error) than the previous population. A fairly large number of the bars in the sample means histogram thus appear to have zero height. Comparing the distribution of the sample means with the normal distribution might be easier if the x axis covered a smaller range.

- Change the series of numbers in AG6:AG25 so that the x axis of the sample means histogram goes either from 40 to 59 or from 41 to 60. Recalculate the spreadsheet.

- Recalculate the spreadsheet several times and observe the "fit" between the sample means histogram and the normal distribution line. Compare this to the fits you saw in the previous two populations.

Skewed populations require the largest sample sizes for sample means to be approximately normally distributed. If the population's skewness were to affect the distribution of sample means, there would be a tendency for the histogram bars to the right of the mean to go above the normal line while those to the left of the mean would have a tendency to lie entirely below the normal line. Although this population is quite skewed, there should be little or no sign of that in the distribution of sample means. It is, however, not difficult to create a distribution so severely skewed that the distributions of the means of samples of size 30 are also clearly skewed. Such distributions are rarely encountered with real data. The rule of thumb that samples of size 30 are large enough for the assumption of normality of the distribution of sample means is just that—a rule of thumb.

- Save the workbook.

- Open the File menu on the Menu Bar. Select "Close." This will close the chap6.xls workbook. Open the File menu again and select "New." This will provide you with a new blank workbook.

▼ The *t* Distribution

In the great majority of situations where the sampling distribution of the mean is applied, the population standard deviation is unknown. Instead, the standard deviation of a single sample must be used. Although the *expected value* of a sample standard deviation is the population standard deviation, a sample standard deviation is a random number, and its use can be thought of as adding uncertainty to the sampling distribution.

In the early part of the century William S. Gosset, a British industrial research scientist who worked for the Irish brewer Guinness, showed that better results were obtained when the sampling distribution of the mean was treated not as following the normal distribution but as following a similar distribution, which he termed the *t* distribution. The use of a different probability distribution in Excel would cause little difficulty except for the fact that Excel is inconsistent in its treatment of continuous probability distributions.

As you know, the normal distribution has two variables, μ and σ. An important property of that distribution is that a problem involving any normal distribution can be converted to a problem involving the standard normal distribution (which has $\mu = 0$ and $\sigma = 1$) by using the standardization formula (which converts x to z, or vice versa).

The *t* distribution, by contrast, has three variables: μ, σ, and a third variable called the *degrees of freedom* or *dof*. For problems involving the sampling distribution of the mean, the value of the degrees of freedom variable is generally $n - 1$, where n is the size of the sample from which the standard deviation was calculated.

As in the case of the normal distribution, standardization can be used with the *t* distribution to convert a problem involving one set of values for μ and σ to a *t* distribution with $\mu = 0$ and $\sigma = 1$. No such simple procedure, however, exists to convert between *t* distributions having different values for the degrees of freedom. There is thus not a single standardized *t* distribution; there are an infinite number of them. All of them have $\mu = 0$ and $\sigma = 1$, but they differ in their values for dof.

Excel provides four functions to handle the normal distribution: NORMDIST, NORMSDIST, NORMINV, and NORMSINV. The first two are distribution functions, and the second two are inverse distribution functions. The two with an "S" in the name are for the standard normal distribution while the other two work for any normal distribution (and require that the values for μ and σ be given as arguments). All of these functions are cumulative; the probability they associate with a value for the random variable is the probability of a random variable being less than or equal to that value.

By contrast, there are two functions for the *t* distribution, TDIST and TINV. The first is a probability distribution function and the second is an inverse distribution function. Both provide a relationship only for standardized *t* distributions. They both take the value of the degrees of freedom as an argument. Neither of them are cumulative. Furthermore, both of them handle only positive *t* values. Despite these differences, we can get the same information from these two functions as we did from the normal functions. We just have to keep in mind how what we want relates to what the functions provide.

Consider the diagram below showing the density function for a standard *t* distribution. If an argument of TDIST is set equal to the value of *t* in the diagram, TDIST will return either the area of both shaded regions or the area of just the shaded region to the right, depending on the value of another argument. Notice that the two regions are always equal in size, so that if TDIST is asked to give the area of both regions, the result is exactly twice what it would be if TDIST were asked to give the area of just one region. The value of *t* must be positive, a negative value for *t* will result in an error message. Since the *t* distribution is symmetric (and the standard *t* has mean 0), the value for the upper boundary of the left tail will have the same absolute value (but negative sign) as the lower boundary of the right tail.

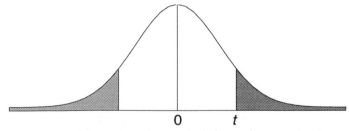

Suppose we want to determine the probability of a standard *t* variable being between two values, both of which are positive or both of which are negative. We can use two calls to TDIST, each of which uses the absolute value of the boundary values, to determine the one-tail probability. The difference between the two one-tail probabilities is the value we want.

Unfortunately, whether we want the one-tail area of the right-most value minus the left-most value, or vice versa, depends on whether the values are both positive or both negative. Since the answer is a probability, and probabilities must be positive, this problem can be solved by taking the absolute value of the difference.

TINV has an argument set equal to a probability. It interprets that probability as the area of *both* tails, and it returns the value of t shown in the diagram. Unlike TDIST, TINV has no argument allowing us to indicate that our problem involves only the area of one tail. Since the area of one tail is always merely half the area of two, this is not a serious problem. Notice that the t value returned is always positive.

▼ Looking at the t Distribution

To better understand the t distribution, we will compare it to the z distribution using the same approach we used to compare the distribution of the sample of sample means with the normal distribution for all sample means.

- Save the new workbook as chap6b.xls.

- Under the Tools menu on the Menu Bar, select options and switch recalculation from manual back to automatic.

- Double click the Sheet1 worksheet tab and change its name to "t vs z."

- In the row of cells A1:D1, enter the labels "Value," "z," "t," and "dof."

- In cell E1 enter the number "10." This will be the value for the degrees of freedom of the t distribution we plot.

- In the column A2:A82 enter the series of numbers which goes from -4 to 4 with an increment of 0.1.

The first z and t probabilities will go in row 2. As was the case with the other probability distributions we have plotted, the first formula is a special case. By using care with the formulas entered in row 3, we will be able to copy those formulas to all of the other 80 rows.

- In cell B2, enter the Excel formula to determine the probability of a standard normal variable being less than the value in cell A2. The displayed value will be very close to zero, 3.17E-05.

- Select cell C2. Click the Function Wizard button.

- Under the "Math & Trig" category, select ABS. This is the absolute value function. Click the "Next>" button.

The ABS function has only one argument ("number"). That argument will contain a formula taking the difference between two probabilities calculated by TDIST.

- Click the small Function Wizard button inside the ABS dialog box beside the "number" argument field.

- Under the "Statistical" category, select TDIST. Click the "Next>" button.

The TDIST dialog window shows three arguments:

1. **x**—the value of the random variable for which you want a probability. This must be a standard *t* variable ($\mu = 0$, and $\sigma = 1$). This value *must* be positive.

2. **degrees_freedom**—the value of the degrees of freedom for the standard *t* variable given as the *x* argument.

3. **tails**—either the number "1" or the number "2," depending on whether you want the probability (area) of one or both tails.

We will use the absolute value function again to be sure that the value in the "x" argument field is positive.

- Click the small Function Wizard button beside the "x" argument field.

- Select the ABS function, and go to its dialog box.

- Enter the address of the "-4" in row A in the "number" dialog box. First be sure the insertion point is in the argument field and then either click the cell with the mouse pointer or enter "A2."

- Click the "OK" button.

You will return to the TDIST dialog window with "ABS(A2)" in the "x" argument field.

- Click the mouse pointer in the "degrees_freedom" field and then click the mouse pointer on the number "10" in cell E1. The argument field should contain "E1."

- Click the mouse pointer in the "tails" argument field. Enter the number "1." As soon as you do that, "0.001259166" will appear in the "Value" field of the dialog box.

- Click the "OK" button. You will return to the (first) ABS dialog box with "TDIST(ABS(A2),E1,1)" in the "number" argument field. Notice that this is highlighted. Click the mouse pointer on the right side of the argument field to remove the highlighting and place the insertion point at the end.

- Enter a minus sign. Again click the small Function Wizard button beside the "number" argument field. Again select the TDIST function.

- When the TDIST dialog box opens, enter the number "4.1" in the "x" argument field. Put the same values in the "degree_freedom" and "tails" fields which you did before (E1 and 1, respectively). Click the "OK" button.

You will return to the ABS dialog window. Notice that the "number" argument field now contains a formula which is too long to be entirely seen. Look at the "Value" field. It should contain 0.000186877.

- Click the "Finish" button.

Cell C2 should display 0.000187. This is the difference between the tail area of 4.1 and the tail area of 4.0, which is also the area between −4.0 and −4.1. Notice the different approach between this and the formula in cell B2. In B2 we simply entered the probability of a standard normal variable being less than −4.0 rather than between −4.0 and −4.1. We took a shortcut with the normal distribution because the probabilities are so small that the difference won't be visible in a graph. This is not the case, however, with the *t* distribution which thus requires extra care.

The formulas in row 3 will be similar. Each will calculate the probability of a random variable (*z* for column B, standard *t* for column C) falling between −3.9 (the value in column A for that row) and −4.0 (the value in the previous row).

- Select cell B3. Enter an Excel formula which will take the probability of a standard normal variable being less than the value in cell A3 and subtract from that the probability of a standard normal variable being less than the value in cell A2. Be sure to use relative addresses to refer to A2 and A3. The displayed value should be 1.64E-05. Start by entering an equal sign, then use the Function Wizard twice to use NORMSDIST.

- Select cell C3. Click the Function Wizard button. Select the absolute value function (ABS).

- When the ABS dialog window appears, click the small Function Wizard button beside the "number" argument field. Select TDIST.

- When the TDIST dialog window opens, click the small Function Wizard button beside the "x" argument field. Select ABS again.

- Be sure the insertion point is in the "number" argument field. Click the "-3.9" in column A or simply enter its address, A3. Be sure you use a *relative* address. The "Value" field should display "3.9," the absolute value of the number in cell A3. Click the "OK" button.

- When the TDIST dialog window reappears, the "x" argument field will have "ABS(A3)," which is what you want.

- Click the mouse button in the "degrees_freedom" argument field to put the insertion point there. Click the "10" in cell E1 or enter the address. Make this address *absolute* so that it will not change when the formula is copied.

- Enter the number "1" in the "tails" argument field. The "Value" field should immediately display 0.001480504. Click the "OK" button.

- When the ABS dialog window reappears, the "number" argument field will contain "TDIST(ABS(A3),$E$1,1)" and will be highlighted. Click the mouse pointer on the right side of the field to remove the highlighting and place the insertion point at the end.

- Enter a minus sign. Again click the small Function Wizard button beside the "number" argument field. Again select TDIST.

- Either use the Function Wizard or directly enter the formula in the "x" argument field to determine the absolute value of the contents of cell A2 (the previous row to the one referred to below). Be sure the reference to A2 is *relative*.

- Enter the same values in the remaining two fields as before. Again, be sure the reference to the cell with the degrees of freedom is *absolute*. The number appearing in the "Value" field will be 0.001259166. Click the "OK" button.

- The ABS dialog box will reappear with a long expression in the "number" argument field. Check that the "Value" field displays 0.000221338, which is the absolute value of the difference between the tail area of 3.9 and that of 4.0. If the display is correct, click the "Finish" button.

Cell C3 will display 0.000221, the same value as was in the "Value" field of the ABS dialog window except rounded to fewer digits. The next step is to copy the formulas in B3 and C3 down through row 82.

- Select the region B3:C82. This is most easily done by entering this range address in the Name Box.

- Open the "Edit" menu on the Menu Bar. Select "Fill" on the drop-down menu, and "Down" on the cascade menu. The formulas will be copied. To check your work, examine row 38. Cell A38 should display

-0.4, cell B38 should display 0.036041, and cell C38 should display 0.034837. We're now ready to plot the two distributions.

▼ Plotting the *t* and the *z* Distributions

The values in columns B and C are probabilities associated with small intervals (0.1). The plot of these probabilities will have shapes which are very close approximations to the shapes which the density functions would have. The values along the horizontal axis correspond to values which the random variable might equal. The closer the plot is to the horizontal axis, the less likely are those values to occur. By comparing the plots of the *t* and *z* distributions, we can tell which values are more likely to occur in one distribution rather than the other by seeing which distribution's plot is higher above the section of the horizontal axis corresponding to those values.

- Select the region A1:C82. This is most easily done by entering that address range in the Name Box.

- Scroll your worksheet so that cell D1 is in the upper left-hand corner. Be sure to not to deselect the region A1:C82.

- Click the Chart Wizard button.

- Click the Chart Wizard mouse pointer in cell D2 and drag it to the cell in the lower right corner of the portion of the worksheet visible on your screen. Be careful not go beyond the visible region of cells so your worksheet will not start scrolling.

- Since A1:C82 was selected when you clicked the Chart Wizard button, the Step 1 window should appear with that range already entered (it should show "=$A$1:$C$82"). If it does not, simply enter "a1:c82" in the range field. Click the "Next>" button.

- Select the "Line" plot on the first row of the examples shown in the Step 2 window. Go to the next step.

- Select format 2 in the Step 3 window. This will result in the least clutter in the plots. Proceed to the next step.

- In the Step 4 window you must tell Excel to use the numbers in column A (the "First 1 Column") for the *x* axis labels. Once you do that, the preview in the Step 4 window should immediately show two very similar bell-shaped curves. Proceed to the next step.

- In the last (Step 5) window, set the title to "t versus z distribution." Click the "Finish" button.

- Scroll your worksheet so that cell D1 is again in the upper left-hand corner. The plot should fill most of your screen.

- Change the value of the degrees of freedom by changing the number in cell E1. Start by reducing the value to 8, then to 5, then to 2, then to 1. Does reducing the value of the degrees of freedom make the two plots more alike or less alike?

- Increase the value of the degrees of freedom. Try 20, 100, 1000, 10000, and 100,000. It may seem that the line for the *z* plot completely disappears. Actually, it is simply becoming better covered by the *t* plot line. Look carefully at the places where the plot curves most sharply and you may see indications that the two lines are not perfectly superimposed. If you can't tell a difference, scroll the worksheet back to where you can see the numbers in columns B and C. If the two plots were identical, the numbers would be identical (except for B2 and C2—those two will differ because of the "shortcut" we took with the *z* distribution). If you can't see a difference between the numbers in columns B and C, increase the widths of those columns. This will enable Excel to display the numbers with more precision, making the (slight) difference clearer.

As you can see, as the degrees of freedom increases, the *t* distribution becomes more like the normal distribution.

- Change the degrees of freedom back to 1.

When the degrees of freedom is 1, the *t* distribution is most unlike the normal. The difference is similar for other values of the degrees of freedom. The tails are "fatter" for the *t* distribution than they are for the normal. Although both of these distributions have the same standard deviation (1), the *t* distribution appears more spread out than the normal distribution. Since the tails are higher and the peak is lower, how would the width of an interval symmetrically distributed around the mean with given area compare for the standard *t* and *z* distributions? This issue will be discussed again below.

▼ Using Excel to Solve Problems on the Distribution of Sample Means

Problems on the distribution of sample means are not important because they are useful. They are important to help you connect an understanding of the normal distribution with an understanding of confidence intervals and hypothesis tests, highly useful tools of statistical inference. There are two classes of problems on the distribution of sample means:

those for which the population standard deviation (or variance) is known, and those for which only a sample standard deviation is known. The first class of problems is solved much like the very similar normal distribution problems. The primary difference is that the standard error (standard deviation of sample means) must be calculated from the equation $\sigma_{\bar{x}} = \dfrac{\sigma}{\sqrt{n}}$. Consider the following example:

A soft drink bottling machine fills each bottle with an average of 2.05 liters with a standard deviation of .03 liters. Within what region symmetrically distributed around the mean will 95% of the means of samples of 50 bottles fall?

- Double click the Sheet2 worksheet tab. Change its name to "sigma known."

- Enter the following labels in cells A1:A9: "Mean," "Std Dev," "n," "Std Err," "Prob," "zL," "zH," "x bar L," and "x bar H."

- Enter the values from the problem above in cells B1:B3 adjacent to the labels in column A.

- Enter an Excel formula in cell A4 which will divide the value of the standard deviation by the square root of *n*. The displayed value should be 0.004243.

- Enter the number ".95" in cell B5.

- Using the same technique used in Chapter 5, enter the formulas in cells B6 and B7 which will display upper and lower *z* values for the central interval with area .95. This will require using the NORMSINV function. B6 will display -1.95996, and B7 will display 1.959961.

- Enter the formulas in cells B8 and B9 which will convert the *z* values in cells B6 and B7 to $\bar{x}$ values. This conversion should be done using the following formula:

$$\bar{x} = \mu + \sigma_{\bar{x}}$$

The difference between this formula and that used in Chapter 5 is that *z* value is multiplied by the standard error rather than by the population standard deviation. The displayed value for cell B8 should be 2.041685, while that for B9 should be 2.058315. Thus 95% of the means of sample of size 50 will lie between 2.041685 and 2.058315.

Now consider the following problem:

A soft drink bottler has selected a random sample of ten bottles from a bottle-filling machine designed to fill bottles with an average of 2.05 liters. The average fill in the sample was 2.00 liters with a standard deviation of .12 liters. If the machine was actually putting an average of 2.05 liters in all bottles, what is the probability that a sample of ten bottles could be selected with a sample average of 2.00 or less?

This problem requires the *t* distribution because the only standard deviation known is that of a single sample.

- Double click the Sheet3 worksheet tab to display this blank worksheet. Change its name to "sigma unknown."

- Enter the following labels in cells A1:A8: "mu," "s," "n," "std err," "x bar," "t," "TDIST," "Answer."

- In cells B1:B3 enter the population mean (2.05), the sample standard deviation (.12), and the sample size (10). In cell B5 enter the value for $\bar{x}$ (2.00). These are the data provided by the problem.

- In cell B4 enter the formula which will calculate the standard error. The standard error is calculated from the sample standard deviation just as it was from a population standard deviation; divide the standard deviation by the square root of *n*. The displayed value should be 0.037947.

- In cell B6 enter the formula which will standardize the number in cell B5. The formula to standardize the *x* value is the same as that used in the previous problem, although the symbols are usually slightly different:

$$t = \frac{\bar{x} - \mu}{s_{\bar{x}}}$$

The symbol *t* is used instead of *z* because sample means will be treated as following the *t* distribution. The symbol for the denominator is $s_{\bar{x}}$ instead of $\sigma_{\bar{x}}$ to indicate that the standard error used here is derived from a sample standard deviation (*s*) instead of a population standard deviation (σ). When the correct formula is entered in B6, it will display the value -1.31762.

Before using TDIST, it is helpful to have a clear picture of what area in the density function corresponds to the probability wanted to determine how to use TDIST. For this problem, the density function and the area are shown on the top of the next page.

Compare this diagram with that shown on page 180. If we give TDIST the absolute value of -1.31762 and ask for the one-tail probability, it will

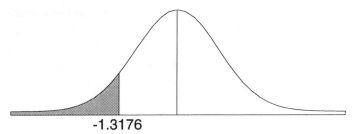

-1.3176

return the area of the tail to the right of (+)1.31762. But the area of this tail is the same as the one above which we want.

- Select cell B7, click the Function Wizard button, and choose TDIST.

- In the "x" argument field, enter the expression which will take the absolute value of the number in cell B6.

- In the "degrees_freedom" argument field enter an expression which will subtract 1 from the number in cell B3. The degrees of freedom equals $n - 1$.

- Enter the number "1" in the "tails" argument field. The number 0.11009272 will appear immediately in the "Value" field. Click the "Finish" button, and the same number will appear in cell B7.

- Since this is the value we want, enter a formula in cell B8 which will make the contents of that cell equal the value of cell B7. The probability of a sample of ten bottles having an average fill less than 2.00 liters is .110093.

Consider this problem:

A soft drink bottler has selected a random sample of 12 bottles from a bottle-filling machine. The average fill in the sample was 2.00 liters with a standard deviation of .09 liters. What is the probability that the average fill for a sample of 12 bottles will be within .05 liters of the actual average fill for all bottles?

A diagram of the density function with the relevant area is shown below. The smallest value a sample mean can have and be on the boundary of the area is $\mu - .05$. The largest value a sample mean can have is $\mu + .05$.

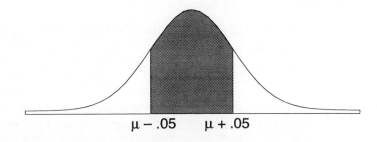

$\mu - .05$ $\mu + .05$

In this problem we are given a value for s and n, but we don't have a numeric for the two $\bar{x}$ values, and we don't have a value for μ. The expressions which are given for $\bar{x}$ ($\mu \pm .05$) will enable us to find the corresponding t values because the value for μ will cancel out.

- Enter the values for s and n in the appropriate places on the worksheet. The standard error will be calculated automatically from these values and should be displayed as 0.025981.

The calculation the t value corresponding to the x value of $\mu + .05$ is:

$$t = \frac{\bar{x} - \mu}{s_{\bar{x}}} = \frac{(\mu + .05) - \mu}{s_{\bar{x}}} = \frac{.05}{s_{\bar{x}}} \, .$$

Notice that μ is not present in the final expression.

- Select cell B6. Enter the formula which will divide the number .05 by the standard error in cell B4. The displayed value should be 1.924501.

How do we use TDIST with this problem. Compare the diagram above with the one showing the probability given by TDIST on page 180. The center region above is the complement of the two shaded tails shown on page 180. The shaded area above can be calculated by having TDIST determine the two tail probability associated with the positive t value and subtracting that probability from 1.

The formula currently in cell B7 determines the one-tail area associated with the t value. Let's change it to the two-tail area:

- Select cell B7. Click the Function Wizard button. The TDIST dialog window will appear with the argument fields filled out as they were when the formula in B7 was created.

- Change the "1" in the "tails" argument to "2." Click the "Finish" button. The value displayed in cell B7 should be 0.080535.

- Select cell B8. Enter the Excel function which subtracts the value in cell B7 from 1.

The answer to the problem, as displayed in cell B8, shows that the probability that the mean of a sample of 12 bottles will be within .05 liters of the mean of all bottles is .919465.

Let's examine the use of the TINV function to solve a couple of problems:

An advertising agency wants to determine whether a new campaign for Crunch-O cereals has increased consumption among 8- to 12-year-olds who eat cold cereal. Prior to the campaign, those in the population group consumed an average of 12 oz of Crunch-O per month. If the campaign had no effect, average consumption would remain at 12 oz. A sample of 15 children was chosen whose consumption after the campaign averaged 13.9 oz with a standard deviation of 3.1 oz. Assuming the campaign had no effect (and the population average remained at 12 oz), what sample average would be exceeded by only 5% of all samples?

A diagram of this situation is shown below. The shaded area to the right has a given area of .05. The problem is to determine the boundary value, $\bar{x}$ for that area. This is done by first using TINV to determine the value of t such that the probability of a standard t having a greater value is .05, and then converting that t value to an $\bar{x}$ value.

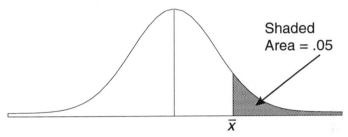

- Enter the following labels in cells D1:D8: "mu," "s," "n," "std err," "upper tail," "TINV Prob," "t," "x bar."

- In cells E1:E3, enter the values given in the problem: $\mu = 12$, $s = 3.1$, and $n = 15$.

- In cell E4 enter the formula to calculate the standard error. The displayed value should be 0.800417.

- Enter the upper tail area, .05, in cell E5.

Refer back to the picture on page 180. In order to use TINV, we must determine the *two-tail* probability which would give us the t value corresponding to the $\bar{x}$ value in the picture above. If we were to add a left tail to the picture above corresponding to the area to the left of $-\bar{x}$, the area of that tail would also be .05 because of the symmetry of the t distribution. Thus the two-tail area is exactly twice the one-tail area.

- Enter the formula in cell E6 which will double the value in cell E5. The displayed value should be 0.1.

- Select cell E7. Click the Function Wizard button. Select TINV from the "Statistical" category. Move to the TINV dialog box.

- In the "probability" argument field, put the address for the two tail probability you have just calculated. In the "degrees_freedom" argument field, enter an expression which will subtract 1 from the value in cell E3. Click the "Finish" button. The displayed value should be 1.761309. This t value needs to be converted to an $\bar{x}$ value.

The formula for converting a t value to an $\bar{x}$ value is very similar to that used to convert a z value to an x value:

$$\bar{x} = \mu + ts_{\bar{x}}$$

- Enter the formula in cell E8 which will add the mean (in cell E1) to the product of the t value (in cell E7) and the standard error (in cell E4).

The answer, 13.40978 oz, is the sample average amount of cereal which would be exceeded by only 5% of the sample of 15 children assuming that the average amount eaten by all children was 12 oz.

Let's consider a slightly different version of the problem:

An advertising agency wants to determine whether a new campaign for Crunch-O cereals has increased consumption among 8- to 12-year-olds who eat cold cereal. Prior to the campaign, those in the population group consumed an average of 12 oz of Crunch-O per month. If the campaign had no effect, average consumption would remain at 12 oz. A sample of 15 children was chosen whose consumption after the campaign averaged 13.9 oz with a standard deviation of 3.1 oz. Assuming the campaign had no effect (and the population average remained at 12 oz), within what interval, symmetrically distributed about the mean, would 95% of sample means fall?

The diagram for this problem is shown below. The shaded central region has an area of .95, and the values of $\bar{x}_L$ and $\bar{x}_H$ must be determined.

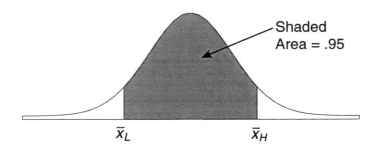

- Since the mean, sample size, and standard deviation for this problem are the same as those for the previous problem, copy the region D1:E4 to G1:H4. An easy way to do this is to select D1:E4, place the mouse pointer on the boundary of the selected region, press and hold the Ctrl key while dragging the boundary to the new location.

- Add the following labels to cells G5:G10: "Mid Prob," "TINV Prob," "t," "x bar L," "x bar H," and "width."

- In cell H5 enter the given probability of a sample mean having a value in the central region, .95.

Compare the shaded region shown in the diagram above with that required by TINV (shown in the diagram on page 180). The probability required by TINV is the *complement* of that given in the problem, and is shown in the diagram above by the nonshaded region under the density function. Since the area under the entire density function is 1, the area of the nonshaded region is 1 minus the area of the shaded region.

- Enter the formula in cell H6 which will calculate 1 minus the value in cell H5. The displayed number should be 0.05.

- Select cell H7. Click the Function Wizard button. Select TINV and go to the dialog window.

- In the "probability" field enter the address for the TINV probability, H6. In the "degrees_freedom" field enter the expression which will subtract 1 from the value given in the cell where the number of observations is (H3). Click the "Finish" button. The value displayed in H7 should be 2.144789.

This t value is the t value corresponding to $\bar{x}_H$. There is also a negative t value corresponding to $\bar{x}_L$. Since both have the same absolute value, the negative t value must be –2.144789.

- Enter the formula in cell H9 which adds the product of the positive t value (in H7) and the standard error (H4) to the mean (H1). The displayed value should be 13.71672.

- Enter the formula in H8 which will do the same as that in H9 except with the negative t value. Since the standard error is (always) positive, adding the product of the negative t value and standard error is the same as subtracting the product of the positive t value and standard error. The displayed value should be 10.28328.

- In cell H10 enter the formula which will calculate the difference between the value in cell H9 and that in cell H8. The displayed value should be 3.433449.

The answer to this problem is that 95% of the means of samples of size 15 will be between 10.28328 and 13.71672.

Let's consider the effect of the degrees of freedom on the width of this interval by determining the change in the width of this interval which would occur if the sample had a size different from 15 (but with the same standard deviation).

- Change the value of n (H3) to 10. Observe what happens to the t value (H7), the standard error (H4), and the interval width (H10). (With a sample of size 10, the interval width should be 4.435216.) Switch the value in H3 back and forth between 15 and 10 until you have determined the way all three of these values change.

When the sample size goes down, the degrees of freedom also decreases. This causes the *t* value to increase (to 2.262159 when *n* is 10). Refer again to the diagram on page 180. As the value of *t* goes up, the boundary moves further from the mean, 0, of a standard *t* distribution. Since the *t* value of the boundary for the left tail has the same absolute value (but negative sign), it too moves away from the mean and the interval becomes larger. Conversely, if the sample size (and degrees of freedom) becomes larger, the width of the interval containing the central 95% of *t* values decreases. Since the *z* distribution is the limit of the *t* distribution as the degrees of freedom increases toward infinity, the width of the interval containing 95% of *z* values must be narrower than the corresponding interval for any *t* distribution.

When the number of observations goes down, the standard error goes up. This reinforces the effect of the change in the *t* value caused by the change in degrees of freedom. Conversely, an increase in sample size causes the standard error to go down which reduces the width of the central interval. The impact of the change in the standard error is much larger than the impact of the change in the degrees of freedom of the *t* distribution.

▼ Exercises

1. A bottle-filling machine is designed to fill bottles with an average fill of 2.02 liters. A sample of 20 bottles is selected. The average fill of the bottles in the sample is 1.99 liters and the standard deviation is .09 liters. Assume that the machine is operating properly and really is filling *all* bottles with an average fill of 2.02. What is the probability that a random sample of 20 bottles could have a sample average fill of 1.99 or less? Assume that the filling process is normally distributed.

2. For the question above, determine an interval symmetrically distributed about the population mean of 2.02 liters within which would fall 90% of the means of samples of 20 bottles.

3. The average time required for students to complete the registration process at a university has been 55 minutes. A university administrator is trying a new procedure. Under this procedure, the registration times of 25 randomly selected students are recorded, resulting in a sample mean of 50.2 minutes and a sample standard deviation of 8.7 minutes. Assuming that there has been no improvement in the average time with the new procedure, determine the probability that the mean time

for 25 students would be 50.2 minutes or less. Assume that student registration times are normally distributed.

4. A bolt-making machine is designed to produce bolts whose length is normally distributed with an average of 2 inches and a standard deviation of .1 inches. If the machine is working properly, what is the probability that a sample of ten bolts would have an average length of 2.05 inches or more?

5. For the problem above, determine the value of the length of the bolts such that only 5% of the samples of 20 bolts would have means less than that length.

6. Decreasing the number of degrees of freedom causes the shape of the standard *t* density function to change. The function goes up in the tails and down in the middle. This change is similar to that which happens with the normal density function when the value of the standard deviation is increased. Is it the same? Investigate this by changing the "t vs z" worksheet. Change column B so that NORMDIST is used rather than NORMSDIST so that you can vary the value for the standard deviation. Use a low value (1 to 4) for the degrees of freedom of the standard *t* distribution. Now change the standard deviation of the normal curve so that the tops of the two curves are the same height. Are the two curves identical? If not, describe the differences. Print the plot showing the two curves with the same heights. Put your name on the header, and use the title to document the value for the dof of the *t* curve and the value of σ for the *z* curve.

7. When samples of size 30 are chosen, the distribution of sample means is fairly close to the normal distribution even when the population follows the skewed distribution we tried last. According to the standard rule of thumb for the central limit theorem, this should not be the case for smaller sample sizes. Investigate the case of samples of size 15. Reload the chap6.xls spreadsheet, but be sure to turn off automatic recalculation *before* you open it. Change the formulas in column AF so that they calculate the average of the first 15 cells in each row instead of the first 30. Also change the standard deviation of the normal curve (cell AI3) so that it reflects the new sample size. Although it is not necessary, it might speed up recalculation if you deleted the second 15 in each row. If the population's skew comes through in the distribution of sample means, you should tend to see bars on the right side of the distribution above the normal line while those on the left are below the normal curve. Recalculate the spreadsheet several times to check if this is the case. Rescale the horizontal axis so that you can see more of the plots. Print out some of the plots to show what you have seen.

Chapter 7

Confidence Intervals on a Population Mean

Inferential statistics generally involves a straightforward application of the concepts of a sampling distribution. One of the techniques of inferential statistics is interval estimation. Suppose you need to know the mean of a population, but only data from a (properly drawn) sample is available. How can you take information from a sample and use it to *infer* information about a population? The best single-value (or *point*) estimate you can give for a population mean is the sample mean. It is best in the sense that no other calculation can be made of the data in the sample yielding a single number which is likely to be as close to the population mean as is the sample mean.

Using the sample mean as an estimate of the population mean has one drawback—it is certain to be wrong! A sample mean, as we saw in the previous chapter, is a continuous random variable. A population mean, on the other hand, is not a random variable. It is a fixed value, even though it is unknown. The probability that a continuous random variable will ever precisely equal a fixed value is zero. Therefore, the probability that any sample mean will ever precisely equal the population mean is zero. Clearly statistics needs a technique for providing estimates of a population mean which can sometimes be correct.

The sampling distribution of the mean provides a technique for determining intervals within which a sample mean may lie with nonzero probability. These problems, examples of which were worked in the previous chapter, are worded like this, "Find an interval symmetrically distributed around the population mean which will contain $x\%$ of sample means." By using the t distribution, it is possible to use a sample standard deviation to solve this type of problem. The interval boundaries are found by evaluating the following expression:

$$\mu \pm t s_{\bar{x}}$$

The center of this interval is μ, the population mean. The lower bound is below μ by an amount equal to $t s_{\bar{x}}$ while the upper bound is above μ by the same amount. The value of *t* is determined by the size of the *x*% in the problem and by the size of the sample (degrees of freedom). The value of the standard error, $s_{\bar{x}}$, is determined by the sample standard deviation (*s*) and the sample size (*n*).

In most situations the value of μ is unknown. If we knew μ, there would be no point to estimating it with a sample! If we don't know the value of μ, there's no way we can calculate the boundaries of an interval symmetrically distributed around μ which contains a given percentage of sample means. Even though its value is unknown, both μ and the the interval around μ still exist. If we pick a sample, there is no way of knowing whether or not the mean of that sample lies within the interval. But we do know the *probability* that it lies within the interval. How can this be used? Consider the diagram below of a density function of a sampling distribution of the means.

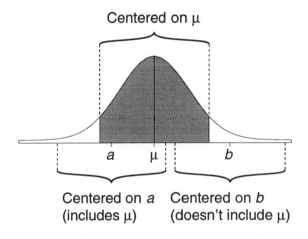

Suppose the shaded central region, which is centered on μ, has an area of .95. The portion of the horizontal axis below the shaded region represents the range of values, symmetrically distributed about the mean, within which a single sample mean has a .95 probability of falling. If we know nothing about the population, then we can't know the actual values of the boundaries of that range. If a sample is drawn and its mean is calculated, we cannot know for sure if that mean lies within the range of values (as does *a* in the diagram) or outside the range (like *b*). But we know it has a 95% chance of being inside the range and an only 5% chance of being outside the range.

Suppose we construct an interval of the same width as the unknown interval around this sample mean. We can do this by adding and subtracting $ts_{\bar{x}}$ from the sample mean, which we can calculate entirely from the data of the sample. This value, $ts_{\bar{x}}$, is called the *sampling error*.

Notice that if the sample mean lies with the range containing 95% of the sample means (like *a*), the interval centered on it will include μ. If the sample mean lies outside the range containing 95% of the sample, then the interval centered on it will not contain μ. Since there is a 95% probability that the sample mean does lie within the range, there is a 95% probability that this interval centered on the sample mean will include the unknown value of μ. Such an interval is called a *95% confidence interval*. Intervals can be constructed to other confidence levels, such as 80%, 90%, or 99%, by using the appropriate value for *t* in the expression for the sampling error.

▼ Using Excel to Determine Confidence Intervals

- Start Excel with a new blank workbook and save it in a file named chap7.xls.

- Double click the "Sheet1" worksheet tab and change its name to "CI on Mu."

Consider the following problem:

A manufacturer wants to test a batch of light bulbs for lumen output. A sample of light bulbs was tested with the following results:

1326, 1336, 1351, 1365, 1209, 1343, 1259, 1365, 1308, 1349

Determine a 95% confidence interval estimate for the mean lumen output of all light bulbs in the batch. The lumen output of all bulbs can be assumed to be normally distributed.

- In cell A1 enter the label "Data." In cells C1:C9 enter the following labels in the order given: "n," "mean," "std dev," "std err," "conf level," "t," "samp error," "lower bnd," "upper bnd."

Column D will contain the statistics given by the labels in the same row of column C.

- In cells A2:A11, enter the data from the problem.

Many of Excel's built-in functions will automatically ignore blank cells. This will be used to create a worksheet which can determine confidence intervals for samples of varying size.

- Select cell D1. Click the Function Wizard button. In the "Statistical" category choose COUNT.

- When the Step 1 dialog window opens, be certain an insertion point is in the "value1" argument field. If it is not, click the mouse pointer in that field.

- Click the mouse pointer on the column heading of column A. (The column heading is the gray square at the top of the column with the letter "A" in it). The argument field will contain "A:A." Doing this is equivalent to selecting the entire column, including the label and all of the blank cells. This style of addressing can be used in any function and in the Name Box to refer to entire columns. Multiple columns can be selected by giving the starting and ending column letters. "C:E," for example, would refer to all of columns C, D, and E.

- Click the "Finish" button. Cell D1 will display "10" which is the number of data items in column A, the size of the sample.

The COUNT function only counts cells displaying numbers. It ignores labels and blank cells. It will include functions if they display a number. Many of the other Excel functions designed to do calculations behave the same way.

- Observe the behavior of the COUNT function by entering the number "0" in cell A14. Then delete that number so that the value displayed in D1 is "10."

- Using the "A:A" addressing style, enter the formula in cell D2 to calculate the mean of the numbers in column A. The displayed value should be 1321.1.

- Enter the formula in cell D3 to calculate the standard deviation of all the numbers in column A. The displayed value should be 50.38397.

- Enter the formula in cell D4 to calculate the standard error. Recall that the standard error is the standard deviation (in cell D3) divided by the square root of the sample size (in cell D1). The value displayed in D4 should be 15.93281.

- Enter "95%" in cell D5. Be sure to enter the percent symbol "%." Reselect cell D5 and observe the value in the formula bar.

Excel regards the percent symbol as a type of cell format. Entering a number followed by a percent sign is equivalent to first entering the number as a proportion between 0 and 1 and then clicking the Percent Style button to set that cell's format. The cell will now set to display any value as a percent.

- To see the effect of the percent style, select D5 again and enter the number "95" without the percent sign. The cell will display "9500%"! Select the cell again and enter ".95." Now it again displays 95%.

The formula to be entered in cell D6 will determine the t value corresponding to the level of confidence (.95 for this problem) and the degrees of freedom. The TINV function will convert a probability to a t value, but the probability it expects is not the area of the central region corresponding to the confidence level. Refer to the diagram on page 180. TINV must be given the two-tail probability represented by the two shaded regions. The confidence level corresponds to the area of the unshaded region in the center. These two areas are complementary; they must sum to one. To determine the tail areas, simply subtract the confidence level from one.

- Select cell D6. Click the Function Wizard button and select the TINV function.

- In the "probability" argument field, enter an expression which will subtract the confidence level in cell D5 from one. Check the value displayed to the right of the argument field. It should show the value "0.05."

- In the "degrees_freedom" argument field, enter the expression which will subtract one from the sample size in cell D1. The value displayed to the right of the field should be "9." Click the "Finish" button. The value displayed in cell D6 should be 2.262159.

- Enter the formula in cell D7 to calculate the sampling error. The sampling error, $ts_{\bar{x}}$, is the product of the t value and the standard error. The displayed value should be 36.04255.

- Enter the formulas in cells D8 and D9 to calculate the lower and upper bounds of the confidence interval. The lower bound is the sample mean minus the sampling error while the upper bound is the sample mean plus the sampling error. The displayed values should be 1285.057 and 1357.143, respectively.

The 95% confidence interval on the population mean can be written as:

$$1285.057 < \mu < 1357.143$$

You can determine the 80% confidence interval on the mean by entering ".80" (or "80%") in cell D5. You should get this result:

$$1299.064 < \mu < 1343.136$$

Similarly the 99% confidence interval should be:

$$1269.321 < \mu < 1372.879$$

Notice that the higher the level of confidence, the lower the value of the lower bound and the higher the value of the upper bound. Higher levels of confidence are associated with larger sampling errors and wider intervals than lower levels of confidence. It is desirable for a confidence interval to have as high a level of confidence as possible, but it is also desirable for it to be narrow. What answer do you get from Excel when you ask for a 100% confidence interval?

▼ Using Excel to Determine Required Sample Size

The only practical way of reducing the sampling error without decreasing the level of confidence is to increase the size of the sample. As n increases, the standard error will decrease. The higher degrees of freedom will also slightly reduce the t value associated with a particular confidence level. Larger samples are more expensive to collect and thus some tradeoff between the sample size and the size of sampling error is often needed. In order to investigate that tradeoff, users of confidence intervals will often want to determine the sample size needed to obtain a target sampling error. Since the sampling error, $ts_{\bar{x}}$, requires a standard deviation, it is not really possible to determine the relationship between sample size and sampling error before drawing a sample. It's tough to draw a sample before knowing the sample size required. This problem is so important, however, that we have to assume that some information about the population standard deviation is known. Perhaps historical data can be used or a pilot sample drawn. Assuming that we know something about the *population* standard deviation also sidesteps another issue. If we don't know the size of the sample, what value for the degrees of freedom should be used for the t in the sampling error? Using a value for the population standard deviation enables us to use the z distribution rather than the t distribution for the distribution of sample means. The sampling error in this case is $z\sigma_{\bar{x}}$ rather than $ts_{\bar{x}}$. If we symbolize the sampling error as e, this equation can be written as:

$$e = z\sigma_{\bar{x}}$$
$$= z\frac{\sigma}{\sqrt{n}}$$

Solving for n yields:

$$n = \frac{z^2\sigma^2}{e^2}$$

If the value for *n* is not an integer, the convention is to *round up* to the nearest integer. This formula, including the rounding, is easily evaluated by Excel.

- Double click the "Sheet2" worksheet tab and rename it "n" (the symbol for the size of a sample).

Consider the following problem:

Owners of a fast-food restaurant want to estimate the average amount spent by customers during the lunch hour. A 92% confidence interval is desired with a sampling error of no more than ±$2.00. Based on past experience, they believe the standard deviation of customer expenditures is no more than $5.00. What sample size is needed to achieve this sampling error?

- Enter the following labels in the range A1:A6 of your worksheet: "samp error," "conf level," "z," "sigma," "n1," "n2."

- In cell B1 enter the desired sampling error from the problem, 2. In cell B2 enter the desired confidence level, .92 (or 92%). In cell B4 enter the assumed value for σ, 5.

Cell B3 must contain the *z* value corresponding to the confidence level in B2. This will involve using the NORMSINV function which converts a *left-tail* probability to a *z* value. Furthermore, if you convert the area of the central region corresponding to a confidence interval to the area of the tail to the left of the central region, the *z* value you get will be negative. You want the value displayed in cell B3 to be positive. Refer to Chapter 5, particularly the section beginning on page 140 to review the technique for determining the *z* value you need.

- Enter the formula in cell B3 to convert the confidence level in cell B2 to the appropriate positive *z* value. When the correct formula is entered, the displayed value corresponding to a 92% confidence level is 1.750686.

- Enter the Excel formula in cell B5 which will calculate the value for *n* given in the formula on page 201. Recall that " ^ " is the Excel symbol to raise a number to a power. The expression to square the value of cell B3 would be "B3 ^ 2." When the correct formula is entered, cell B4 should display the value 19.15564.

- Enter the Excel formula in cell B6 which will round the value in cell B4 up to the next integer. Use the CEILING function for this with the number "1" as the value of the "significance" argument. Cell B6 should display the value 20.

This worksheet allows us to easily investigate the trade-offs between decreased sampling error and increased sample size. Suppose, for example, that we wanted to reduce the sampling error by half.

- Change the desired value of the sampling error in cell B1 from "2" to "1." This should cause the required sample size (n_2) to be 77.

Reducing the required sampling error by half more than tripled (or almost quadrupled) the required sample size.

- Reduce the desired sampling error from by half to ±1.00. This should cause the needed sampling size to nearly quadruple again to 307.

As the sampling error gets smaller, it becomes increasingly more expensive (in terms of sample size) to achieve additional reduction.

▼ Simulating the Accuracy of Confidence Intervals

- Double click the "Sheet3" worksheet tab and change its name to "Simul."

Imagine that a hardware manufacturing firm wants to estimate the average life of a radial saw blade which it manufactures. To do this, it chooses a random sample of 15 blades and constructs a confidence interval on the population mean.

Let's examine how this process would work by drawing a sample from a population whose mean we know. We can then determine a confidence interval for that sample, and see whether or not the interval is correct; that is, does it contain the true population average life which we know but the hardware manufacturing firm does not know? Once we have done this for a single sample, we will use Excel's ability to copy formulas to examine the results of confidence intervals for 1,000 different samples.

- Enter the following labels in the "Simul" worksheet: In cell A1 enter the label "Samples." In the range P1:V1, enter the following labels: "Mean," "Std Dev," "Std Err," "t," "Lower Bnd," "Upper Bnd," "Correct?" In cell X1 enter "Conf Level."

The 15 sample values will be placed in a row from columns A through O. The sample statistics will be displayed in the cells below the labels in columns P, Q, and R. The confidence level will be entered in cell Y1. The *t* value corresponding to that confidence level will be entered in the cells in column S and the upper and lower bounds to the confidence interval calculated from a sample will be placed in columns T and U. Formulas will be placed in the cells of column V so that the cell will contain a

"Yes" if the confidence interval for that row is correct (contains the population mean) and a "No" if does not contain the population mean.

- Enter "95%" or ".95" in cell Y1. We'll start with a 95% confidence interval.

Excel's Random Number Generation Tool will be used to simulate the drawing of sample values. The Random Number Generation Tool can draw samples from several different distributions, including the normal distribution. The values for the mean and standard deviation given in the Tool's dialog window are parameters for the population distribution from which the random numbers are drawn, not values for the sample. Let's assume that the life of all saw blades is normally distributed with a mean of 100 hours and a standard deviation of 15 hours.

Our procedure will be to first develop the statistics for one sample and then use Excel's copying ability to extend that to 1,000 samples. In order to provide you with feedback on whether or not the formulas you have entered for the statistics are correct, a "dummy" sample will be used to develop those statistics. When the formulas for the statistics are known to be correct, the dummy sample will be overwritten by a realistic sample using the Random Number Generation Tool.

- In cells A2:O2 enter the series of numbers beginning with 65, incrementing by 5 and ending with 135. This can be done by entering the number "65" in A2 and "70" in B2 and either selecting those two cells and dragging the fill handle to O2 or by selecting the entire range and opening the Edit menu, choosing Fill and then Series.

- In cells P2 and Q2 enter Excel formulas to calculate the mean and standard deviation of the numbers in the range A2:O2. Use relative cell addresses.

The values displayed in cells P2 and Q2 should be 100 and 22.36068, respectively.

- Enter the formula in cell R2 to calculate the standard error by dividing the sample standard deviation in cell Q2 by the square root of 15. The displayed value should be 5.773503.

- In cell S2 enter the formula to calculate the *t* value corresponding to the confidence level in cell Y1. Use an *absolute* cell address reference to cell Y1 so that you will be able to change the confidence level and have the *t* value change automatically and so that you will be able to copy this value to other cells and still have the reference to Y1. You can use a constant value for the degrees of freedom because we won't change the sample size in this lesson. When the formula is correctly entered, the value displayed in S1 will be 2.144789.

- Enter formulas for the lower and upper bounds in cells T2 and U2. The lower bound is the sample *mean* minus the product of the *t* value and the standard error (which is the sampling error). The upper bound is the sample mean *plus* the sampling error. Be sure to use relative cell addresses to refer to the mean, *t* value, and standard error. The displayed value for the lower bound should be 87.61706, and the displayed value for the upper bound should be 112.3829.

Column V will be used to determine whether or not a confidence interval includes the true population mean of 100. The confidence interval for the "sample" currently in row 2 ($87.6 < \mu < 112.4$) clearly does include 100, but the formula needs to be checked to be certain that it can correctly determine when a confidence interval does not contain 100.

The confidence interval includes the value 100 if two conditions are both met. First the value in cell T2 (the lower bound) must be less than or equal to 100 and the value in cell U2 (the upper bound) must be greater than or equal to 100. As is often the case with Excel, there is more than one way to do this, but a method will be explained below which will display the word "Yes" if the confidence interval includes 100 and "No" if it does not.

- Select cell V2. Click the Function Wizard button. Under the category "Logical" select the function name IF.

The IF function has three arguments. Excel evaluates the "logical_test" argument. If it is true, the IF function will return or display the value in the "value_if_true" argument. If the "logical_test" argument is not true, the function will return or display the value in the "value_if_false" argument. You will enter an expression in the "logical_test" argument which will be true if and only if the confidence interval includes 100. Let's skip that argument initially.

- Enter the word "Yes" in the "value_if_true" argument field. Enter the word "No" in the "value_if_false" argument field. These words can be entered either with or without the quotation marks. If you enter them without quotation marks, Excel will later automatically insert them.

The next step is to enter an expression in the "logical_test" argument field which will be true if 100 lies between the values displayed in T2 and U2. This requires two tests in Excel and the logical test is to be considered true only if both tests are true. To do this requires nesting a function.

- Click the Function Wizard button in the IF dialog window beside the "logical_test" argument field. In the "Logical" function category, choose the function named AND. A dialog window for the AND function will open.

The AND function has two or more arguments. Each of these arguments is a logical expression which can be true or false. The AND function returns or displays the value TRUE if all the logical expressions which are arguments are true. If one or more of these expressions is false, the AND function returns the value FALSE.

- Enter the expression "T2<=100" (without quotation marks) in the "logical1" argument field. (The "<=" is the way you indicate "less than or equal to" since there is no key for the symbol "≤.") Since the displayed value of T2, 87.61706, *is* less than 100, this expression is true, and you should see "TRUE" to the right of the argument field where the argument's value is displayed.

- Enter the expression "U2>=100" in the "logical2" argument field (also without quotation marks). Since the displayed value of U2 is 112.3829, this expression is also true, and you will see the value "TRUE" appear in the region in the upper right-hand corner of the window giving the function result.

Did you notice that once you began entering material in the "logical2" argument field, a new "logical3" argument field appeared? In this case we only want two arguments, but the function can accommodate any number by opening a new argument field as soon as the last one begins to be filled.

- Click the "OK" button. You should return to the IF dialog window. The "logical_test" field will contain the embedded AND function: "AND(T2<=100,U2>=100)." Since this is true for the current values of T2 and U2, the function result is "YES." Click the "Finish" button and cell V2 will display "Yes."

- Test the operation of the formula in cell V2 by changing the values in A2:O2. Enter the series of numbers from 100 to 114 with each cell having the value one more than the cell to its left. The 95% confidence interval should have a lower bound of 104.5234 and an upper bound of 109.4766. Since 100 lies below this range, cell V2 should display "No." Now enter the series in A2:O2 going from 50 to 64 (increment 1). Now the lower bound should be 54.52341 and the upper bound 59.47659. Since 100 lies above this range, V2 should again display "No."

We now know that the statistics and confidence interval are calculated correctly and that the test for the correctness of the confidence interval is working. Let's draw the samples.

- Open the "Tools" menu on the Menu Bar and choose "Data Analysis...." The Data Analysis dialog window will open. Choose "Random Number Generation." The Random Number Generation Tool dialog box will open.

- Enter "15" in the "Number of Variables" field and "1000" in the "Number of Random Numbers" field. This will result in 1,000 rows of 15 random numbers. Each row will be a separate sample of size 15.

- Click the small downward pointing arrow beside the "Distribution" field to open the list of choices. Click "Normal."

- Once you have chosen the normal distribution, two fields labeled "Mean" and "Standard Deviation" will appear in the "Parameters" area. Enter the value "100" for the mean and "15" for the standard deviation.

- Select the button beside "Output Range" and enter the address A2 in the "Output Range" field. The first row of data will replace the numbers we have used to set up the sample statistics.

- Click the "OK" button in the dialog window. Since the first sample will replace existing data, Excel opens a warning window. Click the "OK" button in that window. Because of the large number of values being generated, you may get another window warning that selection is so large you will not be able to undo the command. Click the "OK" button in this window as well.

Be patient! The generation of 15,000 random numbers will take a little time. The status bar will say that the values are being calculated, but it won't show an animated indicator. The mouse cursor will have the beloved hourglass shape. Your patience will eventually be rewarded by a screen full of numbers.

The next step is to copy the statistics formulas in columns P through V down through all the rows of samples. Since there are 1,000 samples and they start in row 2, the last row is row 1001.

- Select the region P2:V1001. This is most easily done by using the Name Box. Open the "Edit" menu on the Menu Bar. Select "Fill" then "Down." Copying the first row to the next 999 will take a few seconds.

- Once the copying is done, glance at the cells in column V. Most of them should display "Yes." If they do not, something is wrong. In this case, look at the cells in column S. All of them should have the same value (2.144789). If they do not, you probably did not make the cell address in the formula in cell S2 absolute. Check it and correct if necessary. If it was wrong, recopy cell S2 down the 999 cells below it.

Glancing down column V should convince you that most of the samples result in confidence intervals which do include the true population mean, 100. Some, however, do not. The next step is to have Excel produce a count on the number of samples with correct confidence intervals versus the number of samples with incorrect confidence intervals.

- Scroll your worksheet so that cell V1 is in the upper left corner of your screen.

- Enter the following labels in cell range W4:W6: "Correct," "Incorrect," and "Total."

- Enter the following labels in X3 and Y3: "Number" and "Percent."

- Select cell X4. This cell will contain the number of times "Yes" is displayed in cells in column V.

- Click the Function Wizard button. In the "Math & Trig" category select the function named COUNTIF.

The COUNTIF function will count the number of cells in a range which meet a specific criteria. If the criteria is that the cells display a certain value, only that value need be placed in the criteria argument field. We will use this function to have cell X4 provide a count of the number of times the word "Yes" appears in column V.

- In the "range" argument field enter the cell range V2:V1001.

- Enter "Yes" in the criteria field. This time you *must* include the quotation marks! Click the "Finish" button. The value displayed in cell X4 should be a number close to 950.

- Select cell X5. Use the COUNTIF function to count the number of times "No" appears in the range V1:V1001. You should get a value close to 50.

- Select cell X6 and click the AutoSum button. Press the Enter key. The sum of the number of cells with "Yes" and the number with "No" should be 1,000.

- Select cell Y4. Enter the formula to convert the value in X4 to a proportion of the total by dividing the value in X4 by the total in X6. Note that Excel may not immediately display the value when the formula is entered because it must update the worksheet. Enter a similar function in Y5 to convert the value in X5 to a proportion of the total.

- Select cell Y6 and use the AutoSum button to have it display the sum of cells in cells Y4 and Y5. They should sum to 1.

- Select cells Y4:Y6. First click the Percent Style button ![Percent Style button], then click once the Increase Decimal button ![Increase Decimal button].

The three cells should now display numbers as percentages with one value to the right of the decimal point. Compare the value displayed in cell Y4 with the confidence level you entered in cell Y1.

- Scroll down your worksheet until you find two cells displaying "No." Jot the addresses of the cells in the margin to the left.

- Change the value of cell Y1 from 95% to 99%. Don't forget to type the percent sign.

Excel will take a few seconds to recalculate the worksheet. You can monitor its progress on the status bar.

Recall that when the confidence level is increased, the sampling error (and the width of the confidence interval) increases. Every sample whose 95% confidence interval included the mean will still include the mean when the confidence level increases to 99%. Some of the samples whose 95% confidence intervals did not include the mean will now include the mean because those intervals are wider.

- Check the two cells whose addresses you noted above. Have either or both of them switched from being a "No" to a "Yes?"

- Experiment with lower confidence levels, including 80%, 50%, and 25%. Compare the value of the confidence level with the percentage of the 1,000 samples whose confidence intervals are correct.

The confidence level and the percentage of the 1,000 samples with correct confidence intervals should always be close in value regardless of the value of the confidence level. So what does the confidence level mean? If we choose a sample and construct a 95% confidence interval from that sample, is it correct to say that there is a 95% chance that the population mean lies within the confidence interval?

No. Consider the first sample on your worksheet, the one in row 2. Once that sample is chosen, a 95% confidence interval either contains the population mean or does not contain the population mean. We can determine which is the case by seeing whether or not cell V2 contains a "Yes" or a "No." There is nothing probabilistic about this question. When confidence intervals are used, of course, we usually do not know what the population mean really is. It is as if cell V2 were covered up; we can't see it. But the fact that we don't know whether a particular confidence interval is correct or not does not make the question probabilistic. Once a sample is chosen, the confidence interval either is correct or not correct, and we don't know which it is.

The confidence level tells us the probability that a randomly chosen sample will have a correct confidence interval. If we construct a 95% confidence interval, there is a 95% probability that we will choose a sample whose confidence interval will be correct. The distinction here is subtle. It is the sample and the confidence interval boundaries calculated from that sample which are random. The confidence level tells us the probability that the confidence interval procedure will result in a correct interval. Once a particular interval is calculated, its boundaries are no longer random; they are fixed. The population mean is also not random; it too is a fixed value. Before the sample was chosen, there was a probability, given by the confidence level, that that sample would result in a correct confidence interval. After the sample is chosen, the confidence interval is either correct or incorrect, and our ignorance of that state does not make the issue random or probabilistic.

▼ Exercises

Sometimes the data we wish to analyze are provided on a diskette or in another form which can be directly read by a computer. It is a good idea to have Excel read such data because it reduces the chance for error. Data provided on a diskette can come in a variety of formats. The easiest for Excel is for the data to be in the form of an Excel workbook. Other formats are common, however, and we often have no choice over the formats in which data we want to use are provided.

Besides Excel workbooks, Excel has no difficulty reading data provided in the formats of competing spreadsheet products like Quattro Pro and 1-2-3. The format used by early versions of 1-2-3 has become a popular way to distribute data because this format can now be read by most spreadsheet programs. Files written in this format typically have names which end in .WKS or .WK1.

The most universal format for data is ASCII Text. Data in this form can be read by most computer programs. Data in this form can be in a file with any name, although common endings for files with ASCII data include .TXT, .DAT., and .PRN. There is nothing in the ASCII format which corresponds to the notion of spreadsheet cells. Although Excel can read ASCII text, it needs help determining exactly what items go into individual cells. In most cases, this is easily done.

In these exercises we will use a set of data collected by a battery manufacturer testing the life of a particular model battery. These data are in the file named BATTERY.TXT, and instructions will be given on how to read them. The first step is the same as that used for reading an Excel workbook.

- Click the Open button.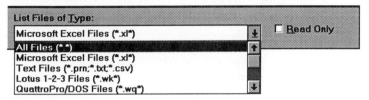

The Open dialog window will initially show only files containing Excel workbooks (and directories or folders). To get the window to show other files (including ASCII files) a setting must be changed.

- Near the bottom left of the Open dialog window, locate the field named "List Files of Type:" (Windows 3.1) or "Files of type:" (Windows 95). Click the small downward-pointing arrow to open the list. If you are using Windows 3.1, the list will look like this:

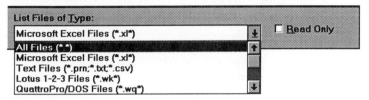

In Windows 95, it will look like this:

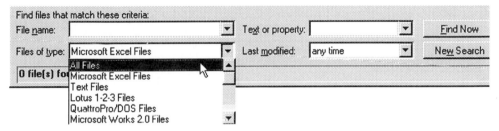

In either case, select "All Files" as shown in the picture. The list will close and "All Files" will appear in the field.

This setting will cause the Open dialog window to show all of the files in the displayed directory.

- In the appropriate fields of the dialog window, select the location of the BATTERY.TXT file. If you are using the data diskette, it will be in drive a: in the "chap_7" directory.

- After selecting the directory, the file name will appear in the "File Name:" filed (Windows 3.1) or "Name" field (Windows 95). The name appearing in the Windows 3.1 field will be "batteries.txt" The name appearing in the Windows 95 field will be "Batteries." Select it and click the "OK" or "Open" button.

Excel will recognize that the data in the file are in the ASCII format. Because this format can be harder for Excel to interpret than other formats, Excel automatically starts the Text Import Wizard and opens the first dialog window. You will notice that the window shows some of the first few lines of the data. Most of the difficulties with using ASCII files occur when there is more than one number in each line. With this file, however, each line has only a single number. Excel has no difficulty with such a file.

- Click the "Finish" button.

Excel tries to treat the ASCII file as a workbook. If you look on Excel's Title Bar you will see the name BATTERY.TXT. Notice that the workbook has only a single worksheet. If you were to make changes on that worksheet and then try to save them, Excel would do its best to write the changed workbook as an ASCII file and would replace the existing BATTERY.TXT with the file it wrote. To avoid this, it is necessary to do the following.

- Click "File" on the Menu Bar. Select "Save As...." The Save As dialog window will open.

- At the bottom of the window is a selection field titled "Save File as Type." You will probably recognize it as similar to the "List Files as Type" field in the Open dialog window.

- The current selection is "Text (Tab delimited)." Click the down arrow to the right of the field and choose "Microsoft Excel Workbook." Notice that the name of the file in the "File Name" field changes from "battery.txt" to "battery.xls."

- Select the drive and directory where you want to save the workbook and click the "OK" button. Notice that the Excel Title Bar now has the name BATTERY.XLS.

1. Based on the data in the worksheet, calculate a 95% confidence interval on the average battery life of all batteries of this type.

2. Suppose the manufacturer wanted future 95% confidence intervals to have a sampling error of, at most, 0.5 hr. Assuming that future population variances are the same as the current sample variance, determine how large a sample would be needed to achieve this sampling error.

3. Produce a chart which shows the relationship between sampling error and required sample size assuming the population has the same standard deviation as this sample of batteries. Do this by creating a series of numbers which goes from 2 to .1 by increments of −0.05. In an adjacent column, determine the sample size required to achieve that sampling error with a 95% confidence interval. Produce a line plot with desired sampling error on the x (horizontal) axis and required sample size on the y (vertical) axis. Give the chart an appropriate title and

print it. Be sure your name is in a header or footer. Describe in words the relationship the chart shows between reduced sampling error and increases in the required sample size.

4. Develop a chart showing the relationship between confidence level and sampling error for a confidence interval of the population mean battery life. First add a new worksheet to your workbook by opening the "Insert" menu on the Menu Bar and selecting "Worksheet." A new worksheet will be created with the name "Sheet2" although Excel will place it in front of the existing "Sheet1." Copy cells A1:A36 from "Sheet1" to the new worksheet. Copy also the cells you used in answering exercise 1 above to the new worksheet. Create a column with the series of confidence levels from 10% to 95% with increments of 5%. In a column to the right enter the formula which will calculate the sampling error associated with each confidence level. Plot this relationship on a line chart with confidence level on the x axis and sampling error on the y axis. Print the chart with an appropriate title and your name in either the header or footer. Describe this relationship and contrast it with the relationship between sampling error and sample size you determined in response to exercise 3.

Chapter 8

▼

Understanding Hypothesis Testing

Hypothesis testing is a technique which lets sample data be used to determine whether or not a characteristic of a population is true. It is used when the need is to answer a yes/no question about the population rather than to determine an estimate of a population parameter. This arises, for example, in quality control when the yes/no question may be, "Is our production system operating properly?" It is used in marketing when the yes/no question might be, "Does the proposed new package lead to higher sales than the old package?"

Hypothesis testing often seems confusing at first to the beginning student, although it is as straightforward an application of sampling distributions as confidence intervals. This chapter will give you a better sense of what hypothesis testing is and what it does. You will use Excel to explore the relationship between the characteristics of a population and those of samples within the framework of hypothesis testing in a way which could not easily be done without a computer. The example used here will be a hypothesis test on a population mean, but the concepts apply equally to all hypothesis tests. The next chapter will deal with the ways you can use Excel to solve hypothesis testing problems and should be read only after you understand what hypothesis testing is about.

There are several steps to solving the typical hypothesis testing word problem. The first step requires setting up the Null and Alternative Hypotheses and determining the appropriate sample descriptive statistics to use in the later calculations. This is often the hardest step, because it is difficult to set up the two hypotheses before you fully understand what hypothesis testing is and what its capabilities and limitations are. Once you understand how hypothesis testing works, you will find it easier to formulate Null and Alternative Hypotheses.

Consider the following quality control example. This problem is a little simpler than the typical hypothesis testing problem in most textbooks, but it's a good starting point to see how hypothesis testing works.

A division of a cereal manufacturer is responsible for packaging the product. When the packaging process is working correctly, the amount of cereal in each box is normally distributed with an average fill of 16 ounces and a standard deviation of 0.50 ounces. A sample of ten boxes is chosen, and the average weight of the ten boxes is 15.43 ounces. Does this provide evidence that the packaging process is working incorrectly?

Although it is unrealistic to assume that we could know anything about the distribution of the weights of *all* the cereal boxes, this example will be easier to explore if we take the standard deviation of 0.50 ounces and the normal distribution as true. The question to be determined through hypothesis testing is whether or not the population mean is really 16 ounces.

▼ The Population and the Null Hypothesis

For this particular problem, the Null Hypothesis is: $H_0: \mu = 16$, and the Alternate Hypothesis is $H_A: \mu \neq 16$. The Null and Alternate Hypotheses are always statements about a population parameter; they are never statements about a sample statistic. They are always constructed so that one of them *must* be true and the other *must* be false. The Null Hypothesis *always* contains an equal sign (including $=$, $\leq$, or $\geq$). The Alternate Hypothesis *never* contains an equal sign. The relational symbol in the Alternate Hypothesis must be $\neq$, $<$, or $>$.

The object of the hypothesis test is to decide whether or not the Null Hypothesis is true. Let's begin by provisionally assuming that it *is* true, and the average fill of all boxes is really 16 ounces. We'll then look at the characteristics of the samples you could expect to get from the population described by the Null Hypothesis by having Excel simulate the choosing of such samples. Finally, we'll decide whether or not the sample described in the problem (with a sample of mean of 15.43) is like those samples. If it is, that's evidence that the sample in the problem is *consistent* with the Null Hypothesis. If it's not, that indicates the sample is *inconsistent* with the Null Hypothesis and provides evidence that the Null Hypothesis is not true.

When we say the average fill is 16 ounces, we're making a statement about the population—all the boxes being filled (which we generally cannot measure directly). The statement also tells something about the weight of any single box of cereal we might measure. If the average weight of all the boxes is 16 ounces, we *expect* the weight of any randomly chosen box to also be 16 ounces. The word "expect" is used here in its statistical sense, not its everyday sense. There is going to be some variation in the weight of individual boxes; no box-filling process can be absolutely perfectly precise. If we regard the actual weight of any box of cereal to be a continuous random number, then the probability is zero that a single box will turn out to have a fill which exactly equals 16 ounces. Most boxes will have a fill close to 16 ounces, and the average fill of boxes chosen will tend to be closer to 16 ounces as the number of boxes chosen increases.

Similarly, if the average weight of all boxes filled is 16 ounces, we *expect* the average weight of a random sample of ten boxes to also be 16 ounces. Just as in the case of an individual box, the average fill of a sample will almost certainly differ from 16 ounces just because of the random nature of the filling process. Finding a sample whose average fill differs a little from 16 does not provide evidence that something has gone wrong with the average fill of all boxes. Finding a sample whose average is very far from 16 would, however, be suspicious. As we saw in Chapter 6, the distribution of sample means has the same mean as the population but a smaller standard deviation. It is thus unlikely that the difference between a sample mean and the population mean will be great. A small difference could well be due to normal random fluctuations, but a large difference could indicate some problem with the population.

▼ How Small a Difference Is Small?

In the example given here, the sample of ten boxes had a mean of 15.43 ounces. This differs from the expected amount by 0.57 ounces. Is this the kind of small difference we expected to happen by chance in a sample of boxes chosen when the average of all (population) is 16? Or is 0.57 ounces too large a difference to explain by chance variability? A small difference would be *consistent* with a population mean of 16, while a large difference would be *inconsistent* with a population mean of 16. If we decide that 0.57 ounces is large, we will conclude that the average fill of all the boxes is not 16. In that case something is wrong with the box-filling process, and it will have to have attention.

Let's examine the question by trying a simulation of the process of filling a box. If the average weight of all boxes is normally distributed with a mean of 16 ounces and a standard deviation of 0.50 ounces, we can use the Random Number Generation Tool to simulate the fill of a single box by generating a random number from a normal distribution with this mean and standard deviation. We can simulate drawing a sample of ten boxes by generating ten such random numbers. In order to see whether a mean of 15.43 from a sample of ten packages is unusual, we will have Excel simulate drawing many such samples and see whether or not a sample mean as different from 16 as is 15.43 is unusual.

- Start Excel if you have not already done so, with a new blank workbook. Save the workbook in a file named chap8.xls. Save it on a hard disk or network drive because it will grow too large to fit on a diskette. Appendix D provides instructions for storing the large file on a diskette at the end of your computer session.

- Double click the "Sheet1" worksheet tab and rename it to "Simul."

- Open the Tools menu and choose "Data Analysis." In the dialog window which opens, choose "Random Number Generation." The Random Number Generation dialog window will open.

- In the Number of Variables field enter "1." In the Number of Random Numbers field, also enter "1." Click the arrow beside the Distribution field and choose "Normal." In the parameters area enter "16" for Mean and "0.5" for Standard Deviation. In the "Output options" area, have Excel place the random number in cell A2. Click the "OK" button.

The value which appears in cell A2 should be very close to 16 and can be thought of as representing the actual amount of product in a single randomly chosen box.

- Simulate the choice of another package by recalling the Random Number Generation Tool. The dialog window will open with the same values as those you filled in before. Simply click the "OK" button, and click the "OK" button when Excel asks if you want to overwrite existing data. A new number will be chosen and written to cell A2. It, too, should be close to 16 but different from the first value.

Let's simulate the selection of a sample of ten boxes.

- Recall the Random Number Generation dialog window.

- Change the value in the Number of Variables field from 1 to 10.

- Click "OK," and again give Excel the "OK" to overwrite existing data. Ten numbers representing random package weights will appear in cells A2 through J2.

- In cell K1 enter the label "Samp Mean." Adjust the width of column K, if necessary, so the text fits in the cell.

- Enter the formula in cell K2 which will determine the average of the numbers in A2:J2. Be sure to use *relative* cell addresses.

- In cell N1 enter the label "Pop Mean." In cell O1 enter the mean of the population, 16.

- In cell L1 enter the label "Diff."

- In cell L2 have Excel determine the *absolute value* of the difference between the sample average in K2 and the population mean in cell O1. Use the ABS function to determine the absolute value and put an expression as the argument which will subtract the contents of cell K2 from O1. Use a *relative* reference to K2 and an *absolute* reference to O1.

The sample mean should be close to 16. Is the difference between the sample mean and the population mean more or less than 0.57 for this sample?

- Draw a different sample of ten by recalling the Random Number Generation dialog window again and clicking "OK" without changing any of the fields. (Click "OK" when Excel asks if you want to overwrite existing data.) Compare the difference between this sample mean and the population to 0.57.

In the problem we're considering, the sample mean is 15.43, which differs from 16 by 0.57. If the average fill of all cereal boxes really is 16 ounces, then a sample mean should be close to 16 but will likely not exactly equal 16. The samples you have just had Excel simulate are drawn from a distribution where we *know* that the mean is 16. The means of the samples you have just chosen were not *exactly* equal to 16, but were close to 16. Were they closer to 16 than 15.43? In other words, do they differ from 16 by less than 0.57? This provides some information on the question of whether a difference of 0.57 is a small difference or a large difference.

▼ Checking More Samples

The result of two samples is suggestive, but the evidence would be stronger if we look at a larger number. Let's have Excel simulate a *thousand* samples.

- Recall the Random Number Generation dialog window.

- Change the field for Number of Random Numbers from 1 to 1000. Click "OK."

- Click "OK" again when Excel asks if you want existing data overwritten.

- Excel may then display a warning box with the message "Selection is Too Large. Continue without Undo?" Simply click the "OK" button. Excel will simulate the drawing of 1,000 samples of size 10.

When Excel finishes generating the random numbers, the cells containing those numbers will be selected (cells A2:J1001). If that cell region is not selected, use the Name Box to select it. Put a border around these numbers to help set them off from the additional numbers we will add.

- On the Formatting Toolbar, find the Borders button .

- Click the small downward-pointing arrow on the right side of the Borders button. A cascaded set of buttons will open.

- On these new buttons, find the one showing a heavy outlining border . Click it. A heavy border will appear around the set of sample values Excel has generated.

Each row in the set of sample values is a simulated sample. To determine the means of these samples and the differences between those means and 16, we need to copy the formulas in cells K2 and L2, which calculate these values for the first sample to the corresponding rows in columns K and L for all the other samples.

- Copy the formulas in K2 and L2 to the cells in their respective columns from row 3 to row 1001.

Since relative addressing was used in K2 and for the sample mean in L2, and absolute addressing was used for the population mean in L2, each cell in column K now displays the mean for the sample in its row, and each cell in column L displays the absolute difference between that mean and the population mean of 16.

- Save your worksheet.

How can we determine how many of the samples had means which differed from 16 by as much as the sample mean in the problem? There are several ways this could be done. One easy way is to sort the samples in order of the magnitude of the difference between their mean and 16 so that those samples whose means differ from 16 by the most will appear at the top.

- Select the region of cells from L2 through L5.

- Open the Data menu on the Menu Bar and choose Sort.

Since you have a selected region, Excel is unsure whether you want only the selected cells sorted or if you want the current region sorted. The *current region* consists of a rectangular block of cells which are not empty and which are adjacent to the selected cells. Excel will select the current region by expanding the selected area until a row and column are encountered which are completely blank. If you had only selected a single cell (say, L2), Excel would have known you wanted the entire current region sorted since it wouldn't make sense to sort one number.

- In this case we want the entire *current region* sorted. Be sure the radio button labeled "Expand the selection" is selected. Then click the Sort button.

A new dialog window will open, and behind it you will see that Excel has selected a rectangular region of cells including the samples, their means and differences, the sample numbers, and the first row which contains the column labels you have entered.

- At the bottom of the dialog window is a pair of radio buttons in a section labeled "My List Has." Click the button labeled "Header Row."

- Click the arrow beside the selection field at the top the dialog window labeled "Sort By."

- In the list which opens you are to choose which column you want the data sorted by. For those columns which you have entered text labels, the labels will appear in the list. Other columns are indicated by their column label. Since we want the data sorted by the difference between the sample mean and 16, choose "Diff" (at the end of the list). This is the label you put in cell L1 and tells Excel you want the data sorted by the numbers in column L.

- Click the "Descending" radio button to the right of the field displaying "Diff" so that Excel will sort from highest to lowest.

- Click the "OK" button, and Excel will sort all of the simulated samples by the value of the difference between each sample's mean and 16.

Arrange your worksheet so that you can see the values at the top of column L, the difference column. In the entire set of 1,000 samples which Excel simulated, the one with the mean furthest from 16 is now in row 2. The difference between that sample's mean and 16 is shown in cell L2. Is it greater than or equal to 0.57? If not, then none of the 1,000 samples had a mean which differed from 16 by as much as the one in the problem. Perhaps the value in cell L2 is greater than 0.57. If so, see how many of the values in cells below L2 are also greater than 0.57. It is very unlikely (though not impossible) that there are more than three or four samples out of 1,000 with means which differ from 16 by as much as 0.57, and it is very likely that none of the 1,000 samples had a mean which differed from 16 by so much.

▼ An Unusual Sample or a Process Gone Bad?

What has this exercise shown? If the average fill were 16 and 1,000 samples of ten boxes were chosen, none or few of the samples would have means which differed from 16 by 0.57 or more. Thus a difference in a sample mean of 0.57 is *not* the kind of difference you would expect from a randomly drawn sample. It is not a small difference. It is a large difference—one very unlikely to occur by chance. A sample of ten boxes having a mean of 15.43 is thus *not* consistent with all boxes being filled, on average, with 16 ounces.

Knowing this, what do we conclude if, one day, a sample of ten boxes is drawn with a mean of 15.43? Although it is *possible* that the difference is due to chance, the probability of this is very low. There is another explanation, however. If something has gone wrong with the filling process, the population mean might no longer be 16. If the population mean had fallen, say, to 15.40, a sample mean of 15.43 might not be surprising at all. In this case, of course, something has gone wrong which needs correcting. Since a sample mean of 15.43 is so unlikely if nothing has gone wrong, it would be reasonable to conclude from such a sample mean that something has gone wrong. In this case we would *reject* the Null Hypothesis that the population mean (μ) equaled 16, and conclude that the Alternate Hypothesis ($\mu \neq 16$) is correct.

Suppose the sample of ten boxes instead had an average weight of 15.89 ounces? The difference from 16 in this case is 0.11. Scroll through the values in column L until you find a value less than 0.11. What row is this value in? All of the numbers above it are greater than .11. Since the largest number is in row L2, the total number of values in column L which exceed 0.11 is the row number of the first number less than 0.11 minus 1. How many of the thousand samples have means greater than 0.11? What proportion of the thousand samples does that represent?

This proportion is liable to be at least .40, probably more. This shows that there is a high probability that a sample mean can differ from 16 by 0.11 or more. This is a difference which could likely occur by chance; it is thus a *small* difference which is *consistent* with all boxes being filled, on average, with 16 ounces. With such a sample we would *not* conclude that something has gone wrong with the process. We would *fail to reject* the Null Hypothesis.

▼ Summary

Here's a quick summary of the steps we went through in determining that something had gone wrong with the process of filling cereal boxes:

1. The Null Hypothesis was assumed to be correct ($\mu = 16$).

2. Under that assumption, Excel simulated the drawing of 1,000 samples. The assumption was used when the Random Generation Number Tool was told to generate numbers with a mean of 16.

3. The mean of each of the samples was calculated.

4. The difference between each of the sample means and the *expected* value of the sample means (16) was calculated.

5. The differences were sorted from highest to lowest so we could easily determine how many of the samples had means which differed from the population by at least as much as the sample described in the problem.

Had we calculated the proportion of the 1,000 samples with differences at least as great as that of the sample in the problem (0.57), we would have been approximating a probability, and that probability would have been close to zero. This is the probability that a single sample of ten boxes chosen when the process was working perfectly would have a mean further from 16 than the sample mean given in the problem (15.43). This probability, called the *p* value, can be calculated precisely from the distribution of sample means using the techniques explored in Chapter 6, and it is a far easier process than generating a thousand samples.

▼ Determining the *p* Value

- Double click the "Sheet2" worksheet tab and change the name to "p value."

Since in this case the distribution of the fill of all cereal boxes is known to be normal and the standard deviation of the fill of all cereal boxes is known, the distribution of the means of samples is the normal distribution. The steps required to determine the *p* value involve determining the standard deviation of sample means and converting the sample mean given in the problem, 15.43, to a z value, which is called the sample z (or z statistic). The standard error is given by the formula $\sigma_{\bar{x}} = \dfrac{\sigma}{\sqrt{n}}$. The sample z is calculated by using the standard error and the population mean to standardize the sample mean: $z = \dfrac{\bar{x} - \mu}{\sigma_{\bar{x}}}$. The final step in calculating this (two-tailed) p value is to determine the probability of a standard normal random variable having an absolute value greater than the sample z.

First put descriptive labels in the worksheet.

- In cell A1 enter the label "Population Parameters."

- In cell A2 enter "Mean," and in cell A3 enter "Standard Deviation."

- In cell A5 enter "Sample Statistics," in cell A6 "Mean," and in cell A7 "Sample Size."

- Adjust the width of column A so the cells are wide enough to hold the labels.

Enhance the formatting of this worksheet with underlining.

- Select cells A1 and B1 by clicking cell A1 and, while holding down the (left) mouse button, dragging the mouse cursor to cell B1.

- Do the same with cells A5 and B5 except press the Ctrl key while you select these cells. If done correctly, this will result in cells A1:B1 and cells A5:B5 being selected at the same time.

- Click the small downward pointing arrow to the right of the Borders speed button.

- In the cascaded set of buttons which appear, find the button showing a heavy underline and click it. You should see a thick line below each of the formatted cells.

Enter additional labels.

- In cell A9 enter the label "Standard Error."

- In cell A10 enter "Sample z." Before pressing the Enter key, take the mouse cursor (which should be in the shape of a vertical "insert" line), and, while holding down the left mouse button, move it across the letter z. A portion of the text will become surrounded by black. You want only the letter z and the space to the right of the letter z to be so surrounded.

- With the letter z selected, click the Italics button on the Format Toolbar. This will make the z have an italic face, which is a standard for many (but not all) statistics texts.

- In cell A11 enter the label "p value." Give the *p* an italic face using the same technique as was used with the *z* above.

- Enter the data given by the problem in column B to the right of the corresponding labels. The population mean is 16. The population standard deviation is 0.50. The sample mean is 15.43, and the sample size is 10.

The remaining three items are calculated from these numbers.

- In cell B9 enter the formula to calculate the standard error by dividing the population standard deviation by the square root of the sample size. The displayed value should be 0.158114.

- In cell B10 enter the formula to calculate the sample *z* by subtracting the population mean from the sample mean and dividing the difference by the standard error. If entered correctly, the displayed value in cell B10 will be -3.605.

The *p* value is the probability that a normally distributed random variable would be less than −3.605 or more than +3.605. This probability is represented by the shaded area in the normal probability distribution function below (note that the size of the tails in the diagram is not to scale):

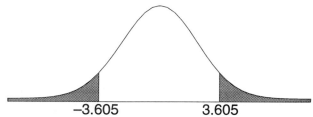

Recall that the NORMSDIST function gives the probability of a normally distributed variable being less than the value given in the function's argument. The area of the left tail will be the value returned by NORMSDIST if the argument is −3.605. To get the area of both tails, this amount must be doubled.

- Enter the formula in cell B11 to determine the area of both tails in the diagram above with the interval boundaries determined by the value of cell B10, not the constant shown in the diagram. If you have the correct formula, the displayed value in cell B11 will be .000312.

As more and more samples of size 10 are drawn, the proportion of those samples whose means would differ from 16 by 0.57 or more will get closer to the *p* value, .000312. This is a very low proportion, and confirms our finding that a sample mean of 15.43 is *not* consistent with the claim that all the cereal boxes, on average, are filled to 16 ounces. With this sample we would *reject* the Null Hypothesis.

Suppose the sample mean had been 15.89 rather than 15.43? What would the p value have been then? You can quickly determine this by replacing the 15.43 in cell B6 with 15.89. The p value becomes .486616. In other words, if all boxes were filled with an average of 16 ounces, just under half of all samples of ten boxes would have means which differed from 16 by as much or more as 15.89 differs from 16. Is this close to the proportion you determined for your 1,000 samples? This is a high proportion and makes it reasonable to conclude that the average fill of all boxes might really be 16 and that the sample's average of 15.89 was due to chance. In this case, we would *fail to reject* the Null Hypothesis. Note that this is not the same as concluding that the Null Hypothesis is true. The fact that the sample is consistent with the Null Hypothesis does not mean that we have shown that it is true, a point which will be explored more below.

▼ From *p* Value to Conclusion

Hypothesis testing is essentially a process which determines whether or not the sample selected has characteristics which make it likely to have been drawn from a population described by the Null Hypothesis. The p value quantifies this relationship between the sample and the Null Hypothesis.

A small p value is evidence that the sample is not the kind of sample which would be expected from the population described from the Null Hypothesis. This leads to the conclusion that the population must be different from that described by the Null Hypothesis. The Null Hypothesis is rejected.

A large p value, on the other hand, tells us that the sample *is* the kind of sample one might expect to draw by chance from a population like that described by the Null Hypothesis. In this case we wouldn't conclude that the population must be different from that described by the Null Hypothesis. The Null Hypothesis is *not* rejected.

Whether or not a sample leads to rejection of the Null Hypothesis depends on how low the p value is. In this example given here, the p value was extremely low. In many, perhaps most, problems, the question is bound to arise of how low the p value must be before the Null Hypothesis is rejected. In many of the hypothesis testing problems which beginning students encounter, the problem will provide a significance level, also referred to as α. For that problem, the significance level is the threshold. If the p value is less than the significance level, the Null Hypothesis is rejected. If the p value is greater, the Null is not rejected. Providing a significance level neatly solves the problem of how low a p value is low, but it begs the larger question of what the value of the significance level *should* be. We will explore this issue below.

▼ Formulating the Null and Alternate Hypotheses

To solve a typical hypothesis testing word problem, you have to first determine the Null and Alternate Hypotheses. One principle to keep in mind is that the Null Hypothesis must describe the population and must give an expected value for the sample. A Null Hypothesis must have an equal sign ($=$); it cannot have a not equal ($\neq$) or a greater than ($>$) or a less than ($<$) sign. Most statistics texts formulate one-tailed Null Hypotheses with greater than or equal to ($\geq$) or less than or equal to ($\leq$) signs. In practice, these are treated as equals signs when the tests are performed (a few statistics texts use equals signs even in one-tailed Null Hypotheses). The reason for these restrictions on the relationships expressed by the Null Hypothesis is that the Null Hypothesis must tell what the population *is*, not what it *is not*. It would have been impossible to generate the simulated samples in this chapter without a specific value from the Null Hypothesis for the average fill of all boxes.

If a problem asks for evidence of a particular situation, that situation is formulated as the *Alternate* Hypothesis. This is because you only come to a conclusion in hypothesis testing when you *reject* the Null Hypothesis. If you reject the Null Hypothesis, you have evidence of the Alternate Hypothesis. For this reason, many students find it easier to formulate the Alternate Hypothesis first, and the Null Hypothesis as the logical opposite of the Alternate Hypothesis.

▼ Significance Level

A Null Hypothesis describes a population and tells us what to expect from a sample. The hypothesis is tested by randomly selecting a sample and calculating the appropriate sample statistic (such as the sample mean). The Null Hypothesis is rejected if the sample statistic is very different from what the Null Hypothesis leads us to expect.

For a hypothesis test on a population mean, the Null Hypothesis gives a value for the population mean. That value is also the expected value of a sample mean. The mean of the sample we have to analyze will very likely differ from the expected value, but is that difference due to chance, or is it evidence that the Null Hypothesis is wrong and is not providing the true expected value? Differences due to chance are usually small, while differences due to an incorrect Null can be large.

The *p* value provides a measure of the difference between the actual sample statistic of the test sample and the expected value of the sample statistic implied by the Null Hypothesis. The *p* value is the probability that if the Null Hypothesis is true, another sample of the same size as that used for the analysis would have a statistic (e.g., sample mean) at least as different from the population parameter (also mean) as the analysis sample.

Since chance can cause small differences between the actual and expected value of a sample statistic, a small difference could occur by chance with a large probability. The *p* value for a small difference between the analysis sample's mean and the Null's expected mean would be large. A *small* difference can occur with a *large* probability. A large *p* value is evidence that the difference between sample and population mean is likely to have occurred by chance. In that case the Null Hypothesis would not be rejected. Instead we would conclude that the difference between the analysis sample's actual mean and the expected mean given by the Null Hypothesis is due to chance.

On the other hand, a large difference between the sample mean and population mean can occur only with small probability. A small *p* value is evidence that chance is not a good explanation for the unexpected sample mean. If chance can't explain the difference, the Null Hypothesis must be wrong and isn't really giving the expected value of the sample mean.

If the *p* value is small, the Null Hypothesis is rejected. If the *p* value is not small, the *p* value is not rejected. An obvious question to ask is, "How small does the *p* value have to be for the Null Hypothesis to be rejected?" This is the issue we will explore in this chapter.

▼ How Small a *p* Value Is Small?

The typical hypothesis testing problem will provide a *significance level* for a test. That significance level is, for that problem, the threshold for the *p* value. If the *p* value is less than the significance level, the Null Hypothesis is rejected. If the *p* value is greater than the significance level, the Null is not rejected. Having a significance level solves the problem, but it also begs the question. When a hypothesis test is performed outside of a course in statistics (in the "real" world), the person doing the test has to decide for herself what the significance level should be. How is that decision made?

▼ The Consequences of Error—Type I versus Type II

Hypothesis testing can never be an infallible method of determining the characteristics of a population. Depending on a sample to provide evidence about a population is always risky since we can never be certain the sample isn't unrepresentative. It's good to remember that the benefit of hypothesis testing also comes from the fact that it depends on a sample, because analyzing the entire population may be impossible or prohibitively expensive. Hypothesis testing is often the only practical way of investigating a population. The investigator using it, however, must explicitly consider the consequences of the unavoidable error which might occur with a hypothesis test.

Consider the problem analyzed above. A cereal packaging company wants to be sure that the average fill of cereal in all boxes is exactly 16 ounces. They monitor this process by selecting a sample and performing a hypothesis test. If the hypothesis test reveals a problem, the company does whatever is necessary to correct the problem. Suppose the hypothesis test gives them the wrong answer? What impact does that have?

There are two types of wrong answers. One possibility is that the filling process is working properly, but by sheer bad luck the company happens to select a sample which is not representative and which leads to the erroneous conclusion that something is wrong. The consequence of this error is needless expense. Equipment may be taken out of service for expensive testing; perhaps the production of cereal may have to be stopped or slowed until the cause of the problem is determined. The company's revenue may suffer. These costs would be gladly paid to fix a problem, but if there is no problem they are needless. Concluding that there is a problem when, in fact, there is no problem, is an example of *Type I* error.

The other possibility is that the filling process has broken, and the average fill of cereal boxes is either too high or too low, but again by sheer bad luck the company happens to select a sample which is not representative and which leads to the erroneous conclusion that something is *not* wrong. In this case, the company continues to incorrectly fill the boxes, unaware of the need for correction. Depending on whether the boxes are underfilled or overfilled, this could result in product waste, higher than expected production costs, regulatory troubles, or loss of confidence by consumers. These are potentially costly problems which the company also wants to avoid. Concluding that there is no problem when one really exists is an example of *Type II* error.

Ideally, of course, the company wants to avoid, or at least minimize, both types of error. The only way to reduce the likelihood of both types of error is to collect more data. This is itself a costly action. If Type I and Type II errors are very rare, it may make more sense to accept the risk of bearing the costs associated with them than to bear the costs of additional testing. We will assume that the company has decided that it can't afford to test samples of more than ten boxes, although the cost of additional data collection should be balanced against the costs of errors. In this chapter you will explore the relationship between the significance level and the balancing of Type I and Type II errors.

▼ Simulating Type I Errors

In this exercise we will use the Random Number Generation Tool to generate samples drawn from a population whose mean is 16. Each sample will be used to test the Null Hypothesis that the population mean is 16. Since this Null Hypothesis is true, the only error that can be made is to reject this Null Hypothesis. Rejecting a true Null Hypothesis is Type I error, and we will see how many samples result in Type I error.

• Double click the "Sheet3" worksheet tab and rename it "Type I."

• Use the Random Number Generation Tool to generate 1,000 samples ("Number of Random Numbers" = 1000) of size 10 ("Number of Variables" = 10) drawn from a normal distribution with mean 16 and standard deviation 0.5. Have the Tool place the output beginning in cell A2. This is exactly the same process you went through to generate the 1,000 samples on "Sheet1." If you haven't quit Excel since doing that, the Random Number Generation Tool will already have the correct entries in all fields of the dialog window, and you need merely click the "OK" button.

Each row of ten values will be treated as an independent sample. Each hypothesis test will be performed using *only* data from the sample. When an investigator does a hypothesis test, he will only have data from a single sample. We will pretend that 1,000 investigators each has access to only one sample. Although we know that the true population mean really is 16, no investigator can know that. Thus no investigator can ever know whether or not his hypothesis test has led him to a correct or an incorrect conclusion.

Since all data used for the hypothesis test must come from the sample, we must use each sample's sample standard deviation. This means using the t distribution rather than the normal distribution. Once the mean is standardized, it will be called the sample t or t statistic. Before proceeding, let's do a little formatting.

- Select the entire set of random numbers. If you have just generated the numbers, they will already be selected. Otherwise, select cell A2. With the Shift key held down, press the End key and the right arrow key. With the Shift key still held down, press the End key and the down arrow key.

- Open the Format menu on the Menu Bar and choose "Cells." In the dialog box which opens, click the folder tab at the top which says "Borders." In the area of the dialog box on the left labeled "Border," click the field beside "Outline." A line should appear in that field. In the area to the right labeled "Style," click the field which has a double line, the one on the top right. Click the "OK" button.

It's usually easier to use the Borders button than to use the Format menu as you did here, but this method offers a few more options.

The first row will be used for labels. Before doing that, activate the option in Excel to have text labels occupy multiple lines within a cell by following these instructions:

- Select the entire first row of the worksheet by clicking the Row Heading for row 1.

- From the "Format" menu choose "Cells."

- In the dialog box which opens, click the folder tab at the top labeled "Alignment."

- Click the small field beside "Wrap Text." An x should appear in the field. Click "OK."

- Enter the following labels in row 1 of the worksheet:

- In cell A1 enter the label "Samples."

- In cell K1 enter "Sample Mean."

Notice how the cell (and its row) became taller. The "Wrap Text" option allows words to move to a new line within a cell.

- In L1 enter "Sample Standard Deviation."

- In M1 enter "Standard Error."

- In N1 enter "Sample *t*." The *t* can be made italic after it has been entered by selecting it (moving the mouse cursor across the *t* with the left mouse button pressed) and the clicking the Italics speed button on the Formatting Toolbar.

- In O1 enter "*p* Value." Make the *p* italic.

- In P1 enter "Reject or Not?"

▼ Constructing 1,000 Hypothesis Tests

With each of the 1,000 samples, we want to construct a separate hypothesis test on the question of whether or not there is evidence that the filling process is working improperly. This will be done first for the first sample (in row 2). The tests will be done on the remaining 999 samples by copying the formulas from row 2 downward.

The Null and Alternate Hypotheses for this test are:

$$H_0: \mu = 16 \text{ and } H_A: \mu \neq 16.$$

The first step is to calculate the sample statistics.

- In cell K2 enter the formula to calculate the mean of the values in A2:J2.

- In cell L2 enter the formula to calculate the sample standard deviation of the values is A2:J2.

- In cell M2 enter the formula to calculate the standard error (the standard deviation of the means of samples of size 10). Recall that this is the sample standard deviation divided by the square root of the sample size (10, in this case).

The easiest way to express the square root of 10 is to use the square root function with 10 as the argument, SQRT(10). Notice that this requires Excel to actually calculate the square root of 10. Since we plan to make another 999 copies of the formula, we can save Excel a little work if we substitute the "SQRT(10)" in the formula with the actual square root of 10.

- Select "SQRT(10)" in the formula in cell M2 by moving the mouse cursor across that text while holding down the left mouse button. When selected, the background behind SQRT(10) will be black and the lettering will be white. Be sure that the background behind "=L2/" is still white. Once the correct area is selected, press the F9 function key on your keyboard. The text "SQRT(10)" will then be replaced by the number which is the square root of 10 (approximately 3.16227766016838). Press the Enter key, and the value for the standard error for the first sample will appear.

The sample *t* is calculated according to the following formula:

$$t = \frac{\bar{x} - \mu}{s_{\bar{x}}}$$

- Enter the following formula in cell N2 to calculate the sample *t*. Use the number 16 for μ. The formula is "=(K2-16)/M2."

The *p* value for the first sample equals the probability of a random variable with the standard *t* distribution and 9 (*n* – 1) degrees of freedom having an absolute value greater than the absolute value of the sample *t*. In the diagram below, the *p* value equals the area of the shaded regions.

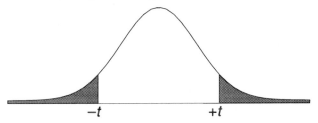

- Select cell O2 and click the Function Wizard button. Select TDIST from the "Statistical" category.

Recall that the "x" argument corresponds to the +*t* in the diagram above. It must be positive. Even if the value in N2 is positive, the sample *t* will be negative for some of the samples.

- Use the ABS function in the "x" field to calculate the absolute value of the sample *t* in cell N2.

- The "degrees_freedom" field should have *n* – 1. Since *n* = 10 for these samples, simply enter the number "9" in this field.

- Enter the number "2" in the "tails" field. This will cause TDIST to return the area of both tails as shown in the diagram.

- Complete the hypothesis tests for the remaining 999 samples. Copy the formulas in cells K2 through O2 down their respective columns to row 1001. A quick way to do this is to use the Name Box to select K2:O1001, and use "Fill" on the Edit menu.

Column O now contains the *p* values for the test of the Null Hypothesis that the population mean is 16—which is correct for these samples. Look down at the values to see what *p* values look like for samples drawn from a population which is correctly described by the Null Hypothesis. Since the p value is a probability, which must be less than 1, most of these values should be large.

Given a significance level, we can complete the hypothesis test for the first sample. If the p value is less than the significance level, the conclusion would be to reject the Null Hypothesis—which would be wrong in this case. Although the p value for the first simulated sample might correctly fail to reject the Null Hypothesis, at least some of the hypothesis tests based on the remaining 999 simulated samples may lead to an erroneous conclusion. What proportion of the 1,000 samples would result in an incorrect rejection of the Null Hypothesis?

▼ Significance Level and Type I Error

All of the samples which result in rejection of the Null Hypothesis will be in error in this case because the Null Hypothesis is true. These will be the samples which have p values less than the significance levels. Let's set up a table in Excel which will allow us to enter a significance level and will calculate the proportion of samples with Type I error.

Enter the following text labels:

- In cell R2 enter "Incorrect Tests."

- In cell R3 enter "Correct Tests."

- In cell R4 enter "Proportion Incorrect."

- In cell R5 enter "Significance Level."

Adjust the width of column R so that these labels fit in their cells. Column S will be used for the data values. The value for the significance level will be entered in cell S5. The initial value for the significance level will be .10, but that value will be changed once the worksheet is set up.

- Enter the value "0.1" in cell S5.

With a significance level we can determine whether the sample would lead to rejection or failure to reject the Null Hypothesis. Rejection will occur if the p value is less than the significance level. We can use the IF function in Excel to perform this test.

- Select cell P2. Click the Function Wizard button. Select the IF function in the "Logical" category.

- Enter the expression in the "logical_test" argument field which is *true* if the p value for the sample in row 2 (cell O2) is less than the significance level in S5. Use a *relative* address for the p value and an *absolute* address for the significance level so the expression will copy correctly. The expression should be "O2<$S$5." If it is true, the Null Hypothesis is to be rejected.

- In the "value_if_true" argument field enter the word "Reject." This should be in quotes, but the Function Wizard will automatically add them if you don't.

- In the "value_if_false" argument field enter the phrase "Fail to Reject." Click the "Finish" button.

- Copy the contents of cell P2 down through P1001. Adjust the width of column P so that "Fail to Reject" fits.

Most of the cells in column P should display "Fail to Reject," but you should have no difficulty finding cells with "Reject."

Cell S2 needs to have a count of the number of tests which "Reject" the Null Hypothesis (incorrectly), and cell S3 needs a count of the number which "Fail to Reject" (correctly). Excel's COUNTIF function can be used to make this count.

- Select cell S2. Click the Function Wizard Button. Select the COUNTIF function in the "Math & Trig" category.

The COUNTIF function has two arguments. The "range" argument contains the address of the range of cells which are to be tested and counted. The "criteria" field can either have an expression which is *true* for those cells in the range to be counted and *false* for those cells not to be counted or it can have a value which the counted cells must equal. We will use the latter approach.

- In the "range" argument field, enter the address of the range of cells for which we want a count of the number of negative values. These are the cells which subtract the significance level from the *p* value, P2:P1001.

- In the "criteria" argument field enter the word "Reject" as it was entered in the IF function. As was the case then, it can be entered with or without quotes. If you enter it without quotes, The Function Wizard will automatically add the quotes when you click "OK." If you entered this formula with COUNTIF directly in a cell (without the Function Wizard) you would have to use quotes. The COUNTIF function will take each cell in the range and determine if its value is "Reject." If so, it will be included in the count, and the total count will display in S2.

- Enter the formula in cell S3 (using COUNTIF) to determine the number of cells in P2:P1001 with "Fail to Reject." Verify that the numbers displayed in S2 and S3 sum to 1,000.

- Enter the formula in cell S4 which determines the proportion of the 1,000 hypothesis tests which are incorrect. This can be calculated by taking the value in S2 and dividing it by 1,000.

- Use the Percent Style button on the Formatting Toolbar to have the values in S4 and S5 display as percentages. Significance levels are sometimes expressed as a percentage and sometimes as a proportion. Use the Increase Decimal button on the Formatting Toolbar so that both percentage show two places to the right of the decimal point.

To better examine the relationship between significance levels, we will create a table which tabulates the relationship between the value of the significance level and the percent of samples with incorrect hypothesis tests.

- Double click the "Sheet4" worksheet tab and rename it "Error Count."

- Create a table on the "Error Count" worksheet by entering labels as shown in the picture below. This will require using formatting techniques used earlier in this chapter (see page 230).

	A	B	C	D	E
1	Empirical Probabilities of Erroneous Hypothesis Tests				
2	Significance Levels	Type I	Type II-Large Difference	Type II-Small Difference	
3	0.1%				
4	1.0%				
5	5.0%				
6	10.0%				
7	15.0%				
8					

Enter values for column B (Type I error) in this table by using the following procedure

- Select cell A3 (with "0.1%") and click the Copy button on the Standard Toolbar to copy the contents to the Windows clipboard.

- Return to the "Type I" worksheet. Select cell S5 (the significance level). Click the Paste button on the Standard Toolbar. The "0.1%"

will be copied from the clipboard and the workbook will be recalculated.

- Once the recalculation has finished, select cell S4 (the proportion incorrect). Click the Copy button to copy the cell contents to the clipboard.

If you were simply to paste the contents of S4 on a new worksheet, the cell formula would be copied. This is not what you want. Instead you want the current *value* of the cell to be copied.

- Return to the "Error Count" worksheet and select cell B3. Do not click the Paste button! Instead, open the Edit menu on the Menu Bar and select "Paste Special...." A dialog window will open. Click the button beside "Values" as shown below, then click "OK."

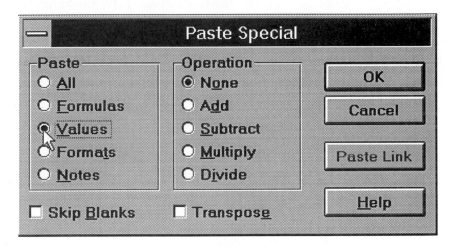

You will notice that cell B3 now displays "0.001." This is indeed the *value* of cell S4 on the "Type I" worksheet, but without the formatting as a percentage. If you want to display the value as a percentage, click the Percent Style button on the Formatting Toolbar, and then click the Increase Decimal button on the same toolbar.

- Repeat the same operations with the other significance levels in row A of the "Error Count" worksheet. Copy each value to cell S5 on the "Type I" worksheet, wait for S4 to be recalculated, and then copy its value back to the corresponding cell in column B of the "Error Count" worksheet.

The values displayed in column B of the Error Count table should be very close to the significance levels in column A. The significance level of a hypothesis test *is* the probability of Type I error. The smaller the significance level, the less likely is Type I error to occur. Based only on this, the smaller the significance level the better.

▼ Significance Level and Type II Error

Let's now investigate the relationship between significance level and Type II error. Type II error can only occur when the Null Hypothesis is false and a test fails to reject it. For the problem we are considering, Type II error can occur only if the average fill of all boxes is something other than 16. The average can be close to 16 or far from 16, but if there is any difference at all, the Null Hypothesis is wrong and should be rejected. As you will see, the likelihood of Type II error depends on how far the true average is from that given in the Null Hypothesis.

▼ Large Difference Between Actual and Hypothesized Mean

We will first consider the case where the actual average fill of the cereal boxes is quite different from that given by the Null Hypothesis. The Null Hypothesis says the average is 16 ounces; we will consider the case where the actual average fill is 15 ounces. You may not consider the difference between 16 ounces and 15 ounces a large difference, but for the cereal company this would amount to a substantial error for an average fill.

- Double click the worksheet tab labeled "Sheet5" and rename it "Type II."

- Bring up the dialog window for the Random Number Generation Tool by selecting "Data Analysis" from the "Tools" menu. If you haven't quit Excel since generating the sample for the "Type I" worksheet, the fields in the dialog window will already be filled out. In this case, change the Mean from "16" to "15." If all the fields are blank, enter "10" for the Number of Variables, "1000" for the Number of Random Numbers, select "Normal" for the Distribution, enter "15" for the Mean, "0.5" for the Standard Deviation, and enter "A2" for the Output Range.

- Click "OK," and click "OK" again when the warning appears offering to continue without undo.

- Draw a double border around the random number as you did on the "Type I" worksheet. Make the border red this time by clicking the down arrow beside "Color" and then clicking the small red square.

The calculations which need to be done on this worksheet are, in most cases, identical to those on the "Type I" worksheet. Rather than reentering them, we can copy them from that worksheet.

- Click the "Type I" worksheet tab. On that worksheet, select the range of cells K1:P1001 (use the Name Box). Click the Copy button on the Standard Toolbar. This copies the formulas which are the contents of those cells to the Windows clipboard.

- Return to the "Type II" worksheet and select cell K1. Click the Paste button on the Standard Toolbar. This copies the contents of the Windows clipboard to the range of cells with K1 in the upper left corner. Examine one cell in each column and verify it contains the correct formula.

Since no significance level has been entered yet in S5, all the cells in column P will display "Fail to Reject." Notice that the copying operation does not adjust the column width.

- Adjust the width of column P so "Fail to Reject" fits in the cells.

Next we will copy the results table. It will have to be changed after copying, however.

- Return to the "Type I" worksheet, select cells R2:S5, and copy them to the clipboard.

- Select cell R2 on the "Type II" worksheet and click the Paste button.

- If the significance level in S5 is not 10%, change it to that value.

On the "Type I" worksheet, a hypothesis test was incorrect if it rejected the Null Hypothesis, because the Null Hypothesis $H_0: \mu = 16$ was true. On the "Type II" worksheet, however, the mean is 15, not 16; thus a hypothesis is incorrect if it fails to reject the Null.

- Select cell S2 on the "Type II" worksheet. Click the Function Wizard button. The dialog window for the COUNTIF function will appear with the argument fields filled out as they are in the formula in S2.

- Change the "Reject" in the "criteria" argument field to "Fail to Reject." Click the "Finish" button.

- Select cell S3 and click the Function Wizard button. Change the value in the "criteria" argument field from "Fail to Reject" to "Reject." Click the "Finish" button.

Verify that the numbers displayed in S2 and S3 sum to 1,000. With a 10% significance level, all or almost all of the samples will correctly reject the Null, and the Proportion Incorrect should be 0.00% or close.

The proportion which is incorrect is an estimate of the probability of Type II error. Notice that the probability of Type II error is quite different from the significance level.

- Return to the "Error Count" worksheet. As you did in the case of Type I errors, copy the significance levels in column A, one at a time, to the "Type II" worksheet in cell S5 and then copy the *value* of the resulting proportion of incorrect tests back to the corresponding cell of column C in the "Error Count" worksheet.

Lower significance levels result in a higher proportion of tests having Type II error, the opposite of the situation with Type I error. In cases where the true population mean (15 in this case) is far from the hypothesized mean (16 in this case) fairly low significance levels (around 10%) virtually eliminate Type II error. Thus while larger significance levels reduce the probability of Type II error (but increase the probability of Type I error), it's not hard to find a significance level for which both probabilities are low.

▼ Small Difference Between Actual and Hypothesized Mean

Let's now consider the case where the actual average fill is not 16 (the Null Hypothesis is wrong), but the difference is not large. We will do this on simulated samples from an average fill of 16.2 ounces. Since the Null Hypothesis is still wrong, a correct hypothesis test would still reject the Null Hypothesis.

First generate 1,000 new samples drawn from a population with mean 16.2.

- Return to the "Type II" worksheet. Recall the Random Number Generation Tool dialog window. If you have not quit Excel since its last use, all the fields will already have the correct values except for "Mean." Change the value in the "Mean" field from 15 to 16.2. If you need to provide values for the other fields, use those given on page 237.

- Using the same method used previously, copy each of the significance levels in column A of the "Error Count" worksheet to cell S5 of the "Type II" worksheet and copy the value of the proportion incorrect shown in cell S4 to the corresponding cell in column C of the "Error Count" worksheet.

Examine the table in the "Error Count" worksheet. For both columns of Type II errors, the proportion of error should go down as the significance level goes up. However, at each significance level, the proportion of errors when the difference between the hypothesized and actual means is small (column C) should be larger than those when the difference is large (column B). The investigator can control the probability of

Type I error by setting the significance level, but cannot control the probability of Type II error since that depends largely on the unknown difference between the actual and hypothesized population means.

The inability to know the extent of Type II error is the reason most statisticians prefer the phrase "fail to reject" the Null Hypothesis to "accept" the Null Hypothesis. The problem with saying that we *accept* the Null Hypothesis is that the probability that the Null Hypothesis is wrong (Type II error) is unknowable and could be large. Statisticians are comfortable, however, with the phrase "reject" the Null Hypothesis even though that, too, could be wrong. The error here is Type I, and we can at least know the probability of that occurring and keep it low.

▼ Exercises

In performing the first hypothesis test discussed in this chapter, we were concerned with the probability that the mean of a sample of ten boxes would differ from 16 by more than 0.57 (the amount by which the sample mean given in the problem, 15.43, differed from 16. That probability was estimated empirically by actually looking at 1,000 sample means and seeing how many had means which differed from 16 by more than .57. It was also determined analytically by calculating the p value.

1. If another 1,000 samples were drawn, what is the probability that the number of means which differ from 16 by more than 0.57 would be exactly 0? Exactly 1? Exactly 2? Three or more? Given these answers, do you think your set of 1,000 samples was typical of all the possible sets of 1,000 samples? Why or why not? (Hint: Use the binomial distribution to answer this question. The number of trials is 1,000, and the probability of success is the p value.)

2. Using the second sheet of your workbook find a value for the sample mean which will produce a p value of exactly .01. Start with 15.4, and increase the digit in the tenths place (initially "4"—the digit just to the right of the decimal point) until the p value switches to a value greater than .01. Then reduce the tenths place by one so the p value is again less than .01 and add a "5" to the hundredths place (the digit just to the right of the tenths place). Adjust the "5" up and down until you find the value for the hundredths place that keeps the p value just below .01. Then add a "5" to the thousandths place (just to the right of the hundredths) and make the same adjustment continuing to the right until the p value which appears in your worksheet displays exactly as .01. What is the z value associated with this sample mean? This z value is the *critical z* for a significance level of .01. Suppose you were given

a problem just like that given at the beginning of this chapter, but with a different sample mean. What values for that sample mean would result in a p value less than .01? Explain.

3. Format the table on the "Error Count" worksheet to approve its appearance and print it out. Be sure your name is on the printed sheet.

4. The *power* of a hypothesis test is its ability to avoid Type II errors. What does the table you just printed say about the power of this test and the difference between actual and hypothesized population mean? Is the power high or low if the difference is small?

5. Suppose that we had generated another set of simulated samples and told the Random Number Generation Tool to use a mean of 16.1. Would a correct hypothesis test have rejected or failed to reject the Null Hypothesis that $\mu = 16$? Why?

6. In the set of simulated samples described in the previous question, would you have expected the proportion of incorrect tests for each significance to be more or less than the proportions for the samples you investigated?

Chapter 9

Hypothesis Testing of a Population Mean

Excel provides powerful tools which make it easy to perform hypothesis tests on a population mean. This chapter will provide you with instructions and exercises to help you gain proficiency in using Excel for this, but does assume you have a basic understanding of the procedures involved in performing a hypothesis test.

▼ Critical Values versus *p* Values

Two different approaches are used for hypothesis testing: the critical value approach and the *p* value approach. For tests in which the significance level is known, these two approaches are equivalent. They will always give the same answer. Both are easy to do with Excel, and both will be covered in this chapter. The critical value approach is more traditional, but the increased use of computers has made the *p* value approach increasingly popular.

▼ *z* Distribution versus *t* Distribution

Hypothesis testing on a population mean is based on the sampling distribution of the mean which is treated as following either the normal distribution or the Student's *t* distribution. The normal distribution is the correct one to use for problems in which the variance or standard deviation of the population is known.

If the standard deviation of the population is not known, and a sample standard deviation is used instead, the *t* distribution is the correct distribution to use. In the case of very large samples, the *t* distribution would have a large value for the degrees of freedom. Such a *t* distribution is very close to a normal distribution, and the error associated with using the normal distribution may be very small. Some textbooks use the normal distribution in this situation because tables for the normal distribution are easier to use than tables for the *t* distribution, and more accurate *p* values can be determined from a normal distribution table than from a *t* distribution table. Computers eliminate this advantage of the normal distribution, and there is no reason not to use the *t* distribution whenever the population standard deviation is unknown regardless of the sample size.

▼ Two-Tail Tests on a Population Mean, σ Known

Consider the following problem:

A manufacturing firm purchases sheet metal from a supplier who maintains that the average thickness of the metal sheets is 15 mils and that the standard deviation of the metal sheets is .1 mills. The manufacturing firm selects a sample of 50 sheets and determines that the sample mean is 14.982 mils. At the .05 level of significance, is there evidence that the population average claimed by the supplier is incorrect?

The first step is to determine the Null and Alternate Hypotheses. The Null Hypothesis is: $H_0: \mu = 15$, and the Alternate Hypothesis is $H_A: \mu \neq 15$.

No sample standard deviation is given by the problem. Instead we have the claim of the supplier that the population standard deviation, σ , equals .1. Thus the normal distribution is the correct distribution to use. The test is two-tailed because the Null Hypothesis is subject to rejection if the sample mean were either above or below 15.

First prepare a workbook in Excel for this chapter.

• Open Excel with a new blank workbook.

• Under the "File" menu choose "Save As," and save the worksheet as chap9.xls.

• Double click the "Sheet1" worksheet tab at the bottom of the Excel window and rename it "2-Tail, Sigma Known."

• In Cell A1, enter the text, "Population Data."

• In Cell A2, enter the text, "Hyp Mean."

• In cell A3, enter the text, "Std Dev."

• In cell A4, enter the text, "Std Err."

The headings in this table will be highlighted by increasing the font size.

- Select cell A1. In the formatting toolbar, find the font size tool 10 ▾ . Click the down arrow on the right and then click the "14," on the list which opens. Do not worry about the text spilling beyond the cell boundary.

- Enter additional labels as shown in the picture below. Adjust the heading labels to 14 points, and the other labels to 10 points. Change the *n*, the *z*'s, and the *p*'s to italic face as shown. When finished, your worksheet should look like this:

	A	B	C	D	E	F	G	H	
1	Population Data			Sample Data			Test Statistic		
2	Hyp Mean			Mean			Sample *z*		
3	Std Dev			*n*					
4	Std Err								
5									
6	Significance Level			*p* Value			Critical *z* Values		
7	Alpha			2 Tail			Lower		
8							Upper		
9	Decision								
10	*p* value								
11	Critical *z*								
12									

Next enter the data values from the problem.

- In cell B2, enter the population mean given by the Null Hypothesis.

- In cell B3 enter the population standard deviation.

- In cell E2 enter the sample mean, 14.982.

- In cell E3 enter the size of the sample, 50.

- In cell B7 enter the significance level (α), .05.

The remaining cells contain formulas performing calculations on these values.

The standard error is placed under "Population Data" in this worksheet to emphasize that it is calculated here from the population standard deviation. The formula for the standard error is:

$$ \mathrm{SE}(\bar{x}) = \sigma_{\bar{x}} = \frac{\sigma}{\sqrt{n}} $$

- In cell B4 enter the Excel formula to calculate the standard error. The displayed value should be 0.014142.

- The formula for the sample z is:

$$z = \frac{\bar{x} - \mu}{\sigma_{\bar{x}}}$$

In cell H2, enter the Excel formula for the sample z. The displayed value should be -1.27279.

The decision of whether or not to reject the Null Hypothesis depends on whether or not this sample is like those likely to be chosen at random from a population for which the Null Hypothesis is true. If the Null Hypothesis is true, the population mean is 15, and samples should have means close to 15. This sample has a mean of 14.982. Is that close enough to 15 that it is reasonable to believe the difference is due to chance, or is it so far from 15 that such a sample is unlikely to have been drawn from a population with mean 15? To reject the Null Hypothesis, the probability of a randomly chosen sample having a mean which differs from 15 by at least as much as 14.982 differs from 15 must be less than the significance level (.05 in this case). In that case we decide the difference is too great to be due to chance and the difference must be due to the population mean being different from 15. If the probability is greater than the significance level, we conclude that the Null Hypothesis could be true and the different sample mean could be the result of chance.

The decision of whether or not to reject the Null Hypothesis thus involves a comparison between the sample z and the significance level. Before this comparison can be done, either the sample z must be be converted to a probability (the p value approach), or the significance level must converted to a z value (the critical value approach).

▼ The *p* Value Approach

The p value approach involves converting the sample z to a probability that a z value will have an absolute value which exceeds the absolute value of the sample z. For this problem, that probability is represented by the shaded area in the density function depicted on the next page.

Excel's NORMSDIST function can be used to determine this area. NORMSDIST has a single argument and provides the probability of a standard normal variable having a value less than that argument. This is represented as the area to the left of the argument on the probability density function. If the argument for NORMSDIST were -1.27279 (the

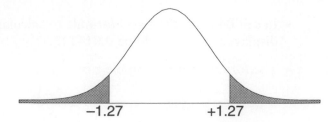

sample *z* for this case), the area of the left shaded tail in the density function above would be returned. If NORMSDIST were given the positive value 1.27279, the area to the left of that value would be returned. This would be equivalent to 1.0 minus the area of the right shaded tail. What we want here is the area of *both* shaded tails. An easy way to get that would be to double the value NORMSDIST would return if given a negative parameter, -1.27279 in this case.

Although the sample *z* in this case *is* a negative number, the formula for the *p* value should be one which would work even if the sample *z* were positive. A way to ensure that the parameter given NORMSDIST is negative is to take the negative of the absolute value of the sample *z*.

- Enter the following formula in cell E7: "=2*NORMSDIST(-ABS(H2))." The value 0.203092 will be displayed.

If the *p* value is less than the significance level, the Null Hypothesis should be rejected. If the *p* value is greater, the Null Hypothesis should not be rejected. For this problem, the *p* value, .203092, is clearly greater than the significance level, .05, so the Null will not be rejected. An Excel formula can make this decision.

- Select cell B10. Click the Function Wizard button and choose the IF function in the "Logical" category.

The IF function has three parameters. The first, "logical_test," is the relationship to be tested. In this case, we want to have Excel test whether the *p* value is less than the significance level. The *p* value is in cell E7 and the significance level is in cell B7.

- In the "logical_test" field, enter "E7 < B7." Notice that after you enter this test, the word "FALSE" appears just to the right of the field. This is because the current value of E7 is *not* less than the current value of B7. This may change, however, for different hypothesis tests.

- In the field labeled "value_if_true," enter the text "Reject." This is what the function will display whenever the condition E7 < B7 is true.

- In the "value_if_false" field, enter the text "Fail to Reject." Click the "Finish" button. Cell B2 should show "Fail to Reject," the correct result of this hypothesis test.

The Null Hypothesis was not rejected in this test because the sample mean was close enough to the hypothesized population mean (15), that chance could explain the difference with a probability (p value) higher than the significance level. If the sample mean had been further from 15 than 14.982, chance would have been a less likely explanation, and the Null Hypothesis would have been rejected. The sample mean of 14.982 is so close to the value the supplier claims is the average for all the metal sheets, that the conclusion of the test is that we do not have evidence that the supplier's claim is incorrect.

What if the mean had been further from 15? Select cell E2 and enter 14.95, which is further from 15 than is 14.982. Notice how the value of the sample z increases (in absolute value) to -3.53553, and the p value decreases to .000407, which is less than the significance level. What is now the value of cell B10?

Change the value of E2 back to 14.982. Let's now consider how Excel can be used to test a Null Hypothesis using the critical z approach.

▼ The Critical Value Approach

Rather than converting the sample z to a probability, the critical value approach converts the significance level to a z value. These z values define "critical regions," as shown in the diagram below.

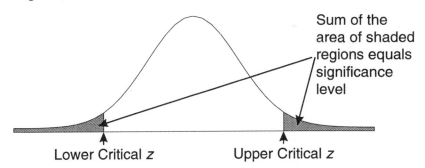

The critical regions refer to those z values which are greater than the upper critical z or lower than the lower critical z. The probability of a z value falling within the critical region is equal to the shaded area which is equal to the significance level. Notice that the area of each tail for a two-tail critical region is half the significance level.

The determination of a critical value requires an inverse distribution function. For the z distribution this is NORMSINV.

- Select cell H7 and click the Function Wizard button. Choose "NORMSINV" from the "Statistical" category. (Be sure not to choose the similar NORMINV. Look for the "S" in the middle.) Notice the description of this function at the bottom of the Function Wizard window. Click the "Next" button.

The dialog window for the NORMSINV function has only one parameter, "probability," the probability of getting a z value less than the value the function returns. For the lower critical z in the diagram above, that probability is the area of the left tail. Since the area of both tails is given by the significance level (in cell B7), the correct probability for the lower critical z is half that.

- Enter in the "probability" field of the dialog box an Excel expression which will divide the value of cell B7 by 2. Click the "Finish" button. The lower critical z value, -1.95996, should appear in cell H7.

- Select cell H8. Enter an Excel formula to determine the value of the upper critical z. There are several acceptable ways of doing this. All will result in cell H8 displaying a positive number with the same absolute value as that displayed in H7.

Since it is always the case that the upper and lower critical z's have the same absolute values, it is common for just the positive value to be referred to as the critical z.

We can now determine whether or not to reject the Null Hypothesis by comparing two z values, the test statistic and the critical z. If the test statistic lies within the critical region, the Null Hypothesis is rejected. The test statistic will lie within the critical region if its absolute value exceeds the absolute value of a critical z (both of which have the same absolute value). Let's automate this decision as we did the p value decision.

- Select cell B11 and click the Function Wizard button. Select the IF function. In addition to the "Logical" category, you can also find it in the "Most Recently Used" category since it was used with the p value approach.

- Enter this expression in the "logical_test" field: "ABS(H2) > H8." The ABS function returns the absolute value of the value of H2, the sample z, and H8 contains the absolute (positive) value of the critical z. As soon as this is entered, the word "FALSE" will appear to the right of the field, since the absolute value of cell H2 is 1.27279 which is *not* greater than the positive critical z which is 1.959961.

- In the field labeled "value_if_true," enter the text "Reject." In the field labeled "value_if_false," enter the text "Fail to Reject." Click the "Finish" key.

Both cell B10 and B11 should have the same value, namely "Fail to Reject." Change the sample mean in cell E2 from 14.982 to 14.95. Notice that the test statistic changes to -3.53553, which has an absolute value greater than the critical z, which remains unchanged. The values of cells B10 and B11 both change to "Reject." This shows that the final decision of whether or not to reject the Null Hypothesis is the same whether the p value approach or the critical value approach is used.

This worksheet will enable you to perform any two-tail hypothesis test when sigma is known, by simply setting the values of cells B2, B3, E2, and E3 to the values appropriate for that problem. Consider the following problem:

A quality control inspector wants to check the manufacturing process in a plant which makes scales for home use. The scales are tested by having them weigh a precise reference weight which weighs 120 pounds. When the manufacturing process is working properly, the measured weight given by all scales averages 120 pounds with a standard deviation of .015 pounds. The inspector chooses 30 scales and weighs the reference weight with each of them. The average weight reported by this sample of scales is 120.01 pounds. Does the inspector have evidence at the .01 level of significance that the manufacturing process is not working properly?

The Null and Alternate Hypotheses for this problem are $H_0: \mu = 120$ and $H_A: \mu \neq 120$.

- Enter the hypothesized population mean, population standard deviation, sample size, sample mean, and significance level in the appropriate cells. When you have done this correctly, the sample z will be 3.651484, the p value will be .000261, and the upper critical z will be 2.575835.

The Null Hypothesis is rejected. Yes, the inspector does have evidence that the manufacturing process is not working properly.

▼ One-Tail Tests on a Population Mean, σ Known

- Double click on worksheet tab "Sheet2" and rename it "1-Tail, Sigma Known."

Consider the following problem:

A mail-order furniture company has been receiving complaints from customers concerning delays in receipt of merchandise shipped to them. The furniture company suspects the fault lies with the trucking firm it employs to ship the furniture to its customers. The trucking firm assures the furni-

ture company that the average time from shipment to delivery is no more than 15 days with a standard deviation of 4 days. The furniture company decides to check this by selecting a random sample of 50 shipments and determining the precise time between shipment and delivery. The furniture company decides that a significance level of .02 is appropriate for this issue.

The concern here is that average delivery time may exceed the 15-day standard. There is no concern that the average may be less than 15 days. This makes a one-tail test appropriate here. When the furniture company takes its sample, it will calculate the sample mean. If the sample mean is less than 15 days, there would be no reason to do any further calculations. A sample mean which is less than 15 cannot possibly provide evidence that the population mean exceeds 15. If, however, the sample mean exceeds 15, a procedure is followed to determine if the high sample mean could be due to chance.

Many statisticians would formulate the Null and Alternate Hypotheses as follows:

$$H_0: \mu \leq 15$$
$$H_A: \mu > 15$$

Other statisticians, however, while keeping the Alternate Hypothesis the same as that shown above, would formulate the Null Hypothesis as:

$$H_0: \mu = 15$$

If it is necessary to calculate a test statistic, the value for the population mean (μ) used in the calculation would be that given by the second form of the hypothesis test. In other words, for the purposes of calculating a test statistic, an inequality in the Null Hypothesis is treated as an equality.

Suppose the furniture company selects a sample, and the sample mean is 17. Since this value exceeds 15, further computation is necessary to determine if chance can be excluded as an explanation for the high sample mean.

- Select the first worksheet by clicking the worksheet tab labeled "2-Tail, Sigma Known." This will return you to the worksheet with the two-tail hypothesis test. Much of the calculations on this worksheet are the same as those used for the one-tail test, and they can simply be copied.

- Select cells A1 through H11.

- Click the Copy speed button on the standard toolbar ▣. This will copy the contents of the selected cells to the clipboard.

- Click the worksheet tab at the bottom of the window labeled "1 Tail, Sigma Known," bringing it to the screen.

- Select cell A1.

- Click the Paste speed button on the standard toolbar ▣. The contents of the previous worksheet will be copied to the current worksheet.

Change the data in the worksheet to reflect the values for the current problem:

- In cell B2 enter the hypothesized population mean.

- In cell B3 enter the population standard deviation given in the problem, 4.

- In cell E2 enter the sample mean, 17.

- In cell E3 enter the sample size, 50.

- In cell B7 enter the significance level, .02.

The formula for the sample z is the same for one- and two-tail tests, and the correct value, 3.535534, should appear in cell H2.

The formulas for the p value and for the critical z values need to be changed, and the wording of one cell needs to be changed.

- Change the label "2 Tail" in cell D7 to "1 Tail."

- Double click cell E7. The formula in the cell will appear in place of the value.

The current formula is =2*NORMSDIST(-ABS(H2)). This formula doubles the area of one tail, which is appropriate in the two-tail test case. For a one-tail test, the doubling should be removed.

- Hold down the left mouse button and drag the text cursor across the "2*" so that it (and *only* it) is selected (black background with white letters). Press the Del or Delete key. The corrected formula, =NORMSDIST(-ABS(H2)) should appear. Press the Enter key. The correct value is .000204.

The critical z values for a two-tail test divide the significance level in two parts. The two critical z values define two tails whose *combined* areas equals the significance level. A one-tail critical z defines a single tail whose area equals the significance level.

- Select cell H7 and observe its contents in the formula bar.

The current formula, =NORMSINV(B7/2), divides the significance in cell B7 by 2. For a one tail critical value the division by two should be removed.

- Remove the "/2" from the formula. The corrected formula is =NORMSINV(B7). Press the Enter key. The displayed value should be 2.05375.

- Make any necessary changes to cell H8 so that its value will be the positive number with the same absolute value as that of cell H7.

In a one-tail test, only one of the two critical *z*s is correct for that test. If the sample data are not consistent with the Null Hypothesis, the correct critical *z* will have the same sign as the sample *z*.

The formulas for the decision rules are the same for one- and two-tail tests. For the current data, you should see "Reject" in cells B10 and B11. This result indicates that the furniture company should conclude that the trucking firm's claims are not accurate and that the average delivery time for all shipments exceeds 15 days. If the population mean were 15, the probability of a random sample of 50 deliveries having a mean delivery time of 17 or more is low enough that chance is excluded as an explanation for the high sample mean. If the sample mean were closer to 15, this would not have been the case.

Change the value of cell E2 to 16 (be sure to press the Enter key). The decision should change to "Fail to Reject Null Hypothesis," indicating that the furniture company does not have evidence at the desired level of significance that the average of all delivery times exceeds 15 days. A sample mean of 16 is close enough to 15 that it could have happened by chance. The *p* value shows that the probability of this is almost .04, which is greater than the significance level of .02. What would happen if the significance level were .05? Check this by changing cell B7 to .05, pressing the Enter key, and observing the decision. Change B7 back to .02 before proceeding.

▼ A Warning About One-Tail Tests

Earlier you created an Excel worksheet which completely automates a two tail test. This is not, however, the case with the worksheet for a one-tail test.

Consider, for example, the possibility that the average delivery time for the sample of 50 chosen by the furniture company was 13 days. Enter the value 13 for the sample mean in cell E2. Notice that the decision reported by the worksheet in this case is "Reject" the Null Hypothesis, indicating evidence that the trucking firm's claims are incorrect. But this is wrong! A sample mean of 13 days is consistent with the trucking firm's claim that the average of all delivery times is less than 15 days. That assertion cannot be rejected by a sample which is consistent with the claim. For such a sample, no calculations of *p* values or critical *z* by Excel are needed. In the case of one tail tests, the Excel worksheet should be used *only when the sample statistic is consistent with the Alternate Hypothesis.*

▼ Hypothesis Tests on a Population Mean When σ is Unknown

In the great majority of real hypothesis tests on a population mean, no information about the population, including the population standard deviation, is available. In these cases the sample standard deviation, *s*, must be used, and the *t* distribution is used instead of the normal distribution (although the error in using the normal distribution is minuscule when the sample size is large).

Textbook problems concerning hypothesis tests on a population mean when σ is unknown sometimes provide the sample mean and standard deviation, but sometimes the sample data are provided instead. Determining the mean and standard deviation becomes part of the problem—a more realistic situation. Excel can, of course, easily determine these sample statistics. Some textbooks provide the data for problems on a diskette. In this section we will cover the use of such data.

Although you have produced separate worksheets for the one- and two-tail tests for the case when σ was known, these will be combined into a single worksheet for the case when sigma is unknown. It is very important to recognize that Excel cannot determine for you whether a one-tail or two-tail test is appropriate for a particular problem. Furthermore, in a one-tail test, Excel cannot determine for you if the sample is inconsistent with the Alternate Hypothesis. As you saw earlier, if the sample is inconsistent with the Alternate Hypothesis, calculated *p* values and critical values are incorrect, as would be a decision to reject the Null Hypothesis. The use of Excel, or any other computing tool, can never substitute for an understanding of basic statistical principles.

Prepare a new worksheet for the case when sigma is unknown.

- Double click the worksheet tab "Sheet3" and rename it "Sigma Unknown."

- Return to the previous worksheet, "1 Tail, Sigma Known."

- Copy cells A1:H11 from this worksheet to the the "Sigma Unknown" worksheet.

This worksheet will now be a copy of the previous worksheet. Several modifications need to be made. Either select each cell in turn and make the changes in the formula bar or double click and make the change in the cell.

- Change the "z" in cells G2, G6, and A11 to a "t."

- Select cells A5 and A6. From the "Insert" menu choose "Rows." Two blank rows will be inserted in your worksheet below row 5. This will move the text "Significance Level" from row 6 to row 8.

Since the standard deviation will come from a sample rather than from a population, move the cells referring to the standard deviation and standard error from "Population Data" to "Sample Data."

- Select cells A3:B4 and move them to D4:E5. If you wish to review the "drag-and-drop" method for moving cells, see page 31.

- Using the drag and drop procedure, move the contents of cells A12:B13 to B12:C13 (move one cell rightward).

- Copy the contents of cells B12:C13 to B15:C16. The "drag and drop" procedure for copying is also explained on page 31.

- In cell A12, enter the text "1 Tail."

- In cell A15, enter the text "2 Tail."

- In cell D10, enter the text "2 Tail."

- Change the text in cell G9 from "Lower" to "1 Tail."

- Change the text in cell G10 from "Upper" to "2 Tail."

- Erase the contents of the following cells by selecting each and then pressing the Del or Delete key: E9, H9:H10, and C12:C16.

- Click the row heading for row 6 to select the entire row. Open the Edit menu on the Menu Bar and click "Delete." The entire row will be deleted, which will have the effect of moving all of the contents of cells below up one row.

At the completion of these steps, your worksheet should look like the picture on the next page.

The calculations for the standard error and for the test statistic (sample t or t statistic) are correct. Using a sample standard deviation does not

	A	B	C	D	E	F	G	H
1	Population Data			Sample Data			Text Statistic	
2	Hyp Mean	15		Mean	13		Sample *t*	-3.53553
3				*n*	50			
4				Std Dev	4			
5				Std Err	0.56569			
6								
7	Significance Level			*p* Value			Critical *t* Values	
8	Alpha	0.02		1 Tail			1 Tail	
9				2 Tail			2 Tail	
10	Decision							
11	1 Tail	*p* value						
12		Critical *t*						
13								
14	2 Tail	*p* value						
15		Critical *t*						

change the way they are computed except that the standard deviation comes from a sample rather than from a population.

The use of the *t* distribution rather than the normal distribution does require changes within Excel, however, both in the function names and to account for the differences in the way Excel's functions handle the two distributions.

For the *t* distribution, Excel provides the probability for an interval of values greater than the value given it as a parameter. Furthermore, Excel will not accept a negative parameter for its *t* distribution function.

- First change the one tail *p* value. Select cell E8 and click the Function Wizard button. Select "Statistical" under "Function Category" and "TDIST" under "Function Name." Click the "Next" button.

There are three parameters. The first, "x," is the value defining the interval for which the function will return a probability. For a *p* value the test statistic (the sample *t* value) is the proper value for this parameter. However, since TDIST will only accept a positive parameter, we need to specify that Excel should use the absolute value of the test statistic.

- Since the test statistic (sample *t* or *t* statistic) is in cell H2, enter ABS(H2) for the "x" parameter. The value "3.53553..." should appear in the box to the right of the parameter field

- The second parameter is the degrees of freedom, which is the sample size minus one. Since the sample size is in cell E3, enter E3-1 for the degrees of freedom parameter. A "49" should appear to the right of the parameter field.

- The third parameter, tails, can only have the value 1 or 2. If the parameter is 1, Excel returns the probability associated with the interval of values greater than the "x" parameter. If the tails parameter is 2, Excel returns twice this probability. For a one-tail *p* value, the correct value for this parameter is 1.

- As soon as you enter a 1 for the tails parameter, the *p* value will be displayed in a box at the upper right corner of the Function Wizard box. That value should be a little over 0.00045. Click the "Finish" button and the same value will appear in cell E9.

There are two methods of calculating the two-tail *p* value. One method would be to use TDIST exactly as you did in the one-tail case except the "tails" argument is "2" instead of "1." There's an even easier method of converting the one-tail area to a two-tail area:

- Select cell E9. Enter the Excel formula which doubles the value of cell E8. The value displayed in E9 should be 0.0009.

To determine the critical *t* values, we must convert the significance level to *t* values, an operation which requires an inverse distribution function. For the *t* distribution, this is TINV, which works quite differently from NORMSINV, which we used to find critical *z* values. Consider the diagram below.

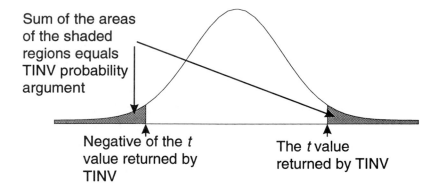

Sum of the areas of the shaded regions equals TINV probability argument

Negative of the *t* value returned by TINV

The *t* value returned by TINV

The Excel TINV function will interpret the probability given it as a parameter as the area of *both* tails in the diagram. Unlike the TDIST function, there is no argument which will allow us to set the number of tails. TDIST returns the *t* value which is the lower bound of the upper tail. The upper bound of the lower tail would be negative but would have the same absolute value.

- Select cell H8 and click the Function Wizard button.

- Select "Statistical" under function category and "TINV" under function name. Click the "Next" button.

We want Excel to give us a *t* value such that the probability of a greater *t* will equal the significance level. We can't simply use the significance level as the "probability" parameter because TINV will divide that probability between both tails as shown in the diagram. To force the area of *one* tail to equal the significance level, the "probability" parameter of TINV needs to be twice the significance level.

- The significance level is in cell B8. Therefore in the "probability" argument field, enter an expression which will calculate twice the value in B8. Use an *absolute* address for cell B8. The field to the right of the argument filed should display 0.04.

- Enter the expression in the "degrees_of_freedom" which will subtract 1 from the sample size (which is in cell E3). Also make the reference to E3 *absolute*.

- At the top of the Function Wizard window the correct one tail critical *t* value, slightly over 2.109873, should appear. Click the "Finish" button, and this value will be shown in cell H8.

The determination of the two-tail critical *t* is very similar.

- Copy the contents of cell H8 to cell H9. Since absolute cell references were used in cell H8, the value of H9 will be the same as H8 after the formula has been copied.

- Select cell H9. Click the Function Wizard button. The window for TINV will appear with the parameters filled out as they were for cell H9.

- For the two tail critical *t*, the probability parameter is the significance level. It currently is twice the significance level. Alter the contents of the "probability" argument field so that it refers to the significance level rather than doubling the significance level. The value 0.02 should appear to the right of the "probability" field.

- The value of the two tail critical *t* at the top right of the Function Wizard window should start with 2.40488. If it is, click the "Finish" button.

Notice that there is no simple relation between the one-tail critical *t* and the two-tail critical *t* as there was in the case of *p* values. The two-tail critical *t* is not twice the one tail critical *t*. The inverse probability function (TINV) must be used to calculate both.

In the previous worksheets, two critical *z* values were given for two-tail tests. The lower value was always negative and always had the same absolute value as the upper value. For this worksheet, only the absolute value is shown, which is the standard convention in statistics.

The final step is to add the decision rules. For decisions based on a p value, the Null should be rejected if the p value is less than the significance level.

- Select cell C11 for the decision rule for one-tail tests based on the p value. Use the Function Wizard to select the IF function (in the "Logical" or "Most Recently Used" categories).

- The one-tail p value for a one-tail test is in cell E8, and the significance level is in cell B8. In the "logical_test" parameter field enter an expression which will be true if the p value is less than the significance level.

- In the "value_if_true" parameter field, enter the text "Reject."

- In the "value_if_false" parameter field, enter the text "Fail to Reject." Click the "Finish" button. The displayed value of C11 should be "Reject."

- Select cell C14 for the decision rule for the two-tail test.

- Use the IF function as you did in the one-tail test. The single change is that two tail p value in cell E9 instead of the one-tail p value should be tested against the significance level in the "logical_test" argument field. Enter "Reject" and "Fail to Reject" in the two "value" argument fields as you did previously. Click the "Finish" button. The displayed value of cell C14 should also be "Reject" the Null Hypothesis.

When using a critical t criteria, the Null Hypothesis should be rejected if the absolute value of the sample t exceeds the absolute value of the critical t.

- Copy the contents of cell C11 to C12. Select C12 and click the Function Wizard button. The IF dialog window will open with the argument fields filled out. The "logical_test" field will have to be completely changed, but the copying saves the need to reenter the text in the two "value" fields.

- In the "logical_test" enter an expression which will be true if the absolute value of the sample t (in cell H2) is greater than the one-tail critical t (in cell H8.) Use the ABS function within the argument field to calculate the absolute value of the value of H2. Click the "Finish" button. "Reject" should display in cell C12.

- Copy the contents of C14 to C15. With C15 selected, click the Function Wizard button. Here again, only the "logical_test" argument field will have to be changed.

- Enter an expression in the "logical_test" field which will be true if the absolute value of the sample t (in H2) exceeds the two-tail critical t (in H9). The only difference between this and the expression used in cell C12 is this time you refer to the two-tail critical t instead of the one-tail critical t.

All of the decision rules should have the value "Reject." Sometimes the results of a one-tail test will differ from those of a two-tail test. Both one-tail tests, however, should always have the same value, as should both two-tail tests.

Change the value for the sample mean (E2) to 13.7. The two one tail Decisions should be "Reject" while the two-tail decisions are "Fail to Reject."

▼ Using the Worksheet

Consider the following problem:

The average balance in a particular type of savings account in a large, multibranch bank has been $2,500. A new branch has opened, and the manager wants to determine if the average balance for this type of account in the branch differs from $2,500. A random sample of 30 accounts is chosen. The sample mean is $2,399, and the sample standard deviation is $250. At the .05 level of significance, does the manager have evidence that the average balance at the new branch differs from $2,500?

A two tail hypothesis test is appropriate for this problem. The Null and Alternate Hypotheses are:

$$H_0: \mu = 2{,}500$$
$$H_A: \mu \neq 2{,}500$$

- Enter the hypothesized population mean, $2,500, in cell B2.

- Enter the sample data (mean = $2,399, $n = 30$, and standard deviation = $250) in the appropriate cells in column E. Note that it is perfectly acceptable to enter numbers with dollar signs and commas. ($2,399 and 2399 are both acceptable).

- Enter the significance level, .05, in cell B8.

If entered correctly, the p value (two-tail) should be 0.034939, and the critical t (also two-tail) should be 2.045231. Under "Decision" the worksheet indicates "Reject Null Hypothesis." So the answer is yes, the manager does have evidence that the average balance at the new branch differs from $2,500.

▼ Using Named Ranges

Often a hypothesis testing problem will provide the complete sample data rather than the sample statistics. It is a simple matter for Excel to compute these statistics directly. A feature in Excel allows you to give a name to a range of cell addresses. This can increase the versatility of worksheets designed to solve a class of problems.

Consider the following problem:

The manager of a firm in the business of telephone solicitation is interested in determining if the installation of new telephone equipment has increased the average sales per worker. Last year, average sales per worker for the month of July were $3,987. As soon as the month of July ended this year, the manager selected a sample of 20 workers and determined the level of sales per worker. These were:

$2,958, $2,215, $4,146, $6,138, $2,893, $2,085, $2,588, $2,218, $3,341, $1,283

Based on this sample, does the manager have evidence, at the .05 level of significance, that average sales for all workers this July exceeded the average of July of last year?

The correct test for this problem is one tail, and the Null and Alternate Hypotheses are:

$$H_0: \mu \leq \$3,987 \text{ or } H_0: \mu = \$3,987$$

$$H_A: \mu > \$3,987$$

- Enter the hypothesized mean, $3,987, in cell B2.

- Double click the worksheet tab at the bottom of your Excel window labeled "Sheet4" and rename it "Data."

- Enter the sample data in column A on the Data worksheet.

- Select the set of sample data (A1:A10).

- Click the cursor in the Name Box (which should show a cell address for one of the numbers in the sample–probably A1 or A10).

- Replace the cell address in the Name Box with the name "data," and press the Enter key. This will give a *range* name to the sample data which can be used in worksheet formulas.

- Click the worksheet tab "Sigma Unknown" to select the worksheet with the formulas.

We will now replace the numbers under "Sample Data" with formulas to calculate the appropriate statistics.

- In cell E2 enter the formula =AVERAGE(data). Notice that this formula refers to the range name of the sample data on the next worksheet. The value which appears in this cell should be $2,987. Notice that Excel continues to use the same *format* (dollar signs and commas) used previously.

- In cell E3 enter the formula =COUNT(data). The COUNT function determines the number of numeric values in the range, which is the same as the sample size, n. The value should be 10.

- In cell E4 enter the formula =STDEV(data). This calculates the sample standard deviation of the data. The value should be $1,353.

What is the conclusion in this case? Notice that the decision for the one-tail test is "Reject Null Hypothesis." This, however, is wrong. The reason can be found in the sample mean, which is $2,987 (2986.5). Since this sample value is less than $3,987, it cannot be used to reject the Null Hypothesis and accept the Alternate Hypothesis because it is consistent with the Null, not the Alternate Hypothesis. *A necessary condition for rejecting the Null Hypothesis (and concluding that there was evidence that the average sales for all workers exceeded $3,987) is that the sample mean must exceed $3,987.* Thus the correct conclusion is to fail to reject the Null Hypothesis and to conclude that there is no evidence that the average sales of all workers exceeds $3,987. Whenever sample data are consistent with the Null Hypothesis, it is always correct to fail to reject the Null Hypothesis regardless of the "Decision" indicated by the worksheet.

Using a name range has an important advantage. Suppose that the manager chooses a larger sample than indicated in the problem. Suppose that the sample was of size 15, and, in addition to the ten values given above, the following five values were also chosen:

$4,200, $3,900, $2,800, $4,400, and $2,910

- Select the "Data" worksheet, and add these five values in column A *after* the ten values already there. The new values should go into cells A11:A15.

- Open the Insert menu on the Menu Bar and select "Name." A cascade menu will open. Select "Define..." from that menu. The Define Name dialog window will open.

- Under "Names in Workbook" you should see the name "data." Click that name with the mouse pointer, and the word "data" should then appear in the top field of the dialog window.

- The bottom field of the dialog window is titled "Refers to:." That field should contain the cell addresses of the range with the name "data" ("=Data!$A$1:$A$10"). Move the mouse pointer across that address so that it is "highlighted." The dialog window should look like that shown below.

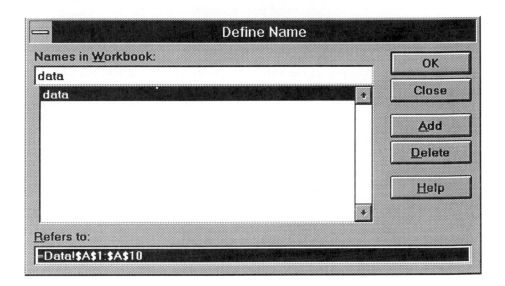

- Place the mouse pointer on cell A1 and select the range containing all of the data by pressing the (left) mouse button and dragging the pointer down to cell A15. The contents of the "Refers to:" field should change to "=Data!$A$1:$A$15", the addresses you have just selected with the mouse. You have redefined the address of the range of cells with the name "data."

- Click the "OK" button and return to the "Sigma Unknown" worksheet. Notice that the sample statistics have changed. The sample mean is now $3,205, *n* is now 15, and the sample standard deviation is $1,198 (1198.224).

Once you redefined the "data" range name, all of the formulas referring to that name automatically changed to reflect the new definition. You can thus use this worksheet to do hypothesis tests on any amount of data without revision as long as you enter the data somewhere in the workbook and give the range containing the data the name "data."

▼ Using Data on a Diskette

You can also read data from a file and bring the file into the worksheet. The simplest way of doing this is to read the file into a workbook and then copy the data from that workbook to the current one.

Consider the following problem:

A car manufacturer has launched a special ad campaign for a particular model car. The manufacturer wants to determine if average sales per dealer for this model exceed 60 during the month following the campaign. A random sample of dealers was surveyed and asked how many of that particular model were sold in the month. The responses were coded and are available in the file cars.txt.

Based on the response to the survey, does the manufacturer have evidence (at the .05 level of significance) that average sales for all dealers during the month exceeded 60?

The test for this problem would be one tail. The Null and Alternate Hypotheses are:

$$H_0: \mu \le 60 \text{ or } H_0: \mu = 60$$
$$H_A: \mu > 60$$

- Enter "60" into the cell on the "Sigma Unknown" worksheet for the hypothesized sample mean (B2). Be sure the significance level (cell B8) is .05.

- Click the Open File button on the Standard Toolbar . A dialog window will open in which you locate the cars.txt file.

There are three fields which you need to adjust: "Drives," "Directories," and "List Files of Type."

- Click the arrow beside the "Drives" field and click the letter by the drive where the cars.txt file is located. For example, if you are reading the file from a diskette, you probably should choose a:. If the file is on a hard disk or a network drive, choose the appropriate drive.

- Click the arrow beside the "List Files of Type" field and click on the choice "Text files (*.prn,*.txt,*.csv)."

- The "Directories" field will display a graphic representation of the directories on the drive you have chosen. If the file is in a directory (such as "chap_9"), double click the mouse pointer on the icon for that directory. The "Directories" field will display any subdirectories within that directory. If the file is in a subdirectory, double click the subdirectory name.

- Click the arrow beside the List Files of Type field and click on the choice "Text files (*.prn,*.txt,*.csv)."

Once the correct directory is selected, you will see the file name, cars.txt, in the long field on the upper left side of the dialog window below "File Name."

- Click on the name cars.txt and then click on the "OK" button. Excel will open the first Text Import Wizard dialog window.

As you will see in that first window, this file only contains one data number per line with a label on the first line. Since the label has three words with spaces, we do not want Excel to regard the space character as a delimiter.

- Click the "Next>" button. Be sure the small square to the right of "Space" in the group of delimiters *does not* have a check in it. Click the "Finish" button.

Excel will create a new workbook with the name (on the Name Bar) "CARS.TXT." The data will be in column A with the label in the first row.

- Select the entire set of data. An easy way of doing this is to select cell A1. Press the "Shift" button on your keyboard, and, while pressing the "Shift," press and release the "End" key, and then press and release the key with the downward pointing arrow. This should select cells A1:A51.

- Click the Copy button.

- Open the "Window" menu on the Menu Bar.

At the bottom of the menu is a list of the open workbooks. This list should include "CARS.TXT" (with a check mark in front of it) and "CHAP9.XLS," the workbook with the hypothesis testing formulas. Click the mouse pointer on the name "CHAP9.XLS." Your screen should immediately display that workbook.

- Click the "Data" worksheet tab to bring it to the top.

- On the "Data" worksheet, select cell A1.

- Click the Paste button. The data on the number of cars sold will be copied to column A of the "Data" worksheet.

- Open the "Insert" menu and select "Name..." then "Define." When the Define Name dialog window appears, redefine the name "data" so it includes the data in column 1 (including A1, the cell with the label).

- Return to the "Sigma Unknown" worksheet by clicking its worksheet tab.

The sample mean shown on the worksheet should be 62.64. Because of the previous formatting, the value may appear as $63.

- Remove the dollar signs from cells B2, E2, and E4 by selecting each cell and then clicking the Comma Style button ▨.

- Increase the number of displayed decimal places for cells E2 and E4 by using the Increase Decimal button ▨.

Is there evidence that the average number of cars for all dealers exceeded 60? Notice that the sample mean, 62.64, *is* greater than 60 and is thus consistent with the Alternate Hypothesis. The calculations appearing on the worksheet enable us to determine whether or not chance is a likely explanation for the high sample value. An examination of the one-tail *p* value (0.020569) shows that probability to be less than the significance level, and thus the decision shown on the worksheet is to reject the Null Hypothesis.

The Null Hypothesis is rejected. Yes, there is evidence at the .05 level of significance that the average sales for all dealers that month exceeded 60.

▼ Exercises

Use the Excel worksheets you have developed to answer the following hypothesis testing questions. State the Null and Alternate Hypotheses, indicate whether or not you reject the Null Hypothesis and provide a yes or no answer to the question asked.

1. A milk bottle-filling machine is operating properly when the average amount of milk placed in each bottle is exactly 1 gallon with a standard deviation of .02 gallons. A random sample of 50 bottles was chosen, and the average amount of milk in the sample was 1.01 gallons. At the .01 level of significance, is there evidence that the machine is not working properly?

2. A testing agency wishes to test the effectiveness of a new brake design in a particular automobile. The brakes are claimed to be able, with an average driver, to stop an automobile traveling at 40 mph in less than

50 feet. A random sample of drivers is chosen to test the brakes and the stopping distances are as follows:

49, 42, 46, 29, 48, 55, 43, 48, 50, 46, 41, 46, 37, 40, 39

Based on this sample, is there evidence at the .05 level of significance that the average stopping distance for all drivers is less than 50 feet?

3. The director of retail operations wants to assign enough tellers to a group of bank branches that the average amount of time any customer will have to spend waiting in line will be less than 120 seconds during peak hours. A random sample of customers was chosen during those peak hours and the amount of time spent waiting in line by each customer was carefully measured in seconds. The data are coded in the file bank.txt. Based on these data, is there evidence at the .01 level of significance that the average amount of time spent by all customers is less than 120 seconds?

Chapter 10

▼

Inferences on a Population Proportion

Some types of data cannot be averaged. In the period prior to an election, polls are taken to measure support for the various candidates. Imagine that you are involved in conducting such a poll for a particular candidate who is hoping to win an election. The first step would be to select a random sample. Once the sample is selected, data would be collected from each person in the sample to determine whether or not that person intends to vote for our candidate. The simplest type of data we might have for each member of the sample is a "yes" or "no." The entire set of data would be a collection of yes's and no's. How can you take an average of data like these? You can't. Instead, you describe the sample by calculating the proportion of people in the sample who said "yes." You can then use the sample proportion to make inferences about the proportion of people in the population who support the candidate much as you used sample data to make inferences about a population mean when the data were of the type that could be averaged.

Once you have a basic understanding of confidence intervals and hypothesis tests of a population mean, you are most of the way to also understanding inferences on a population proportion. The concepts are the same, but some of the mechanics are a little different. Inferences on a population mean are based on the distribution of sample means. Inferences on a population proportion are based on the distribution of sample proportions.

Inferences on proportions are made on "binomial" data—the same kind of data encountered with the binomial distribution. Each individual observation can have only two values, traditionally called "success" or "failure." When the proportion of a sample which falls into a certain category is calculated, an observation in that category is a "success." The rest are "failures." Even though an election (and a poll) may have more than two choices, whenever the proportion favoring a certain outcome is determined, an observation either favors that outcome or does not favor that outcome.

▼ Sampling Distribution of the Proportion

The sampling distribution of the proportion comes directly from the binomial distribution. In the binomial distribution, the random variable is the "number" of successes. In the sampling distribution of the proportion, the random variable is the "proportion" of successes. When a sample is chosen from a population, the sample size, n, can also be thought of as the binomial n trials. The population proportion of successes (π) is also the probability that a single observation selected from the population will be a success and is thus the same as the binomial π. The binomial random variable— number of successes or x—is converted to the proportion of successes (p_s—not to be confused with p value) by dividing by n.

The simple conversion of the binomial random variable to the sample proportion of successes makes it easy to determine the mean and standard deviation (standard error) of sample proportions. The mean of sample proportions is the binomial mean divided by n and the standard deviation of sample proportions is the binomial standard deviation divided by n, which results in the following:

$$\mu_{p_s} = \pi$$

$$\sigma_{p_s} = \sqrt{\frac{\pi(1-\pi)}{n}}$$

As we saw in Chapter 4, under certain conditions (large n, π not too far from 0.50), the normal distribution approximates the binomial distribution. Subject to the same limitations, it also approximates the distribution of sample proportions and is traditionally used for this. As we will see, in the case of hypothesis testing it is possible to use the binomial distribution directly which will give somewhat more accurate results.

▼ Confidence Intervals on a Population Proportion

As was noted in chapter 7 (see the discussion beginning on page 196), determining a confidence interval is closely related to the sampling distribution problem where an interval symmetrically distributed around the mean containing a given percentage of sample values is determined. For example, suppose we knew the population π and wanted to determine the interval around π which would contain a desired percentage of all the sample p_s's. Using the normal approximation, the boundaries would be $\mu_{p_s} \pm z\sigma_{p_s} = \pi \pm z\sqrt{\dfrac{\pi(1-\pi)}{n}}$. If we wanted the interval containing 95% of the values of sample proportions, the appropriate z value would be approximately 1.96.

A confidence interval on a population proportion would be centered on a single sample proportion, but would have the same width ($\pm z\sigma_{p_s}$) as the interval above. There is, however, a problem. The value of σ_{p_s} is dependent on π, and π is unknown (its value is being estimated with the confidence interval). The traditional solution is to substitute the value of p_s from the sample. One justification for doing this is that the value of $\pm z\sigma_{p_s}$ is not highly sensitive to small changes in the value of π (a proposition which will be explored more in an exercise). Therefore if p_s is reasonably close to π, using it in place of π to calculate σ_{p_s} should be acceptable. The formula for a confidence interval on π is thus:

$$p_s \pm \sqrt{\dfrac{p_s(1-p_s)}{n}}$$

This can be easily implemented with Excel.

- Start Excel with a new blank workbook and save it as chap10.xls.

- Change the name of the "Sheet1" worksheet to "CI on Pi."

- Enter labels so your worksheet looks like the picture below. The larger labels are 14-point font and the smaller are in 10-point font. Manually adjust the column width so that the columns are wide enough to accommodate the 10-point labels. Allow the larger labels to continue to the unused adjacent cells.

	A	B	C	D	E	F
1	Sample Data			Confidence Interval		
2	n			Level		
3	ps			z value		
4	std err			samp err		
5				lower bound		
6				upper bound		
7						

Consider the following problem:

A candy manufacturer wants to estimate the impact of an advertising campaign in a metropolitan area by measuring brand recognition for a new confection marketed for children. A random sample of 350 children from the area was chosen and the children were asked if they knew of the new brand. Of these, 112 recognized the new brand. Based on this sample, provide a 95% confidence interval estimate of the proportion of all children in the area who would recognize the new brand.

- Enter the value of n, 350, in cell B2.

- Have Excel calculate the value of p_s in cell B3 by entering a formula which divides 112 by 350. Then "highlight" the formula by dragging the mouse cursor across it on the formula bar (with the left mouse button pressed). After the formula is "highlighted," press the F9 function key. The formula will be replaced by its value, 0.32.

- Enter the formula in B4 to calculate the standard error as $\sqrt{\dfrac{p_s(1-p_s)}{n}}$.

  One way of doing this is to have the Function Wizard display the dialog window from the SQRT function ("Math & Trig" category) and enter the expression for $\dfrac{p_s(1-p_s)}{n}$ in the "number" argument field. Be sure to include the parentheses, and remember that multiplication must be shown explicitly with "*." If the formula is entered correctly, the displayed value will be 0.024934.

- Enter "95%" (without quotes) in cell E2. Be sure to include the percent sign, which will cause Excel to interpret the value as 0.95 (verify in the formula bar).

The z value in cell E3 is the absolute value of the boundaries of a region in the center of the standard normal distribution whose area is given in cell E2. This is illustrated in the picture on the next page. The shaded central region has an area equal to the confidence level. The two boundaries are labeled z and $-z$. Both have the same absolute value and it is this value which is needed in E3.

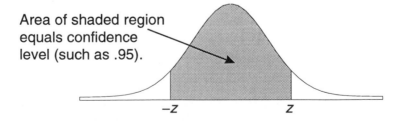

Area of shaded region equals confidence level (such as .95).

$-z$ z

Determining the z value requires using the NORMSINV function. That function has a single argument: "probability," and provides the z value for which the area to the left in the density function equals the "probability" argument. There are two different ways of doing this. One way would be to enter an expression for the "probability" argument which would calculate the area of the left tail from the value of E2. This is a simple expression, but the value returned by NORMSINV would be –z, a negative number. This means the formula in E2 would have to convert the negative value provided by NORMSINV to a positive value, perhaps by using the ABS function. The other way would involve putting an expression in the "probability" argument which adds the area of the central region to the area of the left tail. That sum is the area to the left of the positive z value on the right in the picture. With this area for a probability, NORMSINV would return the positive z value.

- Using either of the methods described above, enter a formula in cell E3 which will determine the z value for the confidence level in E2. With 95% in E2, the displayed value will be 1.959961. Be sure this is displayed as a positive number.

- The sampling error is the product of the z value (in E3) and the standard error (in B4). Enter the formula in E4 to calculate this. This displayed value will be 0.04887.

- The lower bound is the value of p_s minus the sampling error, and the upper bound is p_s plus the sampling error. Enter the formulas in cells E5 and E6 respectively. The displayed values will be 0.27113 and 0.36887.

The 95% confidence interval on the proportion of all children in the area who recognize the brand name is between 0.27113 and 0.36887.

- Check the worksheet by changing the value of n to 275, the confidence level to 99%, and the value of p_s to .45. The lower bound of the 99% confidence interval is 0.372725, and the upper bound is 0.527275. Be sure cells E5 and E6 of your worksheet display these values.

▼ Determining Sample Size for a Desired Sampling Error

Larger samples generally result in narrower confidence intervals. Although it's desirable for confidence intervals to be as narrow as possible, sample size is usually the primary factor determining the cost of a statistical study. As a result, it is not uncommon for researchers to want to know how big a sample will be required to obtain a confidence interval of a certain width or a certain sampling error (the sampling error is half the width of the confidence interval).

The formula for the sampling error is $e = z\sqrt{\dfrac{\pi(1-\pi)}{n}}$, although p_s must be used in place of π. Solving for n yields: $n = \pi(1-\pi)\dfrac{z^2}{e^2}$.

When the value of n obtained from this formula is not an integer, the convention is to round *up* to the next larger integer.

Since the sample size determination must be made prior to selecting the sample, we generally do not have a value for π or even a value for p_s. This situation is analogous to that faced when determining the sample size required for a given confidence interval on a population mean. In that case, it was σ which was unknown. The problem here turns out not to be as difficult as it was in that case, however. Unlike σ, π is bounded—its value must be between 0 and 1. Once the confidence level (which determines z) and the desired sampling error are determined, the value of n is determined by $\pi(1-\pi)$. The closer π is to 0.50, the larger this expression. If we have no idea of the actual value of π, we simply use the value 0.50. The sample size we would calculate from this value might be too large—which means the actual sampling error obtained from the sample cannot possibly be larger than the desired value. It's better to discover that your estimate is more accurate than you expected rather than less accurate. On the other hand, if we are certain that π cannot possibly equal 0.50, choosing another which is still closer to 0.50 than π will reduce the calculated value of n (thus saving money), and *still* ensure a sampling error no larger than the desired level.

- Change the name of the "Sheet2" worksheet to "n," and switch to it.

- Enter labels to your worksheet so that it looks like the picture below.

	A	B	C	D
1	Sample Size Determination			
2	pi			
3	conf level			
4	samp err			
5	z			
6	n1			
7	n			

Consider the following problem:

A computer manufacturer wants to survey individuals who have bought a new model of a home computer to determine the proportion who report that they are satisfied with their purchase. For past models, the proportion has always been at least 80%. The manufacturer has strong reason to believe that no fewer than 70% could possibly report being satisfied. If the manufacturer wants to be able to estimate a 99% confidence interval with a sampling error of ±2%, how big a sample would be required?

Since the data in this problem are expressed as percentages, we will enter it in Excel as percentages. Remember that to Excel the difference between a percentage and a proportion is formatting, so that entering a number with a percent sign causes the actual number stored in the cell to be the corresponding proportion.

- Enter "70%" as the value of π in cell B2 and "99%" as the confidence level in cell B3. Enter "2%" for the sampling error in cell B4.

The z value needed in cell B5 is the same type of z value used in the previous worksheet. It is the absolute value of the boundaries of the central region of a normal density function whose area equals the confidence level.

- Enter a formula in cell B5 which will determine the z value for the confidence level in B3. With 99% in B3, cell B5 should display the value 2.575835.

Cell B6 will contain the formula for n shown above. The value obtained from this formula will not be an integer. Cell B7 will be used for a formula which rounds the value of cell B6 up to the next integer.

- Enter the Excel formula which will calculate $\pi(1-\pi)\dfrac{z^2}{e^2}$. In place of π, z, and e, you will use cell references to their locations in the worksheets. Remember that you must explicitly tell Excel where to multiply by using Excel's multiplication symbol (the asterisk). To square a number (or raise it to any other power), you use the exponentiation symbol, " ^ ." The value which should be displayed in B6 is 3483.335.

To round a number up to the next integer, use the CEILING function in the "Math & Trig" category. That function has two arguments. The "number" argument should refer to B6. The "significance" argument is the value you want the answer to be divisible by. This should be set equal to the number "1," indicating that you want the answer to be an integer (divisible by 1).

- Enter a formula using the CEILING function in cell B7 which will round the value displayed in cell B6 up to the next integer. The displayed value should be 3484.

Remember that the sample size is the primary factor determining the cost of a statistical study. Let's see how some of the factors determined by the computer manufacturer in this problem affect the sample size.

What effect does the sampling error have on the sample size? Smaller sampling errors mean more precise estimates, so the computer manufacturer would like them to be as small as possible.

- Change the sampling error from 2% to 1%. The needed sampling size will shoot up to 13,934.

Reducing the sampling error by half approximately quadruples the sample size. The value of n (before rounding up) will exactly quadruple.

- Change the value of π from 70% to 30%. Notice this has no effect on the size of n.

Since π enters the determination of n only through the expression $\pi(1-\pi)$, there is no difference between using 70% (.70) and 30% (which is $1-.70$). In both cases the value .70 will be multiplied by the value .30 (and that product will be multiplied by $\dfrac{z^2}{e^2}$).

- Change the confidence level from 99% to 90%. The lower confidence level reduces the required sample size by more than half to 5,682.

▼ Hypothesis Tests on a Population Proportion

When the normal approximation is used for the distribution of sample proportions, hypothesis tests on a population proportion are very similar to hypothesis tests on a population mean. Somewhat greater accuracy can be achieved by converting a hypothesis test on a population proportion to a binomial problem and using the binomial distribution. Without computers it would be quite difficult to use the binomial approach and few textbooks cover it for this reason. With Excel, the binomial distribution is no more difficult to use than any other probability distribution. Since it is the traditional approach, the normal approximation for the distribution of sample proportions will be explored first.

▼ Hypothesis Tests on π Using the Normal Approximation

- Switch to the "Sheet3" worksheet and change its name to "Hyp Test on Pi."

- Prepare your worksheet by making it look like the picture below. This involves using 14-point font for the large labels, using italic face for *z* and *p*, where appropriate, and manually adjusting column widths to hold the 10-point labels. The line below "Normal Approximation" can be made by selecting the region A6:H6, clicking the small downward pointing arrow beside the Borders button on the Formatting Toolbar, and then clicking the button showing a dark underline.

	A	B	C	D	E	F	G	H
1	Population Data			Sample Data			Significance Level	
2	Hyp Prop			Samp Prop			Alpha	
3				n				
4				Std Err				
5								
6	Normal Approximation:							
7	Test Statistic			Approx *p* Value			Critical *z* Values	
8	Approx Samp *z*			1 tail			1 tail	
9				2 tail			2 tail	
10								
11	Decision (Approx)							
12	1 Tail	*p* value			2 tail	*p* value		
13		Critical *z*				Critical *z*		
14								

Let's consider the following problem:

An airline has established an on-time goal that requires that at least 95% of its flights will arrive on time. A random sample of 120 flights for the current week was chosen, and 110 of those flights arrived on time. Is there evidence at the .05 level of significance that the goal is not being met?

The first step, as in all hypothesis testing problems, is to formulate the Null and Alternate Hypotheses:

$$H_0: \pi \geq .95 \text{ and } H_A: \pi < .95$$

This is a one-tail test. The next step is to determine whether the sample is consistent with the Null Hypothesis. It would be consistent if the proportion of planes which arrived on time in the sample was greater than or equal to .95. The sample proportion $p_s = \dfrac{110}{120} = .9167$. The sample is thus *not* consistent with the Null Hypothesis. We must then determine whether this low sample proportion might reasonably be due to chance. Similar to the case of a hypothesis test on a population mean, this is done by determining the answer to the following question, "If the Null Hypothesis were true, what is the probability that a sample this size would have a sample proportion at least as far from what was expected as this sample?" If that probability is low (less than the significance level), we conclude that chance is not a reasonable explanation, and the Null Hypothesis is rejected. If that probability exceeds the significance level, we conclude that chance might be the explanation and fail to reject the Null Hypothesis. In assuming that the Null Hypothesis is true, we assume that $\pi = .95$, since this is the value given by the Null most likely to result in a sample proportion less than .95. If $\pi = .95$, we would also expect (in the statistical sense) that $p_s = .95$.

- Enter this value for the population proportion assuming the Null Hypothesis is true in cell B2.

- Enter the significance level for this problem in cell H2.

- Enter the sample proportion in cell E2. Do not simply enter ".9167." Instead, have Excel divide 110 by 120 and then convert the answer to a number. This will improve the accuracy with which this number is represented. Although the gain is small, there is no reason not to take advantage of it.

- Enter the sample size, n, in cell E3.

- Enter the formula in cell E4 which will calculate the standard error, the standard deviation of sample proportions σ_{p_s}, using the formula on page 270. In this case use the hypothesized population proportion in B2 for π rather than the sample proportion. The displayed value should be 0.019896.

- In cell B8 calculate the sample z from the formula $z = \dfrac{p_s - \mu_{p_s}}{\sigma_{p_s}}$. As shown by the formula on page 270, $\mu_{p_s} = \pi$. Use the hypothesized value for π in cell B2. The displayed value should be -1.67542.

The p value is the probability that a standard normal random variable will have a value less than -1.67542. If this were a two-tail test, this probability would be multiplied by 2. For this problem, the sample z is negative. For other problems, the sample z may be positive. To use Excel's NORMSDIST function to get a tail area, the value of the argument *must be* negative. (This is discussed in more detail in the context of a two-tail test starting on page 245.)

The NORMSDIST function has one argument named "z," referring to the upper bound of the left tail of the standard normal distribution for which an area is desired. For this problem, the value is that shown in cell

B8. We must put an expression in the "z" argument field which will make the value in that field negative regardless of the sign on B8.

- Select cell E8, click the Function Wizard button and choose NORMSDIST. In the "z" argument field enter an expression which takes the negative of the absolute value of cell B8. The Excel ABS function can be used to take the absolute value. The displayed value should be 0.046926.

- Enter the formula in cell E9 which doubles the value in cell E8. The displayed value should be 0.093853.

The calculation of critical values is the same as was given in the discussions starting on pages 247 and 251. An abbreviated explanation is given below.

To calculate the critical z values, use NORMSINV to convert the significance level to a z value. Always display a positive value. The NORMSINV function has a single argument ("probability"). Since NORMSINV is cumulative, it returns the upper bound of the lower tail region whose area equals the value of that argument. That means that if you set the argument equal to the significance level (which is less than .50), the z value returned will be negative. What you want is the absolute value of that negative number. There are several ways of doing this. One approach is to set the "probability" argument equal to the significance level and invert the sign of the returned z value (by preceding it with a minus sign or by nesting it in the ABS function). The other approach would be to set the "probability" argument equal to 1 minus the significance level.

- Using any acceptable method, enter a formula in cell H8 which will display a positive one-tail critical z for the significance level shown in H2. The displayed value for the .05 significance level should be 1.644853.

To determine the two-tail critical value, the "probability" argument should be half the significance level. Here also, the z value should be a positive number.

- Enter a formula in cell H9 which will determine the two-tail z value for the significance level in H2. The displayed value should be 1.959961.

The final step is the decision of whether or not to reject the Null Hypothesis. The procedure here is identical to that used in the decision for hypothesis tests of a population mean and is implemented in Excel using the IF function (in the "Logical" function category). Using the p value approach, the Null Hypothesis should be rejected if the p value is less than the significance level. The one-tail p value is used for one-tail tests and the two-tail p value is used for two-tail tests.

- Select cell C12. Using the IF function, enter a formula which will display "Reject" if the one-tail p value is less than the significance level and "Fail to Reject" otherwise.

- Select cell G12. Enter a similar formula to display "Reject" if the two-tail p value is less than the significance level and "Fail to Reject" otherwise.

The decision on the one-tail test should be "Reject," while the decision on the two-tail test should be "Fail to Reject."

Using the critical value approach, the Null Hypothesis should be rejected if the absolute value of the sample z is greater than the critical z. One critical z is used for one-tail tests, another is used for two-tail tests.

- Select cell C13. Using the IF function, enter a formula which will display "Reject" if the absolute value of the sample z (in B8) is greater than the one-tail critical z (in H8).

The decision under the critical value approach should be identical to that under the p value approach. C13 should display "Reject" and cell G13 should display "Fail to Reject."

Since the problem we are dealing with here is a one-tail test, the conclusion which we would draw is that the Null Hypothesis should be rejected. At the .05 level of significance we would conclude that there *is* evidence that the airline's goal is not being met. This conclusion, however, is based on the normal distribution approximating the binomial, and the approximation could be a source of error. The fact that the p value is so close to the significance level (and that the absolute value of the sample z is so close to the critical z) is a source of concern. This sample is so close to the "Reject"/"Fail to Reject" margin, that we cannot have great confidence in any conclusion. We can, however, eliminate the error associated with the normal approximation by using the binomial distribution to analyze this problem.

▼ Using the Binomial Distribution to Test Hypotheses on π

Reread the problem on page 275. If $\pi \geq .95$, the expected number of on time flights in a random sample of 120 would be $\pi \times n$ which would be an amount greater than or equal to 114. In this sample, however, only 110 flights were on time, less than expected if the Null Hypothesis were true. The p value is the probability that if the Null Hypothesis is true

($\pi = .95$), a random sample of 120 flights would by chance have a number of on-time flights as different or more different from what was expected as did this sample. In other words, if the probability of a single flight being on time is .95, what is the probability that in 120 flights the number of on-time flights would be 110 or less?

If the probability of a flight's being on time is independent (which was implicitly assumed in using the normal approximation), the number of on-time flights in a sample of 120 is binomially distributed. If the normal distribution is used to approximate the binomial, the probability is 0.046926, the same as the one-tail p value obtained above using the normal distribution as an approximation for the distribution of sample proportions. With Excel it is as easy to use the binomial distribution as the normal distribution. The probability given by the binomial distribution is the correct p value while that given by the normal distribution is only an approximation.

We will add to the current worksheet so that it can be used to handle the binomial distribution approach for all hypothesis tests on a population proportion. The first step is to add the labels shown in the picture below. Carefully note the row numbers; these labels go below the portion of the worksheet you have already used.

	A	B	C	D	E	F	G	H
14								
15	Binomial Approach							
16	Number of Successes			Prob of x			Exact p Values	
17	Sample			< or =			1 tail	
18	Expected			> or =			2 tail	
19								
20	Decision							
21	1 tail			2 tail				

- Enter the number of successes for this sample in cell B17. For this problem, a success is a flight arriving on time. The number of successes is the number of flights which arrived on time in the sample of 120.

- Enter the formula in cell B18 which will calculate the expected number of successes which is $n \times \pi$. Use the cell addresses for n and the hypothesized value for π located in the upper portion of the worksheet. The value displayed in cell B18 should be 114.

If the Null Hypothesis were true, the expected number of on-time flights would be 114 (or more). The actual number of on-time flights was 110. The p value is the probability, assuming that π really is 0.95, that in another sample of 120 flights the number of on-time flights would differ from the expected value by as much or more than it did for this sample.

Since the expected value was 114 (or more), the number of on-time flights in a second sample would differ as much or more if it were 110 *or less*. The *p* value is the binomial probability that the number of successes will be less than or equal to 110 given 120 trials and a probability of success on each trial of 0.95. The formula for this binomial probability will be entered in cell E17.

- Select cell E17 and click the Function Wizard button and select the BINOMDIST function from the "Statistical" category. Enter the word "true" in the last ("cumulative") argument field, and the value returned by the function will be a *cumulative* probability, that is, the probability of obtaining a number of successes less than or equal to the value referred to by the "number_s" argument, which should refer to the cell containing the number of successes in the sample. The "trials" argument should refer to the cell in the worksheet with the value of *n* and the "probability_s" argument should refer to the cell with the hypothesized value of π. When the correct references have been entered in the argument field, the value appearing in the "Value:" field in the upper right corner of the dialog window will be 0.078629947. The displayed value in the cell will be this same value rounded.

The value displayed in cell E17 is the exact (one-tail) *p* value for this problem.

In some hypothesis tests of a population proportion, the expected number of successes will be less than those obtained in the sample. Assuming the sample is not consistent with the Null Hypothesis, a one-tail *p* value would be the binomial probability that another sample would have a number of successes greater than or equal to the number in this sample. To enable this worksheet to be used for these problems it will be necessary to calculate that binomial probability. This can be determined by calculating one minus the cumulative probability of the number of successes being one less than the number of successes in this sample. In other words, the probability of 110 successes *or more* is one minus the probability of 109 successes *or less*.

- Enter the formula in cell E18 which will calculate the binomial probability of a number of successes greater than or equal to the value given in cell B17. The number of trials and the probability of success on each trial are the same for this calculation as they were for the previous calculation. The value displayed in cell E18 should be 0.96155.

The one-tail *p* value for any problem will be either the value in cell E17 or the value in cell E18. How can we know which is the correct one? Unless the number of successes in the sample happens to be exactly the expected number, one of those two values will be less than .5 and the other will be greater than .5. If the number of successes in the sample is not consistent with the Null Hypothesis, the p value must be less than .5. As was the case with hypothesis tests on a population mean, the worksheet can't determine if the sample is or is not consistent with the Null. If the sample is consistent, there is no need to calculate a p or critical value because the Null Hypothesis cannot be rejected. Our calculation of the p value can, therefore, reasonably assume that the sample is *not* consistent with the Null Hypothesis.

- Enter a formula in cell H17 which gives that cell the value in E17 if E17 is smaller than E18, and the value in E18 otherwise. The value displayed in cell H17 should be .07863.

The p value for a two-tail hypothesis test using the binomial approach will be exactly double the one-tail p value.

- Enter a formula in cell H18 which display a number twice that displayed in cell H17. The displayed value should be .15726.

All that is left is the decision under the binomial approach, which is exactly the same as the p value decision used in the normal approximation approach except that the exact p values determined by the binomial distribution are compared to the significance level rather than the approximate p values determined by the normal approach.

- Enter formulas in cells B21 and E21 which will display either "Reject" or "Fail to Reject" depending on whether the one- or two-tail p values, respectively, are less than or more than the significance level. For the values currently in the worksheet, both cells should display "Fail to Reject."

▼ Which Approach Is Correct, Binomial or Normal?

It is interesting to note in this case that the two approaches give different answers. The result of the normal approximation approach (in cell C12 or C13 is "Reject," while that of the binomial approach (in cell B21) is "Fail to Reject." Which approach is correct?

The answer, of course, is that the p value determined by the binomial approach, .07863, is correct, not the p value determined by the normal approximation approach, .046926. The latter value is an *approximation* of the former, not a very good approximation since the error is over half the approximate value. Why was the error so bad?

As we explored in the chapter on the normal distribution, the normal distribution approximates the binomial best if n is large and if π is close to

0.5. The value for π for this problem, 0.95, seems far from 0.5, but many textbooks give the rule of thumb that it is safe to use the normal approximation if $n \times \pi > 5$ and $n \times (1-\pi) > 5$. Did the values for this problem meet that test?

Another factor which caused the normal approximation to lead to the wrong conclusion in this problem is that the p value is close to the significance level. Had the p value been further in value from the significance level, the error involved with the normal approximation might not have mattered.

While it can be argued that the use of the binomial distribution usually adds little to the result obtained with the normal distribution, the obvious rejoinder is to question why any procedure, like the use of the normal approximation to test hypotheses of population proportions, which introduces error should be used in preference to a procedure giving a more accurate answer. Virtually all textbooks teach the normal approximation because it is easier to use that procedure with statistical tables. With computer programs like Excel, that advantage disappears.

▼ Exercises

Use the Excel worksheets you have developed to answer the following questions. In the case of hypothesis testing questions, state the Null and Alternate Hypotheses, and determine the approximate p value using the normal distribution as well as the precise p value using the binomial distribution. Indicate whether or not you reject the Null Hypothesis and provide a yes or no answer to the question asked.

1. The management of a baseball stadium is interested in determining whether or not a new ad campaign has been successful in convincing more than 20% of people attending a game to purchase hot dogs. A sample of 200 people at the game was surveyed, and 33 reported having bought hot dogs. At the .05 level of significance, is there evidence that the ad campaign was successful?

2. An advertising firm wants to determine the proportion of children aged 10 to 15 who report that Coke is their favorite soft drink. They want to be able to develop a 95% confidence interval estimate on this proportion with a sampling error of at most ±0.015. The firm is uncertain about what that proportion will be; past studies have found values ranging between 0.40 and 0.70. How large a sample should the firm choose? Report the effect of the assumed value of the true proportion by answering this question for the following assumed values for π:

0.40, 0.50, 0.60, and 0.70. If the firm has no idea which value is correct, which would you recommend they use and why?

3. An administrator of an institution which was previously a women's college and is now coeducational claims that at least half of the current students are male. A random sample of 200 students was selected, and 90 of them were male. At the .05 level of significance, is there evidence that the administrator's claim is invalid?

4. A city council wants to estimate the impact which a local professional hockey team has on the local economy by estimating the proportion of fans attending a game who live outside of the county in which the city is located. A random sample of 150 fans was chosen, and 25 of these were found to live outside the county. Based on this result, provide a 99% confidence interval estimate on the proportion of all fans who live outside the county.

5. A manufacturing firm's quality control process involves measuring the proportion of product coming off a particular assembly line which is defective. Quality standards require that that proportion be no higher than 0.005. If evidence indicates that the proportion of defectives is higher than that amount, the equipment used on that assembly line may be failing and the line must be stopped and the equipment must be inspected. A random sample of 500 product items was taken off the line, and four of them were found to be defective. At the .05 level of significance, should the firm stop the line and inspect its equipment?

6. A confidential survey of all seniors attending a particular university 20 years ago found that 29% of them admitted to having cheated at some point in their college career. In order to determine if there has been a change in behavior, the student newspaper interviewed a random sample of 120 seniors and found that 24 of those admitted to having cheated at some point in their college career. At the .05 level of significance, is there evidence that the proportion of seniors who admit to having cheated has changed from the value found 20 years ago?

7. The management of a baseball stadium is interested in determining whether a new ad campaign has been successful in convincing more than 20% of people attending a game to purchase hot dogs. A sample of 200 people at the game were surveyed and 49 reported having bought hot dogs. At the .05 level of significance, is there evidence that the ad campaign was successful?

Chapter 11

Inferences on a Population Variance

In Chapter 7 we considered the problem of determining the required sample size to achieve a desired sampling error for a confidence interval on a population mean. In order to determine the sample size, it is necessary to have some information about the population standard deviation. One way this might be done is through a pilot study. In such a study a sample is drawn and from that sample an inference about the population standard deviation is made. (Since the standard deviation is simply the square root of the variance, the same inferences can be applied either to a population variance or standard deviation.)

Quality control is another area where inferences about a population variance are important. In any production process some degree of process deviation is inevitable. Maintaining high quality requires that variability to be kept to within acceptable limits. Consider, for example, a firm which manufactured cables used in airplanes to control the flight control surfaces, such as the ailerons, rudder, and elevator. If one of these cables were to break, it could have serious consequences on the pilot's ability to control the airplane. We would naturally expect that an important dimension of quality in these cables would be their strength. The manufacturer of the cables will undoubtedly have an ongoing quality control program involving sampling cable from the manufacturing processing and testing the strength of the sample cable. From such a sample, inferences on the mean strength of all cable can be made, ensuring that the average strength of all cable is sufficient for the job.

Ensuring that the cable is sufficiently strong, *on average*, is not enough. Even if the average strength is sufficient, if the variance in the strength of the cable is large, some of the cable which is manufactured will be far stronger than needed, while other cable will be too weak. If your airplane happened to be the one whose cables broke because they were too weak, you would probably not be consoled by the knowledge that the *average* strength of all the cable made by that manufacturer was sufficient! The way for the manufacturer to avoid this is to monitor not only the average strength but also the *variance* of the strength of the cable being manufactured. If the variance is kept low enough (and the mean is kept high enough), the manufacturer can be reasonably assured that *all* the cable is strong enough to depend on.

The standard procedure for inferences on a population variance differs from the others we have seen. Rather than being based on the sampling distribution of the variance, it is based on the sampling distribution of another statistic. This statistic is called the "chi square" statistic and is calculated according to the following formula: $\chi^2 = \dfrac{(n-1)s^2}{\sigma^2}$.

In this formula, s^2 is a sample variance, which, like all sample statistics, is a random number. Since s^2 is random, so is χ^2. Under the restrictive assumption that the population is normally distributed, the distribution of the χ^2 random number is easier to work with than would be the distribution of the s^2 random number, and this is the reason for its use. Notice that χ^2 cannot be negative, since both s^2 and σ^2 must be positive, and, since n cannot be less than 1, $(n-1)$ must also be positive.

If the population is normally distributed, the chi square statistic follows a distribution which is called the *chi square* distribution. The same term is used to refer to the statistic and to the distribution. The chi square distribution has only a single variable—the degrees of freedom. The degrees of freedom for the problems we will be concerned with will always be $n-1$, where n is the size of the sample.

Excel has two built-in functions for using the chi square distribution, CHIDIST and CHIINV. CHIDIST converts a value of the chi square statistic to a probability, and CHIINV converts a probability to a value of the chi square statistic. In this way they are like the NORMSDIST and NORMSINV functions. Unlike the normal distribution functions, the two chi square functions are not cumulative. Whereas the NORMSDIST function gives the probability of a standard normal variable being *less than* the value given in its argument, the CHIDIST function gives the probability of a chi square variable with the specified degrees of freedom being *greater* than the value given in its argument. Similarly, the NORMSINV function returns a z value for which the probability of a standard normal variable being *less* equals the probability given in the function's argument. The CHIINV function returns a χ^2 value for which the probability of the chi square variable being *greater* equals the probability given in the function's argument.

The two Excel chi square functions are similiar to the the two t distribution functions TDIST and TINV. Refer to the illustration of a standard t density function below. If TDIST were given the value labeled T, it would provide the area of the shaded region which represents the probability of a random variable whose distribution is given by the density function having a value greater than *T*. If TINV were given the area of the shaded region, it would return the value for *T*.

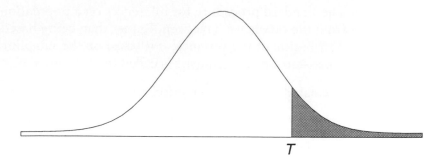

T

There are a few other differences using the chi square distribution from the other continuous distributions we have investigated. Some of these differences will be easier to understand after examining the shape of the density function. We can do this by having Excel prepare a chart of the distribution function for very small intervals. This has the same shape as the density function.

- Start Excel with a new workbook and save it as chap11.xls.

- Rename the "Sheet1" worksheet to "Chart."

- Enter the series of numbers 0, 1, 2, etc., up to 100 in column A.

- Enter the label "DOF" in cell D1. Cell E1 will be used for the chi square distribution's only variable, the degrees of freedom.

- Enter the number "25" in cell E1. This will be the first value for the degrees of freedom we will try.

Column B will be used to enter the probability of a chi square variable having a value between the value given on the same row of column A and that of the previous row. For example, row 6 has "5" in column A. In column B we will enter a formula which will display the probability of a chi square variable having a value between the "5" in A6 and the "4" in A5. One way of doing this is to subtract the probability of a chi square variable being less than 4 (that is, the cumulative probability of 4) from the probability of a chi square variable being less than 5. The difference is the probability of being between 4 and 5.

The CHIDIST function, however, is not cumulative. Rather than provide the probability of a chi square variable being *less* than the value we give it, it provides the probability of a chi square variable being *greater* than the value we give it. The probability that CHIDIST returns for the chi square value of 4 will be greater than the probability it returns for the chi square value of 5. To get the probability of being between 4 and 5, we do the opposite of what would be done with a cumulative probability function; that is, we subtract the probability associated with 5 from the probability associated with 4. Let's start with the value 1.

- Select cell B2. Since we will have to subtract two values returned from CHIDIST, we need to start the formula before using the Function Wizard. Enter an equal sign, then click the Function Wizard button.

- Select the CHIDIST function in the "Statistical" category.

The function has two arguments: "x" is the value for which the function will provide the probability of a chi square variable being larger, and "degrees_freedom" is the degrees of freedom of the chi square distribution for which we want the probability.

- In the "x" argument field enter a *relative* address reference to the cell in the previous row in column A. That cell contains a zero. In the "degrees_freedom" argument field enter an *absolute* address reference to the cell where we have placed the degrees of freedom (initially, 25).

Notice that the number in the "Value" field at the top of the dialog window is "1." The probability of a chi square variable being greater than zero is 1. Remember that a chi square variable must be positive.

- Click the "Finish" button. The Function Wizard will close and we can continue building the formula in cell B2.

- Since we will want to subtract the probability of a chi square variable being greater than 1 (the value in column A for this row), enter a minus sign.

- Click the Function Wizard button again, and select CHIDIST again.

- This time, enter a *relative* address reference to the cell in the same row in column A (which contains the number "1"). Enter an *absolute* reference to the cell containing the degrees of freedom, as in the previous case. Although the value given this time (1) is different from that given last time, the probability appearing in the "Value" field will again be 1. That value is actually very slightly less than 1, but so slight that Excel expresses it as a 1. Click the "Finish" button.

- The formula is now finished. Press the Enter key and the value "6.36E-14" will display in B2. This is an extremely small number, but still greater than 0.

- Copy the formula in cell B2 down to cell B101. Since the two uses of CHIDIST in the formula in cell B2 use relative addresses for "x," those addresses should change as the formula is copied. The address of the degrees of freedom, however, should not change since an absolute address was used in the "degrees_freedom" argument. If error values appear in the cells to which you copied the formula, check to be sure you have the correct cell references in B2.

We can treat the values in column A as chi square values, and we will next chart the probabilities in column B against those values.

- Click the Chart Wizard button. Make the upper left corner of your chart about the center of cell C2. Drag the Chart Wizard mouse pointer to about the middle of the cell visible in the lower right corner of your screen so that the chart will be as large as possible without the worksheet scrolling.

- In the first dialog window for the Chart Wizard, indicate that the data for the chart are in the range a2:b101.

- In the next two dialog windows, have Excel use the simplest possible line plot, without any symbols marking the specific points plotted.

- In the "Step 4" dialog window, you will have to tell Excel to use the first column (column A) for the chart's horizontal (x) axis.

- In the "Step 5" dialog window, choose the option not to have a legend, and title your chart "Chi Square Distribution." Click the "Finish" button.

Your chart should look much like the picture on the next page.

Notice that although the graph is bell-shaped, it is not symmetric. The degrees of freedom of the chi square distribution is also the mean. The mean of the distribution on your screen is, therefore, 25.

Where exactly is the point on the graph directly above the mean? In the case of the normal and t distributions, the peak of the graph lies directly above the mean. To check whether this is also true of the chi square distribution, let's have Excel put the vertical axis on the value 25.

- Activate the chart by double clicking the left mouse pointer with the mouse pointer inside the graph. The graph is in active mode when it is surrounded by the active mode boundary: ▬▭.

- With the graph activated, place the mouse pointer on the horizontal axis on a spot where the density function is clearly above the axis (say, between 17 and 37). Double click the left button. The Format Axis dialog window will open.

- Click the "Scale" file folder tab.

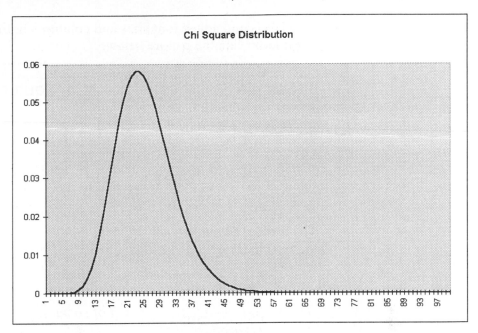

- Change the "1" in the field labeled "Value (Y) Axis Crosses at Category Number" to "25" and click the "OK" button.

With the *y* axis drawn directly above 25, it is clear that the point on the graph directly above the mean is not at the peak but to the right of the peak. The positive or right skew of the chi square distribution causes the extreme positive values to pull the mean to the right.

- Click the mouse pointer outside the chart to take it out of active mode.

- Change the value for the degrees of freedom to other values. Try a number of values between 2 and 200. Change the position of the *y* axis so that it lies above the mean (the degrees of freedom) in each case. Pay attention to the effect these changes have on the apparent skewness of the chart and to the range of values for which the probabilities are clearly nonzero. You will notice that for larger values, not all of the density function will appear on your graph given the range of chi square values we are showing.

The fact that the density function of the chi square distribution is not symmetric and is not centered on zero will affect the nature of confidence intervals using this distribution.

▼ Confidence Intervals on a Population Variance

- Rename the "Sheet2" worksheet to "CI on Var" and switch to it.

- Enter the labels and adjust font sizes and column lengths so that your worksheet looks like the picture below.

	A	B	C	D	E
1	Sample Statistics			Chi Square Values	
2	n				
3	Std Dev				
4					
5					
6	Population Values				
7	Upper Var				
8	Lower Var				
9	Upper Std Dev				
10	Lower Std Dev				

Consider the following problem:

A large bakery produces a national brand of cookies. Experience has shown that the temperature at which the cookies are baked affects their taste. It is important to maintain as little variation as possible in the baking temperature so as to maintain the consistency required of a national brand. A random sample of 25 batches of cookies was selected, and the standard deviation of the temperature at which those cookies were baked was 2.13° F. Based on this result, and assuming the distribution of temperatures is normal, construct a 95% confidence interval on the standard deviation in the baking temperature of all batches of cookies.

- Enter the values for n, the sample standard deviation, and the confidence level (as a proportion or with a percent sign) in cells B2, B3, and E2, respectively.

When we determined a confidence interval from a statistic which followed the normal or t distribution, the first step was to determine the z or t values corresponding to the confidence level desired. Similarly, when determining a confidence interval for a population variance or standard deviation, the first step is to determine the χ^2 values corresponding to the confidence level. For the t and z distributions, the two values always had the same absolute values and differed only in sign. This is not the case with the chi square distribution, however.

Consider the chi square density function in the illustration on the next page which shows the two values as χ_L^2 and χ_R^2. If these correspond to the values for the 95% confidence interval, the area of the white region between them must be .95. The area of each shaded tail region is .025. Unlike the case with the t and z distributions, the two values are not equidistant from the mean because the distribution is not symmetric.

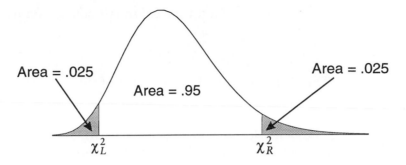

To find the values for χ_L^2 and χ_R^2, use the CHIINV function. This function requires that we provide it with the area to the *right* of the value it returns. For the 95% confidence interval, the area to the right of χ_R^2 is .025, and the area to the right of χ_L^2 is $.95 + .025 = .975$. We will need to provide CHIINV with expressions which will work even if the confidence level in cell E2 is changed. The central area is always equal to the level of confidence (expressed as a proportion). The sum of both tail areas is one minus the central area, and each tail is half the sum. The area to the right of χ_R^2 is the area of one tail. The area to the right of χ_L^2 can be calculated either as the area of the right tail plus the central area or as one minus the area of the left tail.

- Select cell E3, which will contain the formula to determine the value of χ_R^2. Click the Function Wizard button and select the CHIINV function in the "Statistical" category.

- The dialog window shows two arguments. In the "probability" argument field, enter an expression which will calculate the area of the right tail in the picture above given the confidence level (the area of the central region).

- In the "degrees_freedom" argument field, enter an expression which will subtract one from the sample size given on the worksheet. The number in the "Value" field should be 39.36406014. Click the "Finish" button and this value (rounded) will display in cell E3.

- Select cell E4 and use the Function Wizard to call up the CHIINV dialog window. Enter an expression in the "probability" argument field which will calculate the area to the right of χ_L^2 from the confidence level in the worksheet. Enter the same expression in the "degrees_freedom" argument field used in E3. Click "Finish." The value displayed in E4 should be 12.40115.

Taking the formula for the chi square statistic on page 285 and solving for σ^2 gives: $\sigma^2 = \dfrac{(n-1)s^2}{\chi^2}$.

The sample data in the numerator of this formula are known for this problem. The confidence interval on σ^2 is found by evaluating the formula for each of the two chi square values corresponding to the confidence level. Note that since we are dividing by the chi square value, the *higher* confidence level limit is found when we use the *lower* chi square value, and vice versa.

- Select cell B7. Enter the Excel formula which will calculate σ^2 according to the formula above using the lower chi square value in E4. Notice that the formula requires the sample variance (s^2), while the worksheet contains the sample standard deviation (s). The displayed value should be 8.780285.

- Select cell B8 and enter the Excel formula to calculate the lower bound of the confidence interval on the variance by using the higher chi square value in E3. The displayed value should be 2.766117.

- Enter formulas in cells B9 and B10 which will determine the boundaries of the confidence interval on the population standard deviation. Each boundary is simply the square root of the corresponding variance boundary. The displayed values should be 2.963155 and 1.663165.

The 95% confidence interval on the variance of the temperature for all batches of cookies is 2.8 to 8.8, while the 95% confidence interval on the standard deviation of the temperature is approximately 1.7 to 3.0.

Check your worksheet by using it to solve the following problem:

A manufacturer of light bulbs is monitoring the life of 60-watt bulbs made under a new process. A sample of 150 bulbs was chosen, and the standard deviation in the life of those bulbs was 23.5 hours. Based on this result, and assuming the life of light bulbs is normally distributed, determine a 90% confidence interval on the standard deviation of all bulbs produced by that process.

Your worksheet should show that the 90% confidence interval is from 21.47137 hours to 25.99324 hours.

▼ Hypothesis Tests on a Population Variance

Prepare a worksheet for hypothesis tests on a population variance.

- Switch to the "Sheet3" worksheet and rename it "Hyp Test on Var."

- Enter labels on the worksheet so that it looks like the picture below.

	A	B	C	D	E	F	G	H	I
1	Population Data			Sample Data			Significance Level		
2	Hyp Sigma			*n*			Alpha		
3				*s*					
4									
5	Test Statistic			*p* Values			Critical Chi Sq Values		
6	chi sq			1 tail			1 tail	upper	
7				2 tail				lower	
8							2 tail	upper	
9								lower	
10	Decision								
11	1 tail								
12	2 tail								

Probably the most common hypothesis test on a population variance tests whether the variance has exceeded some target level. This is the type of test which would arise in quality control since the object there is to keep the variance as low as possible. The tests for whether a population variance is below a certain value or differs from a certain value (two-tail) is similar. We will develop a worksheet for all types of tests, but the first example will be a typical quality control type problem.

A laundry detergent company packages its product in boxes labeled as containing 64 oz. Although some variation in the amount of detergent placed in each box in unavoidable, it is desirable for that variation to be kept as low as possible. If too much detergent is placed into the box, it may spill over and be wasted. If too little is placed into the box, customers may be unhappy and the company may face regulatory difficulties. Given the characteristics of current filling technology, a standard deviation in the amount of fill in each box of 1.6 ounces is normal and unavoidable. A higher standard deviation, however, indicates a problem with the process. In order to monitor the process, the firm carefully measures the amount of detergent in a random sample of 50 boxes chosen from each batch. In a recent sample, the measured sample standard deviation was 1.9 oz. At the .05 level of significance, does the company have evidence that the standard deviation in the fill of all boxes exceeds 1.6 oz?

The Null Hypothesis for this problem is $H_0: \sigma \leq 1.6$ and the Alternate Hypothesis is $H_A: \sigma > 1.6$. For this sample, the sample standard deviation *s* is 1.9, which is greater than 1.6. Therefore, the sample is not consistent with the Null Hypothesis and we have to determine if this might be due to chance.

As indicated by the labels, the worksheet we are developing is designed to accept standard deviations (rather than variances) as input. This is an essentially arbitrary choice, but is consistent with the wording of this problem which refers to standard deviations rather than variances.

- Enter the values from the problem in the appropriate places in the worksheet. The value for σ from the Null Hypothesis goes in cell B2, the sample size and sample standard deviation go in cells E2 and E3, and the significance level goes in cell H2.

- Enter an Excel formula in cell B6 which will calculate the value of the chi square statistic for this sample assuming that σ has the value given by the Null Hypothesis (in B2). The formula for the chi square statistic (χ^2) can be found on page 285. The value displayed in cell B6 should be 69.09766.

If the Null Hypothesis is true (interpreted as $\sigma = 1.6$), the expected value of a sample standard deviation would also be 1.6, and the expected value of the chi square statistic would be 49 (the degrees of freedom or $n-1$). The probability that a sample would have a sample standard deviation of 1.9 or more is the same as the probability that a sample would have a chi square statistic of 69.09766 or more. The probability is the p value and can be determined by using the CHIDIST function. This is shown below on a graph of the density function for the chi square distribution with 49 degrees of freedom.

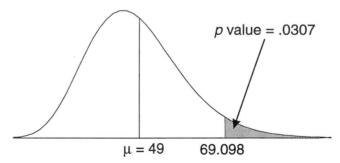

- Select cell E6. Click the Function Wizard button and choose CHIDIST. Since the CHIDIST function returns the probability of a chi square statistic *greater* than that given as the "x" argument, the cell address of the sample chi square statistic should be put in the "x" argument field. The "degrees_freedom" field should contain an expression which will calculate $n-1$. The value displayed as the p value should be .030749.

- In cell B11 enter an Excel formula (using the IF function) which will display the word "Reject" if the p value in E6 is less than the significance level in H2 and "Fail to Reject" otherwise. "Reject" should display in this case.

The test could also be done using a critical value. For this problem, the critical chi square would be the value for which the probability of a greater chi square exactly equals the significance level. To convert the significance level (a probability) to a chi square value, use the CHIINV function.

- Select cell I6 and click the Function Wizard button. Select the CHIINV function. The "probability" argument field should have the address of the significance level, and the "degrees_freedom" field should contain an expression which will calculate $n - 1$ as before. The critical chi square for this problem is 66.33865, which should display in cell I6.

The rejection region lies above 66.33865. Since the sample chi square (69.09766) is greater, and therefore is in the rejection region, the critical value approach (as it must) also leads to a rejection of the Null Hypothesis.

Since the Null Hypothesis is rejected for this problem, the conclusion is that the company does have evidence that the standard deviation in the fill of all boxes exceeds 1.6 oz. This would provide justification for an investigation of the package-filling process to determine what has broken down.

▼ Two-Tail Test on Population Variance (or Standard Deviation)

Although this is not generally the concern of quality control, suppose the question to be determined was whether or not the sample provided evidence at the .05 level of significance that the standard deviation of detergent fill was *different* from 1.6 ounces. In this case the Null Hypothesis would be $H_0: \sigma = 1.6$, and the Alternate Hypothesis would be $H_A: \sigma \neq 1.6$. This Null Hypothesis could be rejected if the sample standard deviation was less than 1.6, while the one-tail test considered above could only be rejected if the sample standard deviation exceeded 1.6.

As in other hypothesis tests, the two-tail p value is twice the one-tail p value.

- Enter the formula in cell E7 which doubles the one-tail p value in cell E6.

- Enter a formula in cell B12 similar to that in B11 which will display "Reject" if the two-tail p value is less than the significance level and "Fail to Reject" otherwise.

Since the two-tail p value is .061499, which exceeds .05, we fail to reject the two-tail Null Hypothesis. It may seem puzzling that at the same significance level we can find evidence that the population standard deviation *exceeds* 1.6 oz, but we can't find evidence that it *differs* from 1.6. Remember, though, that a sample with a standard deviations below 1.6 could not possibly lead to the conclusion that the population standard deviation exceeds 1.6 oz but could lead to the conclusion that the population standard deviation differs from 1.6 oz. The significance level is the probability of committing Type I error. *If* the true population standard deviation is 1.6 (the Null Hypothesis is true), the probability of incorrectly rejecting that Null will be .05 for both one- and two-tail cases.

Determining the critical chi square values for a two-tail test is almost exactly the same as determining the chi square values for a confidence interval. To translate a significance level to the corresponding confidence level, subtract it from one. In this case, the significance level is 0.05. The critical chi square values are the same as those for a $1 - 0.05 = 0.95$ or 95% confidence interval. Look at the diagram on page 291. The two values, shown there as χ_L^2 and χ_R^2, define two tails with equal areas which sum to 0.05. These are the critical chi square values for a hypothesis test at the 0.05 significance level. The values can be determined by using the CHIINV function and providing that function with the area to the right of each critical value. The area to the right of χ_R^2 is half the significance level, 0.025. The area to the right of χ_L^2 is one minus half the significance level.

- Select cell I8. Use the CHIINV function to determine the upper critical value, χ_R^2, for the significance level and sample size entered on the worksheet. The value displayed in cell I8 should be 70.22236.

- Select cell I9 and use the CHIINV function to determine the value of the lower critical chi square, χ_L^2. The displayed value should be 31.55493.

The critical chi square values are 31.55493 and 70.22236. Since the sample chi square, 69.09766, lies between these two values, the sample is not in the rejection region, and we would fail to reject the Null Hypothesis, the same result obtained with the two-tail p value.

▼ Test on a Population Variance Being Below a Given Value

The remaining hypothesis test to consider is one in which we look for evidence that the population variance is below a given value. Consider the following problem:

The laundry detergent company is evaluating a new package-filling process developed by a group of its engineers. The new process promises to increase quality by reducing the standard deviation in the fill placed into each box. Under the old process, the standard deviation was 1.6 oz. The new process was put into operation and a random sample of 50 boxes filled by that process was chosen. The standard deviation in the fill of those 50 boxes was 1.35 oz. At the .05 level of significance, does the company have evidence that the standard deviation of all boxes filled by the new process is less than 1.6 oz?

The Null Hypothesis for this problem is $H_0: \sigma \geq 1.6$ and the Alternate Hypothesis is $H_A: \sigma < 1.6$. The sample standard deviation is 1.35, not consistent with the Null Hypothesis, so we have to determine if this could be due to chance.

- The only change in the values from the previous problem is the sample standard deviation. Change the appropriate cell in the worksheet to reflect this change.

The worksheet immediately updates. The correct sample chi square value in this case is 34.88379, as is shown in worksheet. The p value shown in the worksheet, 0.936075, is wrong, however. The situation is shown in the diagram on the next page.

The p value for this problem is the probability that if the population variance equaled 1.6 oz (the Null Hypothesis were true), a sample of 50 boxes could be chosen whose sample variance by chance was 1.35 or less. This is identical to the probability that the sample's chi square statistic would be 34.88379 or less. It is this probability which is illustrated in the diagram on the next page of the density function of the chi square statistic.

Compare this diagram with that shown on page 294. In that case, the p value was equal to the area to the *right* of the sample chi square. In this case it is equal to the area to the *left* of the sample chi square. The problem with the formula in cell E6 calculating the p value is that it is calculating the area to the right of 34.884 instead of the area to the left. The correct p value is not .936075 but one minus .936075.

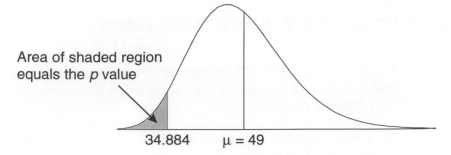

Area of shaded region equals the *p* value

34.884   μ = 49

In other words, the CHIDIST function returns the correct *p* value for problems like the previous one-tail problem where the *p* value is the area of a right tail. To get the *p* value for problems like this one, when a left tail area is desired, we must calculate one minus the probability returned by CHIDIST. Is there a way we can enter a formula which will determine whether the *p* value is the value returned by CHIDIST or by one minus the value returned by CHIDIST?

If we calculate both the area to the right of the sample chi square (the value returned by CHIDIST), and the area to the left of the sample chi square (one minus the value returned by CHIDIST), the correct value is always the smaller. As long as we remember that the *p* value given by the worksheet is only meaningful if the sample is not consistent with the Null Hypothesis, the *p* value can never exceed .5.

Excel has a built-in function, MIN, which takes two or more arguments and returns the value of the smallest. We can use this to have the correct formula for the *p* value chosen automatically.

- Select cell E6. Look at the formula bar for that cell's current contents and write them down in the margin on the left. Erase the contents of that cell by pressing the Delete key. We are now ready to enter a new formula.

- Click the Function Wizard button, and select MIN from the statistical category.

- The dialog box for MIN shows two arguments "number1" and "number2." In the "number1" argument field, enter the formula (without equals sign) which used to be E6 and which you have written in the margin. In the value field to the right of the argument field you should see the number which used to be displayed in E6, .936075. This is the probability of a random chi square variable *exceeding* the sample chi square value.

- Click the mouse pointer in the "number2" argument field. Notice how this causes a "number3" argument field to appear (which we won't use). The MIN function doesn't have a fixed number of arguments and whenever you use the last one in the Function Wizard, a new one will appear until the maximum of 30 arguments have been used.

In the "number2" argument field you should enter an expression which will calculate one minus the probability of a chi square variable being greater than the sample chi square.

- Begin the expression by entering "1-" (without quotes) in the "number2" argument field. Finish by entering the expression which determines the probability of a chi square variable being greater than the sample chi square. That expression, of course, is already in the "number1" argument field. The number appearing in the value field is 0.063924595, which is 1 minus 0.936075405. This is the probability of a random chi square variable being *less* than the sample chi square value

- Click the "Finish" button. Cell I6 will display the value 0.063925 which is the smaller of the values in each of MIN's arguments.

Since this *p* value exceeds the significance level, the Null Hypothesis is not rejected, as shown by the decision in cell B12. The manufacturer does not have evidence at the .05 level of significance that the new filling process reduces the standard deviation (or variance) of the fill in all detergent boxes.

All that remains is to determine the critical chi square value for the lower one-tail test. This is the chi square value for which the area under the density function to the left of the value equals the significance level. Since CHIINV interprets the probability given it as the area to the right of the value it is to return, we must convert the significance level to the corresponding right area by subtracting one.

- Select cell I7. Click the Function Wizard button and choose the CHIINV function. In the "probability" field enter an expression which calculates one minus the significance level. In the "degrees_freedom" field enter an expression which calculates $n - 1$. Click "Finish." The value appearing in I7 is 33.93029.

Since the sample chi square exceeds the critical chi square, the sample does not lie in the rejection region.

▼ Exercises

In Chapter 9 you used Named Ranges as a means of dealing with hypothesis testing problems where the actual data were provided rather than the summary statistics. The problems below would be most easily answered if you altered your current worksheet using the same techniques used there.

1. A machine is designed to fill cereal boxes so that the average fill is 16 oz with a standard deviation of 1.1 oz. A sample of 15 boxes of cereal was selected and measured. The following measurements were recorded:

   16.81, 11.18, 17.36, 14.55, 15.64, 17.29, 20.8, 17.26, 16.07, 14.86, 13.95, 14.51, 17.65, 14.91, 18.41

   At the .01 level of significance, is there evidence that the machine is not meeting specifications with respect to variation?

2. Experience has shown that variability in the output of a bolt-making machine increases shortly before a machine failure. Amalgamated Bolts has determined that properly operating machines produce an average of 1,000 bolts per hour with a variance of 25.0. In order to anticipate a possible breakdown, the output of each bolt-making machine is monitored. As part of this program, the output of one particular bolt-making machine was monitored this week during a random sample of 20 hours. The measurements were as follows:

   1001, 1005, 997, 1000, 994, 1001, 999, 1006, 994, 1004, 998, 1000, 1001, 994, 996, 1000, 1008, 996, 994, 1002

   Based on this sample, is there evidence at the .10 level of significance that this machine is about to break down?

3. A specialty light bulb used by the manufacturer of a computer projection system is supposed to have an average life of 200 hours with a standard deviation of 12 hours. A new supplier of the bulbs has promised the projection system manufacturer light bulbs which have less variation in their life. In order to test this, the projection system manufacturer selected a random sample of 12 bulbs and subjected them to testing. The lifetimes of the 12 bulbs were:

   180.6, 211.9, 175.1, 181.4, 196.5, 188.9, 206.3, 189.7, 223.3, 180.0, 211.3, 193.7

   Based on this sample, does the projection system manufacturer have evidence which supports the new supplier's claims?

Chapter 12
▼

Inferences on Two Population Means

All of the inferential statistics investigated so far have been *univariate*—they were concerned with only a single variable. Techniques that are concerned with more than a single statistic add an important dimension to inferential statistics—the investigation of relationships among two or more variables. The techniques explored in this chapter do not enable the investigation of as many different types of relationships as those in later chapters. The one type of relationship they do handle, however, is an important one: the relationship between the mean of an observation and which of two groups that observation is in. This is a relationship between two variables, one of which is discrete with exactly two values and the other of which is continuous.

All of the techniques considered here have certain features in common. There are always two samples, each drawn from a different population. A sample mean is computed from each of the two samples, and the difference between those two means is calculated. This difference is a random number, like all sample statistics considered earlier, and its distribution is used to make inferences about the difference between the two population means. These inferences can be either confidence intervals or hypothesis tests, but the Excel procedures we will examine have been created with hypothesis testing in mind. Although the hypothesized difference between the two population means can be any value, by far the most common value is zero. A Null Hypothesis with a difference of zero between the means is appropriate for a question which asks, "Is there evidence of a difference in the two population means?" or, for the one-tail case, "Is there evidence that the mean of one of the populations exceeds the mean of the other?"

There are two different ways in which data can be collected for these tests, and they require different analysis techniques. One method is the *paired samples approach*, and the other method is the *independent samples approach*. In the paired sample approach, each observation in one sample is linked to a matching observation in the other sample. The observations are matched so that, ideally, they are identical in all characteristics which might affect the variable whose means are being compared *except* for the difference in the populations from which each is drawn. Since each observation in one sample is matched to an observation in the other sample, the two samples must be the same size. In the independent samples approach, no attempt to match characteristics between observations is made: the two samples are each randomly drawn from their respective populations. The samples may or may not be the same size.

It is always more difficult to select paired samples than independent samples, but the test for paired samples is more sensitive, and, for this reason, is preferable to the independent samples approach. It frequently is the case, however, when the paired samples approach is simply impossible. The paired samples approach is most often used when the data are to be collected from a future experiment over which the investigator has some control. The issue of matching samples is part of a much larger topic called *experimental design,* which is very important in laboratory science where the investigator has considerable control over the process generating the data. Sometimes this is the case in business and economics, but more often it is not.

▼ Inferences from Paired Samples

Consider the following problem:

A tire manufacturer wants to determine if a new rubber formulation will improve tread wear. One set of twelve tires was manufactured with the old formulation, and a another set was manufactured with the new formulation. Both sets of tires were identical in all respects except for the rubber. Six test cars and drivers were chosen for the test. Each car received two tires with the old rubber formulation and two with the new. One of each was placed on the front and one of each was placed on the rear. Each car drove until a tire wore out. That tire's mileage was recorded, and the car continued driving until all of the test tires had worn out. The mileage each tire received is shown in the table on the next page.

Based on the data in that table, does the manufacturer have evidence at the .05 level of significance that the average tread life of all tires made with the new rubber formulation exceeds the average tread life of all tires made with the old rubber formulation?

The Null Hypothesis for these data is $H_0: \mu_{new} \le \mu_{old}$ and the Alternate Hypothesis is $H_A: \mu_{new} > \mu_{old}$. Because of the methods used with inferences on two population means, it is common to formulate the

Car	Tire Location	Total Tread Life in Miles	
		Old Rubber	New Rubber
1	Front	37,661	31,902
	Rear	42,342	41,203
2	Front	31,108	38,816
	Rear	41,239	43,305
3	Front	32,903	35,375
	Rear	42,658	52,353
4	Front	29,829	30,883
	Rear	39,616	49,424
5	Front	34,625	38,724
	Rear	42,650	43,234
6	Front	31,923	34,565
	Rear	39,990	43,861

hypotheses in terms of the difference between the two population means. If $\mu_D = \mu_{new} - \mu_{old}$, an alternative formulation for the Null Hypothesis is $H_0: \mu_D \leq 0$, and for the Alternative Hypothesis: $H_A: \mu_D > 0$. These samples are clearly paired because each tire with the old rubber formulation has a corresponding tire with the new formulation.

The data for this problem are provided in an Excel workbook named "tires.xls" in the subdirectory for this chapter.

- Open the workbook "tires.xls." After opening it, select "Save As…" from the "File" menu on the menu bar and give the workbook the name "chap12.xls." Alternatively you can open a new workbook and enter the labels "Old" and "New" in cells A1 and B1 and enter the data in two rightmost columns of the table below their respective labels. Save this workbook under the name "chap12.xls."

- Change the name of the "Sheet1" worksheet to "Paired."

- Enter the label "Diff" in cell C1. In cells C2 through C13, enter formulas which will calculate the the value in each row in column B (the mileage with the new formulation) minus the value in column A (the mileage with the old formulation). The value displayed in cell C13 should be 3,871. If you used the tires.xls workbook, you will notice that the cell formatting shows negative numbers in parentheses rather than with a minus sign. The value in C2, for example, will display as (5,759).

Each of these values is a random number. Think of them as being selected from a population of differences. Imagine that each tire in the population of tires made with the new rubber formulation was paired with a corresponding tire in the population of tires made with the old formulation and the difference in the mileage of the two pairs was calculated. This would be the population of differences. The formulation of the Null and Alternate Hypothesis which use "μ_D" are referring to the mean of this population of differences. The values you have in column C are a sample from that population and can be used to test hypotheses on the population mean, μ_D. The methods described below are identical to those used in Chapter 9. You may wish to review the methods of testing a hypothesis on a population mean in that chapter.

- Enter the label "Mean" in cell B14, "Std Dev" in cell B15, "Std Err" in cell B16, "t" in cell B17, and "p value" in cell B18.

- Enter formulas in cell C14 and C15 to calculate the average and standard deviation, respectively, of the numbers in C2:C13. The displayed values will be 3092 and 4471.701.

Notice that since the sample mean is positive, it is not consistent with the Null Hypothesis. It will be necessary to calculate a sample t and determine from it if the positive sample mean could reasonably be due to chance.

- Enter a formula in C16 to calculate the standard error by dividing the sample standard deviation by the square root of the sample size. The displayed value should be 1290.869.

- Enter the formula in C17 to calculate the sample t for the Null Hypothesis that the population mean is less than or equal to zero. Enter the formula in cell C18 to calculate the one-tail p value from that sample t value. The displayed value should be 0.01777.

Since this p value is less than the significance level, we would reject the Null Hypothesis and conclude that there is evidence that the average tread life of all tires made with the new rubber formulation exceeds that of all tires made with the old formulation.

Notice that the standard error and means you have calculated could also be used to calculate a confidence interval on the difference between the average tread life of the two populations of tires.

▼ Using the Analysis Tool for a Paired Samples Test

Although analyzing data from paired samples is very straightforward, Excel provides an Analysis Tool for this very task. The Analysis Tool automatically does all of the calculations and produces an output. The output, however, is in the form of numbers rather than formulas. As a result, the tool must be used each time the data change. It is not possible using an Analysis Tool to develop a worksheet which will automatically recalculate when the data change.

- Open the "Tools" menu on the Menu Bar and click "Data Analysis...." If "Data Analysis..." is not present on your Tools menu, see Appendix A.

- When the Data Analysis dialog window opens, scroll down through the list of Analysis Tools and choose "t-Test: Paired Two Sample for Means." The dialog window for this Tool will open.

- In the fields for the "Variable 1 Range" and "Variable 2 Range," enter the cell address ranges for the columns with the mileage for the "Old" and "New" rubber formulations, respectively. Include in these ranges the cells in the first row containing the labels "Old" and "New."

- In the "Hypothesized Mean Difference" field enter the number "0."

- Click the small box beside the word "Labels" so that an "X" appears. By doing this you tell the analysis that the first cell in the variable ranges contains a label. It is always good to do this because it enables the Analysis Tool to use your labels in the output.

- The "Alpha" field should contain the significance level, 0.05. The Excel Analysis Tools generally seem to start assuming this is the significance level you want, but you can change it to another value.

- Click the button to the left of "Output Range" and enter the address D1. The output of the Analysis Tool will be placed immediately to the right of the data already entered in the worksheet.

- Click the "OK" button. The output will be written to columns D, E and F, and the cells containing that output will be selected. As with all the output of all the Analysis Tools, the column widths are not adjusted to fit the output which you must do next.

- Open the "Format" menu on the Menu Bar. Select "Column" and from the submenu which opens select "AutoFit Selection." This will adjust the widths of the columns so that you can see the output of the Analysis Tool.

As you examine the output of the Analysis Tool, you will notice that it provides a number of statistics, such as the means of each sample, which we did not calculate before, and omits some (such as the mean sample difference) which were calculated before. These means are useful because they help you determine how the Tool made its calculations. Look, for example, at the sample t (labeled "t Stat") in cell E10. It has the same absolute value as the sample t earlier calculated in cell C17, but a different sign. The differences in column C were calculated by subtracting the values in column A from those in column B (that is, B – A). However, the Analysis Tool calculated the differences as A – B. In the case on one-tail tests, it is important to check the means of each sample to ensure that the sample data are not consistent with the Null Hypothesis. It is also wise to include labels with the data analyzed so that the output will be clearly labeled.

In addition to giving both one-tail and two-tail p values, the output of the Analysis Tool also includes critical t values. The value given in the Tool's dialog window is used to determine these values. Notice that the output does not indicate if the Null Hypothesis is rejected. When you use an Analysis Tool to do a hypothesis test, you must still determine if the Null Hypothesis is rejected including whether or not the sample is consistent with the Null Hypothesis (for one-tail tests). Notice that the output does not include a standard error of the mean of the differences. It cannot, therefore, be used to derive confidence intervals.

▼ Tests of the Difference of Means for Independent Samples

When samples drawn from two populations are not paired, they are called *independent* samples. Such samples need not be the same size. Excel provides three different Analysis Tools for hypothesis tests on independent samples. The appropriate one to use depends on the information you have on the variances of the two populations. There are three possibilities, and each requires different calculations:

1. You know the two population variances. This situation arises primarily in statistics texts since the usual situation is one in which you know nothing about the populations. In this case a sample statistic with a z distribution can be calculated from the data in the two samples.

2. You don't know the population variances, but you believe they are equal or are willing to assume they are equal. Even if the two population variances are equal, the two sample variances will differ purely by chance. Each sample variance is an estimate of the same population variance, and the appropriate approach is to combine the two sample

variances so as to get a better estimate of that common population variance. This estimate is referred to as the *pooled sample variance*. From the two sample means and the pooled sample variance, a sample statistic with a t distribution can be calculated. The degrees of freedom of the t distribution is $n_1 + n_2 - 2$, where n_1 and n_2 are the sizes of the two samples.

3. You don't know the population variances, but you believe they are unequal or do not want to assume they are equal. This situation is what statisticians refer to as the Behrens-Fisher problem. A sample statistic is calculated from the sample data. This statistic approximately follows the t distribution, and for this reason some texts refer to it as t', although Excel's output simply designates it as "t Stat." The degrees of freedom is calculated by a formula known as Satterthwaite's approximation and is rounded to the nearest integer. This is then used to determine both p values and critical values using the t distribution.

Let's consider the realistic case where you do not know the variances of the two populations. In this case you must use options 2 or 3 above. It is very likely that you may be uncertain as to whether the population variances are equal or unequal. It is reasonable, therefore, to use both procedures in all problems involving hypothesis tests on the equality of means when the data are independent samples. Although the two tests will result in different p values, in most cases the two p values will be close. Either both will be greater than the significance level or both will be less than the significance level, and they will therefore be in agreement on the rejection of the Null Hypothesis. In this case, doing both procedures establishes that the result of a hypothesis test does not depend on the equality or inequality of population variances.

What if both procedures are done and they lead to different conclusions on whether or not the Null Hypothesis should be rejected? Although rare, this *can* happen. The decision on whether the two populations have equal means in this case depends on whether they have equal variances. There is an Analysis Tool within Excel which tests for the equality of two population variances. This test may be inconclusive, however, and a final conclusion may elude the investigator who really has no additional data on the populations. Fortunately, this is a rare situation whose primary use is to worry students of statistics.

Consider the following problem:

A firm supplying computer display projectors is considering switching to a new supplier of specialty bulbs because of that supplier's claim that its bulbs last longer. The firm has data from tests of sample bulbs of itsold supplier and has recently acquired and tested a sample of bulbs from the potential new supplier. Based on these data, does the firm have evidence at the .05 level of significance that the bulbs from the new supplier have a longer average life than bulbs from the old supplier?

The Null Hypothesis for this problem is $H_0: \mu_{new} \leq \mu_{old}$, and the Alternate Hypothesis is $H_A: \mu_{new} > \mu_{old}$. A necessary condition for the rejection of the Null Hypothesis is that $\bar{x}_{new} > \bar{x}_{old}$ (the sample is not consistent with the Null Hypothesis).

- Select the "Sheet2" worksheet. The data on bulb life are located there, with the sample data for bulbs from the old supplier in column A and those from the new supplier in column B. The first sample is larger than the first.

- Rename the "Sheet2" worksheet to "Independent."

We will first use the Tool that performs the test which assumes that the two populations have equal variances. The output from that test will enable us to check whether or not the sample data are consistent with the Null Hypothesis. If they are not, we will also use the Tool for the analysis assuming the population variances are unequal.

- Click on "Data Analysis..." on the "Tools" menu. On the Data Analysis dialog window select "t-Test: Two-Sample Assuming Equal Variance."

- Enter the range address of the "Old" data in the "Variable 1" field. Include the address of the cell containing the label "Old."

- Enter the range address of the "New" data in the "Variable 2" field, also including the address of the label.

- Enter the number "0" in the "Hypothesized Mean Difference" field, and click the box beside "Labels" so a small "x" appears.

- Click the radio button beside "Output Range" so it is selected and enter the address C1 in the "Output Range field. Click "OK."

- When the Tool has completed writing the output, and the range containing the output is selected, click the "Format" menu on the Menu Bar, select "Column" and then "AutoFit Selection" to adjust the column width so the output can be seen.

The first row of the output, labeled "Mean," gives the value of the sample means. You should have 47.5 for the mean of the sample of bulbs from the old supplier and 52.41666667 for the mean of the sample from the new supplier. This means that $\bar{x}_{new} > \bar{x}_{old}$. Since the Null Hypothesis is $\mu_{new} \leq \mu_{old}$, the sample is *not* consistent with the Null and the reported p values are therefore valid.

Notice the output gives the estimated "Pooled Variance." The most important part of the output is the reported p values. The one-tail p value is .051746314. This is slightly greater than the significance level (.05). On that basis we would fail to reject the Null Hypothesis and conclude that there is not evidence at the .05 level of significance that bulbs from the new supplier outlast those from the old supplier.

Let's now see if the results are different if we assume the two populations have different variances.

- Recall the Data Analysis dialog window. Choose "t-Test: Two Sample Assuming Unequal Variance" (immediately below the previous choice).

- The dialog window for this Tool looks like that of the previous Tool except for the title bar which has the words "Assuming Unequal Variance." Complete the fields of this dialog window exactly as you did the one for the previous Tool except direct the output to cell C16 which will put it directly below the previous Tool's output. Click "OK."

The output of this Tool is similar to that of the previous one. A good check to be sure you haven't made an error is to verify that the reported sample means on this output are the same as they were for the output above it. No "Pooled Variance" is reported since none is calculated if the population variances are believed equal.

The one-tail p value on this output is .025783329, which is less than the 0.05 significance level. Although in most cases these two outputs will lead to the same conclusion, they have not for this problem. The small p value in this procedure indicates that the Null Hypothesis should be rejected, and that we should conclude at the 0.05 level of significance that there *is* evidence that bulbs from the new supplier outlast those from the old! When the two procedures come to different conclusions, how are we to choose?

▼ Testing for a Difference in the Variance of Two Populations

The decision for this problem depends on whether or not the variance in the life of the population of bulbs from the old supplier equals the variance in the life of the population of bulbs from the new supplier. With our samples from each population, we do have some information on this issue. Both outputs provide the sample variances. Take a look at them.

For the sample of bulbs from the old supplier, the variance is a bit less than 90.55. For the sample of bulbs from the new supplier, the variance is just under 21.54. This seems like a substantial difference. Is it possible that such a difference in sample variances could arise if the samples were drawn from populations with the same variance? It certainly is *possible,* but it would be interesting to know how likely such a result would be. If this seems like a hypothesis testing question, good for you! This is exactly what we can do. Excel provides with a method of determining whether or not these samples provide evidence that the two populations have different variance.

To look for evidence of a difference in population variances we can test the Null Hypothesis $H_{0:}$ $\sigma^2_{new} = \sigma^2_{old}$ against the Alternate Hypothesis $H_{A:}$ $\sigma^2_{new} \neq \sigma^2_{old}$. The sample statistic in this case is the ratio of the two sample variances which, under the assumption of population normality, follows the F distribution. If the Null Hypothesis is rejected, we have evidence that the population variances differ. If they differ, the second t-Test output is the correct one for testing the equality of population means.

- Recall the Data Analysis dialog window and select "F-Test Two-Sample for Variances." The dialog window for this Tool is very similar to those you have filled out for the two procedures testing the equality of means. The major difference is that this Tool's dialog window has no field for "Hypothesized Mean Difference." Enter the same cell addresses in the "Variable" fields here as you did for the previous Tools. Select the "Output Range" radio button and direct the output to cell C30, placing it below both previous outputs. Click "OK."

The output from this Tool testing the equality of variances is similar to that to that of the two previous outputs testing the equality of means. Like the others, it provides the two sample means. Check to be sure the sample means in this output are identical to those of the other outputs, verifying that the correct data were used for the analysis. The sample statistic calculated in this analysis is the sample F, 4.204110346. The most important part of the output is the p value (labeled "P(F<=f) one-tail"), which in this case is slightly over .0088. Unfortunately, the Null Hypothesis we want to test ($H_{0:}$ $\sigma^2_{new} = \sigma^2_{old}$) requires a *two-tail* test, and this output gives only a *one-tail* p value (and critical value). Fortunately, it is easy to convert a one-tail p value to its two-tail counterpart: multiply by two. This must always be done when Excel's F test is used in the context of choosing between the two t tests on the equality of two population means.

- Select the region containing the last row of the output (C39:E39). Use the mouse to move that region down one row so that the row below the one-tail p value is blank.

- In (now blank) cell C39 enter the label "2 tail p value." In cell D39 enter a formula which will multiply the value of cell D38 by two. The displayed value will be 0.017676129.

This is a fairly small p value. At the 5% or 2% significance level (but not 1%), we would reject the Null Hypothesis that the population variances are equal and conclude that we have evidence that they are unequal. This, in turn, implies that the proper procedure for testing the equality of the means is the second procedure, which assumes the population variances are different. The low p value from this procedure (just under .026) led to the conclusion that there is evidence that the average life of bulbs from the new supplier exceeded that of the old supplier. This would be the ultimate conclusion from our analysis of the data.

In most cases the need to test a hypothesis about two population means will not require a test of equality of the two population variances because both procedures testing the means will yield the same result. Only in cases where they differ can an F test possibly be useful determining which means test procedure should be relied upon. In the example discussed here, the small p value in the F test led to a rejection of the Null Hypothesis of equal variances—a clear indication that the assumption of unequal variances is the correct choice. But what if the p value in the F test were large and the Null Hypothesis could not be rejected? As we saw in Chapter 8, failing to reject the Null Hypothesis is not the same as *accepting* it because we cannot determine the probability of committing Type II error. A failure to reject the Null Hypothesis that the population variances are equal is therefore *not* a solid justification for choosing to assume they are equal and using that assumption to test the population means. In fact, the only reliable guidance the F test can give us is to choose the assumption of unequal variances. It can't tell us to assume the assumption of equal variances. If a decision on the test of population means depends on the equality of variances (and it usually doesn't), and if the F test results in a p value too large to conclude the variances are unequal, we are left in a kind of statistical limbo. Without additional information it would be difficult to draw any conclusion.

▼ Exercises

1. The paired samples approach was described as being more *sensitive* than the independent samples approach. What, exactly, does this

mean? In the example paired samples problem on tire life, the average tread life of the tires made with the new compound was 3,091.75 miles greater than the average tread life of the tires made with the old compound (40,304 miles versus 37,212 miles). This difference was great enough to conclude the new rubber compound made a significant difference. Suppose we had the same sample data but from independent samples. Would we then have found evidence of a difference? Check this by analyzing the tire data using the two independent samples approaches. Explain why this makes the paired samples approach more *sensitive*.

The data for the problems given below can be found in an Excel workbook in the file named xrcise12.xls. The questions below indicate which worksheet has the data for each problem.

2. A manufacturing firm has plants in two different states and wants to compare the productivity of workers in one plant with workers in the other plant. The managers of each plant were asked to provide output per worker for a sample of 31 days. The resulting data are on the worksheet "Plants A & B." Based on these data, is there evidence (at the 0.10 level of significance) of a difference between average worker productivity (measured as output per worker) in the two plants? Provide the Null and Alternate Hypotheses for this test, give your reasons for rejecting or not rejecting the Null, and provide a yes or no answer to the question of whether there is evidence of difference in average productivity.

3. A long-distance trucking firm wants to determine whether increased maintenance will increase the gas mileage of trucks. A random sample of 25 trucks and drivers who repeatedly drive the same routes was placed on the standard maintenance routine for one week and the intensive maintenance routine for another week. The average gas mileage for each truck under each routine was collected and is presented in the worksheet named "Maintenance," in which the data for each truck are in one row. Based on these data, is there evidence (at the 0.01 level of significance) that the intensive maintenance increases gas mileage? Provide the Null and Alternate Hypotheses, the basis for rejecting or not rejecting the Null, and a yes or no answer to the question of whether intensive maintenance increases mileage.

4. The sales department of a firm is considering enrolling their salespeople in a program in positive sales motivation offered by a national consultant. In order to determine the effectiveness of the program, the firm sends a random sample of 30 salespersons to attend their program and measures their sales over the following month. A control group of 30 salespersons who did not attend the program is also cho-

sen at random, and their sales are also measured during the same month. Total monthly sales for each sample are on the "Motivation" worksheet. Based on these data is their evidence that attending the program would increase the average sales of all salespeople? Provide the Null and Alternate Hypotheses, the basis for rejecting or failing to reject the Null, and a yes or no answer to the question of whether there is evidence that program attendance would increase average sales.

Chapter 13

Analysis of Variance

Analysis of variance (or *ANOVA*) is another technique for testing the equality of different population means. Its name comes from the fact that it uses variance-like measures to make inferences about population means. One of the most useful characteristics of the analysis of variance technique is that it can be extended to any number of populations. Excel's Data Analysis Tools provide three different analysis of variance techniques. These techniques are appropriate for different types of data collection—analogous to the difference between paired samples and independent samples used in the *t* test for differences in two population means.

All of these techniques have certain things in common, however. All of them are designed to test the Null Hypothesis that all the populations from which the samples were drawn have equal means. The Alternate Hypothesis is that at least one of the population means differs from the others. If there are *n* different samples (drawn from *n* different populations) the Null Hypothesis can be symbolized as $H_0: \mu_1 = \mu_2 = ... = \mu_n$. There is no succinct way of expressing the Alternate Hypothesis (except as *not* the Null Hypothesis). The Alternate Hypothesis is true if many different conditions are met including, among many others, none of the population means being equal or all of the population means being equal except one. Analysis of variance techniques also share assumptions about the data. In addition to assuming the samples are random, they also assume the populations are normally distributed and have equal variance.

▼ Single-Factor Analysis of Variance

The (mathematically) simplest form of analysis of variance is the single-factor analysis (also frequently called *one-way* analysis of variance). It is used when the data are like those used in the independent sample approach to a test of the equality of two population means. The only difference accounted for in the sample observations is the different populations from which each observation came. Since, like all ANOVA techniques, the populations are assumed to have equal variance, this technique is an alternative to the *t* test for the equality of two population means assuming equal population variances. It is more versatile than that test because it is not restricted to two populations. When used with two populations, it gives exactly the same (two-tail) results.

In addition to single-factor analysis of variance, Excel has tools for two other types of ANOVA. They are all conceptually similar, and we will take a close- look at how single-factor ANOVA works to gain an understanding of the essentials of any ANOVA procedure.

Let's consider the following problem:

A company is considering two competing sales training courses for new salespersons. In order to compare their effectiveness, with each other and with no course, three groups of five randomly chosen new salespersons are selected. One group is sent to sales training course "A," the second is sent to sales training course "B," and the third receives no training at all. After the two groups have completed their training, sales records for each salesperson for the next two-week period are collected, and the results for each group are shown in the table below.

Course A	Course B	No Course
$2,058	$3,339	$2,228
$2,176	$2,777	$2,578
$3,449	$3,020	$1,227
$2,517	$2,437	$2,044
$944	$3,067	$1,681

Based on the data in the table, is there evidence at the 0.10 level of significance that there would be a difference in the means of all salespersons if they were sent to a training course?

What characteristics of these sample data would lead us to find evidence of a difference in the population means? First, a large difference in sample means is more likely to lead to the conclusion of a difference in population means than would a small difference in sample means. Sample means are randomly distributed around their population means. The means of any set of samples might be closer together or might be further apart than the population means, but sample means are unbiased estimates of population means. Sample means which are far apart are more consistent with differing population means than with identical population means. Second, small sample variance is also more likely to lead to the conclusion that the population means differ than is large sample variance. Small sample variance is consistent with small population variance, and if the population variance is small, the sample means are likely to be close in value to the population means. Differences in sample means are less likely to be the result of chance and more likely to be the result of a difference in population means. We can get a sense of both the difference in sample means and the sample variance by making a chart of the data.

- Open the Excel workbook in the file anova.xls.

- The data for this problem are on the "Sheet1" worksheet in the range B1:D6. Change that worksheet's name to "Sales Course." Change the name of the "Sheet2" worksheet to "Calc."

- Select cells B6:D6 in the "Sales Course" worksheet. Click the arrow beside the "Borders" button on the formatting toolbar and choose the button from the set that opens which will draw a dark underline below the selected cells.

- In cell A7 enter the label "means," and in cell A8 enter the label "grand mean."

- In cells B7:D7 enter formulas which will calculate the average of each column of five numbers. The values appearing in B7 through D7, respectively, should be 2228.8, 2928, and 1951.6.

- Enter the formula in cell D8 which will calculate the average of 15 numbers in B1:D6. The displayed value should be 2369.467.

A rearranged copy of the data will make it easier to produce a chart and show how the ANOVA calculations are done. This copy will be constructed so that changes in the original will automatically update the copy. One way of doing this would be to use a simple equation setting the value of each copy equal to the original. The procedure shown below is roughly equivalent, and you may find it easier.

- Switch to the "Calc" worksheet. Enter the labels "Sample" in cell A1, "x" in cell B1, "Samp Mean" in cell C1, and "Grand Mean" in cell D1. Adjust the column widths to hold the labels.

- Place a dark underline below the labels in A1:D1 with the "Borders" button. The heavy underline selection you made earlier will be the choice displayed on the button for the rest of the session until you make another choice. As long as you want heavy underline in this session, you need only click the button on the toolbar.

- Return to the "Sales Course" worksheet. Select cells B2:B6 (the "Course A" data) and click the Copy Button 📋 on the Standard Toolbar.

- Go to the "Calc" Worksheet. Select cell B2. Open the "Edit" menu on the Menu Bar. Select "Paste Special…." When the dialog window opens, click the "Paste Link" button on the right side (shown below). The numbers will appear to have been copied, but the formula bar will show that they contain a type of equation referring to the cells copied from the "Sales Course" worksheet.

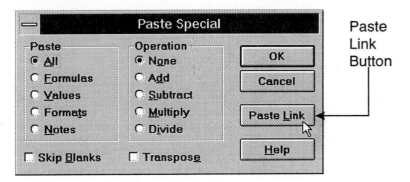

- Select cell B7 in "Sales Course" (the mean of "Course A") and click the Copy button again.

- Return to "Calc" and select the cell range C2:C6. Open the "Edit" menu on the menu bar, select "Paste Special…," and, when the dialog window opens, again click the "Paste Link" button. Each of the cells in C2:C6 will display the number 2228.8, but will actually contain a formula referring to cell B7 in "Sales Course."

- Enter the number "1" in cell A2 and then copy it down to cells A3:A6.

We now have the beginning of a table containing each value (in column B), the sample number in column A, and the sample mean in column C.

- Go to the "Sales Course" worksheet and select cells C2:C6. Click the Copy button. Switch to "Calc." Select cell B7, click "Paste Special…" off the "Edit Menu," and click the "Paste Link" button in the dialog window. The data from "Course B" will now appear directly below that of "Course A."

- Return to "Sales Course." Select cell B7 (the mean of "Course B"), click the Copy button, switch to "Calc," select the range C7:C11, and again make a "Paste Link" by opening the "Edit" menu, clicking "Paste Special…," and the clicking the "Paste Link" Button.

- Enter the number "2" in cells A7:A11.

The data for the second sample now appear directly below the first. The third sample will be placed below the second.

- Using the same procedures as before, create a "Paste Link" reference in cells B12:B16 in the "Calc" worksheet to cells D2:D6 (the "No Course" sample) in the "Sales Course worksheet. Check the formula bar for a cell in the range B12:B16 to be sure it contains the formula "{='Sales Course'!$D$2:$D$6}"and not simply numbers.

- Create a "Paste Link" in cells C12:C16 of "Calc" to the mean of the "No Course" sample in cell D7 of "Sales Course." Each of the cells in C12:C16 should display the value 1951.6, but should show in the formula bar the formula "='Sales Course'!$D$7."

- Enter the number "3" in cells A12:A16 of "Calc."

The last step is for each of the cells in column D of the table to refer to the "Grand Mean" of all the samples.

- Select cell D8 in the "Sales Course" worksheet, which contains the average of all 15 numbers, and click the Copy button. Go to the "Calc" worksheet. Select cells D2:D16, open the "Edit" menu, click "Paste Special...," and then click the "Paste Link" button. Each of the cells in D2:D16 will display the 15-number mean but will contain an equation referring to cell D8 in "Sales Course."

▼ Charting the Sample Values and the Means

The next step will be to produce a scatter plot which graphically displays the sample values, the sample means, and the grand mean.

- Switch to the "Sales Course" worksheet. Position the worksheet on the screen so that cell G1 is in the upper left-hand corner of your screen.

- Click the Chart Wizard button. Place the Chart Wizard mouse pointer approximately in the center of cell G1 and, while holding down the (left) mouse button, drag the mouse pointer to the lower right-hand corner of your screen, being careful not to move it off screen causing the worksheet to scroll. Release the mouse button.

- When the "Step 1" Chart Wizard dialog window opens. Switch to the "Calc" worksheet by clicking its worksheet tab. The dialog window will remain on your screen.

- Place the mouse pointer in cell A1 of the "Calc" worksheet, press the (left) mouse button, and drag the pointer to cell D16, surrounding the entire table with a marquee. Release the mouse button. Click the "Next>" button in the dialog window.

- In the "Step 2" Chart Wizard dialog window, choose the "XY (Scatter)" plot and click the "Next>" button.

- In the "Step 3" Chart Wizard dialog window, select the version of the scatter plot labeled "1," which has no gridlines and shows the points but does not connect them with lines. Click the "Next>" button.

- In the "Step 4" dialog window simply click the "Next>" button.

- Enter a title such as "Effect of Sales Courses on Sales" in the "Chart Title" field in the "Step 5" window. Click the "Finish" button.

The chart which appears on your screen has three columns of points. While most of them are one color (probably black or dark blue), you will notice that each column also has two differently colored points identified in the chart legend. We can make the chart clearer by editing it.

- "Activate" the chart by placing the mouse pointer inside and double clicking. The chart will be surrounded by the active mode boundary.

- Place the mouse pointer over one of the three points in the chart for the "Grand Mean." Click the mouse button once. All three grand mean points will change color.

- Click the "Format" menu on the menu bar. When the menu opens, choose "Selected Data Series...." A dialog window will open with folder tabs at the top.

- Click the "Patterns" folder tab (unless it is already in front). It contains two large areas labeled "Line" and "Marker." We will change it to eliminate the small symbol in each column but connect the locations with a straight line.

- In the "Line" section, click the radio button beside "Custom" to select it. Change the color, if you wish, by clicking the small downward pointing arrow by the current color and clicking the color you want.

- In the "Marker" area, click the radio button beside "None." This will eliminate the small symbol. Click the "OK" button.

The horizontal line shows the value of the grand mean (the mean of all the sample values). If you click the mouse pointer in a blank area in the graph, you will see that the symbols marking the values in each column are now gone.

- Be sure the activation boundary is still around the chart. Place the mouse pointer directly on one of the "Samp Mean" points. As an alternative to using the Format menu, click the *right* mouse button. A small menu will appear beside the mouse pointer. Choose "Format Data Series...." The dialog window which opens is identical to the one you saw earlier.

- Click the "Patterns" folder tab unless it is already on top. In the "Line" area click the radio button beside "Custom." Press the downward pointing arrow to the right of "Style" and choose a dotted line. Do not remove the marker, but be sure the marker and the line have the same color. Click the "OK" button.

The sample means should still have a symbol marking their location in each column, but are now connected by a dotted line, making it easy to see where they are and to compare their relative values.

A few more changes will improve the esthetics of the chart.

- Click the horizontal axis at the bottom of the chart. A small marker will appear at each end. Open the "Format" menu on the menu bar and click "Selected Axis...." (An alternative would be to place the mouse pointer on the axis, click the right mouse button, and choose "Format Axis.")

- Click the "Patterns" folder tab if it is not already on top. In the "Axis" region, click the radio button beside "None." In the "Tick-Mark Labels" region below, click the radio button beside "None." These two actions will completely eliminate the horizontal axis and its numbers.

- Click the "Scale" folder tab. In the field beside "Maximum," replace the number "3" with the number "4." This will extend the chart so that the right most column will be within the graph rather than on the right edge. Click the "OK" button.

- Make sure the edit boundary is still around the chart, but not also around some feature within the chart. If there is a second edit boundary around some feature of the chart, click the mouse pointer on a blank portion of the chart so that second edit boundary will disappear.

- Click the Formula Bar. Enter the label "Course A" in the formula bar (no quotes) and press the Enter key. A box will appear in the center of the chart with that label and surrounded by an edit boundary.

- Place your mouse pointer directly on the edit boundary surrounding "Course A." Press and hold the left mouse button and you will be able to move the label. Position it beneath the first column so that it is below where the horizontal axis used to be.

- Click the mouse pointer in a blank part of the chart so that the edit boundary disappears from "Course A." Click the formula bar and enter "Course B." Move this label below the second column.

- Using the same method, place the label "No Course" below the third column.

It is apparent from the chart that those who took course "B" did better on average than either of the other groups, and those who took no course did the worst, on average. This suggests that the sales courses do make a difference. Without a statistical test, we cannot be certain that the differences apparent in these samples are not simply due to chance—a result of the sample values randomly chosen. The test, single-factor ANOVA, is discussed below.

▼ Determining the Sum of Squares

A population variance is the average sum of squared deviations from the mean. A sample variance is an unbiased estimator of a population variance. To be unbiased, the sum of squared deviations must be divided by the degrees of freedom rather than by the number of observations. An analysis of variance involves calculating several variance-like measures. Each of them is a sum of squared deviations around some measure divided by the degrees of freedom. We will extend the table in the "Calc" worksheet to calculate these measures. Once this worksheet is finished, the results will be placed back on the "Sales Course" worksheet. We will then experiment with samples drawn from different populations to see how the chart and the statistical tests reflect those changes.

- Select the "Calc" worksheet.

Most of the calculations will be done in additional columns added to the present table. Row 1 will contain labels for these columns. In those labels we will use "s bar" to refer to the *sample* means (which differ for each sample) and "g bar" to refer to the *grand* mean which is the same for all samples.

- Enter the following labels in row 1 columns E through J: "x-s bar" in E1, "(x-s bar) ^ 2" in F1, "s bar-g bar" in G1, "(s bar-g bar) ^ 2" in H1, "x-g bar" in I1, and "(x-g bar) ^ 2" in J1. Adjust the column widths. A quick way of adjusting them all at once is to select cells F1:J1 (E1 should already have enough room), open the "Format" menu on the Menu Bar. Select "Column," then select "AutoFit Selection."

- Place a heavy underline under these cells like the one under the labels entered previously.

In all of the formulas below, use *relative* addresses. First enter the formulas for the first row. A simple copy will generate the formulas for the rest of the cells.

- In cell E2 enter a formula to calculate the difference between the *x* value in that row (column B) and the sample mean for that row (column C). The displayed value should be -170.8. In the language of ANOVA, this is a *deviation* from the sample mean.

- In cell F2 enter a formula which will calculate the square of the number in cell E2. This value (29172.64) is a *squared deviation*.

- In cell G2 enter a formula to calculate the difference between the sample mean in that row (column C) and the grand mean (column D). This value, -140.6667, is the *deviation* of the sample mean from the grand mean.

- In cell H2 enter a formula to square the value in G2. This value, 19787.11111, is another *squared deviation*.

- In cell I2 enter a formula to calculate the deviation of the *x* value in that row from the grand mean. The displayed value should be -311.467.

- In cell J2 enter a formula to calculate the squared deviation of the *x* value in that row from the grand mean by squaring the value in I2. The displayed value should be 97011.48.

The next step is to copy these formulas down their columns.

- Select cells E2:J2. Place the mouse pointer over the fill handle in the lower right corner of J2. When the pointer changes to a black cross, press and hold the (left) mouse button and drag the outline border down until it includes row 16. Release the mouse button, and the rest of the table will be filled with numbers.

- Use the "Borders" button to put heavy underlines beneath the last cell in each of the three columns of squared deviations: F16, H16, and J16.

- Enter the label "Sums" in cell A17, "SSW" in cell E17, "SSB" in G17, and "SST" in I17. "SSW" stands for "Sum of Squares Within," "SSB" for "Sum of Squares Between," and "SST" for "Sum of Squares Total."

- In cell F17 use the AutoSum button to enter a formula to add the numbers in column F. The value is 4790788. The numbers in column F are squared deviations, and F17 is a *sum of squared deviations* or a *sum of squares.* Since it is based on the difference between each value and that value's sample mean, it is the sum of squares within each group (or sample), SSW.

- Using the AutoSum button (or other means), enter formulas in cells H17 and J17 to calculate the sum of squares for their respective columns. H17 will display 2531795.733, and J17 will display 7322584.

H17 is the sum of squares between groups (SSB), and J17 is the total sum of squares (SST). The three sums of squares will be used for calculations in the *ANOVA table*

▼ Preparing the ANOVA Table

- Switch to the "Sales Course" worksheet.
- The ANOVA table will be put in the region of cells A10:F13. Scroll your worksheet and enter labels for the table as shown in the picture below.

	A	B	C	D	E	F
10		SS	df	MS	F	p value
11	Between					
12	Within					
13	Total					

The "SS" label stands for "Sum of Squares." The first step will be to create a link between the three cells in that column and the corresponding sum of squares in the "Calc" worksheet.

- Switch to the "Calc" worksheet. Select "SSB" in cell H17 and click the "Copy" button. Switch to the "Sales Course" worksheet and select cell B11. Open the "Edit" menu, click "Paste Special…," and click the "Paste Link" button in the dialog window.
- Using this procedure, create links for "SS Within" and "SS Total" in the "Sales Course" worksheet to the corresponding values in column B of the "Calc" worksheet.

The degrees of freedom of SST is the sum of the sample sizes minus 1. If all the samples were drawn from a single population and were combined into a single sample, this would be the degrees of freedom of the variance of that single sample. In this case there are three samples each of size 5. The degrees of freedom of SST is $5 + 5 + 5 - 1 = 14$.

- Enter the number "14" in cell C13.

If a separate variance were calculated from each sample, the degrees of freedom for each sample would be the simple size minus 1. The degrees of freedom of SSW is the sum of the degrees of freedom of each sample. This is the sum of the sample sizes minus the number of samples. For this problem there are three samples. The degrees of freedom of SSW is $5+5+5-3=12$.

- Enter the number "12" in cell C12.

The variance of SSB is the variance of sample means around the grand mean. There are only as many sample means as there are samples. The degrees of freedom is the number of samples minus one. For this problem there are three samples. The degrees of freedom of SSB is $3-1=2$.

- Enter the number "2" in cell C11.

Notice in the table that the total sum of squares is the sum of the two sum of squares above it, and the degree of freedom of the total sum of squares is the sum of the two degrees of freedom above it.

Dividing a sum of squares by the appropriate degrees of freedom results in a variance-like measure. It is traditional in ANOVA to do this only for the within-groups and between-groups measures.

- Enter formulas in cells D11 and D12 to divide the sum of squares in each row by its degrees of freedom. The displayed values should be 1265898 (D11) and 399232.3 (D12).

- In cell E11 enter the formula which will take the value in cell D11 and divide it by the value in cell D12. The displayed value will be 3.17083.

This number, essentially a ratio of two variances, is a random number distributed under the F distribution. The F distribution is the ratio of two independent chi square distributions, each of which is divided by its degrees of freedom. The assumption of equal values for σ in all populations will cause this to simplify to a ratio of sample variances in many cases. A large value for the between groups variance compared to the within-groups variance indicates that the sample values are relatively closer to the sample means (small sample variation) than the sample means are to the grand mean (large difference in sample means). This is the kind of result which would be expected if the samples were drawn from populations with different means. A p value can be determined by using the F distribution function in Excel to determine the probability that a value as high or higher than that in cell E11 could occur by chance.

- Select cell F11. Click the Function Wizard button. In the "Statistical" function category choose FDIST. There are three arguments for this function. The "x" argument field should have the cell address of the value for which we want the probability that an F distributed random variable will exceed E11. The two "degrees_freedom" arguments are the degrees of freedom of the numerator variance (in C11) and the denominator variance (in C12). Click the "Finish" button and the displayed value in F11 should be 0.078425.

Since this p value is less than the significance level of .10, we would reject the Null Hypothesis and conclude that there is evidence that the averages of all salespersons sent to the two courses and those sent to no course are not equal.

▼ Analyzing Simulated Samples

We can use Excel's Random Number Generation Tool to simulate new samples for the chart and ANOVA table. In order to meet the assumptions of analysis of variance, these random numbers will be drawn from a normal distribution.

- Open the "Tools" menu. Select "Data Analysis…," and choose "Random Number Generation" from the dialog window.

- On the Random Number Generation dialog window, enter "3" in the "Number of Variables" field (to overwrite the three columns of data in A1:D8) and "5" in the "Number of Random Numbers" field (for the five rows of data to be overwritten). Select "Normal" in the "Distribution" list and enter "2000" and "300" in the "Mean" and "Standard Deviation" fields, respectively. Click the "Output Range" radio button and enter the cell address for the upper left-hand corner of the existing data table (B2). Click the "OK" button. Click the "OK" button in the window warning you that data will be overwritten.

- Examine the new p value and look at the chart.

What we have done is simulate drawing three samples from a population with mean 2000 and standard deviation 300. The sample means and standard deviations will, of course, differ due to chance. The correct result of an analysis of variance would be to fail to reject the Null Hypothesis that the three samples are drawn from populations with the same mean. Large p values are what would be expected.

It is easy to draw an additional set of samples from the same population because the Analysis Tool will retain the values you previously entered. Try drawing additional samples from this population.

- Open the "Tools" menu and click "Data Analysis." Three dialog windows will appear in sequence; simply press the Enter key as soon as each appears, and a new sample will be drawn. Do this a dozen times or so, and look for a relationship between the p value and the chart. If you get a p value greater than .80 or less than .10, print its chart. Remember that to print just the chart, double click it ("activate" it) before choosing "Print Preview." In the page header, put your name and the p value.

- You must take the chart out of active mode (click off the chart on the worksheet) before drawing additional samples.

Even though ANOVA should always produce large p values when the samples are all drawn from the same population, if you choose enough samples you will occasionally see ANOVAs with small p values—caused by random differences in samples. These small values would cause you to reject the Null Hypothesis. Since the samples are all drawn from the same population, it would be incorrect to reject the Null Hypothesis—an example of Type I error.

Let's next examine how ANOVA handles data when the samples are drawn from populations which don't have equal means. It is not quite as convenient in Excel to generate repeated sets of samples in this case, but we will make it as easy as possible by continuing to draw the first two samples from the same population and drawing only the third sample from a population with a different mean.

- Recall the Random Number Generation dialog window. Change the value in the "Number of Variables" field from "3" to "2" and click "OK" until the values are generated. This will generate new values for the "Course A" and "Course B" samples but not the "No Course" sample.

- Again recall the Random Number Generation dialog window, this time to generate new values for the "No Course" sample from a population with a different mean.

- Change the value in the "Number of Variables" field from "2" to "1." Only one column of numbers will be written.

- Change the value in the "Mean" field from "2000" to "2100." This is the new population mean for this sample.

- Change the address in the "Output Range" field from "$B$2" to $D$2 (or D2). This will place the numbers in the "No Course" sample. Click "OK" (twice) so they will be generated.

Examine the graph and the p value. It is likely that this result is not very different from those obtained when all three samples were drawn from the same population. The p value is probably above .10, too high to conclude from the samples that the population means differ (even though we know they do). Furthermore, it's quite likely that the "No Course" sample, drawn from the population with the highest mean, doesn't even have the highest sample mean. Let's look at a few more samples drawn from these different populations. The easiest way to do this is to simply rerun the Random Number Generation Tool with the last set of values and then rerun it with the changes needed for the other sample or samples.

- Recall the Random Number Generation Tool. Repeatedly click "OK" (or press the Enter key) until a new set of numbers is generated. Since the tool was last used for the "No Course" sample, that sample will be regenerated.

- Again recall the Random Number Generation Tool. Make the changes needed to have it draw new values for the two "Course" samples. Change "Number of Variables" to "2," "Mean" to "2000," and "Output Range" to "$B$2." Click "OK" until the new random numbers are generated. Examine the chart and ANOVA table again.

- Generate yet another set of samples by first recalling and re-running the Random Number Generation Tool without change. This will result in new numbers for the two "Course" samples. Again recall the tool and make the changes needed to generate the "No Course" sample ("Number of Variables"= 1, "Mean" = 2100, "Output Range" = $D$2). After the new values are generated check the chart and ANOVA table.

- Repeat the process of generating the two sets of samples a few more times. Each time the Random Number Generation Tool must be run twice. The first time, run it unchanged from the previous time. The second time, change the three fields (Number of Variables, Mean, and Output Range) to generate the rest of the data.

You should see from this exercise that ANOVA cannot reliably detect a difference between population means when the difference is only 100 and population variances are 300. Failure to reject the Null Hypothesis in this case is an example of Type II error. Avoiding this error requires some combination of a larger difference in population means, a smaller variance, or larger samples.

- Regenerate the two sets of samples except change the value of "Mean" for the "No Course" sample from "2100" to "3000" (and leave the others at "2000). This time you should get a quite different result. The ANOVA p value should be quite small (less than .01), and the chart should clearly show the third sample as having a mean clearly greater than the other two. If you don't get this result, regenerate the two sets of samples a couple of more times.

- Regenerate the two sets of samples again. This time change the "Mean" of "No Course" back to "2100" (leaving the other two at "2000"). Change the "Standard Deviation" of *both* sets of samples from "300" to "30." Even though the difference in the means is again only 100, the reduced variance of the population makes it easy for ANOVA to detect the difference from the samples. The *p* value should be very small and the chart should clearly show higher values for the "No Course" sample than for the other two samples.

▼ Using the One-Factor ANOVA Tool

Excel has an analysis tool which will automatically create an ANOVA table and will also display other statistics not shown on the ANOVA table we have created. Like all analysis tools, it must be rerun whenever there is a change in the data.

- Select "Data Analysis…" from the "Tools" menu on the Menu Bar.

- Choose "Anova: Single Factor," which is located at the top of the list. You will probably have to scroll the list of tool up to see it.

- Enter the cell addresses of the sample data in the "Input Range" field. The addresses should contain the sample labels in the first row, so the address you enter should be B1:D6.

- Click the square beside "Labels in First Row" so that an "x" appears.

- The "Alpha" value allows you to specify a significance level for a critical *F*, a statistic not present in the ANOVA table prepared earlier. Enter "0.1" in this field. This corresponds with the significance level given in the original problem.

- Click the radio button beside "Output Range" to choose it and enter the cell address A15 in the field to the right. This will place the tool's ANOVA table directly below the one already on the sheet.

- Click "OK." As soon as the output is written, and while it is still selected, open the "Format" menu on the Menu Bar, select "Column" and then select "AutoFit Selection." If part of the output is covered by the chart, click the chart once and move it out of the way by placing the mouse pointer on the chart and dragging it (with the left mouse button pressed) to the right.

The output consists of a summary table providing the sums, means and variances of the data in each sample and an ANOVA table. Except for minor formatting differences and the presence of a critical F value (which should be 2.80679302), the table produced by the Analysis Tool should be identical to the table prepared earlier above it. If the two tables are not the same on your worksheet, you have made an error, probably in the dialog window of the Analysis Tool. Recall that dialog window and pay special attention to the "Input Range" field. Does it have either B1:D6 or $B$1:$D$6? Is the "Labels" box checked?

▼ Two-Factor Analysis of Variance

Excel provides two analysis tools for two-factor analysis of variance (also called *two-way* analysis of variance). Two-factor analysis attempts to additionally control for factors other than which population an observation came from which might affect the observed value. The difference between two-factor and one-factor analysis is similar to the difference between the paired samples and independent samples in Chapter 12. One of the two-factor analysis tools is termed "Without Replication," and the other is termed "With Replication." There are a several other common terms used for these analyses which you may see. The two-factor analysis without replications is often called *two-way analysis without interaction* or *randomized block* design. The two-factor analysis with replication is also known as *two-way analysis with interaction* or *factorial* design. The Excel terminology will be used here.

▼ Two-Factor Analysis without Replication

Consider the following problem:

In recent years, a number of "ergonomic" computer keyboards have become available. A business office wants to determine if the keyboard design has any effect on the speed of typists. Five typists of varying ability are chosen at random. Each is given the opportunity to become familiar with each keyboard prior to taking a test with that keyboard, and each typist is tested with all three keyboards. The results of that test are shown on the next page (the numbers represent words per minute typed).

Is there evidence (at the .01 level of significance) that average typing speed differs among the three keyboards?

One of the factors which strongly influences a typist's speed is that person's skill. Two-factor analysis of variance provides a technique which

		Keyboard	
Typist	A	B	C
1	51	57	72
2	109	112	117
3	47	43	51
4	98	98	107
5	70	69	77

accounts for the fact that much of the difference in typing speed is owing to ability differences among the typists, not keyboard differences.

- The data for this problem are on Sheet3 (cells A1:D6) of the anova.xls workbook. Select that worksheet and change its name to "Blocked." (This name will be explained below.)

The data in the worksheet are arranged the same as the data in the table. This follows a convention in statistics in which the characteristic distinguishing the data in one column for that in another is the characteristic to be analyzed. The characteristic distinguishing one row from another is controlled by the researcher and is used to permit better identification of the difference to be analyzed. It is standard terminology to refer to the column differences as *treatment* and the row differences as *blocking* or *blocks*. Think of an agricultural experiment to determine the effectiveness of different fertilizers on plant growth. Plant growth is also affected by other conditions, such as amount of water, soil characteristics, and amount of sunshine. In order to test the fertilizer, numerous small sections of land (*blocks*), which have identical soil, water, and sun, would each get plants which received each of the test fertilizers (*treatments*).

- Open the "Tools" menu, select "Data Analysis…," and choose "Anova: Two-Factor Without Replication."

- In the "Input Range" field, enter the cell range which contains the data and the labels for both the rows and columns. Note that with this Analysis Tool "labels" means both row labels and column labels. You cannot simply have column labels as was done with the data for one-factor ANOVA.

- Click the box beside "Labels" to place an "x" in it indicating that the cell range includes row and column labels.

- Change the value in the "Alpha" field to "0.01." This will cause the output to have the correct critical F values. This is unnecessary if the p value is used for the decision on the Null Hypothesis.

- Click the radio button beside "Output Range," and enter the address "E1" in the field to the right. Click "OK." When the Tool finishes writing the output, select the following menu sequence: "Format," "Column," and "AutoFit Selection."

The organization of the output is similar to that of the one-factor ANOVA. The summary table provides summary statistics for each column *and* each row in the data. The ANOVA table also has more entries than did the one-way ANOVA table, but the structure of the calculations within the table is very similar.

Separate sums of squares are calculated and provided for the rows and columns (many statistics texts would use the terms *blocks* and *treatments* to mean the same thing). The "Rows" sums of squares are calculated from the difference between each value and the average of the three values in that row. That difference is then squared, summed for all columns, and multiplied by the number of values in each row (the number of columns). The "Columns" sum of squares is computed exactly as the "Between Groups" sum of squares was in single-factor ANOVA. The difference between each number and the average of the numbers in the same column is determined, squared, summed for all rows, and then multiplied by the number of values in each column (number of rows).

The calculation of the error sum of squares is a bit different. For each number the sum of the average of all numbers in the row plus all numbers in the column is computed. That sum is then subtracted from the grand average of all the data. The difference between the value of that number and this result is then determined, squared, and added for all the numbers in the data. The error sum of squares is analogous to the single-factor "Within Groups" sum of squares.

The total sum of squares is calculated the same as in single-factor ANOVA: the difference between each value and the grand average of all the data is calculated, squared, and summed for all the data. The total sum of squares is also the sum of the row, column, and error sums of squares.

The degrees of freedom of the rows sum of squares is the number of rows minus 1, which is 5 for this problem. Dividing the rows sum of squares by its degree of freedom gives the rows mean squares, which is a measure similar to a variance. Similarly the degrees of freedom of the columns sum of squares is the number of columns minus 1. Dividing the columns sum of squares by its degrees of freedom gives the columns mean square error, another variance-like measure. The degrees of freedom of the error sum of squares is the product of the rows sum of squares and columns sum of squares degrees of freedom. Dividing the error sum of squares by its degrees of freedom yields the mean square error.

Two F values are given in the printout, along with their p values and corresponding critical values. The significance level for the critical values is set by the number in the "Alpha" field of the Tool's dialog window. The values in the "Rows" row of the table is appropriate for the Null Hypothesis that the means of populations from which each row was drawn are all equal. The low p value (5.42004E-08 or 0.0000000542) provides a strong basis for rejecting that Null Hypothesis and concluding that there is a difference in the population row means. This result, however, does not address the problem which the analysis is designed to solve. The rows correspond to the different typists. Rejecting the Null Hypothesis means that there is a real difference in the average typing speed of different typists, something we knew before analyzing the data. The only value of the "Rows" test is to help identify a situation in which we have erroneously chosen a control factor which is not strongly related to the outcome measure (typing speed) in which we are interested. This problem clearly does not suffer from that error.

The more important result is found in the "Columns" row of the ANOVA table. The low p value in that row (a bit less than .00343) is a strong basis for rejecting the Null Hypothesis of no difference in the population means of the three keyboards. By rejecting that hypothesis, we have evidence (at the .01 level of significance) that the keyboard *does* make a difference in average typing speed.

▼ Two-Factor Analysis with Replication

Two factor analysis of variance with replication is a technique for examining the relationship between two different characteristics believed to affect a particular outcome. It differs from the two-factor analysis without replication in the following ways.

1. Usually the investigator is interested in both factors, unlike the typical situation with two-factor analysis without replication where one of the factors is used as control or "blocking."

2. There is more than one observation for each set of values of the factors.

3. In addition to the effect of each factor, the analysis also looks at "inter-actions," the possibly different effect associated with combinations of factors.

These issues will be clearer as we look at an example:

A perfume manufacturer has test marketed a new perfume in a number of cities. In addition to the scent of the perfume, experience has shown that sales depends heavily on packaging and on advertising strategy. Three different advertising strategies (termed "Sophisticated," "Athletic," and "Popular") and three different package designs were tested along with the new perfume. Each combination was tested in two different markets, and each test market program was six months long. At the completion of the program, the level of sales per thousand women in the market was collected. The results, arranged by advertising strategy and package design, are shown below.

Package Design	Advertising Strategy		
	Sophsticated	Athletic	Popular
1	2.80	2.04	1.58
	2.73	1.33	1.26
2	3.29	1.50	1.00
	2.68	1.40	1.82
3	2.54	3.15	1.92
	2.59	2.88	1.33

These data are also present on Sheet4 of the worksheet in anova.xls.

Based on these data, is there evidence of a difference in population means for different advertising strategies? Different package designs? Interactions between package designs and advertising strategy?

In this example, we would expect to find *interactions* if the effect of the package design depended on the advertising strategy. It is reasonable to expect interactions in this case. Suppose, for example, one of the package designs was somehow more "sophisticated" than the others. It would make sense for this design to have a different (more positive) impact if the perfume were advertised with the "Sophisticated" strategy than if it were advertised with the "Athletic" strategy.

The fact that each "cell" (that is, each combination of a specific advertising strategy and package design) has more than one observation enables us to calculate a mean of those observations and use them to form an additional sum of squares. This will result in *four* sums of squares: one for the rows, one for the columns, one for the interactions, and an error sum of squares. These sums of squares are handled in an ANOVA table in a manner very similar to the previous ANOVA tables.

In two-factor analysis of variance with replication (unlike two-factor analysis without replication) there is no conceptual difference between the columns and the rows. The factor represented by the rows and that represented by the columns are to be analyzed. The situation is thus different from the previous approach where the column factor was the only one to be analyzed while the row factor was designed by the researcher to account for things already known to affect the outcome to be analyzed.

Excel's analysis tool does impose one requirement on the structure of the data: each value of the column factor must occupy a single column on the spreadsheet. Since there are multiple observations per cell, each value of the row factor must occupy *more than one* row. The data in the table on page 333 are organized this way as are the data in the worksheet.

- Switch to Sheet4 of the anova.xls worksheet. Rename that worksheet "Interactions."

- Open the "Tools" menu, select "Data Analysis...," and choose "Anova: Two-Factor With Replication."

- In the "Input Range" field, enter the address for the cell range containing the data table including the labels in row 1 and column A.

Note that in this tool, unlike the two other ANOVA tools, labels *must* be present for *both* the columns and rows, and their addresses *must* be included in the "Input Range" field. There is no "Labels" check box because labels are required.

- The "Rows per Sample" field should indicate how many observations are in each cell. Since Excel requires them to be in different rows, this is equivalent to the number of rows for each value of the row factor. For this problem, the number is "2." Enter that value in the field.

- Make the entries required to have the tool place the output on the same worksheet beginning in cell E1. Click "OK." Once the output is written, use the Format menu to adjust the column widths.

The table of summary statistics is now quite long, although the same basic descriptive statistics given in the previous ANOVA tools are given here as well. For this output the statistics are arranged in a matrix allowing you to determine the values for each cell (each combination of a particular row factor value and column factor value). A good check to be sure the dialog window was filled correctly is to verify that Excel reads two values for each cell, and that the labels given in this output include all the row and column labels in the original data. The rightmost column and bottom row are labeled "Total." These give the summary statistics for all of the observations for each value of the column factor and row factor, respectively.

The ANOVA table is quite similar to all the other ANOVA tables except for the presence of the "Interaction" row. Excel uses the term "Sample" to denote what had been termed "Rows" in the two-factor analysis without replication. "Rows" would have been clearer here since the statistic in that row accounts for differences in the row factor. The calculations of the sums of squares and degrees of freedom are similar to those of the other ANOVAs, and the mean squares (MS), a variance-like measure, is determined by dividing each sum of squares by its degrees of freedom. The three *F* values were calculated by dividing each of the mean square values in that row by the mean square error. The answers to the problem are given best by the three *p* values.

The *p* value of slightly over .0761 for the rows ("Sample") factor indicates that we (just) fail to reject the Null Hypothesis (at the .05 level of significance) that there is no difference in the population means for the different package designs. The *p* value of a bit over .00037 for the column factor provides a strong basis for reject the Null Hypothesis of no difference in the population means of the different advertising strategies. In other words, advertising strategy clearly affects sales, while it appears that package design may not. The *p* value for interactions of slightly over .022 is especially interesting. This low value would lead to rejecting the Null Hypothesis of no difference in the population means of the different interactions. This suggests that while we were unable to conclude that packaging overall had any effect on mean sales, it appears that it does have an effect with certain advertising strategies. It would thus be a mistake to conclude that packaging is not important. A result like this clearly calls for additional research to determine with more precision how the interaction between packaging and advertising strategy works.

▼ Exercises

1. Use one-factor analysis of variance to analyze the data on the effect of keyboards on typing speed in the "Blocked Worksheet." Produce a printout which shows both the results of the one factor and two-factor without replication analysis. Which technique is preferable? Why?

2. The results of the perfume data indicated the presence of significant interaction effects between advertising strategy and package design. For which advertising strategy are these effects important? Answer that

question by using separate one-factor analysis of variance on the data for each advertising strategy to test for differences in the population means of different package designs. Produce a printout showing your results for each strategy. When is package design important?

3. Property taxation requires that appraisers periodically determine the market value of all the houses in a jurisdiction. Ideally this determination is completely objective, and every appraiser would come up with the same value. In practice this is impossible. The tax division of a county government wants to determine if there is evidence of a difference in the averages of appraised values among four different appraisers. In order to determine this, each appraiser is asked to determine the value of four houses. The same four houses are appraised by each appraiser with the following results.

House	Appraiser			
	Mike	Sally	Tom	Jane
1	$101,900	$101,944	$100,967	$100,175
2	$72,744	$76,893	$73,206	$74,820
3	$132,217	$136,232	$131,935	$132,889
4	$211,213	$213,941	$212,735	$213,796

Is there evidence (at the .05) level of significance of a difference in average appraised value among appraisers? Print the results of the appropriate analysis in Excel, and explain why you chose that particular analysis rather than the others. Be sure to provide a yes or no answer to the question and your basis for that answer. (A copy of the data is in Sheet6 of the workbook in anova.xls.)

4. A grocery chain wants to determine if background music affects the average daily sales of stores. A sample of similarly sized stores was chosen and each was randomly assigned to four different groups: no background music, classical, hard rock, and soft rock. The results (in $10,000) are shown below. (These data are also on Sheet7 of the workbook in anova.xls.)

None	Classical	Hard	Soft
13	16	13	13
9	19	14	12
10	11	16	15
17	9	4	9
10	11	15	15

Based on this result, is there evidence at the .05 level of significance music choice would affect average sales for all stores? Print the Excel analysis and explain how you determined your answer. Be sure and give a yes or no answer to the question.

Chapter 14

Simple Linear Regression

Regression analysis gives us a way to investigate the relationship among a group of variables. *Simple* regression analyzes the relationship between two variables. *Multiple* regression removes this restriction and permits the analysis of the relationship among any number of variables. Although the mathematics of multiple regression are a reasonably straightforward extension of simple regression, the increased flexibility makes it a much more versatile and complex analysis tool than simple regression. By studying simple regression before multiple regression, we postpone some of the complexities of regression analysis and focus on the essentials. Another reason to study simple regression first is that the restriction to two dimensions (two variables) makes it easy to represent regression analysis graphically.

When a researcher uses simple linear regression to analyze a set of data, she must already accept certain assumptions. If these assumptions cannot be accepted, some technique other than simple regression will be required to analyze the data. In many (but not all) cases, multiple regression may offer a good technique for analyzing such data.

Data appropriate for simple linear regression consist of observations which each have two different measures. For examples, we might have a sample of houses and, for each house, a measure of that house's size and its selling price. Perhaps we have a sample of families, and for each family we have annual income and annual expenditures on clothing. A classic problem in regression analysis involved data containing the height of individuals and the average height of each individual's parents (the measure of height was adjusted for gender differences).

Simple regression allows us to investigate the relationship between the two measures and answer such questions as "What sales price could be predicted for a house with 965 square feet?" or "Do taller parents tend to have taller children?" or "Of every additional $1 increase in income, how much on average goes to additional expenditures on clothes?" Implicit in these questions is the notion of *causality*. The size of a house determines, or causes, the level of the sales price, and not vice versa. Similarly, tall fathers are responsible for tall sons. The height of the son doesn't determine the height of the father. A family's income determines how much that family spends on clothes; the amount it spends on clothes doesn't determine its income. Note that regression is of no use in determining the direction of causality; that determination must be made before regression analysis is used.

In a causal relationship between two factors, one factor causes changes in the other factor, not vice versa. The causing factor (house size, height of fathers, and family income in the examples above) is termed the *independent variable*. The idea here is that whatever determines the level of that measure is outside, or independent, of the relationship being analyzed between the two measures. Other names for this measure include *exogenous variable* and *x variable*.

The factor experiencing the effect of a change in the independent variable in the relationship (such as house selling price, height of sons, and expenditure on clothes) is termed the *dependent variable*. Its value depends on the value of the independent variable. Other names for this measure include *endogenous variable* and *y variable*.

▼ Linear Relationships

When a set of data is analyzed by simple linear regression the result is an equation which traditionally contains a *y* on the left-hand side of the equal sign and an *x* on the right-hand side. When a value is substituted in the equation for the symbol *x*, the equation provides the computation of a *predicted* value for *y*. The equation is called *linear* because it gives a relationship between the *y* and *x* variables which, when plotted, results in a straight line. Any equation for a line can be written in the following form:

$$y = b_0 + b_1 x$$

Both "b_0" and "b_1" would be numbers in a specific equation; when their values are determined, the equation is determined. Simple linear regression determines the values of "b_0" and "b_1" which "best" fit the data according to a specific criteria. When a linear equation is written in the form shown above, "b_0" is sometimes called the *y intercept* and "b_1" is called the *slope*. Let's use Excel to explore these meanings.

- Open the Excel workbook in the file simpreg.xls. Go to the first worksheet, which is titled "b0 & b1."

- In cell B17 enter the number "1." This will be an intercept value.

- In cell B18 enter the number "2." This will be a slope value.

- Select cell B2. This cell will contain a y value to go with the x value of −3. Each cell below it will contain the y value to go with the x value beside it.

- Enter the Excel formula in cell B2 which will take the value in cell B17 (which is "b_0"), and add to it the value in cell B18 ("b_1") times the value in cell A2 ("x"). Make the references to cells B17 and B18 *absolute* and the reference to A2 *relative*.

This formula is the Excel version of the equation of a line given above. With the values for "b_0" (1) and "b_1" (2) given above, the form of the equation is $y = 1 + 2x$. If −3 is substituted for x, the value of y is −5. This value should be displayed in B5.

- Copy the formula in B2 to B3 through B15. If error values are displayed in any of the cells, select B5 and double check it. Be sure the references to B17 and B18 are *absolute* and A5 is *relative*. If the value in A5, 0, is substituted for x in the equation $y = 1 + 2x$, the result is 1. This is the value which should be displayed in B5. Similarly, the value in B15 should be 21.

- Click the Chart Wizard button. Place the Chart Wizard mouse pointer approximately in the center of cell C1, press the left mouse button and drag the pointer to the approximate center of the cell in the lower right corner of your screen. Release the mouse pointer.

- When Step 1 dialog window of the Chart Wizard opens, enter the address of the range of cells containing the table of x and y values, A1:B15. Click the "Next>" button.

- In the Step 2 dialog window, choose "XY (Scatter)." Go to the next dialog window.

- In the Step 3 dialog window choose format number 6, which shows lines but no small squares or other symbols for the data points.

- In the Step 4 dialog window, be sure Excel knows the data are in columns, and that the first column is for "x data." If Excel has this wrong, the small chart in the dialog window will have two lines. When you correct it, only one line will be charted. Click the "Next>" button.

- In the Step 5 dialog window, indicate that Excel should not add a legend. Click the "Finish" button.

If the data for an Excel chart change, Excel will normally rescale the axes so that all of the new data will fit. We will change the values of the slope and intercept to see how the line changes. In this case, a rescaling of an axis will make it more difficult to see exactly how the line changes. To avoid this, we can "fix" the vertical axis so that Excel will not change it.

- Place the mouse pointer on the chart and double click the (left) mouse button to "activate" the chart.

- When the chart is in active mode (with the cross-hatched boundary), place the mouse pointer on the vertical axis and click it once. A small square box (edit handle) should appear at each end of the axis as shown in the picture below.

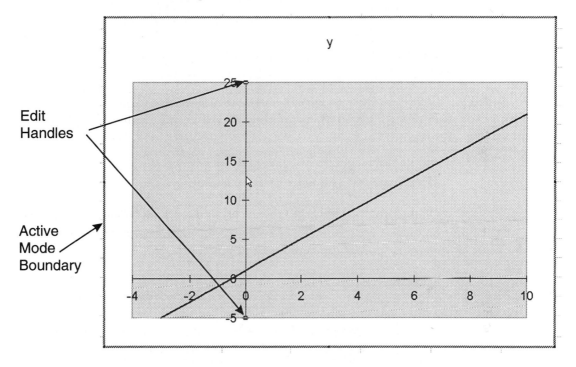

- With the edit handles visible at each end of the axis, open the Format menu on the Menu bar. Click "Selected Axis…." The Format Axis dialog window will open.

- Click the "Scale" folder tab at the top of the window. On the left side of the window is a series of fields under the title "Value (Y) Axis Scale." There is a column of check boxes below the word "Auto." Click the boxes beside the words "Minimum" and "Maximum" to *remove* the x's in the boxes. The window should look like the picture on the next page. Click the "OK" button. Click a part of the spreadsheet off the chart to take the chart out of edit mode.

By changing the value of the intercept (in B17) and the slope (B18), the line will change. Observe how these changes work in the steps below so that you can think of a line you see in terms of its intercept and slope.

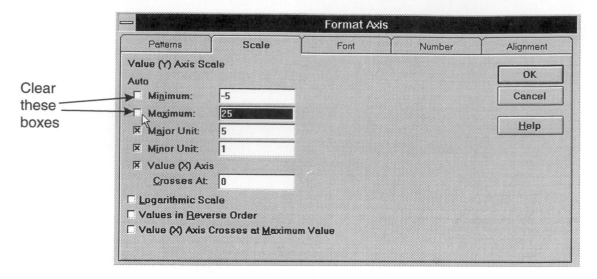

Clear these boxes

Notice also the relationship between the x and y values in columns A and B

- Change the value of the intercept to 5. Observe where it crosses the vertical axis. Change it to 10, 15, and then 20.

- Change the intercept back to 1. Make the slope larger and note the effect it has on the line. Try values of 5, 10, 15, and 20. After each change, look at the x and y values in columns A and B.

- Make the slope 0. Look at the relationship between the values of x and y in the table. Change the intercept to 15 and reexamine the table.

- Keep the intercept at 15. Make the slope increasingly negative. Try values of -2, -5, -10, -50. Study the relationship between x and y in the table after each change.

When a line has a positive slope, increasing x values are associated with increasing y values. When a line has a negative slope, increasing x values are associated with decreasing y values. A positive slope indicates a *positive* or *direct* relationship between x and y. A negative slope indicates a *negative* or *inverse* relationship between x and y.

What happens to the relationship between the values in columns A and B when the slope is 0? A horizontal line has a special significance because it represents *no relationship* between the two variables. Changes in the value of the x variable in column A have no effect at all on the y variable in column B and knowing x doesn't affect our best guess of y. The basis of some of the goodness of fit tests for a regression line involves comparing the relationship implied by the line which "best" fits the data with a horizontal line—equivalent to comparing the "best" relationship to no relationship at all.

▼ The Simple Linear Regression Model

When we use simple linear regression to analyze a data sample, we are making certain assumptions about those data. We assume, for example, that a linear relationship exists between two measures or variables in the population which can be represented by the following equation:

$$Y = \beta_0 + \beta_1 X + \varepsilon$$

Compare this equation to the equation on page 339. The equation here shows a relationship in a population; that is why capital Y and X are used here rather than lowercase y and x. It is also why Greek letters β_0 and β_1 (*beta*) are used rather than b_0 and b_1. The meanings of β_0 and β_1 here are the same as b_0 and b_1 in that earlier equation. β_0 is the y axis intercept and β_1 is the slope of the line. Both of the β's are fixed numbers—population parameters. Like other population parameters (such as μ), we generally do not know their value and seek to estimate them by analyzing a sample of data drawn from the population.

The most important difference between the equation above and the one on page 339 is the "ε" (the Greek letter *epsilon*). Unlike the β's, ε is a random number. Its presence means that the relationship cannot be perfectly represented by a straight line. Even if we knew β_0 and β_1, we still couldn't perfectly predict Y. There is a difference between the actual value of Y and what the value would be if the relationship were perfectly linear. That difference is ε, and its value differs randomly for each observation. ε is usually regarded as representing the effect of a large number of individually insignificant and independent factors which affect the value of Y *other than* X. Regression analysis requires certain assumptions about the distribution of ε: it is normal with a mean of zero and a constant variance. The values of ε are assumed independent of one another.

▼ Fitting a Line to Sample Data

The values of β_0 and β_1 are estimated by selecting a sample of data and then finding that line which best "fits" the data according to a specific criterion: minimizing the sum of squared errors. This estimation line is represented by the following function:

$$\hat{y} = b_0 + b_1 x$$

The $\hat{y}$ is termed the "predicted" value of y given by the linear equation and is often called "y hat." Recall that each observation in the population has a value for ε associated with it and these values cause the population values not to have a precise linear relationship. When a sample is chosen, the sample values will not lie precisely on a straight line. As a result, there will generally be a difference for each observation between the value of $\hat{y}$ and the value of y. This will be clearer if we consider a specific example.

A firm which manufacturers a particular type of hardware fastener wants to determine the relationship between monthly operating cost and monthly output for its manufacturing plants. Each plant submits a report each month which includes this information, and from these reports the firm has selected a sample showing output (in thousands of pounds) and operating cost (in thousands of dollars). Based on this information, what is the relationship?

The data for this problem can be found on the "Line Fit" worksheet of the workbook in simpreg.xls. We will use the procedures above to try to manually fit a line to the output and cost data and see the relationship between the visual fit between the line and data and the sum of squared errors.

- Switch to the "Line Fit" worksheet.

The worksheet already contains observations with x and y values in columns A and B, respectively. Column C (labeled "y hat") will contain a second set of y values derived from a line whose intercept and slope will be entered in C16 and C17 using the same procedure as was used on the previous worksheet.

- Enter the value "2" in cell C16 and "1.5" in cell C17.

- Enter formulas in cells C2:C15 which calculate the y value associated with the corresponding x value in column A for a line whose intercept and slope are given in C16 and C17. These formulas will be very similar to the ones you entered in column B on the "b0 & b1" worksheet. Be sure to multiply the value in C17 (b_1) by x (column A) and not y. Also be sure the addresses for b_0 and b_1 in the equation are *absolute*. When the correct formulas are entered, cell C2 will display the value 3.575, and cell C15 will display 6.29. These values are called the *predicted y values*.

The goal of fitting a line to the data is to come up with the values for the slope and intercept which result in values in column C which are "closest" to those in column B (predicted values close to actual values). For regression, "close" is defined in terms of the sum of squared errors.

- Enter the formulas in cells D2:D15 which will, for each row, calculate the value in column B minus the value in column C. It is these differences which are to be collectively minimized. Cell D2 should display -2.0550, and cell D15 should display 3.6100. These values are often called the *errors* or *residuals*, and fitting a line involves a way of collectively minimizing them.

- Use the AutoSum button to enter the formula in cell D16 which will calculate the sum of the numbers in D2:D15. The displayed value should be 99.4750. This is the *sum of the errors.* The sum is positive, like most of the individual errors. On average, the actual values exceed the predicted values.

- Enter formulas in cells E2:E15 which will calculate the square of the corresponding value in column D. E2 should display 4.223025, and E15 should display 13.0321. These are the *squared errors*.

- Enter the formula in E16 which will calculate the sum of the values in E2:E15. This is the *sum of squared errors.* The value displayed in E16 should be 1004.186.

- Enter the label "SSE" (for sum of squared errors) in cell E17. This is a commonly used abbreviation in statistics.

As stated above, regression fits a line to the data by determining the value of the intercept and slope which minimizes the sum of squared errors (in E16). You may wonder why the sum of errors (in D16) isn't minimized instead. To examine this and the relationship between fit and sum of squared errors, we will plot the data and the line given by the value of the slope and intercept in C16 and C17.

- Select the region A1:C15.

- Scroll your worksheet down so that the top row visible is row 16.

- Use the following procedure to make the largest possible chart in the area on your screen below row 17. Click the Chart Wizard button. Place the mouse pointer in cell A18, press and hold the (left) mouse button, and drag the pointer to the cell in the lower right corner of your screen, being careful not to cause the screen to scroll. Release the mouse button.

- The Chart Wizard Step 1 dialog window should appear with the address of the previously selected region in the "Range" field. Since absolute addresses are used, this should appear as "=$A$1:$C$15." Check it to be sure and click the "Next>" button.

- In the Step 2 dialog window, choose "XY (Scatter)."

- In the Step 3 dialog window, choose format 1 which shows symbols at the data points but no connecting lines. Move to the Step 4 window.

- Check the Step 4 window to be sure Excel knows your data are in columns, the first "1" column is to be used for "X Data," and the first "1" row is to be used for "Legend Text." Examine the small preview plot in this window. You should see two sets of data plotted; the symbols used to show the points should have different shapes and different colors. Look at the legend on the preview plot and identify which points correspond to "y hat." They should appear to lie along a straight line. We will convert the representation of those points to a line, and you need to remember which they are because we will remove the legend in the final chart to give the plot area more room.

- Move to Step 5. Select "No" under "Add a Legend." Click the "Finish" button.

- Scroll your worksheet so that row 16 is again at the top.

- Place the mouse pointer inside the chart and double click to "activate" it.

- Place the mouse pointer over one of the "y hat" points and single click. Many (or all) of the points should change color ("light up"). Be sure you have the points which all lie along a line.

- Open the Format menu on the Menu Bar and click "Selected Data Series…." The Format Data Series dialog window will appear.

- Click the "Patterns" folder tab at the top of the dialog window. In the area titled "Line" click "Custom." In the area titled "Marker" click "None." Click the "OK" button.

- Place the mouse pointer on a part of your worksheet off the chart and click once to take the chart out of active mode. The chart should show a line with no point symbols where the "y hat" points were.

Clearly the line does not "fit" the data points very well; it is too low. As we noted before, most of the errors are positive; the points lie above the line. We will adjust the line so that the fit improves and observe what happens to the sum of squared errors (in E16). What about the sum of errors?

- Enter the number "17.28357" for the intercept and "0" for the slope. What happens to the sum of errors (D16)? (It should be 0). This horizontal line clearly doesn't fit the data very well. Jot down the value of the sum of squared errors (SSE).

- Enter the number "28.18786" for the intercept and "-2" for the slope. What is the sum of errors (D16) this time? (It should again be 0.)

What is going on here? It turns out that any line that goes through the point whose x value is $\bar{x}$ (5.452143 for these data) and whose y value is $\bar{y}$ (17.28357) will have a zero sum of errors. Both of the two lines you just examined went through that point. Lines containing this point may not fit the data well! Although the horizontal line was a poor fit, it was better than the second line. The SSE reflected this, increasing from 1027.219 to 2778.444.

- To see a line which fits the data much better, try an intercept value of "1.5" and a slope of "3.2." The SSE for this line is 113.6625, much smaller than was the case before.

- Look carefully at the line and the data points. Does the line look just a bit high and perhaps a bit too steep? Adjust the intercept and slope to improve the fit. Try to reduce the sum of squared errors as low as possible. You should easily be able to find a line whose SSE is less than 100. Can you find one whose SSE is less than 70? Less than 65?

▼ Determining the Regression Line

Calculating the slope and the intercept of the line which minimizes the sum of squared errors is very straightforward and similar to the calculations done in ANOVA. The formulas for the regression coefficients (intercept and slope) are:

$$b_1 = \frac{\sum (x_i - \bar{x})(y_i - \bar{y})}{\sum (x_i - \bar{x})^2}$$
$$b_0 = \bar{y} - b_1\bar{x}$$

The numerator of the expression above for b_1 is often represented by the symbol SP_{xy} (for Sum of Products). The denominator, which you should recognize as the sum of squared deviations of x from its mean, is represented by SS_x.

Since SS_x *must* always be positive, the sign of the slope of the regression line is determined by the sign of SP_{xy}. When a set of data has a positive relationship small values of x will generally be associated with small values of y. Since these small values will be below the mean, both $(x_i - \bar{x})$ and $(y_i - \bar{y})$ will be negative and their product will be positive. Large values of x will generally be associated with large values of y. Both $(x_i - \bar{x})$ and $(y_i - \bar{y})$ will still be positive and their product will be positive. When these are added up, they result in a positive value for SP_{xy}. On the other hand, if there is a negative relationship between x and y, small values of x tend to be associated with large values of y. In this case $(x_i - \bar{x})$ will be negative but $(y_i - \bar{y})$ will be positive, causing their product to be negative. When x is large and y small, the two expressions switch signs, but their product is still negative. Summing up these negative values will make SP_{xy}, and b_1 also, negative.

These formulas require a lot of arithmetic, but they are easy to set up in Excel.

- Switch to the "Regression" worksheet where you will find a copy of the same output and cost data and the labels for calculating the values of b_0 and b_1. Columns D, E, and F require $\hat{y}$, which will be calculated after the regression coefficients.

- Enter formulas in B17 and C17 which will calculate the average of the data values in their respective columns. B17 should display 5.45 and C17 should display 17.28. Note that these cells have an Excel format which limits their display to two decimal places. You can use the Increase Decimal button to display more precision, but regardless of display, Excel uses full precision in calculations.

- Using either Paste Link or a simple formula with an absolute address, set the cells in the range G2:G15 so that they will refer to cell B17 and will display the same value displayed in B17.

- In the region H2:H15, enter the formula which will calculate the difference between that row's value for x in column B and the mean of the x's in column G. H2 should display -4.40, and cell H15 should display -2.59. Use the AutoSum button to display in cell H16 the sum of the values in the column above. The sum should be zero.

- Enter formulas in each cell of region I2:I15 which will square the value in column H of that row. I2 should display 19.378862, and I15 should display 6.7192046. Use cell I16 to calculate and display the sum of the values above. This sum should be 111.15824. This is SS_x. Enter the label "SSx" in cell I17.

- Enter formulas in rows 2 through 15 of columns J, K, and L which give y the same treatment x received in columns G, H, and I. Cell L2 should display 248.4902, and cell L15 should display 54.51713.

- Enter formulas in row 16 of columns K, and L which will display the column sums. K16 should display zero, and L16 should display 1027.22. This is the value of $\sum (y_i - \bar{y})^2$, also called SST. It is not needed to determine the regression coefficients, but will be used later.

- Enter the label "SST" in cell L17.

- Enter formulas in the region M2:M15 which will calculate and display the product of each row's value of $(x_i - \bar{x})$ in column H and $(y_i - \bar{y})$ in column K. The displayed value of M2 should be a little over 69.39 and that of M15 should be just under 19.14. Use M16 to determine a sum of the values in column M. That sum should be approximately 326.648. This is SP_{xy}. Enter the label "SPxy" in cell M17.

Notice that most (all but one) of the values in column M are positive. Look at how these positive values are the result of the signs of the numbers in each row in columns H and K. Both x and y tend to be associated with values on the same side of the mean.

- Select cell B19 which is to contain the regression value for b_1. Enter a formula which will divide the value of SP_{xy} in the worksheet by the value of SS_x. Cell B19 will display the value of the regression line's slope, 2.938587.

Recall that the formula for the intercept is $b_0 = \bar{y} - b_1\bar{x}$. The value for b_1 is in B19, the value for $\bar{y}$ is in C17, and the value for $\bar{x}$ is in B17.

- Enter the formula in B18 to calculate b_0. The result should display as 1.261978.

With these results, we can now write the regression equation as:

$$\hat{y} = 1.261978 + 2.938578x.$$

The slope coefficient can be interpreted as estimating that a one-unit (that is, 1,000 pounds) increase in output results, on average, in a little less than a 2.94 unit (thousands of dollars) increase in monthly operating costs. This is equivalent to just under $2.94 a pound. The equation can be used to predict the average monthly cost for any level of output. We will first use it to provide predicted values for the output levels in the data.

- Using the same approach used on the previous worksheet, enter formulas in cells D2:D15 which will provide a predicted y value ($\hat{y}$) for each x value in the row, using the values for b_0 and b_1 given in cells B18 and B19. The value displayed in cell D2 should be approximately 4.347, while that in D15 should be approximately 9.666.

- Enter formulas in E2:E15 to calculate the difference between the actual y value in column C and the value for $\hat{y}$ in column D (the *errors* or *residuals*). E2 should display -2.83, and E15 should display 0.23. Sum the values of column D in E16. The sum should be zero.

- Enter formulas in F2:F15 to calculate the squared errors. The value in F2 should be approximately 7.99 and that in F15 should be approximately 0.055. Use F16 to calculate and display the sum of squared errors (SSE). The displayed value should be about 67.335. Enter the label "SSE" in F17.

Recall that the regression-determined intercept and slope result in the smallest possible value for SSE.

- Compare the SSE here with that you got when you manually tried to find the slope and intercept which minimizes SSE (cell E16 on the "Line Fit" worksheet).

▼ Using Regression to Predict y Values

The process you used to develop a value for $\hat{y}$ for each of the x values in the data can also be used to provide predicted y values (that is, $\hat{y}$'s) for any x value, not just ones actually in the data.

- Enter the labels "x" and "y hat" in cells C20 and C21.

- Enter the number "5" in cell D20.

- Enter a formula in D21 which will use the value of b_1 in cell B19, the value of b_0 in cell B18, and the value of x in D20 to calculate the regression equation for the x value in D20. The displayed value for D21 will be 15.95491.

The regression analysis enables us to predict that a monthly output of 5,000 pounds would incur an operating cost of $15,954.91. What would be the predicted operating cost for an output of 3,000 pounds?

- Enter the number "3" in cell D20. After you press the Enter key, the value 10.07774 should immediately be displayed in cell D21. The predicted cost of a monthly output of 3,000 pounds would be $10,077.74.

Using regression to predict the y values in this way will yield the most accurate results when the x value is close to the average value of the x's used to determine the regression coefficients (5.45 in this case). Special caution must be used in predicting a y value for an x value outside the range of x values used to determine the regression coefficients (1.05 to 9.98 in this case).

▼ Goodness of Fit—Descriptive Approach

For any set of data, regression analysis will always find the line that fits the data best in the sense of minimizing the sum of squared errors. Even if there is no relationship at all between the two measures, regression will provide the intercept and slope which best fits that "relationship." In this case the "best" fit will not be a "good" fit. As a result, whenever we do regression analysis we need to have, in addition to the estimated parameters (intercept and slope) which define the regression line, an indication of whether the fit between the line and data is "good." We will explore how that is done.

- Switch to the "Data" worksheet. You will find two columns of numbers under the heading "Bad Fit." Select the cells containing the numbers (A3:B16), click the Copy button, switch to the "Line Fit" worksheet, select cell A2, and click the Paste button. The previous data will be overwritten with the "Bad Fit" data.

Changing the data in the "Line Fit" worksheet will also change the data in columns B and C of the "Regression" worksheet. There is a "Paste Link" connection between those "Regression" worksheet cells and the ones in the "Line Fit" worksheet.

- Scroll the screen in the "Line Fit" worksheet so that row 16 is at the top and examine the chart. These data points are not going to be too close to any line.

- Switch to the "Regression" worksheet. Copy the value for the mean of the y values ($\bar{y}$) into the clipboard by selecting cell C17 and clicking the Copy button.

Remember that cell C17 contains a formula for calculating the average of the y values in column C. If we use the Paste button to paste the clipboard, that formula would be copied to the cell we pasted to. We want to paste not the formula but the *current value* of the formula. It is this value (sometime rounded) which is displayed in the cell.

- Switch back to the "Line Fit" worksheet and select cell C16 (the intercept of the line drawn on the chart). Open the "Edit" menu on the Menu Bar and select "Paste Special...." When the "Paste Special" dialog window appears, click "Values" under "Paste" on the left side of the window so the radio button beside it is chosen (as shown at the top of the next page).

- Click the "OK" button in the dialog window. The value for $\bar{y}$ (about 17.35074) will appear in cell C16.

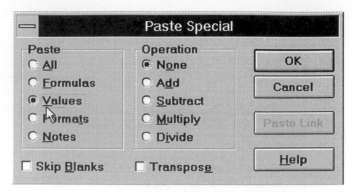

- Enter the value "0" in cell C17 (the slope of the line). Scroll your worksheet and look at the values of $\hat{y}$ in C2:C15. They should all be equal to $\bar{y}$.

- Scroll your worksheet down so that cell A16 is in the upper left corner. Your screen should show the chart with a horizontal line.

Remember that a horizontal line represents no relationship between the x value and the y value. The horizontal line which goes through $\bar{y}$ has a lower sum of squared errors than any other horizontal line.

- Copy the value of $\bar{y}$ in cell C16 to cell F16 (use the Copy and Paste buttons). Also copy the *value* of SSE cell E16 to cell G16 (use the Copy button and "Paste Special" on the "Edit" menu). Enter the label "SSE horiz" in G17. As you make changes to the intercept and slope, compare the changing SSE in cell E16 to the SSE from the horizontal line through $\bar{y}$ in G16.

- Make small changes to the value in C16. You should see the horizontal line shift up and down depending on whether the changes increase or decrease the value in C16. Notice that any change in C16 alone will increase the value of the sum of squared errors in cell E16 (as compared to the original value in G16).

- Copy the value for $\bar{y}$ in cell F16 back to cell C16.

When you went through the process earlier in this chapter of manually fitting a line to the original set of data, you also started with a horizontal line through $\bar{y}$. With those data, it was not difficult to find a value of the slope and intercept which would reduce the sum of squared errors. For the current set of data, it will not be so easy (although it can be done).

- Adjust the values of b_0 and b_1 (in cells C16 and C17) to reduce the value of SSE in E16 below the horizontal line SSE in G16.

Not only is it more difficult to find values for b_0 and b_1 which reduce SSE, but the amount of reduction is less for this data set than it was for the original data set. By using the regression coefficients, we can determine the minimum value for SSE.

- Switch to the "Regression" worksheet. Copy the regression values for b_0 and b_1 (in cells B18 and B19) to the clipboard by using the Copy button. Switch back to the "Line Fit" worksheet. Select cell C16. Paste the *values* in the clipboard by using "Paste Special" on the "Edit" menu.

Despite the fact that it doesn't fit these data very well, the regression intercept and slope are identical to the regression intercept and slope of the previous data. You should know that the probability of two independent samples having the same regression coefficients is close to impossible. Your experience in hypothesis testing should lead you to doubt that the "bad fit" data are really a sample independent of the original data. It is useful, however, in illustrating that we can't tell from the regression coefficients alone whether the fit is good or not.

Compare the values in E16 (SSE with regression line) and G16 (SSE with horizontal line). They are clearly much closer in value to each other than were the corresponding SSE's for the original data (which were 67.33504 for the regression SSE and 1027.22 for the horizontal line SSE). When a regression line fits a set of data well, its SSE is much lower than the SSE of a horizontal line through $\bar{y}$. If *no* line fits a data set very well, the regression SSE will be only a little smaller than the horizontal line SSE.

- Compare the value of the horizontal line SSE in cell G16 of the "Line Fit" worksheet with the value we earlier labeled "SST" in cell L16 on the "Regression" worksheet.

SST was calculated by summing the squared differences between $\bar{y}$ and each y. It is equivalent to the SSE derived from a horizontal line through $\bar{y}$ (if $b_1 = 0$ then SSE = SST). You should also recognize it as the numerator of the expression defining the variance of y. SST and SSE may also remind you of the sum of squared differences which constitute the building blocks of ANOVA. As with ANOVA, a simple relationship exists among the various sums of squares, one of which has not yet been introduced.

- Replace the "SSE horiz" label currently in cell G17 on the "Line Fit" worksheet with the label "SST."

SST measures the "Total" sum of squared differences, or variation, in a set of data. After a regression line is fit to the data, SSE measures the variation that the regression line cannot explain ("Error"). If the line fits the data well, SSE will be substantially less than SST, as we saw above. If no line fits the data well, SSE and SST will be close in value. The difference between SSE and SST is termed SSR, the sum of squares due to "Regression." It can be directly calculated as $\sum (\hat{y}_i - \overline{y})^2$ (this is left for an exercise) or from the relationship $SSR = SST - SSE$.

- On the "Line Fit" worksheet, enter the formula in cell F16 (replacing the current contents) to display the value of SSR by subtracting the SSE in cell E16 from the SST in cell G16. The displayed value is 426.2462. Enter the label "SSR" in cell F17.

As we have seen, the greater the difference between SSE and SST, the better the regression line fits the data. Since SSR is the difference between SSE and SST, an equivalent formulation would be to say that the closer SSR is to SST, the better the regression line fits the data. A common measure of goodness of fit is the r^2 (or coefficient of determination) statistic which calculates SSR as a proportion of SST:

$$r^2 = \frac{SSR}{SST} = \frac{SST - SSE}{SST}$$

An interpretation of r^2 is that it measures the proportion of the total variation in y which is explained by the variation in x. It must have a value between 0 and 1.

- Enter the formula in cell D16 (replacing the current contents) to calculate the value of r^2. The displayed value for this data is 0.0916. Enter the label "r squared" in cell D17.

For the "bad fit" data, slightly over 9% of the variation in the y values is explained by variation in the x values. Let's compare the value of r^2 for these data with that from the original data we used.

- Select the "Data" worksheet. Copy the contents of the original data in D3:E16 to the clipboard. Return to the "Line Fit" worksheet and paste those data in A2:B15.

Notice that the value of r^2 is now over 0.98! For these data over 98% of the variation in the values of y is explained by the variation in the values of x. Note that normally when the data changes like this, the values of the coefficients in C16 and C17 need to be changed to the regression coefficients. In this case, however, the two sets of data we have examined happen to have the same regression coefficients. Hence, we need not copy new values for the slope and intercept from the "Regression" worksheet.

▼ Goodness of Fit—Inferential Approach

The r^2 statistic is descriptive—it tells us how well the regression line fits the particular sample on which it has been estimated. A different, although related, approach to goodness of fit is the inferential approach which looks at the issue from a different perspective. Recall that regression analysis assumes that the sample data on which a regression line is estimated have been selected from a population. In that population the X and Y variables have a relationship which can be expressed by the formula $Y = \beta_0 + \beta_1 X + \varepsilon$. When a regression line is estimated, the resulting regression equation is $\hat{y} = b_0 + b_1 x$. We can regard b_0 and b_1 as *estimates* of β_0 and β_1, respectively. Just as $\bar{x}$ is an estimate of μ, b_1 is an estimate of β_1. Both $\bar{x}$ and b_1 (and b_0, for that matter) are random numbers (*statistics*) whose value will vary from sample to sample and which will never precisely equal their corresponding fixed parameters (μ, β_1, and β_0).

If there is no relationship in the population between y and x, the value of β_1 is zero. In such a case, the value of b_1, determined by regression from a sample will, in all probability, be nonzero just by chance. The inferential approach treats the issue of goodness of fit in a hypothesis testing or confidence interval framework. Two different sets of calculations can be used in regression to implement the inferential approach. For simple linear regression they always yield identical results, but in multiple regression they have different interpretations and different results.

SSE, as we have seen, is similar to the numerator of a variance formula. If SSE is divided by its degrees of freedom, the result is termed MSE (mean square error) or residual variance and represented by the symbol s_ε^2.

$$s_\varepsilon^2 = \text{MSE} = \frac{\text{SSE}}{df}$$

where *df* is degrees of freedom of SSE.

MSE measures the variance of the y values around the regression line in the same way that an ordinary variance is measured around the mean of the y's. It is analogous to a sample variance; the corresponding population variance for which it is an estimate is the variance of the residual values ε in the population equation.

- Select the "Regression" worksheet. Enter the label "MSE" in cell F18. Cell G18 will be used for the formula to calculate and display the value of MSE.

For simple linear regression the value for the degrees of freedom of SSE is $n-2$, where n is the number of observations used in the regression analysis.

- Enter the formula in cell G18 to calculate and display the value of MSE. The displayed value should be slightly over 5.611.

You may recognize this step as similar to those used in analysis of variance. One of the inferential approaches to goodness of fit is an ANOVA approach. At this point we will consider the other approach.

As noted above, b_1 is a random number. It therefore has a distribution (whose mean is β_1) and a standard deviation. As a statistic, its standard deviation is termed a *standard error* just as the standard deviation of $\bar{x}$ is called a standard error. Once we determine the standard error of b_1, we can construct a confidence interval on β_1 and perform hypothesis tests on β_1. These will provide techniques for investigating whether or not there is a relationship between y and x in the *population* from which the sample was drawn.

The standard error of b_1 is easily calculated from MSE and SS_x (the sum of squared deviations of x from its mean—already calculated in cell I16) by the following formula:

$$s_{b_1} = \sqrt{\frac{MSE}{SS_x}}$$

Notice that if the regression line fits the data well, SSE and thus MSE would be small, as would s_{b_1}. A smaller standard error will also occur if there is a high variation in the x values.

- Enter the label "std err b1" in cell A20. In cell B20 enter an Excel formula which will calculate s_{b_1} as shown in the equation above by referring to the cells on this spreadsheet where MSE and SS_x are calculated. The cell should display the value 0.224677.

The statistic b_1 follows the t distribution with $n-2$ degrees of freedom, much as the statistic $\bar{x}$ follows the t distribution with $n-1$ degrees of freedom. We can use this to examine inferential goodness of fit by asking whether this sample provides evidence that the population slope, β_1, differs from 0. This can be done by testing the Null Hypothesis $H_0: \beta_1 = 0$ against the Alternate Hypothesis $H_A: \beta_1 \neq 0$. A sample t (or t statistic) for this hypothesis can be calculated with a formula very similar to that which used to test a hypothesis test on μ:

$$t = \frac{b_1 - \beta_1}{s_{b_1}}$$

Since the Null Hypothesis is that $\beta_0 = 0$, this expression reduces to the value of b_1 divided by its standard error. The smaller the standard error, the larger the t value.

- Enter the label "t" in cell A21. In cell B21 enter the Excel formula which will calculate the sample t value for the Null Hypothesis given above. The value displayed in B21 should be 13.07915.

The final step in the worksheet is to determine the p value for this sample t. This will involve using the TDIST function which can be found in the Function Wizard under the "Statistical" category. Remember that TDIST requires that the t value you give it must be positive, and we have previously embedded the use of the ABS function to ensure a positive value. When TDIST was used for problems involving inferences on a population mean, the degrees of freedom was always $n-1$. For this problem it is $n-2$. Given the Null Hypothesis above, a two-tail test is appropriate.

- Enter the label "p value" in cell A22. Enter a formula in cell B22 which will calculate the two-tail p value associated with the sample t in B21 for $n-2$ degrees of freedom. The displayed value should be 1.84E-08 (or 0.0000000184—a very small value).

The small p value tells us that it is highly unlikely that we could have gotten by chance a sample with a regression value for b_1 which differed from zero as much as this one did if the sample were actually chosen from a population in which β_1 was zero. For any of the usual significance levels, we would reject the Null Hypothesis and conclude that $\beta_1 \neq 0$. There *is* evidence (strong evidence) of a relationship in the population between X and Y. Another way of saying this is to say that the regression, or the regression coefficient, is significant.

Finding that a regression coefficient is significant is the inferential equivalent of a good fit. The value for s_{b_1} could also be used to develop confidence intervals on the value of β_1. This could be done using almost the identical procedure used for confidence intervals on μ. The confidence interval would be $b_1 \pm ts_{b_1}$, where the t value would have $n-2$ degrees of freedom and would have a value determined by the level of confidence. A small standard error will result in a narrow confidence interval and a *significant* coefficient's confidence interval will not include zero.

What kind of result would we get in the case where the regression line does not fit the data well?

- Switch to the "Data" worksheet. Copy the "Bad Fit" data to the clipboard. Switch to the "Line Fit" worksheet and paste the data in the region A2:B15. Switch to the "Regression" worksheet.

Although the regression coefficients are the same in this case, the standard error of b_1 is much higher. This has decreased the value of the sample t and resulted in a p value of .292821. With such a high p value, we would *fail to reject* the Null Hypothesis that $\beta_1 = 0$. This means we don't have very good evidence that there is a relationship in the population between Y and X. We would characterize the regression coefficient (or the regression) as *insignificant*, because the estimated slope is not significantly different from zero.

▼ Excel's Built-In Regression Capabilities

Excel has a number of features which will allow you to easily do a regression analysis on a set of data. These include an Analysis Tool, several built-in functions (which can be accessed through the Function Wizard), and a feature of the Chart Wizard. Although these capabilities duplicate each other, they have somewhat different advantages and disadvantages.

The Analysis Tool produces an output which is much easier to read than the functions. The functions have the advantage of being dynamic in the sense that they update their displayed value whenever a change in the worksheet affects the input data. The Analysis Tool, by contrast, must be rerun whenever the data change. Nevertheless, the Tool is usually preferable for doing regression analysis. For this reason, the functions (INTERCEPT, SLOPE, TREND, FORECAST, and LINEST) will not be discussed in this chapter, although information on them can be found in Appendix B.

- Switch to the "Data" worksheet and copy the "Bad Fit" data (including the labels in row 2) to the clipboard. Switch to the "Sheet5" worksheet and paste the data beginning in cell A1.

- Change the name of the "Sheet5" worksheet to "Bad Fit."

- Using the Chart Wizard, prepare a scatter plot of the data (the same type as on the "Line Fit" worksheet) with the upper left corner in cell C1. Make the chart reasonably wide, but do not let it go below row 15. Check your chart against the one on the "Line Fit" worksheet. Except for the lack of a regression line, they should clearly both be charts of the same data.

- Place the mouse pointer in the chart and double click to "Activate" the chart. Once it has been activated, place the mouse pointer over one of the data points and click once. Most or all of the data points should change color ("light up"), indicating that they have been selected. Open the "Insert" menu on the Menu Bar and select "Trendline..." (or, with the mouse pointer on a data point, click the right mouse button and select "Insert Trendline....") In either case the Trendline dialog window will open.

- Select the "Type" folder tab at the top. Click the picture above "Linear" which shows a straight line fitting a set of data points.

- Select the "Options" folder tab. The section labeled "Forecast" enables you to extend the line to left or right of the data points. Click the box beside "Display Equation on Chart" and the box beside "Display R-squared Value on Chart" so that each box has an "x" in it. Click the "OK" button.

As you may see, sometimes Excel does not place the equation and r^2 value in the best place on the graph.

- Place the mouse pointer over the equation and click once. An active mode boundary should surround the equation and r^2 value. When the mouse pointer is inside the boundary, it has the insertion point shape. Outside the boundary it is a white arrow.

- Move the mouse pointer outside the boundary surrounding the equation and the r^2 value. Place the mouse pointer so that the tip of the arrow is on the boundary. Press and hold the (left) mouse button and drag the outline containing the equation and r^2 value to the upper left corner of the chart where there are no data points.

Excel's presentation of the regression line on a plot is nonstandard in that y is used instead of $\hat{y}$, and b_0 is put after, instead of before b_1.

Compare the chart on this worksheet with that on the "Line Fit" worksheet. This is certainly an easier way of putting a regression line on a scatter plot! What happens if you change the data?

- Select cell A15 (which now contains 9.68). Enter the value "0" in the cell. Observe what happens to the chart when you press the Enter key.

Did the regression line change? Look at the equation and r^2 value written on the chart. Did they change? The answer to both questions should be "Yes."

The fact that changing a single observation caused such a drastic change in the regression line is further evidence of the lack of a good fit with these data. This is a demonstration of the result of the test we performed on the Null Hypothesis that the value of β_1 is 0 and that the nonzero value of b_1 could very well be due to chance.

- Press the Undo button ↶. The value of A15 should return to 9.68. If it does not, manually change it back to 9.68. The line, equation, and r^2 value should return to their original forms.

▼ Using the Regression Tool for Simple Linear Regression

The regression tool can be used for either simple or multiple regression. Its use is very similar to that of the other analysis tools.

- Open the "Tools" menu and choose "Data Analysis...." From the Data Analysis dialog window, choose "Regression."

- Enter the cell ranges for the x and y data in the appropriate fields. As with other Analysis Tools, it is a good idea to have a label in the first row and to include the address of the label in the cell ranges entered in these fields.

- Click the small box beside "Labels" so that Excel will know the first row contains labels rather than data.

- As part of its output, Excel provides confidence intervals on the population β's. Excel always provides the 95% confidence interval for each β, and, unless you indicate otherwise, provides it twice. Let's instead ask Excel to provide us also with a 90% confidence interval by first clicking the box beside "Confidence Level" so an x appears and then changing the "95" in the filed to the right to "90."

- Under "Output Options" select "Output Range." Enter the address "A17" in the field to the right.

There are a number of optional outputs which can be selected from the Regression dialog window. In the section titled "Residuals," you can choose four different optional outputs:

1. **Residuals**—If this is selected, Excel will produce a table showing, for each observation, the value of predicted values ($\hat{y}$), and the value of the *residual* (or error) which is $y - \hat{y}$.

2. **Standardized Residuals**—This choice will cause Excel to produce, in addition to the table of residuals described above, a column showing standardized residuals. Residuals are standardized by dividing them by the error standard deviation (also called the standard error of the esti-

mate) which is calculated as $\sqrt{\text{MSE}}$. Choosing to have Excel output standardized residuals always results in the output of predicted values and nonstandardized residuals regardless of whether or not you also select Residuals.

3. **Residual Plots**—Selecting this will cause Excel to produce a scatter plot with the value of each observation's residual (or error) plotted on the vertical axis and the observation's value for the *x* variable plotted on the horizontal axis. Choosing this also always results in getting the output described in 1 above.

4. **Line Fit Plots**—If this choice is selected, Excel will produce a scatter plot showing both the actual data points and the predicted data points lying on the regression line. For simple (but not multiple) regression, the plot is very similar to the one already drawn on the worksheet by the Chart Wizard, except that the predicted values are shown as points rather than as a line which can, of course, be changed afterwards.

In order to see all of these outputs, check all of the boxes in the "Residuals" section.

The last output choice is for "Normal Probability Plots." A normal probability plot is a chart prepared in such a way that data values are plotted against their quartile values on the standard normal distribution. In such a plot, data which are normally distributed will appear to lie approximately along a line. Excel 5.0 produces a plot of the *y* variable, but it appears to be done incorrectly. Do not choose it.

- Once these choices have been made, click the "OK" button on the dialog window.

- When the Regression Tool has finished writing the output, the column widths will need to be adjusted. While the cell region containing the output is still selected, open the "Format" menu, choose "Column," and then click "AutoFit Selection."

- Click on any worksheet cell to remove the selection highlighting.

The output of the Regression Tool is so large that you may only be able to see a small part on your screen at one time. To get a better view of your worksheet, use Excel's ability to "zoom."

- Click the downward pointing arrow on the right side of the Zoom Control on the Standard Tool Bar `100%` ⬇. A list of zoom factors will open. Try 75%. If your screen still cannot display columns A through L, change the zoom factor to 50%.

One of the effects of adjusting the column widths for the regression output is that the chart at the top of the worksheet has been made excessively wide.

- Adjust the width of the chart to a size more appropriate for its height. Select it by clicking it once with the mouse. Edit "handles" will appear at each corner and in the center of each side. Place the mouse pointer on the handle which is in the center of the right side. Press and hold the mouse button and drag the handle to the left until the chart's width is correct. Then release the mouse button.

- Notice that the Regression Tool has placed one of the charts it has produced on top of the other one. Single click the chart on top and move it so that it is to the right of the scatter plot you produced earlier. Move both charts to the left to keep the information on the worksheet in as compact an area as possible.

- Because of the size of the space used on this worksheet, you may find it easier to follow the discussion below from a printout. If you choose to do this, first click the Print Preview button 🔍. When the screen previewing the output appears, click the "Setup…" button at the top. In the Page Setup dialog window, first click the "Page" folder tab. Under "Orientation" select "Landscape." Under "Scaling" select "Fit to 1 page(s) wide by 1 tall." Select the "Sheet" folder tab. Under "Print" select "Row and Column Headings." This will permit you to determine cell addresses on the printout. Click "OK." After you return to the Print Preview screen, have Excel print the worksheet.

Let's take a tour of the output. First the charts.

1. **"x Line Fit Plot,"** as mentioned above, is similar to the scatter plot you produced earlier with the Chart Wizard. The "x" in the title refers to the label for the x variable (the label in cell A1). A different label would result in a different title. Notice that the Analysis Tool labels both axes in the chart and provides a title and a legend. One result is that the area actually devoted to the plot is small. This can, of course, be changed by editing the chart. The regression line (called "Predicted y" in the legend) is depicted as points rather than as a line. This, too, could be changed by activating the chart, selecting the data points, and then formatting the data series exactly as was done with the scatter plot produced by the Chart Wizard.

2. **"x Residual Plot"** shows the residuals (or errors) plotted against the value of the x variable. Like the line fit plot, the residual plot can be useful in finding "outliers," data points which are much further from the regression line than other points. It is often worthwhile to reexam-

ine those data points, because the large value of their error (residual) might be caused by a data collection or recording error. A residual plot can also be used to provide some evidence on the issue of whether the assumption that the population ε has constant variance is correct.

Next are the items under "Summary Output."

3. **Multiple R** is the square root of the r^2. When given the sign of the x coefficient b_1, this value is often termed the coefficient of correlation and is an alternate measure of the strength of the relationship between the x and y variables.

4. **R Square** is, of course, r^2. There is a convention, followed by many statisticians, to use a lowercase r for simple regression and an uppercase R for multiple regression. Check to be sure the value here agrees with the values you determined on the "Line Fit" worksheet for the same data.

5. **Adjusted R Square** is meaningful only in a multiple regression context where, as a measure of fit, it takes the number of independent variables into account. The unadjusted R^2 always increases when a new independent variable is added, even if there is no real relationship between it and the dependent variable. Adjusted R^2 is useful only to compare models with the same dependent variable; it has no meaning by itself.

6. **Standard Error** is the square root of MSE. It also is called the standard error of the regression or the standard error of the estimate and is a measure of goodness of fit which is also used in calculating other statistics associated with regression. As mentioned above, it is used in calculating standardized residuals.

7. **Observations** is, of course, the number of observations in the data used for estimating the regression equation.

The next section is the analysis of variance section. The table is organized exactly like the ANOVA tables seen in Chapter 13. The first column (df) gives degrees of freedom, the second column (SS) gives sum of squared deviations. The third column (MS—for Mean Square) divides the sum of squared deviations by the degrees of freedom. The fourth column has the F statistic and the last column (labeled "Significance F") gives the p value for that F statistic.

The row labeled "Regression" is calculated from differences between predicted y values for each observation and the mean of the y values ($\hat{y} - \bar{y}$). The entry under the SS column is SSR. Compare this with the value you found on the "Line Fit" worksheet to be sure they are the same.

The row labeled "Residual" would, perhaps, better be labeled "Error." It is the differences between predicted y values and actual y values for each observation $(y - \hat{y})$. The value under SS is SSE and the value under MS is MSE. Check these against the values on the "Regression" worksheet.

The row labeled "Total" is calculated from the differences between each y value and the mean of the y values $(y - \bar{y})$. The number under SS is SST. Check it against the values on the "Regression" worksheet.

The next section provides inferences about the population coefficients (β_0 and β_1). The first row is for β_0 (labeled intercept), and the second row is for β_1 (whose label comes from the label used in the data—"x" in this case). For most purposes for which regression is used, β_1 is of greater interest than β_0 and therefore the inferences on β_1 are more important than those on β_0.

The first column gives the values for the regression coefficients, b_0 and b_1. Verify these values with the ones on the "Regression" worksheet. The second column gives the standard errors for the coefficients. You have calculated the standard error of b_1 on the "Regression" worksheet; check that this worksheet shows the same value. The Regression Tool also calculates and shows the standard error for b_0. The third column gives the value of sample t's for the Null Hypotheses H_0: $\beta_0 = 0$ (in the first row) and H_0: $\beta_1 = 0$ (in the second row). The fourth column gives the p values (two-tail) for the respective sample t's. Compare the t and p values on the second row with those showing on the "Regression" worksheet. The remaining four columns give 95% and 90% confidence intervals for the values of β_0 and β_1.

The last part of the output provides, for each observation, the predicted y value $(\hat{y})$, the residual $(y - \hat{y})$, and the standardized residual. The actual y values are not given in the table, but it would be a simple matter to copy them to an adjacent column.

It is clear from the regression output that there is little evidence of a relationship between x and y for these data. The most compelling evidence of this is the lack of significance of b_1 as shown by its high p value. We noted this previously on the "Regression" worksheet. The output of the Regression Tool includes some additional calculations.

- Compare the p value for the F statistic in the ANOVA table (cell F28) with the p value for the t statistic for β_1 (cell E34). Enter a formula in cell E29 which will display the square of the t value in cell D34. Compare this with the F value in E28.

For simple linear regression, the regression analysis of variance always provides information identical to that provided by the test on the hypothesis $H_0: \beta_1 = 0$. Either can be used as an inferential test of the existence of a relationship in the population between the x and y variables. The confidence intervals on β_1 include zero (as well as both positive and negative values), another way of presenting the lack of significance in this regression. The tests on β_0 also indicate that it is not significantly different from 0, although a test on β_0 does not give us information about the relationship between the two variables.

▼ Exercises

1. Select the "Regression" worksheet. Add two columns to calculate SSR. The first column would determine, for each observation, $\hat{y} - \bar{y}$. The second column would square each of those values. The cell just below this second column would sum all of the values. Confirm that you get the same answer here as you have on the "Line Fit" worksheet. Add to the "Regression" worksheet a calculation of r^2 using the value of SSR calculated here and verify that it is the same as that on the "Line Fit" worksheet.

2. Rename the "Sheet6" worksheet "Good Fit." Copy the "Original" data from the "Data" worksheet to this sheet, but rename the x variable "output" and the y variable "cost." Use the Regression Tool to do a regression analysis of these data. Also prepare a scatter plot of these data. On the same worksheet, use the regression coefficients produced by the Tool to give an estimate of the cost associated with these levels of output (in thousands): 3.8, 5.7, 6.3. Print the worksheet showing the output of the Regression Tool, the Scatter Plot, the original data, and the predicted costs for the three output. Be sure your name is printed in the page header.

3. The "State Revenue" worksheet in simpreg.xls contains 1992 data on median household income and per capita state government revenue. Produce a scatter plot with a superimposed regression line. Use regression analysis to examine the effect of household income on state government revenue. Is there a significant (.01 level of significance) relationship between these two? Based on the regression, by how much, on average, does per capita state revenue change for each $1 increase in median household income? Are any of the states "outliers?" If so, can you explain why? Remove that state and reestimate the regression. Does this change your answer to the question of how much, on average, per capita revenue changes for each $1 increase in median

household income? If so, what is the new answer? Print the worksheet showing the scatter plot and both regressions. Put your name in the page header. (Data is from U.S. Bureau of the Census, *Statistical Abstract of the United States: 1994* (114th edition.) Washington, DC, 1994, pp. 395, 468.)

4. Is there a relationship between a state's median household income and its violent crime rate (incidents of murder, rape, robbery, and assault per 100,000 population)? The "Crime" worksheet provides 1992 data on state median household income and violent crime rate. Produce a scatter plot of these data with a regression line. Use the Regression Tool to analyze the relationship. What proportion of the variation in state crime rates is explained by variation in household income? Is the relationship significant (at the .10 level of significance)? Explain. Print the worksheet showing the scatter plot and regression. Put your name in the page header. (Data is from U.S. Bureau of the Census, *Statistical Abstract of the United States: 1994* (114th edition.) Washington, DC, 1994, pp. 199, 468.)

5. Is there a relationship between a state's household income and its death rate (deaths by all causes per 1,000 population)? The "Death Rate" worksheet in simpreg.xls provides 1992 data by state for median household income and death rates. Produce a scatter plot with regression line and regression analysis of these data. Does higher income lead to higher or lower death rates? Is the relationship significant at the .05 level of significance? What proportion of the variation of death rates is explainable by variation in household income? Print the worksheet showing the scatter plot and regression output. Put your name in the header.

Chapter 15

Multiple Regression

Multiple regression analysis is a straightforward extension of simple regression analysis which allows more than one independent variable. This extension, however, makes multiple regression analysis an incredibly versatile tool which can be used in an enormous variety of statistical problems. A reasonably complete treatment of multiple regression would require a book at least as long as this one already is. This chapter will deal with some of the issues and techniques which frequently arise with multiple regression analysis. Multiple regression analysis provides the analyst with such a variety of techniques that the primary problem is to decide exactly what form the regression equation (or regression *model*) will take, including which independent variables will be used. This typically comes after investigating different possibilities, a process known as *model building*.

Although the basic principles are straightforward, their application to any actual set of data often requires a judgment which comes with experience. There is a skill, almost an art, to regression analysis. One of the reasons for this is that for a given set of data different objectives will likely lead to different regression equations. Regression analysis is often used for prediction, for example, and an equation developed for predictive purposes may well be different from an analytical model developed to better understand the relationship among the variables in a set of data.

For some types of analysis where multiple regression is used, Excel 5.0 is probably not the best software. Although Excel provides the basic regression output, many specialized statistical packages also provide additional output. Excel, for example, does not provide an easy method to determine confidence intervals on predicted values, it lacks some of the diagnostic statistics useful for evaluating the analysis of time series data, and it does not easily permit certain types of hypothesis tests on population coefficients. On the other hand, Excel's matrix handling capability does make it possible to construct these tests and even to create macros for them. No attempt will be made here, however, to cover these more advanced topics in this chapter.

▼ Multiple Independent Variables

Let's consider a simple case involving two independent variables. From this we will be able to see how to interpret the output of a regression involving any number of independent variables.

A music CD chain is trying to determine the effectiveness of television and radio advertising. It has collected data from stores in the chain on monthly record sales and on monthly advertising expenditures for both television and radio advertising. Based on these data, is there evidence of a relationship between expenditures on each type of advertising and sales? Which form of advertising appears to be more cost-effective?

Probably the chain would want to include other information, including market size, market type, average family income, and average age in a model explaining record sales. We're keeping it simple here.

- Open the Excel workbook in multireg.xls and switch to the "CDs" worksheet.

- Summon the dialog window for the Regression Tool by first opening the "Tools" menu on the menu bar and then selecting "Data Analysis…."

The dependent (or *y*) variable is in the column labeled "Sales" which gives monthly sales in thousands of dollars. The two independent variables have the labels "Radio" and "TV" which give monthly advertising expenditures on those two media.

- In the "Input Y Range" field enter the range address A1:A21 which has the level of sales with the label.

- In the "Input X Range" field enter the range address B1:C21. Notice that this range includes two columns containing both of the independent variables. It is a restriction of the Regression Tool that independent variables have to be in adjacent columns.

- Click the square indicating that the address ranges include labels. Direct the Tool to construct 90% confidence intervals on the population coefficients. Choose "Output Range" and have the output written beginning in cell D1.

- Click "OK." Once the output is written, and while the cell range containing it is still selected, adjust the column widths by opening the "Format" menu (on the menu bar), selecting "Column" then "AutoFit Selection."

You may find it easier to follow the discussion below if you print the output. If you do print the page, first choose "Print Preview" on the "File" menu and click the "Setup" button on the preview page. Click the "Page" folder tab, choose "Landscape" orientation and "Fit to 1 page." Click the "Sheet" folder tab and select "Row and Column Headings." You will then be able to find cell addresses on your printout. Select "Header/Footer" and put your name and any other useful information in the header before you print.

For this regression, since there are two independent variables, the regression equation can be written as:

$$\hat{y} = b_0 + b_1 x_1 + b_2 x_2 .$$

In the regression output on your worksheet, b_0 is labeled "Intercept," b_1 is labeled "Radio," and b_2 is labeled "TV."

The estimated coefficient for b_1 is 15.7151. This indicates that each additional $1 spent on radio advertising is expected to increase sales by just under $15.72 assuming all other factors (such as TV advertising) are unchanged. This measure is often called a *partial effect*, because it measures the impact of a change in just one of the independent variables. The partial effect is frequently referred as the change in the dependent variable which would result from a one-unit change in one of the independent variables. It could more precisely be defined as a rate of change, but this would have the same meaning in this context. The estimated coefficient (or partial effect) for b_2 is 12.7583, indicating that an additional dollar spent on TV advertising will increase sales by just over $12.75 (holding radio advertising constant). Based on these estimates, radio advertising looks like a better deal, but there is more to this issue, so don't regard this conclusion as final.

The value for R^2 (cell E5) of a bit over 0.36 indicates that variation in radio and TV advertising account for just over 36% of the variation in sales. Nearly 64% of the variation in sales is accounted for by factors other than radio and TV advertising.

Excel makes it easy to determine the significance of a coefficient or of the overall regression by providing p values. An important step in determining p values is the determination of the statistic's degrees of freedom. Consider an estimated coefficient and the t statistic calculated from that coefficient. It is desirable for the degrees of freedom to be as large as possible. A value for a t statistic can be significantly different from zero if the degrees of freedom is large, and insignificant if the degrees of freedom is small. The degrees of freedom for an estimated coefficient's t statistic in multiple regression is $n - (k + 1)$, where n is the number of observations in the data and k is the number of independent variables. In practice the number of independent variables must be considerably fewer than the number of observations. For data with few observations, that can be a serious constraint. It is *especially* important when using regression for prediction that there not be too many independent variables.

The regression F statistic (cell H12) has a p value of approximately .021. This p value is for the the hypothesis test that *all* population coefficients of the independent variables are zero:

$$H_0: \beta_1 = 0 \text{ and } \beta_2 = 0$$
$$H_A: \text{either } \beta_1 \neq 0 \text{ or } \beta_2 \neq 0 \text{ or both}$$

If the Null Hypothesis were true, it would indicate that there is no relationship between *any* of the independent variables and the dependent variable. The p value tells us that if the Null Hypothesis were true, the probability we could draw a sample whose estimated coefficients (b_0 and b_1) differed from zero by at least as much as the values in the regression output is about .02. This low probability provides good evidence for rejecting the Null Hypothesis and concluding that at least one of the population coefficients must be nonzero.

For simple linear regression, the p value for the F statistic always equaled the p value for the estimated coefficient of b_1's t statistic. The t statistics permit a test of whether an individual population coefficient is zero, while the F statistic can be used to test whether *all* population coefficients are zero. In simple regression these have the same meaning. In multiple regression they do not. The p value for the t statistic for spending on radio (b_1) is approximately .013 (cell H18). This is the probability that a sample with a value of b_1 as different from zero as this value in this sample (approximately 15.715) could be drawn from a population where there were no relationship between spending on radio ads and sales of CDs. This p value applies to the test $H_0: \beta_1 = 0$ and $H_A: \beta_1 \neq 0$. We would reject the Null Hypothesis at a .05 level of significance but not at a .01 level of significance. This p value is low enough to conclude that there is good evidence of a relationship between monthly expenditures on radio advertising and sales of CDs.

The p value for spending on TV advertising is considerably higher, almost .18. Although the size of the estimated coefficient is nearly the same as that for spending on radio advertising, this high p value means we can have much less confidence about the value of the population coefficient on TV spending. If there were no relationship in the population between spending on TV advertising and sales, the probability of a sample having an estimated coefficient as different from zero as this one (12.758) is the p value (.18). At the 10% significance level we would fail to reject the Null Hypothesis that β_2 is zero. A common convention would label the coefficient on TV spending *not significant*, which is short for *not significantly different from zero*.

The fact that the estimated coefficient for spending on radio advertising is larger and more significant that the estimated coefficient for spending on TV advertising points to the conclusion that the music store chain should shift advertising expenditures from TV to radio. Look, however, at the two sets of confidence intervals on the population coefficients for TV and radio advertising expenditures. Notice that the upper bound of the confidence interval on TV spending is higher than the upper bound of the confidence interval of radio spending. This is true for both the 95% confidence interval (cells J18 and J19 which show the upper bound for radio to be 27.63 vs 31.99 for TV) and the 90% confidence interval (cells L18 and L19). The fact that the estimated coefficient for TV advertising is not statistically significant does not mean that spending of TV advertising has been shown to be unimportant. As is the case in all hypothesis tests, failure to reject a Null Hypothesis of no relationship between TV advertising spending and sales is not equivalent to concluding that the Null Hypothesis is correct! You just can't rule it out.

One aspect of model building is the decision of which independent variables to include. As a general rule, variables which are statistically significant in a regression should be included. This does not mean, however, that variables which are not statistically significant should necessarily be excluded. A variable which *should* have a relationship with the dependent variable, in most cases, ought to be included in the regression even if its estimated coefficient is not statistically significant. In other words, the decision of what independent variables to include in a regression is never purely mechanical, particularly if the objective of regression analysis is truly analytical. It doesn't make sense that radio advertising would have a strong effect on sales while TV advertising has no effect at all. Although its significance is low, the TV advertising variable should be retained.

Sometimes the objective of regression analysis is purely predictive. In this case the question of whether or not to keep a particular independent variable can be somewhat more mechanical. The adjusted R^2 (located in cell E6) is helpful in this case. The ordinary R^2 (cell E5) discussed in the chapter on simple linear regression always increases when a new independent variable is added whether or not that variable improves the model's predictive power. The adjusted R^2 will increase only if the presence of the new independent variable improves the model's predictive power. Would elimination of the TV advertising variable improve the regression's predictive power? As a rule of thumb, if the t statistic associated with an independent variable has an absolute value less than 1.0, dropping that variable will increase adjusted R^2. In this regression the t statistic for TV advertising is just under 1.40. Eliminating this independent variable would reduce the adjusted R^2. For predictive purposes, TV advertising should be kept in the model. Although the estimated coefficient is *not* very significant, it is significant enough to contribute to the model's predictive power.

▼ Nonlinear Relationships

Sometimes a relationship exists among two or more variables which cannot be represented as a straight line. In such a case a linear regression can give results which are absolutely misleading. In a case where data on more than one independent variable have been collected, nonlinearities can be present with some, but not all, of the data. For this example we will consider a case where there is only a single independent variable. This simplification will enable us to examine the relationship graphically.

A manufacturer of a precision bearings assembly produced at a number of different identical plants wants to determine the relationship between monthly output and short-run average cost. A sample of 50 monthly reports giving output and short-run average cost from several plants was collected. Based on these data, is there a relationship between level of output and average cost? (The data for this problem can be found in multireg.xls on the "Bearings" worksheet.)

An obvious first step would be to use simple linear regression.

- Select the "Bearings" worksheet. Use the Regression Analysis Tool to perform a regression analysis using monthly "Output" as the x variable and average "Cost" as the y variable. If the dialog window opens with the fields already containing values, they are left over from the last regression and must be changed. Have Excel place the output beginning in cell D1.

- In the "Residuals" section of the dialog window select "Residual Plots."

- Click "OK." Use the Format–Column–AutoFit Selection menu sequence to adjust the column widths for the regression output. If you have done the regression correctly, the value for r^2 (in cell E5) will be 5.19084E-06. The number of observations (in cell E8) will be 50.

- Change the value in the "Zoom Control" on the Standard Toolbar to 50%. Locate the residual plot (which Excel will place to the right of the regression output), and move it so that it is below the portion of the output giving the estimated coefficients and their statistics, and to the right of the residual output. With the chart selected, change the "Zoom Control" back to 100%.

- Excel tends to make residual plots too short. Make the plot taller by selecting it (so that there are "handles" in each corner and in the middle of each side). If you accidentally "activate" it (so that is surrounded by the activation boundary), click the mouse pointer on a location on the worksheet away from the chart. Place the mouse pointer on the handle in the center of the bottom side. The pointer will change to this shape: ⇲. Press and hold the (left) button and drag the handle down until the shape of the chart is more like a square.

It may be useful to print the worksheet. If you choose to do this, first unselect the chart by clicking the mouse pointer on a spot on the worksheet off the chart. This worksheet will print best if you first select "Print Preview" from the File Menu. Click the "Setup" button at the top of the preview screen. Select the "Page" folder tab. Select "Portrait" orientation and scale to fit one page. Click the "Sheet" folder tab and select "Row and Column Headings" in the "Print" section. Click "OK" then "Print."

It appears from this output that there is no evidence of a relationship between output and average cost. The R^2 is extremely low. Also the slope (estimated coefficient for "Output" in E18) is -8.81558E-05, a number which is very close to zero. Even more telling, the p value for the coefficient (H18) is over .98, suggesting that this result is very consistent with a population coefficient of zero—no relationship. This conclusion would, however, be *wrong*.

Economic theory tells us that the relationship between output and short-run average cost should be U-shaped, not linear. Starting with a very low level of output, average cost should decline as the production machinery and other fixed capital become more fully used. If output continues to increase, average cost would again increase since, in the short-run, the machinery cannot be increased and would become overloaded. A U shape is a curve, not a straight line. If this is the case, it is possible that no straight line can do a good job of approximating even a very strong relationship.

▼ Curved Relationships and Residuals Plots

If the relationship between a particular independent variable and the dependent variable were in the form of a simple curve, this would create a

U-shaped (or inverted U-shaped) pattern in the residuals. Consider the charts below.

The left chart shows a scatter plot of data with only a single independent variable. The simple linear regression line is superimposed, and vertical lines are drawn between each point and the regression line. Notice that the relationship between the independent and dependent variable in that chart would be better represented by a curve than by a straight line.

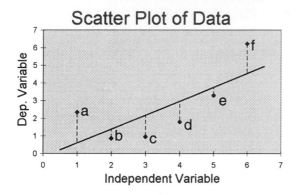
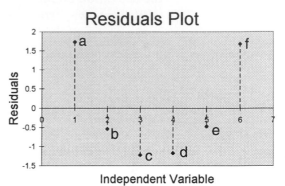

The right chart shows the residuals plot for the same data. Each data point is identified by a letter with the same point in the two charts identified by the same letter. The length of the dotted line between each point and the horizontal axis measures the value of that point's residual.

Consider point *a* in the left chart. It lies above the regression line. The length of the dotted line between it and the regression line is the "error" or residual associated with that value. That length represents the same value as the length of the dotted line on the right between point *a* and the horizontal axis. Points *b*, *c*, *d*, and *e* all lie below the regression line in the chart on the left. Their residuals are negative. Exactly the same pattern is seen on the chart on the right. The point of this is that the curved relationship evident in the chart on the left is also (even more) evident in the residuals chart on the right.

If the curved relationship is apparent in the scatter plot, you may wonder why we bother to also consider a residuals plot. A residuals plot has a fundamental and important advantage when there is more than one independent variable—the usual situation in multiple regression. It is not really possible to do a meaningful scatter plot in this case. Although a scatter plot of the dependent variable against a single independent variable could be done, it would not be useful because it does not account for the values of the other independent variables. If the predicted values from a multiple regression equation were plotted on such a chart, they would not even appear to lie on a straight line. Residuals plots avoid many of these problems and are an often effective means of detecting a curvilinear (or nonlinear) relationship between the dependent variable and one of the independent variables. When Excel is asked to provide residuals plots, it produces one plot for each independent variable in the model.

Let's consider the residuals plot for the precision bearings average cost problem. That plot should be present on your Excel output. Click the mouse pointer once on the chart and use the "handles" to make the chart bigger and taller. Your chart should look like the one below.

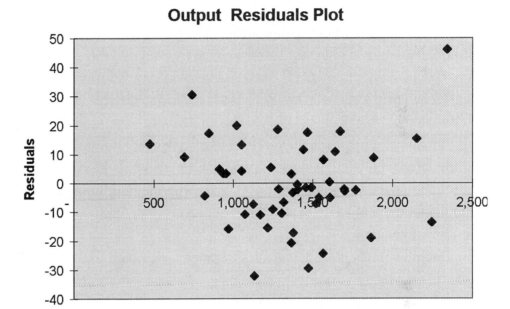

This chart does not show as clear a curved relationship as did the previous chart. Look at it carefully. The data points in the center of the chart are more likely to lie below than above the horizontal axis, while those to the left and right appear more likely to lie above the axis. This is enough of an indication to warrant exploring a curved relationship between output and short-run average cost.

▼ Polynomial Regression

One common technique for estimating a curved regression is with a quadratic regression, which is an example of a polynomial regression. If there is a single independent variable, a quadratic equation would have the following form:

$$\hat{y} = b_0 + b_1 x_1 + b_2 x_1^2$$

This equation is quadratic because it has a squared term. Excel treats it as a separate variable. It's just another x_2 to Excel; the Regression Tool doesn't know where it came from. What changes is your *interpretation* of the results.

Although there is only one independent variable, a quadratic equation can have other independent variables as well as either linear terms (not squared), quadratic terms (squared), or both. The bearings problem only has a single independent variable (output), so we will estimate the equation shown above.

▼ Estimating a Quadratic Regression

The basic method for estimating a quadratic equation will be to create a new column of data in which the values in each cell are the square of the values in the "Output" column. A regression will then be run in which these data will be treated like a separate independent variable.

- Switch to the "Bearings (2)" worksheet. This worksheet is identical to the original "Bearings" worksheet.

- Select any cell in column B.

- Open the "Insert" menu on the menu bar and select "Columns." A new column B will open between the two columns of data. The "Cost" data will move to column C. Column B will be used to put the new output squared independent variable. It has to be beside the "Output" column because Excel requires independent variables to be adjacent.

- Enter the label "Output Sq" in cell B1.

- Enter formulas in the cells in column B so that each cell will display the value which is square of the value in the same row of column A. You will have to adjust the width of column B to see these values. Cell B2 should display 2,122,849, cell B3 should display 2,452,356, cell B4 should display 881,721, etc.

- Open the Regression Tool's dialog window. The entries for the input fields will have to be changed if they have the previous problem's values. Enter the address range of the "Cost" data in the field for the *y* variable and the address range for the columns with both the "Output" and "Output Sq" data for the x variable. Include the cells containing the labels, indicate in the dialog window that labels are included, direct the output to cell D1, and ask for residuals plots.

- Click "OK." When the Tool has finished writing the output, use the Format—Column—AutoFit Selection menu sequence to adjust the column widths containing the output.

- Use the Zoom Control to change the Zoom factor to 50%. Locate the residuals plots. Since this regression has two independent variables, Excel produces two plots. Notice that Excel stacks them so that it is impossible to see the one on the bottom without moving the one on top.

- Select the top residuals plot and move it directly below the plot below it. While it is still selected, change the Zoom factor back to 100% and compare the two residuals plots.

One of the residuals plots shows the residuals values plotted against output. The other shows the same residuals values plotted against output squared. Compare them carefully. Although the two plots are not identical, the pattern of residuals is the same. The plots are not exactly identical because the horizontal scaling is slightly different for the squared term, but you can recognize the common pattern. Since the two plots provide the same information, there is no reason to keep them both.

- Switch the zoom factor back to 50%. Delete the residuals plot for "Output Sq" by selecting it and the pressing the Delete key. Move the residual plot for "Output" below the regression output (the same place used for the regression on the first "Bearings" worksheet). Increase the height of the residuals plot as you did with the previous worksheet.

You may again decide to print this worksheet to better follow the discussion below. Use the same procedure described for the previous regression given on page 373. Adjust the width of column B if needed to see the data values.

While the simple linear regression showed no evidence of a relationship between *output* and average cost, the quadratic regression provides strong evidence of such a relationship. The r^2 (in cell E5) has increased to a value slightly over .20. The F test has a p value (cell I12) of .0052 versus .98 for the simple linear regression. This is sufficient to reject the Null Hypothesis of no relationship between the independent and dependent variables at all typical levels of significance.

Perhaps most striking in the quadratic regression is the significance of both *output* and *output squared*. The p values for the t tests of the significance of each variable are approximately .0015 and .0013 (cells H18 and

H19), respectively. In the simple linear regression where output was the only independent variable, the estimated coefficient was insignificant. As well as being significant itself, the inclusion of *output squared* changes the significance of *output* as well.

The estimated coefficients are in cells E18 and E19, and give the following regression equation:

$$\hat{y} = 90.24 - 0.0863x + 0.0000305x^2$$

The coefficient on *output squared* may appear to be very close to zero, but this must be evaluated in relation to the size of the numbers it is likely to be multiplied by. Look at the values of *output squared* in column B. In many cases, these numbers are in the millions. When such large numbers are multiplied by the coefficient shown above, the product will have a value between 10 and 100, a range which is reasonably large given the *y* values.

▼ Partial Effects in Polynomial Regressions

When each independent variable in a multiple regression equation is included only as a linear term, the coefficient for that variable is also a measure of its partial effect. For polynomial regressions, the measure of the partial effect is not as simple. In estimating the regression considered here, Excel treats *output* and *output squared* as if they were separate independent variables. In determining partial effects, however, they cannot be regarded as separate. There is no way of changing *output* without also changing *output squared*. The estimated partial effect must be determined by taking the derivative of the dependent variable with respect to the independent variable. For a quadratic regression of the form $\hat{y} = b_0 + b_1x + b_2x^2$, the partial effect is not b_1 but $b_1 + 2b_2x$. For this regression discussed here, the partial effect of output on average cost is $-.0863 + .0000611x$. The effect of a change in output on average cost *depends on what the total level of output is*. For small levels of output, increases in output will decrease average cost because the negative term will dominate. As output gets larger, this negative effect will diminish. Eventually the partial effect's term with the *x* will dominate and increases in output will increase average cost. The partial effect of output on cost measures marginal cost. According to economic theory, marginal cost initially declines, reaches a minimum, and then increases. This is exactly the kind of behavior implied by the estimated regression equation.

▼ When Should Polynomial Regression Be Used?

Determining the set of independent variables for a particular dependent variable is much easier than knowing whether the relationship is likely to be linear or curved. As a general rule, it is best to keep a regression model as simple as possible. In some cases, such as the example given here of the relationship between output and average cost, there is good reason to expect a curved relationship and even to have some idea of the general shape of the curve. Other techniques exist within multiple regression analysis for estimating more complex curved relationships. One technique, for example, is to use higher-order polynomials. This could be done by including a cubed term, or perhaps a term raised to the fourth power among the independent variables. This should be avoided in most cases. Although it is appropriate to examine the residuals from a linear regression for evidence of a curved relationship, it is best to avoid higher-order polynomials (and other techniques) unless you have good theoretical reasons to expect the relationship to have some specific shape which can only be represented by a polynomial of order greater than two..

▼ Dummy Variables and Categorical Data

The data used in the regressions we have looked at so far have been continuous. Such measures as output and household income can take on different values, and we expect changes in the values of these variables to have a consistent effect on the value of the dependent variable. Categorical data are different. These data place observations into a particular category, and there may be no obvious ranking to these categories. A fast food chain, for example, may wish to develop a model predicting sales at individual restaurants. One of the important factors affecting sales may be differences in behavior among people living in different regions and different countries. The country or the region where a fast-food restaurant is located may have a big effect on its sales. A variable giving this information is categorical—very different from the continuous variables we have considered so far with regression.

We have considered categorical data in connection with another statistical technique—analysis of variance. We looked at the effect of keyboard design on typing speed (page 329), for example, and the effects of package design and advertising strategy on perfume sales (page 333). Keyboard design, package design, and advertising strategy are all examples of categorical variables, and analysis of variance is designed exclusively to analyze the effect such variables have on a continuous measure (such as typing speed or perfume sales). The dummy variable technique enables multiple regression analysis also to handle categorical independent variables. With this technique, multiple regression analysis can handle any problem which could be analyzed with ANOVA (and will provide the same results). Unlike ANOVA, multiple regression analysis can handle problems involving a mixture of categorical and continuous variables.

A dummy variable is one which has only two possible values—0 or 1. When a dummy variable is used to indicate a single characteristic, observations which possess the characteristics will have the dummy variable made equal to "1" while observations without the characteristic will have it equal to "0." Let's consider the following example.

A university is interested in comparing the performance in the first business statistics class of students who use computers to learn business statistics with those who do not use computers. Data were collected from a sample of statistics students who took courses which either used or did not use computers. Average course grade and GPA were also collected. Is there evidence that those who used computers on average received higher average course grades?

To determine whether there is evidence that students using computers receive higher grades, we would test $H_0: \mu_{computer} \leq \mu_{no\ computer}$ versus $H_A: \mu_{computer} > \mu_{no\ computer}$, holding constant the effect of GPA. This is a one-tail test.

• Select the "Computers" worksheet.

The data in this worksheet will be used to estimate a regression model in which average statistics course grade is analyzed as a function of GPA and whether or not the student used computers to learn statistics. GPA is included because it is expected to have a major impact on the statistics grade, and it may be related to whether or not the student took a course which used computers. Although the column labeled "Use Computers?" has the information for a dummy variable, it cannot be used as is because it does not have just the values 0 and 1. We will need to create a dummy variable from the values in this column. For any observation with the answer "Yes," the dummy variable will have the value "1." When the answer is "No, " the dummy variable will equal "0." Note that the yes/no information is logically exactly the same as 1/0.

The regression tool requires that all the independent variables be adjacent. We will thus first move the current data on computer use out of column C and create a dummy variable in that column.

- Select region C2:C21 and move the data from column C to column D so that each value stays in the same row. Column C will be used to create the dummy variable which must be adjacent to the other independent variables.

- Enter the label "Computer Dummy" in cell C1.

- Select cell C2. Since the observation represented by this row is of a student who did use computers, we want this cell to contain the value "1." Use the Function Wizard button to select the IF function (in the "Logical" category). In the "logical_test" field enter an expression which will be true if the value of cell D2 equals "Yes" (you must include the double quotes). You should see the word "TRUE" in the region to the right of the "logical_test" field where Excel shows the parameter's value.

- When the expression is true, have C2 equal "1," and when it is false have C2 equal "0" (without the quotes). After you click the "Finish" button, cell C2 should display the value "1."

- Copy the contents of cell C2 to cells C3 through cell C21. Check that those adjacent to a "No" in column D (like cell C6) display "0" while those adjacent to a "Yes" display "1."

You now have a completed dummy variable in column C. When running a regression, the data in column C (and *not* column D) will be used as an independent variable.

- Using the Regression Analysis Tool, regress Course Average in column A (*y* variable) against GPA and Computer Dummy in columns B and C (*x* variables). Be sure not to include column D. Have Excel place the output on the same worksheet beginning in cell E2. Residual plots will not be needed.

The estimated coefficients and significance statistics are shown below.

E	Coefficients	Standard Error	t Stat	P-value
18 Intercept	35.98582354	3.33531463	10.789334	5.0277E-09
19 GPA	14.34949132	1.097573966	13.0738262	2.683E-10
20 Computer Dummy	5.86737271	2.031507889	2.88818603	0.01021505

These coefficients provide the following estimated equation:

$$\hat{y} = 35.99 + 14.35x_1 + 5.87x_2$$

where x_1 is GPA and x_2 is the "use computers" dummy variable.

The coefficients suggest that a one point increase in GPA results in an average increase in the course grade of 14.35, holding constant computer use. Observations on those who use computers will have the value "1" for x_2, while those who do not will have the value "0." Those with the value "1" are going to have a predicted grade ($\hat{y}$) which is 5.87 higher than those with the value "0" *and the same GPA*. This coefficient (5.87) is a measure of the value of using computers *controlling for the independent effect of GPA*.

Had we simply regressed average grade against the computer dummy without including GPA we might also have found that those students using computer scored higher grades. In that case, however, *we would not have been sure that this wasn't because better students (with higher GPAs) were more likely to take courses which used computers than weaker students*. If this were the case, the apparent higher grades of those using computers might not have been because of the computer use. It might have been simply that better students (who would have gotten higher grades anyway) happened to be the ones using computers. By including GPA as an independent variable, we have specifically eliminated this possible interpretation. Our results indicate that *regardless of GPA,* students using computers did better than those who did not, a result which is inconsistent with the Null Hypothesis.

This result is equivalent to saying that there is one equation relating GPA and average statistics grade for those who use computers and another equation for those who do not. This situation is shown on the graph on the next page. The dashed line shows the estimated relationship between GPA and average statistics grade for those using computers, while the lower solid line shows the estimated relationship for those not using computers. The vertical distance between the two lines is the estimated value of using computers, the coefficient on the dummy variable, 5.87.

In this equation only one coefficient for GPA is estimated; it applies to both those who do and those who do not use computers. Thus the two lines are parallel, and their common slope is the estimated coefficient on GPA, 14.35. The dummy variable has an effect like a change in the constant term (y intercept or b_0). For those not using computers, the constant term is the constant term from the printout, approximately 35.99, but for those using computers it is that *plus* the coefficient on the dummy variable, or approximately 41.85.

Is the difference statistically significant? The Null Hypothesis we are testing is $H_0: \mu_{computer} \leq \mu_{no\ computer}$. When using dummy variables, think of the equivalent $H_0: (\mu_{computer} - \mu_{no\ computer}) \leq 0$. The estimated coefficient on the dummy variable is an estimate of a β which measures the differ-

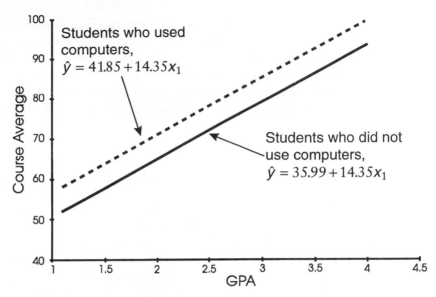

ence between the average grades of those using and not using computers, in other words ($\mu_{computer} - \mu_{no\ computer}$). So the Null Hypothesis could also be written as $H_0: \beta_{computer\ dummy} \leq 0$. The estimated coefficient is 5.87, clearly not consistent with H_0. The reported p value is .0102. This, however, is a two-tail p value. To convert it to a one-tail p value, it must be divided by two giving .0051. This low p value is highly significant, leading us to reject the Null Hypothesis and conclude that there is evidence that those using computers received higher average grades, controlling for the effect of GPA.

▼ Multilevel Categorical Data

Categorical data often have only two levels or values, such as the measure in the example above of whether or not a student used a computer. Any variable giving the answer to a yes/no question has two values. A single dummy variable will, in these cases, enable us to estimate the effects of the categorical variable. Much categorical data, however, have more than two levels or values. Location is one common such variable. An observation in a data set might include a variable indicating the state in which a respondent is located. If observations come from more than two states, the location variable can have more than two values and is referred to as *multilevel.*

A multilevel categorical variable is represented in multiple regression analysis by a *set* of dummy variables. Each dummy variable measures the presence or absence of a *single value* of the multilevel categorical variable. The total number of dummy variables equals the number of different values (or levels) of the categorical variable *minus one*. If, for example, a location variable could have nine different values (referring, for example, to nine different states), there would be *eight* dummy variables each of which would have the value of one or zero for each of eight different locations. If an observation came from the ninth location, for which there is no dummy variable, the value of all eight dummy variables would be zero. When creating a set of dummy variables for a multilevel categorical variable, one of the values will not have a dummy variable; that value is said to be *omitted*. The reason for this, as well as the issue of which value to omit, will be considered in the example below.

Like most American municipalities, the primary revenue for the town of Elder Hollow comes from the property tax. To administer the tax, the value of each piece of property is estimated by a tax assessor. The town's Board of Equalization has the task of ensuring that all taxpayers are treated equally. A complaint from several residents of the Chester Court development asserts that residences in that neighborhood are assessed at a higher level than houses of the same value in the town's other neighborhoods, Armsley Hills and Blawndale. A higher assessment would cause tax bills in Chester Court to be higher than those of identically valued houses in other neighborhoods. In order to test the assertion, you have selected a random sample of residential properties from each neighborhood which have recently sold. The sales price and the assessed value together with the property's neighborhood have been collected. Based on these data, is there evidence that properties in Chester Court are overassessed compared to properties in the other two neighborhoods?

The Null Hypotheses for this problem would be $H_0: \mu_C \leq \mu_B$ and $H_0: \mu_C \leq \mu_A$, while the Alternate Hypotheses would be $H_A: \mu_C > \mu_B$ and $H_A: \mu_C > \mu_A$. These require one-tail tests which means that we will have to modify the two-tail test provided by Excel.

Ideally, each property's tax assessment would exactly equal the sales price, but this ideal can never be achieved in practice. Equity is achieved if there is no consistent difference among neighborhoods of the relationship between sales price and assessed value.

• Select the "Assessment" worksheet. The data for this problem are located there. We will estimate a regression with assessed value as the dependent variable and sales price and neighborhood dummies as independent variables.

There are three values for the "neighborhood" variable. Two dummy variables must be created. Since we are interested in a comparison between Chester Court and the other neighborhoods, Chester Court will be the omitted value. One dummy variable will therefore indicate if an observation is in Armsley Hills and the other will indicate if it is in Blawndale.

- Select the neighborhood data in column C and move it to column E, keeping each value in the same row. The now empty columns C and D will be used for the dummy variables.

- Enter the label "A Dummy" in cell C1. The Armsley Hills dummy will be placed in column C.

- Select cell C2. Use the Function Wizard to enter values for the arguments of the IF function to test whether the contents of cell E2 equals "Armsley Hills." If it does, have the IF function set the value of C2 to 1. If it does not, have the IF function set the value of C2 to 0. C2 should display the value 1. If C2 displays the #NAME? error, you may have forgotten to put quotation marks around "Armsley Hills" in the IF function's "logical_test" argument field.

- Enter the label "B Dummy" in cell D1. Select cell D2 and use the IF function to set the value of D2 to 1 if E2 equals "Blawndale" and 0 otherwise.

- Copy the formulas in cells C1 and D1 down the column of cells to row 31. Carefully check the values of the two dummy variables. Rows 2 through 10 should have "1" in column C and "0" in column D. Rows 11 through 20 should have "0" in column C and "1" in column D. Rows 21 through 31 should have "0" in both column C and column D.

The next step is to use the Regression Tool on these data. Note that the set of dependent variables will include the dummy variables in columns C and D, but not the original neighborhood information in column E.

- Open the Regression Tool dialog window by selecting "Regression" from the "Analysis Tools."

- Enter the cell region address for "Assessed Value" (including label) in the field for the Y range, and the cell region address for "Sales Price" and the two dummy variables (including labels) in the field for X range.

- Click the box to indicate to Excel that your data regions include labels, and indicate that you want the output to start in cell F2. Residual plots are not needed. Click "OK."

- Once the regression output is complete, adjust the column widths of the region containing the output. Be sure to save the worksheet. Compare your output with the one shown at the top of the next page to be sure you have done this correctly.

We will refer to this regression as "Model 1" in the discussion below.

	F	G	H	I	J	K
2	SUMMARY OUTPUT					
3						
4	Regression Statistics					
5	Multiple R	0.991309388				
6	R Square	0.982694302				
7	Adjusted R Square	0.980697491				
8	Standard Error	3180.036929				
9	Observations	30				
10						
11	ANOVA					
12		df	SS	MS	F	Significance F
13	Regression	3	14930247205	4976749068	492.1317868	5.18302E-23
14	Residual	26	262928506.7	10112634.87		
15	Total	29	15193175711			
16						
17		Coefficients	Standard Error	t Stat	P-value	Lower 95%
18	Intercept	-2133.137762	4324.756946	-0.493238762	0.625984356	-11022.8088
19	Sales Price	0.944474339	0.034134647	27.66908195	8.15154E-21	0.874309522
20	A Dummy	2279.492293	2026.167539	1.125026558	0.270856698	-1885.35746
21	B Dummy	-1305.065776	1431.303948	-0.911801982	0.37025011	-4247.155104

Model 1 indicates that, in any neighborhood, for each $1 increase in the market (sales) price, the average assessed value increases by slightly more than 94¢. The estimated coefficient is highly significant. The p value is slightly more than 8.15×10^{-21}, an extremely small value. The entire regression is highly significant as indicated by the p value for the F test (5.18×10^{-23}). The R^2 is over 0.98.

The coefficients of primary interest in this problem are those on the dummy variables. Each coefficient represents a shift in the value of the constant (or y intercept) for observations in that dummy variables group *compared to the omitted group*. For example, the coefficient for the B Dummy is about -1305. This indicates that observations for which the value of the B Dummy is 1 (residences in Blawndale) have an assessed value about $1,305 less than otherwise identical observations in the omitted group (Chester Court). If we were to calculate, for example, the predicted assessed value for a residence in Chester County which sold for $100,000, the value of both the A Dummy and the B Dummy would be 0. The predicted value assessed value would therefore be

$$\hat{y} = -2,133 + (0.9445 \times 100,000) = \$92,317.$$

Since a $100,000 residence in Blawndale would have the value "1" for the B Dummy, its estimated value would be

$$\hat{y} = -2,133 + (0.9445 \times 100,000) + (1 \times (-1,305))$$
$$= 92,317 - 1,305 = \$91,012.$$

This result appears consistent with the complaint of the residents in Chester Court. The lower assessed value for residences in Blawndale would result in lower average taxes on identically valued houses. The estimated coefficient, however, is not significant since its p value is over .185. (The p value shown on the output is slightly over .37, but this is a two-tail p value and must be divided by two to be converted to a one-tail p value.) Although this sample indicates that residences in Chester Court are overassessed compared to those in Blawndale, this result might well be due to chance. Thus, despite the estimated coefficient, this regression *does not* support the contention of the residents of Chester Court.

The contention of Chester Court residents that their houses are overvalued is also contradicted by the positive coefficient on the A Dummy. This dummy indicates that residences in Armsley Hills are assessed even more than identically valued residences in Chester Court by an average of about $2,279. This estimated coefficient, however, is also not significant since its p value is about .135 (one tail). The final conclusion is that this regression does not provide good evidence that Chester Court residences are assessed any differently than residences in the other neighborhoods. This, of course, does not mean that we have evidence that residences in all neighborhoods are assessed identically. A stronger conclusion *might* result from a regression on a larger sample.

The regression provides (weak) evidence that residences in Blawndale have lower assessments while residences in Armsley Hills have higher assessment than identical houses in Chester Court. Suppose we wanted a direct comparison between Armsley Hills and Blawndale? Such a comparison would most easily be made by creating and including a dummy variable ("C Dummy") for Chester Court and omitting either the A Dummy or the B Dummy. Let's consider a regression with the A Dummy omitted and refer to it as "Model 2." It turns out that a simple pattern exists between the estimated coefficients of Model 1 and Model 2, or any pair of regressions estimated on the same data which differ only in which dummy variable in the set is omitted. All independent variables other than the set of dummy variables (only Sales Price in this case) are the same. The intercept of Model 2 will be the sum of the intercept of Model 1 and the coefficient in Model 1 of the omitted dummy variable in Model 2. The estimated coefficients for the dummy variables in Model 2 will be their Model 1 value minus the estimated coefficient in Model 1 of the dummy variable omitted in Model 2. This pattern for the regressions discussed here are summarized in the table at the top of the next page.

Although the value of the coefficients for Model 2 are easy to determine from Model 1, their significance is not as easily determined. For this rea-

Coefficient	Model 1	Model 2
Intercept	−2,133	−2,133 + 2,279 = 146
Sales Price	0.9445	0.9445
A Dummy	2,279	2,279 − 2,279 = 0 (omitted)
B Dummy	−1,305	−1,305 − 2,279 = −3,584
C Dummy	0 (omitted)	0 − 2,279 = −2,279

son, if we want to test whether or not there is evidence that residences in Armsley Hills are assessed more than identically valued residences in Blawndale, the Model 2 regression should be estimated. This is left as an exercise.

▼ Multicollinearity

Although we refer to the explanatory variables in multiple regression analysis as *independent*, it is very rare for them to be independent of each other in the statistical sense. In other words, independent variables tend to be correlated with each other. One of the reasons for this correlation is that two or more independent variables may contain similar information.

Consider the following problem:

A lawn service company is interested in predicting the average annual amount households in a neighborhood will spend on lawn and garden care. A sample of neighborhoods is chosen, and the average amount spent is collected along with average lot size, average household income, and average value of home. Use multiple regression to estimate the determinants of average neighborhood expenditures on lawn and garden care.

- Select the "Lawn Care" worksheet in the workbook in multireg.xls.

The primary problem with these data is that family income and home value may be highly correlated. Those with valuable homes tend to have high incomes, and vice-versa. Both variables are measures of economic well-being which most directly affects the willingness to spend money for lawn and garden care. We would expect, however, the two factors to have positive, but somewhat different, effects. Multiple regression, however, may have difficulty distinguishing between those effects. This is the problem of multicollinearity.

- Use the Regression Analysis Tool on the Lawn Care data. Lawn Care Expenditure in column A should be the *y* variable and the three variables in columns B, C, and D should be x variables. Use labels. Have Excel place the output beginning in cell E2. Residual plots are not needed. When the Regression Tool has completed, adjust the column widths where the output was placed. The estimated coefficients and measures of significance are shown below.

	E	F	G	H	I
17		Coefficients	Standard Error	t Stat	P-value
18	Intercept	-9.736709754	18.10704706	-0.537730405	0.59335535
19	Lot Size	21.21401018	3.076925279	6.894548374	1.3118E-08
20	Avg HH Income	0.000680953	0.001286404	0.529346471	0.59911059
21	Avg Home Value	-0.00018334	0.00060725	-0.30191837	0.76407513

Although lot size has the expected highly significant positive relationship with lawn care expenditures, the results for the other two independent variables are puzzling. The p values of approximately .60 and .76 indicate that neither variable is significantly different from zero. Average house value has a negative estimated coefficient, suggesting that as house values go up, lawn care expenditures go down. This certainly runs counter to intuition. The problem here is multicollinearity arising from the strong relationship between average household income and average house value.

When two independent variables are highly correlated, including both variables in the regression will raise the problem of multicollinearity. In multiple regression analysis, measures of the significance of a single independent variable (including the variable's standard error, t statistic, and associated p value) should be thought of as measures evaluating that variable's contribution to a model containing all other independent variables. Suppose that we have a model estimating the demand for lawn and garden service in which home value is included as an independent variable. How much *additional* explanatory power will be added by also including family income? Not much, since home value already has the information about economic well-being. As a result, the estimated coefficient on family income will be insignificant. What about the coefficient on home value? In a model which already contains family income, the additional explanatory power of home value will be small. It, too, will be insignificant. Although economic well-being is unquestionably an important determinant of the demand for lawn and garden service, including two highly correlated measures may well result in both of them being insignificant! What if one of them is removed?

- Recall the Regression Tool. Change the x variables to include only lot size and average household income. Put the output in the range beginning with cell E23.

The coefficients should now be as shown in the picture below.

	E	F	G	H	I
38		Coefficients	Standard Error	t Stat	P-value
39	Intercept	-14.13588291	10.64538406	-1.327888485	0.19062812
40	Lot Size	21.18292929	3.045324741	6.9558852	9.535E-09
41	Avg HH Income	0.000293061	6.43727E-05	4.552558973	3.75E-05

Although the estimated coefficient for average household income has declined from about 0.0007 to about 0.0003, the coefficient is now highly significant with a p value of 3.75×10^{-5}.

Let's try excluding household income and including average home value.

- Swap columns C and D. One way of doing this is to first select column C by clicking the column heading. Then select "Columns" from the "Insert" menu on the menu bar (or click the right mouse button while the pointer is on the column and select "Insert" from the pop-up menu). This will open a new column C and shift the worksheet contents of the previous C and above one column to the right. Move the contents of column E (Average Home Value) to the empty column C. Delete the now empty column E by clicking on the column heading and then selecting "Delete" from the "Edit" menu on the menu bar (or from the pop-up menu which appears when you click the right mouse button).

- Use the Regression Tool to run a new regression. The fields in the Tool's dialog window will be the same as for the previous regression (x variables in columns B and C) except for "Output Range" which should be set to cell E43.

The estimated coefficients and their significance measures for this model are shown in the picture below.

	E	F	G	H	I
58		Coefficients	Standard Error	t Stat	P-value
59	Intercept	-17.21555708	11.23778421	-1.531935189	0.13224244
60	Lot Size	21.15324399	3.051147558	6.932881347	1.0333E-08
61	Avg Home Value	0.000137695	3.04495E-05	4.522072066	4.1459E-05

Rather than being negative and insignificant as in the first regression, the estimated coefficient for average home value is positive and highly significant.

The multicollinearity between average household income and average home value caused both variables to have insignificant estimated coefficients when both were included as independent variables. Yet when either variable was included as an independent variable without the other, it was highly significant. There is clearly a relationship between economic well-being and expenditures on lawn and garden care (which both variables measure), but it is impossible to get a good estimate on the unique effect of each variable.

One question which multicollinear data poses is exactly which variables should be included in the set of independent variables. Of the three models presented here, which is correct? There is, unfortunately, no clear answer. If the object of the regression analysis is simply prediction, then the model with the highest value for the adjusted R^2 is probably the best. If the object is to understand the relationship among the variables, then the model with both independent variables may be best. The coefficients of variables which suffer from multicollinearity are unbiased, although they have large standard errors.

There are techniques which can be used to verify multicollinearity, but they are beyond the scope of this book. Excel has a Correlation Analysis Tool which could be helpful in finding pairs of potential independent variables which are highly correlated. One method sometimes used involves regressing independent variables on each other. As a general rule, multicollinearity should be suspected whenever including or excluding an independent variable has large effects on the significance of the estimated coefficients of one or more other variables. In the example given here, the collinear relationship existed among only two variables. It is possible, however, for a multicollinear relationship to involve more than two variables. Detecting the exact nature of the multicollinearity can be difficult in that case.

Even when severe multicollinearity is not a problem, real independent variables are never statistically independent. There always is some degree of correlation. We call it "multicollinearity" only when the problem is severe, but it always affects regression analysis. Much of the challenge of determining exactly which set of independent variables to use in regression analysis occurs because the decision to include or exclude one variable very frequently changes the sign and significance of other variables. We will encounter this problem again when we look at model building.

▼ Heteroscedasticity and Autocorrelation

One of the assumptions of ordinary least squares regression is that the population error terms are random, independent, and have constant variance. If the assumption of constant variance of the error term is violated, the data are said be heteroscedastic (or heteroskedastic). If the assumption of independence is violated, the data are said to be autocorrelated. Sometimes these problems can be handled by adding additional variables to a model or by altering the functional form of the estimated relationship. These problems can also be dealt with by using the technique called generalized least squares, a technique beyond the scope of this book which uses information from the residuals to estimate the relationship between the independent and dependent variables.

The most common type of heteroscedasticity arises when the variance of the error term increases (or decreases) as the value of an independent variable increases. The most common type of autocorrelation occurs when the error term has a pattern associated with the observation over time.

Heteroscedasticity occurs most often with cross-sectional data which are data collected from different observation units at the same point in time. It is likely to occur, for example, if the observations are very different in size. This might be the case, for example, if our unit of observation is the firm, and the data mixes small businesses with giant corporations. Heteroscedasticity can also occur in time series data (data collected from the same unit of observation at different points in time). Heteroscedasticity with such data is sometimes seen as an increase or decrease in the error term over time.

Heteroscedasticity can be detected by examining the estimated residuals $(y - \hat{y})$ to see if their variance seems to vary with the value of an independent variable, the observation number, or some other measure. Although there are formal tests which can be performed on the estimated residuals, they are not calculated by Excel's Regression Analysis Tool. Hetereoscedasticity can often, however, be detected by examining residual plots, which the Regression Tool can prepare.

Consider the following problem.

It has long been known that there is an important relationship between economic development and energy consumption. To investigate this relationship, international data on per capita energy consumption (in kilograms of coal equivalent) and per capita gross national product (in dollars) were collected for 1990 (Data is from U.S. Bureau of the Census, Statistical Abstract of the United States: 1994, *CD-ROM version, Washington, DC, 1994, tables 1366 and 1393). Use these data to estimate the effect of per capita GNP on per capita energy consumption.*

- Switch to the "Energy" worksheet. Call up the Regression Tool dialog window.

- In the "Y Range" field, enter the range address of the per capita energy consumption in column B and in the "X Range" field enter the range address of the per capita GNP in column C. Have the output placed in the range beginning with cell D2.

- In the section of the dialog window labeled "Residuals," select "Residual Plots" by clicking it so that an "x" appears in the small box to the left of the words. This will cause Excel to produce a chart showing the value of residuals plotted against each of the independent variables. Since there is only one independent variable in this case there will be only one plot.

- Click the "OK" button. Adjust the column widths.

The chart showing a plot of residuals against the independent variable (Per Capita GNP) will be located on the worksheet to the right of the regression output.

- Click the residuals plot once so that sizing "handles" appear in the four corners and the middle of each side.

- Use the sizing handles to make the chart larger.

The chart should look similar to the one below.

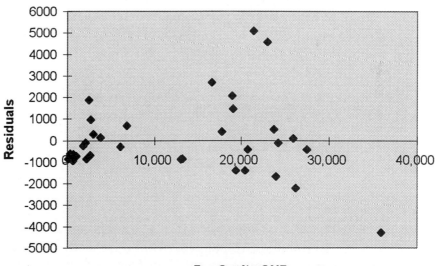

Heteroscedasticity is indicated by the change in the *vertical spread* in the residual values associated with different values of per capita GNP. For those observations with low values of per capita GNP (less than about

$5,000), the points are relatively close together. As per capita GNP increases to about $25,000, the points become more separated. Although heteroscedasticity is fairly evident in this residuals plot, it is easy to mistakenly find heteroscedasticity when there are big variations in the number of observations associated with different values of an independent variable. Spread in the residuals would not be apparent for some value of an independent variable if there are few observations in the sample close to that value. In this case, by contrast, there are roughly the same number of observations with low per capita GNP as with high per capita GNP (up to a bit over $25,000). The relative lack of spread for the residuals for observations with low per capita GNP is *not* an artifact of few observations with low per capita GNP.

If you noticed that these residuals also suggest a nonlinearity, good for you! Note how the residuals at both the low and high ends of the horizontal axis tend to below the axis, while most of the residuals in the middle are above the axis. This model should include a squared term for per capita GNP. Would that correct the heteroscedasticity? This issue is left as an exercise.

Autocorrelation is similar to heteroscedasticity in that it is caused by a pattern in the residuals. In the case of autocorrelation, the pattern is not in the spread of the residuals but in their lack of randomness, their tendency to form a pattern. The most typical autocorrelation occurs in time series data, and is caused by the fact that the effect of a change in an independent variable (which may or may not be included in the model) on a dependent variable can occur over several time periods. Consider the following problem.

The number of oil wells drilled in the United States is known to be affected by the price of oil. Higher prices should lead to more wells drilled. An oil industry trade group wants to determine that relationship more precisely. Data on the number of wells drilled in the United States each year since 1930 were collected along with the average price of a barrel (bbl) of oil that year. Based on these data, what is the relationship? (These data are from Twentieth Century Petroleum Statistics, *Dallas Texas: Degolyer and McNaughton, 1992, pp. 34, 98.)*

The data are on the "Oil" worksheet in the workbook in multireg.xls. In determining a response to price, it is usually necessary to correct a price series to account for inflation. That worksheet also contains the value of the Producer Price Index based on 1982 prices. This index will be used to adjust the price data for inflation.

- Switch to the "Oil" worksheet. Insert a blank column in front of the current column C by first selecting a cell in column C and then either select "Column" from the "Insert" menu on the menu bar or press the right mouse button and select "Insert" from the pop-up menu. The new column C will be used for the inflation-adjusted price of oil.

- Enter the label "Real Price per bbl" in cell C1.

- Enter a formula in cell C2 which will take the nominal (in 1930 dollars) price of oil in cell D2, multiply it by 100, and divide it by the price index in cell E2. Use relative addresses. The value displayed in cell C2 should be a little over 7.9865.

- Copy the formula in C2 to cells C3:C63. The value displayed in cell C63 should be slightly less than 14.1631.

- Use the Regression Tool to estimate a regression equation in which Total Wells Drilled is the y variable and Real Price per bbl is the x variable. Use labels. Request residuals plots. Have the output placed in the region beginning in cell F2.

- After the Regression Tool has completed, adjust the column widths of the region containing the output to fit the cell contents.

The regression output appears to confirm the relationship between price and number of wells drilled. The coefficient on the real price of oil is positive and has a p value of 2.55×10^{-15}, an indication of very high significance. Analysis of the residuals, however, will reveal a problem.

- Scroll your worksheet so that H25 is in the upper left corner of your screen. That cell should contain the label "*Residuals*" and is the last column of a table giving predicted y values and residuals for each observation in the data.

- Click the Chart Wizard button. Use the Chart Wizard mouse pointer to make the chart fill as much space on your screen as possible without causing the worksheet to scroll.

- The data for the chart are the set of residuals in H25:H87. This includes the label, which can be included (but need not be).

- Choose a scatter plot in which only the points are plotted with no connection lines. Your plot should be similar to the one at the top of the next page.

These residuals show a clear up-and-down wavelike pattern. Positive residuals tend to be adjacent to positive residuals. There is a strong indication of autocorrelation. It may be possible to correct for this by respecifying the model to include additional independent variables. These might include "lagged" values from from earlier time periods. A technique other than ordinary least squares regression may also be needed.

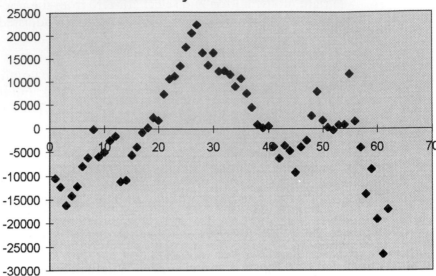

▼ Model Building

The process of model building involves a search for the best way to specify a relationship between a dependent variable and a set of independent variables. A dependent variable is first regressed against an initial set of independent variables based upon a theoretical expectation of the relationship. The results of that regression are used to modify the set of independent variables or even the dependent variable. A second regression is estimated, and the results of that regression are used to make further modification. Since each change in the set of independent variables may change the estimated coefficients and significances of the other independent variables, only a few modifications should be made after each regression. This iterative process continues until the analyst is satisfied that the regression best captures the relationship among the variables. Each step may involve creating new variables as we did in the oil drilling example to create a measure of the price of oil adjusted for inflation. Dummy variables may have to be created and decisions made about which levels to omit. Squared values of independent variables may be added to correct for nonlinearities. Independent variables may have to be checked for multicollinearity, and a decision made of whether to include only some or all such variables. Variables which do not contribute to the model in a logical or statistical sense need to be omitted.

Different analysts approaching the same set of data are not likely to end up with identical regression models. If there are strong relationships among the variables, they should be apparent in different constructed models. Becoming proficient with multiple regression analysis takes practice. It is not possible to provide a set of step-by-step rules which will inevitably lead to the "best" regression models. Nevertheless here are some tentative considerations which a beginner might find useful in the process of model building.

1. Start with the strongest possible regression equation by thinking in advance what types of relationships you expect to find. Is the set of independent variables reasonably complete? If not, can you fill the gaps by gathering additional data? Try to determine in advance what signs you expect for the estimated coefficients. Unexpected signs are "signposts" for areas which need further investigation. Try to determine which variables you expect might have multicollinearity. Don't, however, infer multicollinearity whenever the results look a little "funny" unless you have solid evidence of multicollinearity.

2. Keep in mind that the number of independent variables you can have is constrained by the number of observations. If you have only a few observations, you may not be able to have as many independent variables as you might want. This can be a particular problem if you want to use categorical variables with multiple values since this may require the construction of many dummy variables, only a few of which can be included.

3. Have Excel produce residuals plots. Examine the residuals plots for nonlinearities and heteroscedasticity. For time series data, look for autocorrelation by constructing a plot of the table of residuals Excel produces by observation number. Add squared values of independent variables where nonlinearities are expected.

4. Test for multicollinearity by dropping individual variables and observing whether this increases the significance of other variables which you suspect might be measuring the same or similar factors. Then put the omitted variable back in the regression and drop one of the other variables you suspect of being in a multicollinear relationship. If you confirm multicollinearity, decide exactly which variables to keep. Remember that this decision depends partly on the objectives of the regression analysis.

5. Follow a multiple-step approach. Try to deal with only one problem in each step. Expect to estimate several regressions before you come up with a final model.

▼ A Comprehensive Example

The following problem, although still simpler than most real-world regression problems, will illustrate the step-by-step approach to model building.

A bank wants to determine the factors affecting withdrawals from automatic teller machines (ATMs) located in residential neighborhoods. A sample of daily withdrawals from such machines has been collected together with information thought to affect total withdrawals. This information includes the median value of homes in the neighborhood, the median family income in the neighborhood, the average checking balance of customers living in the neighborhood, the distance to the next nearest ATM, and whether or not the withdrawals occurred on a weekend. Use these data to determine the factors affecting daily withdrawals from this class of ATMs.

What signs would you expect the coefficients for these independent variables to have on total daily withdrawals? Income, home value, and checking account balance should have positive coefficients but may have problems with multicollinearity. Distance to the next ATM should also have a positive sign since the further the distance, the more likely customers are to use the one in their neighborhood. Weekend days might be expected to have higher withdrawals because more recreational spending and more shopping occurs on weekends, and bank offices are closed so customers cannot cash checks there.

- Switch to the "ATM" worksheet in the workbook in multireg.xls. Notice that the data on whether or not withdrawals occurred on a weekend is not in the form of a dummy variable which can be used in regression analysis.

- Construct a dummy variable whose value is "1" for weekend withdrawals and "0" for withdrawals on other days.

- Estimate a regression in which total withdrawals is the y variable, and median home value, median income, average checking balance, distance to next ATM, and the weekend dummy are the x variables. Direct the output to a new worksheet with the name "Run 1." Have Excel produce residual plots.

The estimated coefficients from this regression are shown at the top of the next page. Notice that distance to next ATM has a negative sign, contrary to what is expected. The other coefficients have the correct sign, but median income and median home value are not significant. Possible multicollinearity?

	A	B	C	D	E
16		Coefficients	Standard Error	t Stat	P-value
17	Intercept	69.52701481	10.11810532	6.871544883	1.76399E-08
18	Median Home Value	0.004022096	0.100237489	0.040125669	0.968174458
19	Median Income	0.104543822	0.096207905	1.086644823	0.283111069
20	Average Checking Balance	0.048159307	0.006801364	7.080830427	8.70402E-09
21	Distance to Next ATM	-12.0761525	1.400071802	-8.625380871	5.19594E-11
22	Weekend Dummy	35.16332746	4.631482775	7.592239715	1.56426E-09

- Examine the residual plots. You will note that Excel stacks them on top of each other. They will have to be separated. This may be most easily done by first zooming to 50%. Once the plots are separated, make each a bit taller. Do any show sign of nonlinearities or heteroscedasticity? Pay particular attention to the plot of residuals on distance. This clearly shows evidence of a nonlinearity. None of the plots show evidence of heteroscedasticity.

- Return to the ATM worksheet. Create a new variable which equals distance squared. Run a new regression with all the independent variables previously used plus distance squared. Put the output on a new worksheet titled "Run 2." The estimated coefficients are shown below.

	A	B	C	D	E
16		Coefficients	Standard Error	t Stat	P-value
17	Intercept	34.9204343	10.28778334	3.394359419	0.00148877
18	Median Home Value	0.01899372	0.078872682	0.240814879	0.81084313
19	Median Income	0.17476765	0.076802314	2.275551884	0.02791444
20	Average Checking Balance	0.04681257	0.005354302	8.742983604	4.3171E-11
21	Distance to Next ATM	7.36283735	3.825243965	1.92480203	0.06088635
22	Distance Sq	-2.4924904	0.469723674	-5.30629088	3.6917E-06
23	Weekend Dummy	32.3992403	3.679050953	8.806412492	3.5279E-11

Notice that the coefficient on distance is positive while that on distance squared is negative. If the next closest ATM is very close and is moved away, initially withdrawals from this ATM will go up. If the nearest ATM is very far away, withdrawals go down. This result seems surprising. Perhaps a very distant ATM means that the residents of the neighborhood are less likely to be ATM users at all. The coefficient of distance squared is highly significant; the coefficient of distance has a p value of .06. It would thus be judged significant at the .10 level of significance but not at a level of significance of .05 or below. The theoretical basis for keeping it in the model is strong, however.

The signs of the coefficients on income, home value, and checking account balance are still positive. The coefficient on income, however, has become significant. The reasons for this are not clear.

- Examine the residual plots. You should see no evidence of heteroscedasticity or additional nonlinearities.

- Return to the ATM worksheet. Move the column of data for median income from column C to a location to the right of the other independent variables. This will allow you to estimate a regression without this variable and be able to replace it in a future regression. Estimate a new regression with all variables used in the previous model except median income. Have the output placed on a new worksheet titled "Run 3." There should be five independent variables (including the intercept). The estimated coefficients are shown below.

A	B	C	D	E
16	Coefficients	Standard Error	t Stat	P-value
17 Intercept	36.7402938	10.73258284	3.4232481	0.001348864
18 Median Home Value	0.01380361	0.082498035	0.16732053	0.8678845
19 Average Checking Balance	0.05307057	0.004807246	11.0397042	2.89806E-14
20 Distance to Next ATM	7.05192016	4.000189594	1.76289648	0.084862578
21 Distance Sq	-2.30830796	0.484167834	-4.7675781	2.06921E-05
22 Weekend Dummy	34.8764492	3.677374393	9.48406266	3.33514E-12

The primary reason for dropping median income was to see if there were multicollinearity with median home value. If there were multicollinearity, the significance of the estimated coefficient for median home value should be higher. Is it? The p value for that coefficient on this regression is about .87. This suggests that the low level of significance for median home value *is* not the result of multicollinearity with median income. Instead, median home value seems not to be a factor determining ATM withdrawals.

- Return to the ATM worksheet. Replace the median income variable and remove the median home value variable. Estimate a new regression with the same set of independent variables as the previous regression except use median income and don't use median home value. Place the output on a worksheet titled "Run 4." The coefficients and significance statistics for this analysis are shown below.

A	B	C	D	E
16	Coefficients	Standard Error	t Stat	P-value
17 Intercept	36.2108506	8.687539719	4.16813641	0.00014152
18 Median Income	0.17423281	0.075943952	2.294228982	0.0266079
19 Average Checking Balance	0.04775548	0.003612767	13.21853201	6.3411E-17
20 Distance to Next ATM	7.3671604	3.784032896	1.946907069	0.05794687
21 Distance Sq	-2.488444	0.464370838	-5.35874299	2.9249E-06
22 Weekend Dummy	32.1871907	3.533675725	9.108699616	1.0963E-11

An examination of the residual plots reveals no evidence of nonlinearities or of heteroscedasticity. No irrelevant variables are in the set of independent variables. This, then, is the final model.

▼ Exercises

1. Refer to the problem on page 384. Is there evidence (at the 0.05 level of significance) that homes in Armsley Hills are assessed at a significantly higher rate than homes in Blawndale which sell for the same price? Use the "Assessment (2)" worksheet which is a copy of the one used earlier. Verify that the coefficients in your analysis agree with those in the table on page 386 Print your regression with the title "Assessment - Model 2" and your name at the top of the page.

2. In the problem on page 392, we found evidence both of nonlinearity and heteroscedasticity between per capital GNP and per capita energy consumption. Correct the model to account for the nonlinearity. Use the "Energy (2)" worksheet. Does this correction eliminate the heteroscedasticity? Print out the basis for your conclusion and explain your reasoning.

3. An electric utility is interested in determining whether or not it can develop a model which would be useful in predicting the electricity consumption of a residential user during the month of November. A sample of houses was selected. For each house, total electricity usage (in KWH) was measured. In addition, the size of the house (in square feet), whether or not the house meets the utility's requirement for energy efficiency, the family income of the residents, and the type of heating fuel used was also collected. The data are available in the "Electricity" worksheet. Use these data to develop a model which can be used to predict electricity usage for November.

4. As part of the staff of an electronics industry consortium, you have been asked to investigate the issues surrounding the manufacturing costs of integrated circuits. You have chosen a commonly used memory circuit which is currently manufactured at a large number of "foundaries," as chip manufacturing plants like to style themselves. One issue of concern is whether foundries in the Pacific Rim countries have a cost advantage over those in this country.

   Use the data in the "IC's" worksheet to investigate this issue. These data include the following:

   a) The average manufacturing cost of a lot of 1,000 chips.

   b) The foundry's daily output in millions of chips.

   c) The location of the foundry (PAC=Pacific Rim, SA=South America).

d) The thickness of the silicon "wafer" used by the foundry for manu-facturing the chip (millimeters).

e) Whether or not the firm is vertically integrated; that is, does the firm also make products which use the chip? For example, a firm which manufactured computers as well as manufacturing the memory chip would be vertically integrated.

f) The amount of silicon used per chip (micrograms).

Appendix A

Setting Up the Analysis Tools

Excel regards the Analysis Tools as *add-ins* and does not make them accessible until you take certain steps. If "Analysis Tools…" is not one of the choices on the "Tools" menu on the Menu Bar, there are two possible explanations:

1. The Analysis Tools have been installed but have not been added to the Tools menu.

2. The Analysis Tools have not been installed. After installation, they will have to be added to the Tools menu in a separate step.

A standard installation of Excel will usually install the Analysis Tools onto the machine's hard disk, but will not add them to the Tools menu. It makes sense to start by assuming they have been installed and try adding them to the Tools menu. It will soon be apparent if they have not been installed.

Adding the Analysis Tools to the Tools Menu

Open the Tools menu. Click "Add-Ins" as shown in the picture to the left.

A dialog window will open (shown on the next page). This window shows all of Excel's installed add-ins. Those with x's (or checks) beside them will appear in menus. Two add-ins are needed to use all of Excel's statistical capabilities, "Analysis ToolPak" and "Analysis ToolPak - VBA." They will be the first two choices at the top of the list in Windows 3.1 and appear further down in Windows 95. If they are *not* on the list, the Analysis Tools have not been installed, and you will have do this by following the intructions in the next session. Click the "OK" button. The next time you open the "Tools" menu, "Data Analysis" will be a choice. It will remain on the menu in future sessions unless it is explicitly removed.

If "Analysis ToolPak" and "Analysis ToolPak - VBA" do *not* appear on the menu, they will have to be installed on the machine following the instruc-

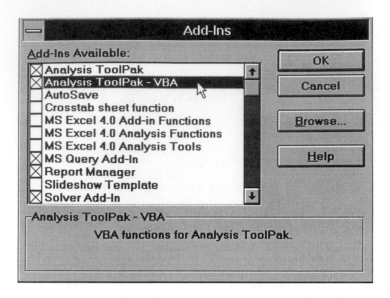

tions below. If your installation is on a network, this installation will probably have to be done my someone responsible for the network.

Installing the Analysis Tools

There are very slight differences between the processes of installing the Analysis Tools depending on whether Excel was originally installed as part of the Microsoft Office package or if it was installed as a stand-alone program. There are also slight differences between the procedures depending on whether the original installation was from diskette or CD ROM. The discussion below provides details specifically for installation in the case when the original installation was a CD ROM of Microsoft Office.

- Exit from Excel and all other Windows software.

- Have your original installation diskettes or CD ROM with you. If you originally installed from CD ROM, place it in your computer's CD reader.

Office Setup

- Locate and double click the Office (or Excel) Setup icon (shown to the left). If you are using Windows 3.1 or Windows for Workgroups. This will begin the setup routine. If you don't have this icon, use "Run" in the Program Manager's "File" menu (Windows 3.1) or on the "Start" menu (Windows 95) to run "setup.exe" on the first diskette or on the CD ROM.

- Click the Add/Remove button on the first dialog window (shown at the top of the next page).

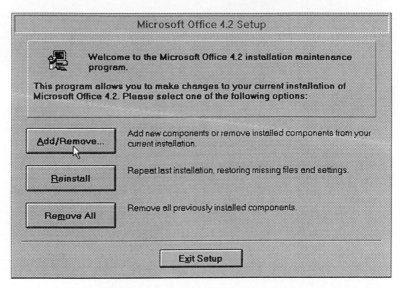

- Highlight "Microsoft Excel" on the list in the next window (shown below). Be sure an "x" appears to the left. Click the "Change Option" button to the right of the list.

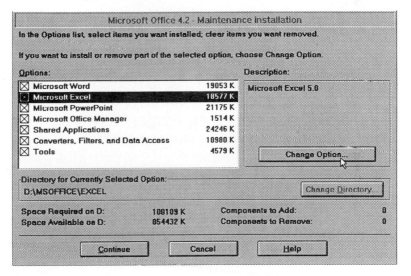

- Highlight "Add-ins" on the list in the next window. Be sure that there is also an "x" to the left. Click the "Change Option" button.

- On the final list, click "Analysis ToolPak" so an "x" appears to the left. Notice the phrase "Components to Add:" on the lower right portion of the window. Verify that this is followed by the number "1." Click the "OK" button.

- The previous dialog window will appear again. Check that it also has "1" after "Components to Add." Click "OK" and the second dialog

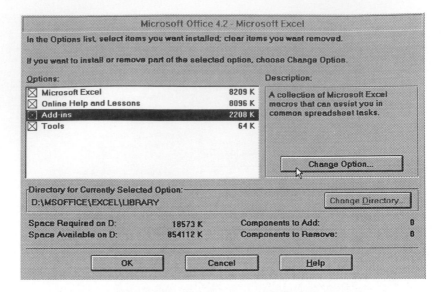

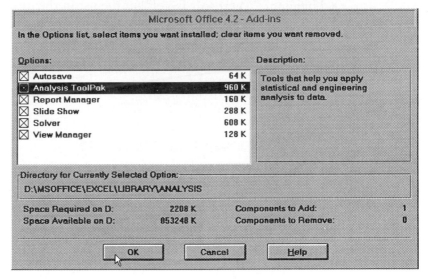

window will reappear. Be sure it also thinks you want to add a component and click "Continue."

If your installation was originally on a CD ROM, the computer will read the CD next and install the Analysis Tools. If your installation was originally on diskette, a sequence of windows will open indicating the diskette number you should insert into the diskette reader. Simply follow the directions.

This process will install the Analysis Tools on your computer's hard disk but will not add them to the menu. After Setup has completed, start Excel and follow the procedures given at the beginning of this appendix to add Analysis Tools to the Tools menu.

Statistical Functions and Analysis Tools

This appendix provides brief information about each of the statistical functions and Analysis Tools. The goal here is to provide information which is not duplicative of that in the on-line help. In some cases, errors or possible errors have been discovered in some of the functions and Tools, and these are noted. These errors may have been corrected in your versions of Excel. Examples of a few of the functions can be found in the workbook statfunc.xls.

Statistical Functions

Each of the functions in the "Statistical" category is discussed below. The argument names are the ones used in the Function Wizard. The discussion usually refers to the values of the arguments as cell or range addresses. Actual values, of course, can also be used as arguments. Note that some arguments are required; their names appear in the Function Wizard in bold type. Some arguments are optional. Some optional arguments appear in the Function Wizard dialog windows only if they might be needed. The AVERAGE function, for example, can accept multiple range addresses. Only two appear initially; if both are used a third will appear.

AVEDEV—Calculates the Mean Absolute Deviation, sometimes used as an alternative to the standard deviation of the values in the cells within the range addresses given in the arguments "number1," "number2," etc. The mean of the values is calculated, the difference between each argument and the mean (the deviation) is calculated, the absolute value of each deviation is determined, and the mean of these absolute values is returned by the function. See the example in the workbook in statfunc.xls.

AVERAGE—Calculates the arithmetic mean or average of the values in the cells within the range addresses given in the arguments "number1," "number2," etc.

BETADIST—The cumulative probability distribution for the beta distribution, also called the standard beta. The range of values for the random numbers are between 0 and 1. The function returns the probability of a random variable whose distribution is the beta distribution with parameters given by the arguments "alpha" and "beta" having a value less than the value given by the value of the "x" argument. The beta distribution can be generalized to a variety of shapes including U-shaped, bell-shaped, symmetric, and skewed. When both "alpha" and "beta" are set to 1, the distribution becomes a continuous uniform distribution. This distribution is not used often in business statistics.

BETAINV—Inverse of the cumulative beta distribution. The function returns the value of the beta distribution such that the probability of a random variable whose distribution is the beta distribution with parameters given by the arguments "alpha" and "beta" is given by the argument "probability." To generate random values from the beta distribution, enter "rand()" (without quotes) in the "probability" argument.

BINOMDIST—Provides either the probability or the cumulative probability associated with the value of a binomial random variable given by the argument "number_s" (number of successes). The "trials" argument is set equal to the number of trials, and the "probability_s" argument is set to the probability of success on each trial. The "cumulative" argument should be set equal either to "true" or "false" (no quotation marks). "True" causes BINOMDIST to return the cumulative probability of obtaining the exact or fewer number of successes given by "number_s." "False" causes BINOMDIST to return the probability of obtaining exactly the number of successes given by "number_s." The use of BINOMDIST and the binomial distribution is covered in Chapter 4.

CHIDIST—chi square distribution. The function returns the probability that a χ^2 random variable will have a value greater than the value given by the "x" argument. The degrees of freedom of the χ^2 distribution is given by the "degrees_freedom" argument. Examples of the use of this function are given in Chapter 11.

CHIINV—The inverse chi square distribution. The function returns the value of a χ^2 random variable such that the probability of another random value exceeding the returned value is given by the "probability" argument. The degrees of freedom is given by the "degrees_freedom" argument. Examples of the use of this function are given in Chapter 11. To generate random numbers from the chi square distribution, use "rand()" (without quotes) for the "probability" argument.

CHITEST—Implements the chi square test for independence which also is used to test for differences in the proportion of successes between different populations. The function determines the p value for the Null Hypothesis that all populations have the same proportions. The "actual_range" argument is the cell range address of a contingency table of values. The "expected_range" argument is the cell range address of a contingency table of expected values assuming the proportions are the same for all populations. This last contingency table must usually be calculated. See the statfunc.xls workbook for an example.

CONFIDENCE—Returns half the sampling error (half the width of the confidence interval) for a population mean. The arguments are "alpha" (one minus the confidence level), "standard_dev" (the standard deviation of the population), and "size" (the sample size). CONFIDENCE uses the normal distribution rather than the t distribution in calculating the sampling error because the standard error is assumed to be the *population* standard error. This limits the usefulness of this function to the rare case when the population standard deviation is known. If the sample standard deviation is used and the sample is large, CONFIDENCE will return a value which is approximately correct.

CORREL—Calculates the correlation coefficient (also called the Pearson product moment correlation coefficient) for two arrays of data. The range addresses of the arrays are provided in the two arguments "array1" and "array2." These arrays need to have the same number of cells and the same number of cells which display numeric values. This function is identical to the PEARSON function.

COUNT—Counts the number of cells in one or more ranges which display numeric values (including dates and text which can be converted into numbers). Cells which are blank or which display nonnumeric text or error values are not counted. Range or cell addresses are provided in the "value1" and optional "value2"… arguments.

COUNTA—Counts the number of cells in one or more ranges which are not empty, including cells which appear empty (e.g. contain blanks) but are not empty. Range or cell addresses are provided in the "value1" and optional "value2"… arguments.

COVAR—Calculates the *population* covariance of two arrays of data. This can be converted to a *sample* covariance by multiplying by $\frac{n}{n+1}$. The range addresses of the two arrays are given in the "array1" and "array2" arguments, which must have the same number of cells and the same number of cells displaying numeric values.

CRITBINOM—This function is related to the cumulative binomial distribution which provides the probability of a given number of successes (or fewer) for a given number of trials and a given probability of success on each trial. CRITBINOM returns the number of successes given the cumulative binomial probability ("alpha"), the number of trials ("trials"), and the probability of success on a single trial ("probability_s"). If the value given for "alpha" is not exactly equal to a binomial cumulative probability, the smallest number of success for which the cumulative binomial probability exceeds "alpha" is returned.

DEVSQ—Calculates the sum of squared deviations from the mean for the values in one or more ranges. This is most useful as an input to other calculations. The sample standard deviation, for example, is the sum of squared deviations divided by $n - 1$. The sum of squared deviations of the y variable in a regression is also called the total sum of squares or SST. The range addresses are provided in the "number1" and optional "number2"… arguments.

EXPONDIST—The exponential distribution. EXPONDIST determines the probability for the cumulative distribution function if "cumulative" is true or the value of the probability density function (which is *not* a probability) if "cumulative" is false. This continuous distribution is related to the discrete Poisson distribution. The Poisson distribution can be thought of as modeling the number of occurrences during a fixed time period. The exponential distribution can be thought of as modeling the period of time between occurrences. The "lambda" argument is the reciprocal of the mean time between occurrences ($\frac{1}{\mu}$). The argument "x" is the value of the time for which a cumulative probability is desired. Suppose the average time required to complete registration at a public university is 3 hours. The probability that registration could be completed in 2.5 hours or less could be determined by EXPONDIST with "x" equal to 2.5, "lambda" equal to $\frac{1}{3}$, and "cumulative" equal to "true."

FDIST—Returns the probability that a random variable drawn from the *F* distribution will have a value *greater* than the value given by the "x" argument. The *F* distribution has two degrees of freedom. The numerator degrees of freedom is given in the argument "degrees_freedom1" and the denominator degrees of freedom is given in "degrees_freedom2."

FINV—The inverse F distribution returns the value of a random variable drawn from the F distribution such that the probability of a *greater* value equals the "probability" argument. The two degrees of freedom are given as in the FDIST function. To generate a random number from the F distribution, enter "rand()" (without quotes) for the "probability" argument.

FISHER—Calculates Fisher's z transformation. This is very seldom encountered in business statistics. It is primarily used in hypotheses tests on the correlation coefficient between two sets of data when the Null Hypothesis is that the coefficient has a value other than 0. Suppose the correlation coefficient between two sets of data is r and we wish to test the Null Hypothesis that the correlation coefficient equals ρ_0.

The test statistic would be: $z = \dfrac{\phi(r) - \phi(\rho_0)}{1/\sqrt{n-3}}$ where $\phi(r)$ and $\phi(\rho_0)$ are the Fisher transformation of the calculated and hypothesized correlation coefficients.

FISHERINV—Calculates the inverse of the Fisher transformation.

FORECAST—This function returns a predicted y value for a single x value whose address is given in the "x" argument. The prediction is based on a simple regression calculated on a set of y values whose range address is given in the "known_y's" argument and a set of x values whose range address is given in the "known_x's" argument. This function is similar to TREND except that TREND can return an array of multiple predicted y values.

FREQUENCY—Provides a count of the number of values in a range of cells which fall within several specified numeric ranges. The output of this function is a vertical array of values. The address of the cell range containing the values to be counted is given in the "data_array" argument. The numeric ranges are defined by a set of "bin" values, each of which is an upper bound of a numeric range (which includes the upper bound if positive but excludes it if negative). The number of values in the output array equals the number of bins. Like all functions which output arrays in Excel, entering the function is tricky. First, select the range of cells into which the output array is to be written (as many cells as "bin" values). Click the Function Wizard button, enter the argument values, and click the "Finish " button. At this point, only a single value will be displayed in the output range. Click the mouse pointer in the formula bar as if you were going to edit the formula. Hold down the Shift and Ctrl keys and, while holding them down, press the Enter key. Values will appear in all of the cells of the output array. An example of the use of the FREQUENCY function is given in the workbook in the file statfunc.xls.

FTEST—This Tool calculates and returns the *p* value from an *F* test on the Null Hypothesis that two arrays have the same variance. The arguments of the function, "array1" and "array2," are the addresses of the two arrays of values whose variances are tested.

GAMMADIST—Returns a cumulative probability if "cumulative" is equal to "true" or the value of the density (which is not a probability) if it is equal to "false." The value of the variable drawn from the gamma distribution to be evaluated is given by the "x" argument. The distribution has two parameters given by the "alpha" and "beta" arguments. The gamma distribution is right-skewed. Small values for alpha result in greater skew. Both the exponential and chi square distributions are special cases of the gamma distribution. The sample variance, s^2, follows the gamma distribution in which $\alpha = \dfrac{n-1}{2}$ and $\beta = \dfrac{2\sigma^2}{n-1}$. The distribution can thus be used for hypothesis tests and confidence intervals on population variances and standard deviations. It has become traditional, however, to calculate the chi square statistic and use the chi square distribution for these problems, doubtless because of the difficulty of constructing a table for the gamma distribution.

GAMMAINV—Inverse of the cumulative gamma distribution. GAMMAINV returns the value of a random variable drawn from the gamma distribution whose cumulative probability is given by the "probability" argument. The parameters of the gamma distribution are given by the "alpha" and "beta" arguments. To generate a random number from the gamma distribution, enter "rand()" without quotes in the "probability" argument field.

GAMMALN—Returns the natural logarithm of the gamma function (*not* the gamma distribution).

GEOMEAN—Returns the geometric mean, a descriptive measure of location favored in certain circumstances over the arithmetic mean when the data consist of ratios, percentages, rates of change, or rates of return.

GROWTH—Calculates predicted values for an exponential growth model. An exponential growth model has the form $\hat{y} = b_0 b_1^{x_1} \ldots b_n^{x_n}$, and is used when data are increasing at an increasing rate, such as biological population growth. The GROWTH function returns an array of any length. Simple versions of this model are sometimes used to predict growth against time; in this case there would only be a single *x* variable measuring time. To see the display of an output array containing more than one value, first select a region of cells for the output array. Click the Function Wizard button, select the GROWTH function, and enter the values in the argument fields. Click the "Finish" button. Only a single value will be displayed in the selected region. Click the mouse pointer in the formula bar as if you were going to edit the formula. Press and hold both the Shift and Ctrl keys and, while holding those keys, press and release the Enter key. All of the cells in the selected region will now display values. The TREND function performs a similar role for the linear model.

HARMEAN—A measure of central tendency rarely used with business data.

HYPERGEOMDIST—Returns the hypergeometric probability of drawing the number of successes given by the argument "sample_s" from a sample of size "number_sample" if the sample is drawn without replacement from a population whose size is given by the argument "number_population" in which there are "population_s" total successes. For example, if you wanted to determine the probability of selecting three aces in five cards from a poker deck, the value of "sample_s" would be 3, the value of "number_sample" would be 5, the value of "population_s" would be 4, and the value of "number_population" would be 52. Note that the probability returned by this function is *not* cumulative, which reduces its usefulness for problems involving large ranges of number of successes.

INTERCEPT—Calculates a simple regression on a set of *y* and *x* values and returns the value of the intercept (b_0). Note that this (and more) is also available in the LINEST function which is capable of multiple regression.

KURT—Returns the measure of kurtosis of a set of data. Kurtosis is a descriptive statistic which adds information about a set of numbers not captured by mean, variance, or skewness. Data with relatively high kurtosis tend to be more "peaked" than data with low kurtosis. The measure is infrequently used but does have application in the analysis of investment returns.

LARGE—Returns the largest ("k" equals 1), second largest ("k" equals 2), to the smallest ("k" equals *n*) value in a range of cells containing *n* numbers.

LINEST—Performs a multiple (or simple) regression analysis on a set of data and returns an array containing the estimated coefficients and (optionally) a number of statistics including r^2, standard errors, SSR, and SSE. An example of the use of this function can be found in the workbook in statfunc.xls. The output of the function is an array. To use the function select a region of cells in which the number of columns equals the number of independent variables plus one (for the intercept) and the number of rows is 5. If only coefficients are desired set the "const" argument to zero and select only one row in the output range. After the region is selected, click the Function Wizard button, select LINEST, and enter the appropriate values in the argument fields. Click the "Finish" button. Only one value will appear in the selected region. With the region still selected, click the mouse pointer in the formula bar as if you were going to edit the formula. Press and hold the Shift and Ctrl keys. While holding those keys, press and release the Enter key. All the cells in the selected region will now display values. If you have more than a single independent variable, some of the cells will display the #N/A error code. This is normal.

LOGEST—Returns estimated coefficients and statistics for an exponential growth model. The output of this function is an array identical to that produced by LINEST except that instead of estimating a linear model it estimates an exponential growth model of the form $\hat{y} = b_0 b_1^{x_1} \ldots b_n^{x_n}$. This is the same model estimated by the GROWTH function. GROWTH returns predicted values while LOGEST returns estimated coefficients and statistics. The statistics (standard errors, r^2, etc., the same as LINEST) must be interpreted with caution. The exponential growth model is estimated by using linear regression in which the dependent variable is the natural log of the y variable in the exponential growth model. This linear regression results in estimated coefficients. The b's in the exponential growth model are the antilogs (Excel's EXP function) of the linear regression's estimated coefficients. The statistics reported by LOGEST come from the linear regression. Thus we cannot, for example, calculate a t statistic on an estimated coefficient by dividing the estimated coefficients reported by LOGEST by its standard error reported by LOGEST. That standard error was calculated from the linear regression's coefficient, the log of the value reported by LOGEST.

LOGINV—The inverse of the lognormal distribution. See LOGNORMDIST for more on this distribution. To generate a random number drawn from the lognormal distribution, enter "rand()" (without quotes) in the argument field for "probability."

LOGNORMDIST—Returns the probability that a lognormally distributed variable will have a value less than the "x" argument. If x is a variable which is lognormally distributed, then ln(*x*) will be normally distributed. The error terms of exponential growth models are typically assumed to be lognormal. Lognormal variables are nonnegative and right-skewed. The extent of skew depends on the size of the variance compared to the mean. A large variance and small mean causes a greater skew. The lognormal distribution is sometimes used to model variables which are known to be skewed and nonnegative such as family income.

MAX—Returns the largest number in one or more cell ranges.

MEDIAN—Returns the median value of a set of numbers in one or more cell ranges.

MIN—Returns the smallest value in one or more cell ranges.

MODE—Returns the modal (most frequently occurring) value in one or more ranges. If there is no modal value (e.g., each value occurs once), the function displays the #N/A error code.

NEGBINOMDIST—Returns the probability that a random variable from the negative binomial distribution will equal the "number_f" argument. The probability is not cumulative. This distribution is useful for problems in which you want to know the probability of obtaining "number_f" failures before you obtain "number_s" successes given that the probability of success in each trial is "probability_s" argument.

NORMDIST—Returns the cumulative probability (or density) of a random variable drawn from the normal distribution with mean given by the "mean" argument and standard deviation given by the "standard_dev" argument having a value less than the "x" argument. If the "cumulative" argument is "true," the function returns the cumulative probability. If it is "false," density—not a probability—is returned.

NORMINV—Returns the value of a normally distributed random variable for which the probability of a smaller random variable equals the value of the "probability" argument. The values of the "mean" and "standard_dev" arguments set the parameters of the normal distribution. To generate a normally distributed random variable, enter "rand()" (without quotes) in the "probability" argument field.

NORMSDIST—Returns the probability of a standard normal (mean equal to zero, standard deviation equal to one) having a value less than the "z" argument.

NORMSINV—Returns the value of a standard normal random variable such that the probability of another standard normal random variable having a smaller value equals the "probability" argument. To generate a standard normal random variable, enter "rand()" (no quotes) in the "probability" argument field.

PEARSON—This function is identical to the CORREL function.

PERCENTILE—Determines a given percentile value in a set of numbers whose range address is given in the "array" argument. Two aspects of this function are unusual. The percentile value is given in the "k" argument and must be a number between 0 and 1 inclusive rather than an integer between 1 and 99 which is more common. Excel's method for determining the percentile value differs from that most widely used in business statistics. Let p represent a percentile value expressed as an integer between 1 and 99 and assume the data have been ordered from smallest to largest. The value of the pth percentile is usually defined as the $\dfrac{p(n+1)}{100}$ th value. Excel instead selects the $\dfrac{pn+(100-p)}{100}$ th value. These two methods give the same value for the 50th percentile, but differ for all other percentiles. If the formula does not yield an integer, Excel interpolates.

PERCENTRANK—The inverse of the PERCENTILE function. When given a range address in the "array" argument and a value in the "x" argument, PERCENTRANK returns the percentile score of that value in the array. See the discussion under PERCENTILE for the method Excel used to determine percentiles.

PERMUT—Calculates the permutations of "number_chosen" objects drawn from "number" objects. Permutations differ from combinations in that order matters for permutations. Excel also has a combinations function, COMBIN, with the same arguments as PERMUT, in the Math & Trig functions.

POISSON—Returns the probability or cumulative probability of drawing the value "x" from the discrete Poisson distribution in which the mean is given by the argument "mean." If the "cumulative" argument is "true," POISSON will return the probability of drawing a value less than or equal to "x." If "cumulative" is "false," the probability of drawing a value exactly equal to "x" is returned.

PROB—Returns the probability of a discrete random variable equaling the value given by the "lower_limit" argument if the "upper_limit" argument is omitted or falling between the values of the two arguments (inclusive) if both are provided. A discrete probability distribution table must be provided the PROB function with the values of the random variable in a range whose address is provided in the "x_range" argument and the corresponding probabilities in a range whose address is given in the "prob_range" argument.

QUARTILE—Returns either the minimum, maximum, or one of the three quartile values of a set of data. The range address of the data is provided in the "array" argument and the value to be returned is provided by the "quart" argument. If "quart" is set to 0 or 4, QUARTILE returns the minimum or maximum values in the data, respectively. If "quart" is set to 1, 2, or 3, QUARTILE returns the corresponding quartile value. As in the case of PERCENTILE, Excel uses a nonstandard definition for quartiles. Assume the data are sorted from the smallest to largest value. The first quartile is usually defined as the $\frac{n+1}{4}$th value. Excel instead uses the $\frac{n+3}{4}$th value. Similarly, the third quartile is usually defined as the $\frac{3(n+1)}{4}$th value. Excel uses the $\frac{3n+1}{4}$th value. Excel's definition of the second quartile (the median) is the same as that usually used.

RANK—Returns the position an individual number would have in a list of values if the list were ordered. The individual number's cell address or value is given in the "number" argument and the address of the range of cells is given in the "ref" argument. If the "order" argument is "true" the position is given as if the list were ordered from smallest to largest. If "order" is "false" or omitted, the position is given as if the list were ordered from largest to smallest. The #N/A error code is displayed if the number is not in the list.

RSQ—Returns the r^2 value of a simple regression of the set of values whose range address is given in the "known_y's" argument against the set of values whose range address is given in the "known_x's" argument. This information (along with other regression derived information) is also provided by the LINEST function which is also capable of multiple regression.

SKEW—Calculates and returns the coefficient of skewness of a set of numbers in one or more cell ranges.

SLOPE—Returns the slope (b_1) value from a simple regression of the set of values whose range address is given in the "known_y's" argument against the set of values whose range address is given in the "known_x's" argument. This information (along with other regression derived information) is also provided by the LINEST function which is also capable of multiple regression.

SMALL—Returns the smallest ("k" equals 1), second smallest ("k" equals 2), to the largest ("k" equals *n*) value in a range of cells containing *n* numbers.

STANDARDIZE—Takes the value given by the "x" argument, subtracts the value given by the "mean" argument, divides the difference by the value given by the "standard_dev" argument and returns the result.

STDEV—Returns the *sample* standard deviation (divides by $n - 1$) of the values in one or more cell ranges.

STDEVP—Returns the *population* standard deviation (divides by N) of the values in one or more cell ranges.

STEYX—Returns the standard error of the regression for a simple regression of the set of values whose range address is given in the "known_y's" argument regressed against the set of values whose range address is given in the "known_x's" argument. This information (along with other regression derived information) is also provided by the LINEST function which is also capable of multiple regression.

TDIST—If the "tails" argument is 1, returns the probability that a random variable drawn from the *t* distribution with degrees of freedom given by the "degrees_freedom" argument will exceed the value of the "x" argument. If the "tails" argument is 2, the probability is doubled. An unfortunate characteristic of TDIST is that a negative value for the "x" argument results in an error code. For this reason, it is wise to embed the absolute value function, ABS, in the "x" argument field whenever the *t* value to be evaluate is calculated on a worksheet. The TDIST and TINV functions were discussed and used starting on page 180.

TINV—The inverse of the *t* distribution. TINV interprets the value of the "probability" argument as the equally divided area of both tails. The positive *t* value (upper tail boundary) drawn from a distribution with degrees of freedom equal to the "degrees_freedom" argument is returned. If the *t* value corresponding to a one-tail probability is desired, the "probability" argument of TINV should be twice the one-tail probability. The TDIST and TINV functions were discussed and used starting on page 180.

TREND—Estimates a simple or multiple regression of the dependent variables whose range address is given by the "known_y's" argument on the independent variables whose range address is given by the "known_x's" argument. The regression is then used to provide estimated *y* values for another set of *x* values whose range addresses are given by the "new_x's" argument. The output of TREND is an array consisting of the predicted values. The number of values in this array equals the number of observations for which there are new *x* values. To see the display of an output array containing more than one value, first select a region of cells for the output array. Click the Function Wizard button, select the TREND function, and enter the values in the argument fields. Click the "Finish" button. Only a single value will be displayed in the selected region. Click the mouse pointer in the formula bar as if you were going to edit the formula. Press and hold both the Shift and Ctrl keys and, while holding those keys, press and release the Enter key. All of the cells in the selected region will now display values. The GROWTH function performs a similar role for the exponential growth model.

TRIMMEAN—Estimates the mean of a set of data after eliminating a proportion of the extreme (highest and lowest) values set by the "percent" argument. Despite its name, the value used in the "percent" argument should be a proportion (between 0 and 1).

TTEST—Calculates a *t* test on the Null Hypothesis that two populations have the same mean. The range address of the sample from the first population is given in the "array1" argument and that from the second population is given in the "array2" argument. The "tails" argument can have the value 1 or 2 and determines whether the test will be one tail or two tail. The "type" argument determines which test will be used. If "type" equals 1, the samples are assumed to be paired samples. If "type" equals 2, the two samples are assumed to have been drawn from populations with equal variance. If "type" equals 3, the two samples are assumed to have been drawn from populations with unequal variance. The function returns the *p* value from this test.

VAR—Estimates the variance of a *sample* of numbers in one or more ranges.

VARP—Estimates the variance of a *population* of numbers in one or more ranges.

WEIBULL—Returns the probability of a random variable drawn from the Weibull distribution with parameters given by the "alpha" and "beta" arguments having a value less than that given by the "x" argument (if the "cumulative" argument is "true"). The Weibull distribution is not often used in business statistics. It is typically used for the distribution of time intervals such as time before failure of a mechanical component.

ZTEST—The purpose of this function is not obvious. If the value of the "x" argument is interpreted as a hypothesized population mean (Null Hypothesis H_0: $\mu \leq x$), and the numbers whose range address is given in the "array" argument are interpreted as a sample drawn from that population, the function returns the p value for the test. An optional argument, "sigma" permits you to give the function the population standard deviation. Only if that argument is given would it be appropriate to use the normal distribution to calculate the p value, as this function does. Without the population standard deviation, the t distribution, not the z distribution, is appropriate. The on-line help description of ZTEST as a two-tail p value which can be used to "assess the likelihood that a particular observation is drawn from a particular population" is inaccurate.

▼ Data Analysis Tools

The Data Analysis Tools are accessed through the Tools menu on the Menu Bar. Appendix A provides instructions for adding "Data Analysis" to the Tools menu if it is not present.

The Data Analysis Tools often duplicate procedures provided by the statistical functions. There are important differences between the Tools and the functions, however. The output of a single Tool generally provides more information than that of a single function. The output of most Tools is formatted and labeled. The functions provide no formatting. The values written by most of the Tools are numbers, not functions. An important consequence of this is that a change in the input data analyzed by a Tool will not change the already written output of a Tool. The Tool would have to be explicitly run on the new data. The displayed value of a cell containing a function, by contrast, automatically reflects any changes in its arguments. Functions can be used directly in Excel formulas; Tools cannot.

The use of most of the Analysis Tools is covered in one or more chapters of this book. The discussion below will primarily cover those Tools *not* otherwise discussed in this book. The objective again is to provide useful information not available through Excel's on-line help.

Anova: Single-Factor—The use of this Tool is covered in Chapter 13.

Anova: Two-Factor with Replication—The use of this Tool is covered in Chapter 13.

Anova: Two-Factor Without Replication—The use of this Tool is covered in Chapter 13.

data have labels, the rows and columns of the output will also be labeled. The entries give the correlation coefficient for the pair of variables in whose row and column the entry lies.

Covariance—Calculates the covariance between all pairs of any number of variables. The difference between the Covariance Tool and the COVAR function is like the difference between the Correlation Tool and the CORREL function. Like the COVAR function, the Covariance Tool provides *population* covariances rather than *sample* covariances.

Descriptive Statistics—The use of this Tool is covered in Chapter 2 starting on page 60. Each of the outputs produced by this Tool can be produced by a single function except the range and the "confidence." The latter purports to be half the width of a confidence interval on the population mean (the standard term for this is *sampling error*). The calculation is wrong, however, because the normal distribution is used instead of the t distribution, an apparent bug. This is similar to the situation with the CONFIDENCE function, except that in the case of the function the standard deviation is an argument. It is at least conceivable that the standard deviation provided there could be a population standard deviation. The descriptive statistics Tool uses the calculated standard deviation. Either the data are a sample, in which case the t distribution should be used, or they are a population, in which case the concept of a confidence interval is meaningless. Note that unless the "Summary Statistics" option is selected in the dialog window, the "confidence" value is the only number the Tool outputs.

Exponential Smoothing—Excel uses exponential smoothing as a form of forecasting. The formula used is $P_{t+1} = \omega A_t + (1-\omega)P_t$, where P_{t+1} is the predicted value in time $t+1$ and A_t and P_t are the actual and predicted values for time t, respectively. The predicted value for time 2 is set to the actual value for time 1. The "damping factor," ω, must be between 0 and 1. If "Standard Errors" are requested, Excel provides for each observation (beginning with number 4) the square root of the mean square error of the three previous observations. Unlike most Tools, the output of this Tool is formulas, not numbers. If the input values change, so will the output of the Tool.

F-Test Two-Sample for Variances—The use of this Tool is discussed in Chapter 12 starting on page 309. It has two bugs. First, the p value and critical F it computes are one tail when the proper test for the equality of two population variances is two tail. This can be corrected for the p value by simply doubling it. Note that the FTEST function returns the correct p value for the same data. To correct the critical F

in the Tools output, the value for alpha entered in the Tool's dialog window should be half the desired two-tail value. Even in this case, the critical *F* is calculated incorrectly if the variance of the data in the "Variable 1 Range" is less than the variance of the data in the "Variable 2 Range."

Fourier Analysis—Fourier analysis is a technique that represents a set of data as a sum of periodic (trigonometric) functions. Widely used for certain engineering problems, the technique is seldom used in business statistics, although it does have some application in sophisticated analysis of time series data.

Histogram—The use of this Tool is discussed in Chapter 2 starting on page 63.

Moving Average—This is a forecasting (or smoothing) technique in which the predicted value is the average of a specified (by the "Interval" field of the dialog window) number of previous values. Excel in fact includes the current period's value in that average. Thus the values provided by Excel must be interpreted as predictions for the *next* period rather than the current period. The standard error, if requested, calculates, for each value, the square root of the mean square error of previous predictions. The number of predictions used for that calculation is the same as the number of data values used in the calculation of the moving average. Unlike most Tools, the output of this Tool is formulas, not numbers. The output will thus automatically change if the input data change.

Random Number Generation—This Tool has been used extensively in this book to explore statistical concepts. Its use to generate discrete random numbers appears in Chapter 3 (page 83) and in Chapter 4 (page 96). It was used to generate uniform random numbers in Chapter 6 (page 174). Its use to generate normally distributed random variables appears in Chapter 7 (page 206), at many locations in Chapter 8, and in Chapter 13 (page 325). The Tool will also generate random numbers from other distributions as well as nonrandom sequences ("Patterned"). It is possible to generate random numbers from any of Excel's inverse probability functions by using RAND() as the "probability" argument. This approach, however, would result in cell values which changed every time the worksheet is recalculated, which may well be undesirable. The functions can be converted to numbers by, for example, selecting their cells, clicking the Copy button, selecting "Paste Special" from the Edit menu, and selecting "Values" to be pasted. The Random Number Generation Tool avoids this problem since its output is numbers.

Rank and Percentile—One or more variables are sorted from highest to lowest, and the rank and percentile of each value are shown. Rank is the position of each value within the sorted order with the largest value assigned rank 1. Excel's method of determining the percentile of each value is based on the same nonstandard method of determining percentiles discussed in the description of the PERCENTILE function.

Regression—The use of this Tool is covered in Chapters 14 and 15. Variables for this Tool must be arrayed in columns (not rows). All independent variables must be in adjacent columns. The "Normal Probability Plots" option does not work correctly and should not be used.

Sampling—Draws a sample from a population. The sample can be random, in which case it is drawn with replacement, or periodic. A periodic sample simply chooses elements from the population which are a fixed number of positions (determined by "period") apart.

t-Test: Paired Two-Sample for Means—The use of this Tool is covered in Chapter 12.

t-Test: Two-Sample Assuming Equal Variances—The use of this Tool is covered in Chapter 12.

t-Test: Two-Sample Assuming Unequal Variances—The use of this Tool is covered in Chapter 12.

z-Test: Two Sample for Means—This performs a z test on the equality of two population means when the population variances are known, but the population means are unknown. This is an unlikely situation to occur in real data, but is often discussed for pedagogic reasons by statistics texts.

Appendix C

Answers to Selected Exercises

Chapter 2

2. In ascending order of per capita GDP: Turkey, Greece, Portugal, Ireland, Spain,..., Luxembourg, Switzerland, United States

Range	Frequency	
$ 0-$ 4,000	0	
$ 4,001-$ 8,000	1	
$ 8,001-$12,000	2	
$12,001-$16,000	4	
$16,001-$20,000	13	
$20,001-$24,000	3	The data are left skewed.

Descriptive Statistics: mean $=16,014.75$, standard deviation $= 4,441.326$, etc. Left skew is indicated by fact that median (16,900) exceeds mean, and coefficient of skewness (-1.230130) is negative.

3. There is an abrupt change in the mean bolt length beginning at sample number 65 (while variance appears to remain constant). This sudden upward shift suggests an assignable cause such as equipment problems.

Chapter 3

2. As n increases, the proportion of stock providing each level of profit should become closer to the probability given in the distribution. For all portfolios, $E(x)=8.00$ and $VAR(x)=4,086$. As n increases, there should also be a tendency for the portfolio mean and variances to converge on these values although the same kind of deviation is possible here as in the table printed for problem 1.

Chapter 4

1. a) 0.5832, b) 0.023711, c) .00002656, d) $=0.4168$

2. a) 75, b) 7.9844, c) 0.0499, d) since the number of cars requiring repair must be an integer, $P(60 \leq x \leq 90) = 0.9481$

Chapter 5

1. $z = 1.2816$, $x = 75 + (1.2816)(10) = 87.8155$

2. $P(x < 16) = P(z < -2.2222) = 0.0131$

3. $(25.7264, 30.2736)$

4. $P(x > 55) = P(z > -1.4583) = 0.9276$

5. The use of the correction for continuity substantially improves the normal approximation for the binomial.

Chapter 6

1. $P(\bar{x} \leq 1.99) = P(t \leq -1.49071) = 0.0762$

2. $(1.9852, 2.0548)$

3. $P(\bar{x} \leq 50.2) = P(t \leq -2.75862) = 0.0055$

4. $P(\bar{x} \geq 2.05) = P(z \geq 1.581139) = 0.0569$

5. $z = -1.64485$, $\bar{x} = 1.9632$

Chapter 7

1. $(6.893, 8.149)$

2. $n=52$

3. Sample size is inversely proportional to the square of sampling error. As sampling error increases, required sample size decreases exponentially (that is, at a decreasing rate). Another way of looking at this is that as sampling error *decreases*, sample size must be increased at an *increasing* rate. It becomes very difficult to continue reducing the sampling error.

Chapter 8

1. $P(x = 0) = 0.7318$, $P(x = 1) = 0.2286$, $P(x = 2) = 0.0357$, $P(x \geq 3) = 0.0040$

2. $\bar{x} = 15.5927255$ results in $p = .0100000$. $z = -2.575830106$. p value less than .01 would result from problems asking for sample means less than 15.5927255 or greater than 16.4072745.

4. The greater the difference between actual and hypothesized means, the greater the power of the test.

5. Correct result would be to reject because a mean of 16.1 means that $\mu = 16$ is *not* true.

6. More. The power of the test would be low because the hypothesized and actual means are so close.

Chapter 9

1. $H_0: \mu = 1$, $H_A: \mu \neq 1$. Reject the Null. Yes, there is evidence the machine is not working properly.

2. $H_0: \mu \geq 50$, $H_A: \mu < 50$. Reject the Null. Yes, there is evidence that average stopping distance is less than 50 feet.

3. $H_0: \mu \geq 120$, $H_A: \mu < 120$. Fail to reject the Null. $\bar{x} = 122.1778$, which is consistent with the Null Hypothesis. No, there is not evidence that the average amount of time spent by all customers in line is less than 120 seconds.

Chapter 10

1. $H_0: \pi \leq 0.20$, $H_A: \pi > 0.20$. Approximate $p = .107963$. Precise $p = .123895$. Fail to reject the Null Hypothesis. No, there is not evidence that the ad campaign was successful.

2. If $\pi = 0.4$, $n = 4,098$. If $\pi = 0.5$, $n = 4,269$. If $\pi = 0.6$, $n = 4,098$. If $\pi = 0.7$, $n = 3,586$. By using $\pi = .5$, the largest sample size is chosen. This assures that the sample will be large enough achieve the desired sampling error regardless of the true value of π.

3. $H_0: \pi \geq .50$, $H_A: \pi < .50$. Approximate $p = .07865$. Precise $p = .089482$. No, there is not evidence that the claim is invalid.

4. $(.088287, .245047)$

5. $H_0: \pi \leq .005$, $H_A: \pi > .005$. Approximate $p = .170786$. Precise $p = .108319$. No, the firm should not stop the line and inspect its equipment (but it might worry about a p value so close to the significance level).

6. $H_0: \pi = .29$, $H_A: \pi \neq .29$. Approximate $p = 0.029801$. Precise $p = .033265$. Yes, there is evidence that the proportion has changed from the value found 20 years ago.

7. $H_0: \pi \leq .20$, $H_A: \pi > .20$. Approximate $p = .055806$. Precise $p = .049353$. Based on the precise p value, the answer is yes, there is evidence the ad campaign was successful.

Chapter 11

1. $H_0: \sigma \leq 1.1$, $H_A: \sigma > 1.1$. p value $= 1.64 \times 10^{-7}$. Reject the Null Hypothesis. Yes, there is evidence that the machine is not meeting specification with respect to variation.

2. $H_0: \sigma^2 \leq 25, H_A: \sigma^2 > 25$. $s^2 = 17.5263$, consistent with the Null Hypothesis. Fail to reject the Null Hypothesis. No, there is not evidence that the machine is about to break down.

3. $H_0: \sigma \geq 12, H_A: \sigma < 12$. Since $s = 15.26228$, the sample is consistent with the Null Hypothesis. Fail to reject the Null Hypothesis. No, the evidence does not support the new supplier's claim.

Chapter 12

1. Using independent samples, we would not have found evidence of a difference even though the difference in the sample means was the same as in the paired sample approach. The independent sample approach would require a greater difference in the sample means before we could conclude that there was a difference in the population means. Remember that failing to conclude that there is a difference does not mean that we conclude that there is not a difference. We are left unsure. The paired sample approach is more sensitive because it can lead us to a clear conclusion with a smaller difference in sample means.

2. $H_0: \mu_A = \mu_B, H_A: \mu_A \neq \mu_B$. Independent samples. For these data, the procedures assuming equal and unequal population variances yield the same two-tail p value, .3283. Fail to Reject the Null Hypothesis. No, there is not evidence of a difference in average productivity.

3. $H_0: \mu_{Std} \geq \mu_{Int}, H_A: \mu_{Std} < \mu_{Int}$. Paired samples approach. $\bar{x}_{Std} = 6.836$ $\bar{x}_{Int} = 6.76$. The sample data are consistent with the Null Hypothesis. No, there is not evidence that intensive maintenance increases mileage.

4. $H_0: \mu_{Prgm} \leq \mu_{Ctrl}, H_A: \mu_{Prgm} > \mu_{Ctrl}$ Independent samples approach. $\bar{x}_{Prgm} = 576.69$ $\bar{x}_{Ctrl} = 670.20$ The sample data are consistent with the Null Hypothesis. No, there is not evidence that program attendance would increase average sales.

Chapter 13

1. Using one factor analysis, the p value is .8276. This would lead to a failure to reject the Null Hypothesis and there was not evidence of a difference of keyboards on typing speeds. The two-factor approach is preferable because it is more sensitive and showed a difference where the one-factor approach could not.

2. The p values for each strategy are Sophisticated, .3729; Athletic, .0285; Popular, .8610. Package design is only clearly important with the Athletic strategy.

3. Use two-factor ANOVA without replication because it controls for other factors affecting house value. The p value for the Null Hypothesis that the population average of all appraisers is the same is .0285. Reject the Null. There is evidence of a difference in the average appraisals of different appraisers.

4. One-factor analysis. The p value for the Null Hypothesis that all stores have the same average is .9444. Fail to reject the Null Hypothesis. There is not evidence of a difference in the population average sales for the different types of music.

Chapter 14

2. If $x = 3.8$, $\hat{y} = 12.4286067$. If $x = 5.7$, $\hat{y} = 18.011921$. If $x = 6.3$, $\hat{y} = 19.775073$.

3. Regression with all states: $\hat{y} = -313.47 + 0.0940x$. By this equation, state revenue increases about 9.4¢ for each dollar increase in median household income. One outlier, Alaska, probably because of the effect of oil revenue. Regression with Alaska omitted: $\hat{y} = 0.1624 + 0.0409x$. This regression suggests an effect half as great: each dollar increase in median income increases state revenue about 4.1¢. Both regressions are significant.

4. Regression equation: $\hat{y} = 617.43 - 0.001793x$. Only 0.1009% of the variation in state violent crime rates is explained by variation in median household income. The relationship is not significant ($p = .82$).

5. Regression equation: $\hat{y} = 13.25 - 0.0001556x$. Higher state household incomes appear to lead to lower death rates. About 38% of the variation in death rates can be explained by variations in household income. The relationship is highly significant.

Chapter 15

1. The Null Hypothesis in this case would be $\mu_A \leq \mu_B$ and the Alternate Hypothesis would be $\mu_A > \mu_B$. With Armsley Hills as the omitted dummy variable, the p value for the Blawndale dummy is .060213144. This is, however, a *two-tail* p value. Since the test requires a *one-tail* test, the appropriate p value is half the reported value or .0301. Since this is less than the significance level the Null Hypothesis would be rejected. Yes, there is evidence that homes in Armsley Hills are assessed at a higher rate than homes in Blawndale.

2. With per capita GNP squared added as an independent variable, the regression equation is $\hat{y} = 89.6060 + 0.5024 \times x_{GNP} - 0.000009952 \times x_{GNP}^2$.

An examination of residuals plotted against GNP still shows that for low values of per capita GNP the vertical spread is small, while for larger values (between 20,000 and 30,000) the vertical spread is large. There is thus still evidence of heteroscedasticity.

3. Since the objective here is *prediction*, the value of the adjusted R^2 is key. Since adjusted R^2 is sensitive to the number of independent variables, it is important to eliminate independent variables which do not add sufficient explanatory power. Two dummy variables are required to account for all fuel types, but the real importance lies in whether or not electricity is used as a fuel, and this can be done in a single dummy equalling "1" if electricity is used for heat and "0" otherwise (or vice versa, of course). The resulting equation is:

$$\hat{y} = 136.23 - 42.69 d_{\text{Enrgy Eff}} + 62.12 d_{\text{Elec Heat}} + 0.083 x_{\text{House Size}}$$
$$+ 0.0023 x_{\text{Fam Income}}$$

Dummy variables are represented by d, and continuous independent variables by x. The adjusted R^2 for this is 0.5954.

4. The relationship between output and average cost is clearly nonlinear, and should be handled by adding an output squared term. There is multicollinearity between the amount of silicon and the thickness of the wafer. Omitting either of these causes the coefficient on the other to become significant. Foundaries which use less silicon, or thinner wafers, have significantly lower costs. The "integrated" dummy has low significance. It's inclusion is optional. It certainly would not be wrong to drop it from the model. Several models can conclusively demonstrate that foundaries in the United States have a significant cost advantage over Pacific Rim foundaries. They also appear to have an advantage over South American foundaries, although the significance is not as high. The following regression equation has an R^2 of almost 0.99:

$$\hat{y} = 480.48 - 9.72 x_{\text{Output}} + 0.0987 x_{\text{Output}}^2 + 57.62 d_{\text{PAC}} + 54.30 d_{\text{SA}}$$
$$+ 9.25 x_{\text{Thickness}} + 3.75 d_{\text{Integ}} - 5.64 x_{\text{Silicon}}$$

Appendix D

Storing a Large File on a Diskette

In some of the chapters, including 6 and 8, the Excel workbook you create will be too large to fit on a diskette. If you are using a machine in a computer lab, you may not be able to leave files on the machine's hard disk or on a network after you finish your session with the computer. This appendix explains a method which will enable you to shrink the Excel workbook so that it can fit on a diskette and later re-expand the workbook so that you can write it temporarily to a hard disk or network disk in a later computer session. This method uses two programs, zip.exe and unzip.exe provided on the data diskette.

Compressing a Workbook and Storing it on Diskette

The instructions below assume that you want to store the file named *chap6.xls* which is currently in *c:\temp*. You should change the names to suit your situation. For example, in chapter 8 the file's name would be chap8.xls. Your file may be on another disk with a letter other than "c:" (almost certainly if you are using a network disk), and the directory may have a name other than "\temp." Determine the location of your file before following the steps below.

- Exit Excel, but do not leave Windows.

- Switch to the DOS prompt. In Windows 3.1, you can do this by opening the "Main" program group in the Program Manager and double clicking the "MSDOS Prompt" or "DOS Prompt" icon.

- Switch to the directory in which your workbook file is located by entering the following two DOS commands:
  ```
  c:
  cd temp
  ```

- Enter the following DOS command:
  ```
  dir
  ```
  and be sure your file appears in the listing. If it does not, you are not in the right directory.

- Place the data diskette in drive *a* and issue the following command:
  ```
  copy a:\zip.exe
  ```
  This will copy the program zip.exe to the same directory as your Excel workbook.

- Remove the data diskette from drive *a* and insert the diskette on which you want to store your workbook. Enter this command:
  ```
  zip a:chap6 chap6.xls
  ```
  This will create a compressed version of chap6.xls (named chap6.zip) on the diskette.

- Leave the DOS prompt and return to Windows by entering the command:
  ```
  exit
  ```

Restoring a Compressed File from a Diskette

If you want, in a later session, for Excel to read a workbook you have previously stored on a diskette in compressed form, follow the instructions below. This should be done *after* you have started Windows but *before* starting Excel.

- Go to a DOS prompt and switch to the drive and directory where your workbook will be stored (assumed to be c:\temp) using the same instructions given above.

- Place the data diskette in drive *a* and enter the following command:
  ```
  copy a:unzip.exe
  ```
  This will copy the unzip.exe program to the directory where the Excel workbook will go.

- Remove the data diskette from drive *a* and insert the diskette with the stored workbook (chap6.zip). Enter the following command:
  ```
  unzip a:chap6
  ```
  This will recreate the chap6.xls file in the c:\temp directory.

- Enter the command:
  ```
  exit
  ```
  You will return to Windows and can now start Excel and read in *chap6.xls* from the *c:\temp* directory.

General Index

434